BEYOND REASONABLE DOUBT

THE WARREN REPORT AND LEE HARVEY OSWALD'S GUILT AND MOTIVE 50 YEARS ON

MEL AYTON
with DAVID VON PEIN

Copyright 2014 by Mel Ayton and David Von Pein

All Rights Reserved

No part of this book may be reproduced, stored in a retrieval system, or transmitted in any form, by any means, including mechanical, electronic photocopying, recording or otherwise, without the prior written permission of the publisher, except by a reviewer who wishes to quote brief passages in connection with a review written for inclusion in a magazine, newspaper or broadcast.

Requests for permission should be directed to:
strategicmediabooks@gmail.com

or mailed to:

Permissions
Strategic Media Inc.
782 Wofford St.
Rock Hill, SC 29730

13-ISBN 978-1-939521-23-1
10-ISBN 1-939521-23-8

Table of Contents

PREFACE iii

CHAPTER ONE 7
    A NATIONAL OBSESSION

CHAPTER TWO 27
    GOVERNMENT INVESTIGATIONS – THE WARREN COMMISSION
    AND THE HOUSE SELECT COMMITTEE ON ASSASSINATIONS

CHAPTER THREE 59
    DAMNING EVIDENCE

CHAPTER FOUR 85
    THE SINGLE-BULLET THEORY, THE HEAD SHOT,
    AND THE GRASSY KNOLL

CHAPTER FIVE 117
    CONSCIOUSNESS OF GUILT

CHAPTER SIX 149
    AN INCONVENIENT TRUTH

PHOTOS 173

CHAPTER SEVEN 187
    THE USUAL SUSPECTS

CHAPTER EIGHT 225
    THE CIA-DID-IT THEORY

CHAPTER NINE 259
    THE NEW ORLEANS DEBACLE

CHAPTER TEN 285
    OSWALD'S DEFENDERS

CHAPTER ELEVEN 313
    THE CASTRO CONNECTION

CHAPTER TWELVE 345
    THE JFK ASSASSINATION LEGACY

NOTES & SOURCES 377

APPENDIX 1 413

APPENDIX 2 441

BIBLIOGRAPHY 457

PREFACE

BY JFK ASSASSINATION RESEARCHER DAVID VON PEIN

The assassination of President John F. Kennedy on November 22, 1963, is one of the most studied and most controversial events in the history of the world. It was a pivotal and life-changing event for many people around the globe.

Ever since the President was killed on the streets of Dallas, Texas, rumors of conspiracy, cover-up, witness coercion, altered evidence, hidden assassins, corrupt and dishonest governmental and police officials, and a host of other rumors and speculation about President Kennedy's murder have flourished and grown to monumental proportions.

But does the evidence in the JFK case, coupled with some ordinary common sense when evaluating many of the conspiracy theories, really point in the direction of conspiracy?

When discussing the assassination with many conspiracy theorists at various forums on the Internet, I've noticed a disturbing trend that seems to permeate almost every forum. I call it the 'Anybody But Oswald' philosophy that many conspiracists have adopted.

Regardless of how much evidence is presented which indicates Lee Harvey Oswald's guilt in the two murders

PREFACE

he was charged with committing in Dallas on November 22, 1963, the members of the Anybody But Oswald club will find some way to disregard that evidence. They will merely claim that all of the evidence against Oswald (and there's a great deal of it, as this book will show) has been planted, faked, manipulated, or manufactured in order to frame the 24-year-old ex-Marine named Oswald for the murders of both John F. Kennedy and Dallas policeman J.D. Tippit.

A good example of this type of 'Everything's Fake' mentality exhibited by conspiracists (particularly on the Internet) comes up quite often when discussing the murder of Officer Tippit and the bullet shells associated with that crime.

The conspiracy advocates love to bring up the fact that Dallas police officer J.M. Poe, who was the first law enforcement officer to handle two of the four bullet shells that were found at the scene of Tippit's murder, could not provide any proof that he had marked those shells with his initials, thereby creating a break in the chain of custody for those two shells. According to some of the conspiracy theorists, this break in the chain of possession is apparently supposed to mean that Oswald couldn't possibly be the person who shot and killed Officer Tippit.

But those conspiracy theorists almost always totally ignore the other two bullet shells that were found at the Tippit murder scene. And those other two shells, which were initially discovered by two separate civilian witnesses, did not go through the hands of J.M. Poe at all. Those other two shells were turned over to two other Dallas police officers (one shell each), with those two officers each marking their respective shell with their initials.

Therefore, the argument that is commonly made by the conspiracy theorists about how the two "Poe" shells indicate Oswald's innocence or indicate some kind of tampering with the evidence in the Tippit case is an argument that does not hold any water at all. Because the two non-Poe shells, which were positively linked to Lee Harvey Oswald's revolver, clearly establish the fact that Oswald was Tippit's murderer.

That example regarding the Tippit bullet shells is just one of many such examples illustrating how conspiracy theorists have twisted and misrepresented the evidence in the JFK and Tippit cases.

As will be shown in many places throughout this book, President Kennedy's assassination has been falsely shrouded in mystery and cloaked within a web of perceived "conspiracy" for fifty years. But the contents of this book will demonstrate that Lee Harvey Oswald murdered President John Fitzgerald Kennedy and will also demonstrate that conspiracy very likely played no part in Oswald's actions on that terrible Friday in Dallas back in 1963.

David Von Pein

CHAPTER ONE

A NATIONAL OBSESSION

> *"There are fast tragedies, like 7 seconds in Dealey Plaza. And there are slow tragedies like the cost of believing nonsense for five decades."*
> —David Aaronovitch, *The Times*
>
> *"The past is never dead. It's not even past."*
> —William Faulkner, *Requiem For A Nun*

Three questions have haunted the United States for the past 50 years: "Was the President killed by a single gunman? Was Lee Harvey Oswald part of a conspiracy? Did the Warren Commission discover the whole truth of what happened on November 22, 1963?"

The assassination of President Kennedy was the kind of tragedy a nation suffers only once in a generation and was every bit as powerful and as shocking as the attack on the World Trade Center in New York on September 11, 2001. Arguably, it was more dangerous than 9/11. America was in the middle of the Cold War. Kennedy had just faced down the Soviet Union over the Cuban missile crisis. Vice President Lyndon Johnson was hurriedly sworn in as commander-in-chief, but he and all the chiefs of the U.S. military knew that an attack on the President could possibly be the first shot of a Third World War. U.S. intelligence agencies were aware that Soviet contingency war planning included the elimination of America's leaders. In a private phone call not long after the assassination, Lyndon B. Johnson, who assumed office on the death of the President, confided in a senior member of Congress that he feared 40 million Americans might die in a nuclear exchange following JFK's assassination in Dallas.

Within months after the Dallas tragedy, the Kennedy assassination turned into a national obsession. Fifty years since the publication of the Warren Commission Report, which reported on the circumstances of the tragedy, the crime has become the 'Great Whodunit' of the last century. Following the Warren Report's publication in September 1964, each new book or private investigation promised to reveal the 'real truth' about the circumstances surrounding the tragedy.

As decades passed, new books and new revelations by conspiracy theorists changed the story of the assassination into a web of intrigue and deceit. Americans were left to wonder if the truth about JFK's death had been covered up by powerful forces – Would we ever make sense of the events of November 22, 1963?

In many ways it was inevitable the American public would try and rationalize the tragic events of November 1963 and place the assassination in a conspiratorial context. For many, the realization that the perpetrator was a pathetic figure like Lee Harvey Oswald took away meaning to the life and leadership of President Kennedy. If JFK had died for one of the causes he fought for, the assassination myth may never have been advanced. The American psyche could not deal with this disturbing fact and it became difficult to accept. Accordingly, Americans turned to irrational explanations for the tragedy and they have held a tight grip on the public consciousness ever since. As Peter Landesman, director of the movie *Parkland* said, "The dialogue about the conspiracy theories goes in circles and it's like arguing about God. I think people have a very difficult time believing or understanding that such a small, insignificant creature like Lee Harvey Oswald could kill arguably the greatest celebrity leader we had in the 20th century. But there is just no evidence for anything else". [1]

Initially, the Warren Commission's report was well received. However, within a year of its publication the skeptics picked through its findings because the Warren Commission was flawed from the start. But not because the commissioners or the staff themselves were part of a conspiracy to bury the truth. As Philip Shenon demonstrates in his book *A Cruel and Shocking Act*, the Warren Commission and its midlevel investigative staff was objective. He portrays the investigators as men as holding a great deal of integrity and zeal in pursuing many angles. Shenon also found nothing that gave him pause at the idea of Oswald as the assassin of President Kennedy.

Instead, the CIA competed with the FBI for control of evidence and narrative; each agency had eyes on Oswald, but neither acted properly to contain him, even as the future assassin was placed under special surveillance. Accordingly, crucial details about the assassination were buried out of selfish considerations by the head of the FBI, J. Edgar Hoover, and key CIA personnel including James Jesus Angleton, who put pride and reputation of themselves, their colleagues, and the then undiminished reputations of their agencies above full disclosure. There is plenty of evidence to suggest that the intelligence agencies destroyed valuable documentation after the killing in a rush to cover up incompetence.

However, the information buried was not connected to the FBI or CIA being any part of the assassination, but rather their knowledge of Oswald beforehand and their failure to ensure the information was properly disseminated to other agencies (e. g. the destruction of a note, delivered to the Dallas FBI by Oswald in November 1963, or information the CIA held in its possession re: Oswald meeting with Cuban embassy personnel or possibly Cuban intelligence officers in Mexico City). Both these agencies quickly tried to withhold any information indicating they were aware of Oswald's movements for fear of criticism they did nothing to stop him. They were trying to hide their incompetence. The CIA distanced itself in the wake of the assassination not only to cover its back, but to prevent disclosure of sources and methods. Shenon concludes that these acts of omission helped to guarantee the flourishing conspiracy culture.

Accordingly, pro-conspiracy books and newspaper revelations of assassination-related stories that had escaped close scrutiny began to chip away at the Commission's lone-assassin conclusions. Assassination researchers alleged a home cine film had apparently revealed how Kennedy had been shot from the right front, indicating two or more shooters; some researchers believed that shots had been fired from the infamous "grassy knoll", situated in Dealey Plaza, the site of the Dallas assassination. New witnesses spoke of how Oswald and his killer, Jack Ruby, had known one another. Independent researchers and New Orleans District Attorney Jim Garrison alleged that Oswald had been tied in with anti-Castro Cuban groups who conspired to murder the President. Numerous 'eyewitnesses' came forward to tell incredible tales of multiple shooters. A number of conspiracy writers claimed they had recorded 'confessions' from individuals who purportedly confessed they had participated in the assassination and cover-up.

Some conspiracy allegations, especially those involving the American government's attempts to assassinate Cuba's President Fidel Castro, were so convincing that 13 years after the assassination the U.S. House of Representatives formed the Select Committee on Assassinations (HSCA) to look into the circumstances surrounding the President's death. They also decided to investigate the assassinations of Civil Rights leader Martin Luther King and JFK's brother, Senator Robert F. Kennedy. (The committee abandoned the RFK investigation due to lack of funds.) The 1976-1979 investigation concluded that Lee Harvey Oswald acted alone when he shot the President, but at the last minute the committee changed its mind after hearing evidence from acoustics experts who examined a Dallas Police sound recording of the assassination. The evidence they presented concluded that a shot allegedly had been fired at the President from a position other than the Texas School Book Depository. The committee concluded that the President *"was probably assassinated as a result of a conspiracy."*[2]

The HSCA also expressed suspicions that elements of the Mafia, or anti-Castro activists, or both, may have taken part in the plot. It said pointedly that two living American Mafia bosses, Carlos Marcello and Santos Trafficante, *"had the motive, means, and opportunity to kill President Kennedy."*

Most conspiracy theorists eventually abandoned the idea that the Mafia was responsible for the President's assassination. During the 1980s, the idea that the CIA had a hand in the 'conspiracy' took off and to this day a majority of the skeptics believe the Agency was culpable. However, many researchers continue to claim that other suspect groups, including anti-Castro, pro-Castro, military-industrial complex rogue groups and even President Johnson, had been responsible.

Today, there is a consensus amongst the American public that it is a "historical fact" that President Kennedy had been killed by a group of conspirators and that:

- The accused assassin, Lee Harvey Oswald, was innocent, a "patsy"; alternatively, conspiracists expressed the notion that Oswald was indeed guilty of shooting President Kennedy but was aided by co-conspirators.

- A second gunman had fired the fatal shot from the infamous "grassy knoll."

- J. Edgar Hoover and the FBI, Lyndon Johnson, southern racists and the Joint Chiefs of Staff, pro-Castro Cubans, anti-Castro Cubans, the

KGB, rogue elements of the CIA and/or the Mafia, the military-industrial complex, and Texas oilmen were fingered as responsible for the assassination of the President. All of these purported plots are labyrinthine in their complexity.

- Lee Harvey Oswald had worked for American foreign and domestic agencies like the CIA, FBI, or Military Intelligence.

- A vast network of state and federal government officials, including Warren Commission members, had conspired to "cover-up" the facts to prevent the American public from knowing the truth.

- There were also additional reasons why the idea of conspiracy became embedded in the American consciousness. JFK conspiracy theories became a lucrative industry in the United States and their enduring popularity made them into a 'money-spinner'. Vested interests kept the conspiracy myths alive. Annual JFK assassination conventions were organized. Speakers included major figures in the conspiracy debate. However, the conferences' agendas were skewed in favor of conspiracy theories and were attended only by committed conspiracy believers.

Six million visitors a year visit the JFK assassination site, where "researchers" peddle books, autopsy pictures, and signed "grassy knoll witness" photos. The visitor can experience a virtual Disneyland of assassination themes, from limousine rides which trace JFK's route from Love Field to Dealey Plaza to bus trips which follow Oswald's escape route. It is a multimillion-dollar industry promoting books, videos, CD-ROMs, T-Shirts, and even board games. Conspiracy theories also brought the assassination into the world of entertainment with the release of Oliver Stone's conspiracy movie *JFK* in 1991. Following the release of the movie, conspiracists were invigorated and continued to promote conspiracy allegations well into the new millennium and beyond.

In the late 1970s, conspiracy theorists believed they had won the conspiracy/no conspiracy debate after the House Select Committee on Assassinations published their conclusions. However, the media had ignored the most important part of the HSCA's report. Two weeks before its findings were due to be published, committee members arrived at virtually the same conclusions as the Warren Commission, but quickly amended them only on the basis of acoustical evidence which had been presented at the last minute. In 1982, the conclusion about the acoustics evidence was found to be in error by a prestigious panel of scientists chosen by the National Academy of Sciences. They reported that the police recording which had been used by the HSCA did not indicate that a shot had been fired from the infamous 'grassy knoll', thus invalidating the HSCA's single piece of evidence which purportedly proved a conspiracy. Members of the NAS panel reiterated their belief that the HSCA acoustics evidence was bogus as late as 2001, but it was ignored by the mainstream media.

As a result of Stone's movie, a new generation of Americans came to believe in an alternative but demonstrably false history of the assassination. President Ford, who served on the Warren Commission, said, "The trouble with the movie, experts tell me, is eighty percent of the people who go to movies are between the ages of sixteen and twenty-four. None of those were alive when JFK was killed. So they're getting a totally distorted story about that tragedy." Ford said his own son had seen the movie and had praised it. The former President had to sit him down and explain Stone's untruths.[3]

Although Stone's movie was a travesty, there was one positive effect it had on the government – the release of government files about the assassination that had been sealed for a generation. The mid-1990s release of JFK assassination documents, numbering some four million pages, was organized by the Assassination Records Review Board (ARRB), a board of overseers appointed by the government. The newly-released files helped to negate numerous claims by conspiracists, but it did not end the debate. Conspiracy writers simply changed tactics and continued to distort the true facts about the case by skewing the meaning of many documents and using some documentary evidence to prop up their case for conspiracy.

Conspiracy writers continued to claim that there was evidence 'proving' that not only were groups like the CIA responsible for the assassination, but the photographic, ballistics, and medical evidence had been faked by the government. Books which claimed a government 'cover-up' contained complex and esoteric articles, written by self-proclaimed 'scientific world authorities'. Using highly technical language, these self-proclaimed 'experts' pronounced the Zapruder home movie film of the assassination, autopsy X-rays, photographs, and other

BEYOND REASONABLE DOUBT

scientific evidence had been faked. Led by lawyer Mark Lane, conspiracy believers accused the CIA of having a hand in the assassination. The Agency became an easy target after newspaper revelations about CIA malfeasance, military black ops, and an 'out-of-control military-industrial complex' became widely publicized.

When facts are presented that explain inconsistencies in the evidence, conspiracy theorists disingenuously allege that the evidence has been tampered with. If parts of the media support the lone-assassin explanation for the assassination, they accuse them of covering up the "consortium / establishment / government" conspiracy. If an agency of the U.S. Government determines that the idea of a conspiracy is groundless, it is instantly dismissed. Their theories are attractive to people who share a muddled, careless, or deceitful attitude towards gathering evidence and often find themselves drawn to each other's fantasies. If you believe one wrong or strange thing, you are more likely to believe another.

JFK assassination conspiracy theories have been successfully debunked by writers like Patricia Lambert, Gerald Posner, Vincent Bugliosi, John McAdams, Jean Davison, Priscilla Johnson McMillan, and a host of other knowledgeable authors. However, the debate has continued for five decades because conspiracy theories are like the legendary Hydra—cut off one of its heads and a score of others will replace it.

The wealth of evidence challenging conspiracy ideas has also been largely ignored by the media, who still refuse to marginalize the crackpot theories which pop up every year or so. Additionally, most journalists have shown a remarkable ignorance about the facts of the assassination and have demonstrated their inability to navigate the voluminous literature on the crime. Their motives have been clear to many researchers – conspiracies remain very appealing because they are powerfully seductive, offering mystery and intrigue to the reader. Additionally, a conspiracy with a valid aim suggests control; the psychotic actions of a lone individual suggest chaos – journalists are aware that people are always looking for simple and straightforward answers. As Patricia Lambert has written, "Contrary to today's conventional wisdom, it wasn't a handful of cranks that drew the country into the conspiracy camp. It was the mainline media."[4]

For example, journalist Jefferson Morley was partly responsible for fueling the undeserved skeptical reaction to Vincent Bugliosi's 2007 book which revealed how conspiracy writers had abused the JFK assassination evidence and revealed that each and every conspiracy that had developed over the years was nothing more than wishful thinking. Morley wrote, "Since 2000, five tenured academic historians have published books on JFK's assassination. Four of the five concluded that a conspiracy was behind the 35th president's murder." However, it is also true that 'academic historians' have been instrumental in propagating false histories, including David Irving who wrote many 'holocaust denial' books and Hugh Trevor-Roper who believed 'Hitler's Diaries' were genuine.[5]

The motives of various 'conspiracy witnesses' were also never closely scrutinized by the media. After the assassination, every witness was in the spotlight. Many were confused about what they had witnessed and some even changed their stories after they realized they had been mistaken. As acclaimed author Patricia Lambert wrote in *False Witness*, her excellent study of New Orleans District Attorney Jim Garrison, "LIFE magazine (in 1966) may have played a greater role in turning the majority of Americans away from the conclusions of the Warren Report than any book written. In those days, most of the country still relied heavily on the print media for its news. LIFE... was still an entrenched and honored part of the American scene. For an institution as conservative and important to endorse such an idea seemed, in itself, to validate the notion of conspiracy."[6]

Other witnesses stonewalled after they realized they were attracting attention, fame, and money. During the 1970s, riding high on the publicity surrounding the new congressional investigation into Kennedy's death, new 'witnesses' came forward to report they had recovered their memories and were 'ready to talk'. The result was a flood of distortion and misinformation. Their tales were rightly denounced by government investigators and anti-conspiracy writers, but conspiracy advocates uncritically accepted their preposterous stories.

Some of the methods conspiracy writers have used include playing the conspiracy game of 'A knows B who knows C who knows D, therefore A must know D'; disparaging every witness who did not prop up their conspiracy allegations; contorting statements made during interviews conducted with assassination witnesses; reckless use of Warren Commission eyewitness testimony and the wrongful use of the physical evidence. Essentially, conspiracists who have claimed the physical evidence and witness testimony proves a JFK conspiracy have been hoodwinked by the sham stories concocted by numerous individuals who have ingratiated themselves into the conspiracy story for political or vainglorious motives.[7]

For example, many conspiracy writers accepted Beverly Oliver's uncorroborated claims that Lee Harvey Oswald and Jack Ruby knew each other. She appeared in the 1988 documentary, *The Men Who Killed Kennedy,* as an important 'witness', yet she is not even mentioned in the Warren Report. She was discovered to have lied when she told researchers she had used a type of camera not in production in 1963, and she embellished her 1970 story so many times only the gullible now accept her claims.[8]

Another typical 'witness' was Marita Lorenz. Her story was convincing to many Kennedy assassination/Castro/CIA documentary makers. Lorenz exaggerated her tale of having been one of Fidel Castro's mistresses to construct an elaborate tale of a CIA/anti-Castro conspiracy. Edwin Lopez, a former researcher for the HSCA, investigated her claims and told Gerald Posner, "Mark Lane was taken in by Marita Lorenz. Oh God, we spent a lot of time with Marita... It was hard to ignore her because she gave us so much crap, and we tried to verify it, but let me tell you – she is full of shit. Between her and Frank Sturgis (ex-Watergate burglar) we must have spent over one hundred hours. They were dead ends... Marita is not credible."⁹

Many 'witnesses' promoted their untrue stories for years before researchers proved they were bogus. Ricky White said his father, a former Dallas police officer, had left a diary after his death in which he confessed to his role in the 'conspiracy'. The diary conveniently disappeared but not before a Texas company tried to market the 'Roscoe White' story as a book or film. Oliver Stone considered buying the 'Roscoe White' story for $750,000 but eventually changed his mind.¹⁰

The way conspiracy theorists have been able to promote their stories can partly be placed at the feet of government. Step by step the mistakes made by the Warren Commission – from the incineration of the autopsy report to the disappearance of the president's brain – inadvertently led to the birth of a thousand conspiracy theories. And nearly all of the suspicious events that followed – the malfeasance of the FBI, the misdirection of the CIA, the obstruction of the Secret Service – were designed to protect the various agencies and officials responsible for the President's safety.

The Warren Commission was also split on the issue of Oswald's motive. As Philip Shenon wrote: "(Chief Counsel J. Lee Rankin) thought that Oswald's quest for fame – not his Marxism – was a much more likely explanation of his motives, a view shared by some of the commissioners". Rankin worried that "...(Wesley) Liebeler's suggestion that Oswald's pro-Castro views led him to kill Kennedy might be seized on by conservative law-makers who wanted to blame Cuba for the assassination".[11]

Accordingly, the commissioners decided they were "unwilling to assign any particular motive or get involved in psychiatric theories or terminology".[12] Earl Warren was also unwilling to ascribe Oswald's Marxist principles to the issue of motive as he was aware that blaming a 'communist' would severely damage diplomatic efforts by the United States to reach an accord with the Soviet Union and Cuba. The American public were therefore left wondering – what were Oswald's 'true' motives?

If the Warren Commission had received full disclosure from the FBI and CIA, questions about Oswald and his suspicious activities in the weeks leading up to the assassination may have been immediately answered. And if the FBI and CIA had been more forthcoming with the HSCA, some 'mysteries' may never have taken hold. If the information about Oswald which they held on file had been released there would have been little room for the conspiracy theorists to maneuver.

The HSCA must also take some of the blame in which conspiracy theories flourished. The committee worked under financial constraints and political considerations and accordingly failed to pursue many leads which could have stopped much speculation. And if the committee had been more generously funded, they would have investigated further the spurious claims that an audio tape recording of the assassination proved there were two gunmen shooting at the President.

The CIA was also culpable in the way they tried to handle the conspiracy allegations. Allen Dulles, a former head of the CIA, for example, who was appointed by President Johnson as a Warren Commission member, failed to tell his fellow commissioners about the assassination attempts against Castro. This information could have led investigators to dig deeper into Oswald's visits to the Cuban and Russian embassies in Mexico City shortly before the assassination. A thorough investigation of Castro's purported role in the assassination may have followed.

The CIA had legitimate reasons for withholding files from the Warren Commission. During the Cold War, information concerning the electronic bugging and surveillance of the Russian and Cuban embassies in Mexico City was deemed sensitive (as it is to this day). The National Security Agency's capabilities and the methodology of its electronic intercepts are the most highly guarded of secrets. Information gleaned from bugging is protected on the grounds that it may inevitably lead to undercover agents coming under suspicion.

Although the majority of CIA and FBI files were released to the public by the ARRB in the mid-1990s, some files remained locked. However, the CIA's claims that they were protecting national security interests can no longer be justified 50 years on. The non-release of these files, including those of Agency officers William Harvey (sealed until 2063) and George Joannides, only helps fuel suspicion that a cabal of operatives, known to be involved in an enterprise designed to either kill or topple

Fidel Castro, enlisted Lee Harvey Oswald or used Oswald as a "patsy" in a conspiracy to kill President Kennedy. [13]

Although it is important that all CIA files pertaining to the assassination be released, it is unlikely conspiracists will find anything which would suggest CIA culpability. G. Robert Blakey, who was the lead counsel during the HSCA investigation, and David Belin, a counsel to the Warren Commission and executive director of the *Commission on CIA Activities Within the United States* (Rockefeller Commission), have stated they had access to all the unpublished material from the CIA and there was no 'smoking gun'.

The Dallas Police, who conspiracists say colluded with the U.S. Government in covering up a purported conspiracy, was careless with Oswald, but there is no evidence to show they were conspiratorially involved. However, the Dallas Police Department was perhaps not as careless as the FBI. For Director J. Edgar Hoover, the assassination was a disaster. The FBI had a file on Oswald which traced his movements back to his time in the Soviet Union. Two weeks before the assassination, Oswald visited the local FBI office in Dallas and angrily complained about the harassment his wife had been receiving from its agents who were trying to keep track of the ex-Marine Russian defector. This information was not revealed until 1975. The FBI also failed to keep Oswald under observation during the Presidential visit. And it is in this sense—and this sense only—that the "cover-up" is an historical truth.

The Kennedy family is also partly responsible for allegations of a cover-up. They sought a limited autopsy, for instance, not because they feared the ballistics evidence but because they hoped to avoid exposing Kennedy's health problems, including Addison's disease. The documents released by the ARRB show how the Kennedys inadvertently fed the conspiracy machine by asking many of those present at the autopsy to promise not to talk about the procedure for 25 years. Conspiracy theorists pointed to this wall of silence as 'proof' of a continuing cover-up, when in fact the doctors were merely adhering to the wishes of the family. Beyond the autopsy, Robert Kennedy may have worried that the Warren Commission might stumble onto the government's plots to kill Castro. He did not want the Warren Commission investigating Cuba. The plots against Castro had nothing to do with the JFK assassination, but the Warren Commission should have been informed. The new President, Lyndon Johnson, must also share some of the blame for the way in which conspiracy rumors developed. In the hours following the assassination, he feared that a public hysteria would demand revenge for the death of President Kennedy. At the very least, his hopes for détente with the Soviet Union would be dashed. Some believed a world war would be imminent if evidence had been found that the Soviets or Cubans were behind the murder. Although intelligence agencies, using sophisticated methods, confirmed that Khrushchev and Castro were not involved, President Johnson was fearful that suspicions alone could lead to conflict. The government therefore decided they must convince the public that the President's death was the work of a lone madman, not of some vast Communist conspiracy.

NATIONAL OBSESSION

In the context of the time, President Johnson's strategy was well intentioned, but many leads pointing to Oswald's peripheral connections with foreign agencies were ignored or swept under the carpet. Johnson was fearful that there had indeed been a conspiracy to kill Kennedy and this would have dire consequences for Soviet-American relations. He may have had some hand in wanting the Warren Commission to disprove allegations of conspiracy at any cost to historical truth. If there was a conspiracy he did not want it laid at the door of the Kremlin. And he fed the conspiracy rumors by telling close aides he believed a conspiracy had existed. Additionally, JFK's brother, Robert, was desperate the Commission not reveal the previous administration's attempts to kill Castro.[14]

The actions of Presidential administrations that followed may also explain why the American public became open to persuasion by conspiracy theorists. The American people faced a litany of lies, distortions, and half-truths by government agencies and the White House during the administrations of Kennedy (attempted assassinations of foreign leaders), Johnson (Vietnam war), Nixon (Watergate), and Reagan (Iran-Contra), therefore allegations of a cover-up did not appear unusual or outrageous.

Hopes were raised in 2007 that the conspiracy theories had all been successfully debunked when Vincent Bugliosi published his 1600-page book, *Reclaiming History*, which examined every theory and every conspiracy claim. The former Los Angeles lawyer, who became famous for his prosecution of hippie killer Charles Manson, wrote a devastating no-nonsense

25

approach to assassination scenarios which had been built upon innuendo, speculation, and a distorting of the evidence in the case. It was hoped his work, which was described by writer Scott Turow as a book "that will be read for centuries," would put an end to false stories about the death of JFK. That hope was dashed when polls came out following the book's publication which indicated a majority of Americans were still convinced a conspiracy had been responsible for the President's murder. Six years later, polls revealed a majority of Americans still clung to that belief.[15]

CHAPTER TWO

GOVERNMENT INVESTIGATIONS – THE WARREN COMMISSION AND THE HOUSE SELECT COMMITTEE ON ASSASSINATIONS

> *"We ducked the question of motive."*
>
> —Burt Griffin, Warren Commission Counsel

> *"I believe history will be kind to President Johnson, the Warren Commission, the FBI, the CIA, and all the other parties involved in perhaps the greatest cover-up this nation has experienced. The bottom line is that the correct guilty party was identified and this nation's peace was preserved. In 1963, those were the two most important things. Unfortunately, a consequence of these decisions was the sacrifice of the U.S. government's credibility."*
>
> —Former FBI Agent James P. Hosty Jr.

> *"...the HSCA's finding of a fourth shot from the grassy knoll has been so thoroughly discredited that it has become an indelible stain on its legacy, a very large asterisk to its otherwise excellent reinvestigation of the assassination."*
>
> —Vincent Bugliosi, *Reclaiming History*

THE PRELUDE

1964 was an election year in the United States and the Democratic Party was confident President John F. Kennedy would be re-elected to a second term in office. Opinion polls reflected his growing popularity and his

BEYOND REASONABLE DOUBT

expected Republican Party opponent was the right-wing Senator Barry Goldwater, although rumors that Richard Nixon would enter the arena persisted and Nelson Rockefeller was still being hailed as a Republican liberal contender. However, in November 1963, as the President was about to begin his campaigning for a second term in office, America suddenly changed direction as the country witnessed the most notorious political murder in its history.

President Kennedy was in Texas primarily for political reasons – to heal a rift in the Democratic Party and to raise funds for the coming campaign. He told his friend, Senator George Smathers, he wished he could escape the trip which he called "a pain in the neck". It had in fact been a political week. On Monday, November 18, he spoke to audiences in Tampa and Miami Beach. That night, he flew back to Washington for a two-day interlude of official business. At a White House reception for the Justices of the Supreme Court, Jacqueline Kennedy returned to her work after a two-month hiatus after the death of her infant son in August. On Thursday, the President and his wife embarked on their journey to Texas.

There were warnings that the President's reception might be hostile. Lately, Texas had been in an unfriendly mood toward the Kennedy Administration. This arose partly from the Civil Rights Movement which Kennedy had supported; partly it was aroused by right-wing militant groups like the John Birch Society, who detested Kennedy's liberal policies. Vice President Lyndon Johnson, a Texan, was frequently vilified. Ambassador to the United Nations, Adlai Stevenson, had recently been spat upon and hit with a picket sign in Dallas. Placards were being distributed bearing the President's picture and the legend "Wanted for Treason". Even Texas Governor John Connally was worried and argued against a motorcade through Dallas but withdrew his objection. Some of JFK's aides were uneasy about the trip.

Yet Thursday's visits to San Antonio, Houston, and Fort Worth were warm and enthusiastic. Everything was obviously going well. But there had been a note of doom. In Fort Worth, Kennedy and his wife discussed the risks that a President inevitably faces when he makes public appearances. JFK aide Kenneth O'Donnell mentally recorded the President's response, "(Kennedy said) If anybody really wanted to shoot the President of the United States, it was not a very difficult job. All one had to do was get (into) a high building some day with a telescopic rifle and there was nothing anybody could do to defend against such an attempt."[1]

This was not the first time that Kennedy had worried about his own mortality. After his election in November 1960, he retired to his father's estate in Palm Beach. On Sunday morning, December 11, 1960, a car slowed down and came to a halt across the street from the Kennedy residence. Inside the house were members of the Kennedy family, including John and Jackie Kennedy and their children. According to Secret Service files, the driver of the car was a retired 73-year-old postal clerk from Belmont, New Hampshire, named Richard P. Pavlick, who had previously made threats against the life of President-elect Kennedy.[2]

Pavlick's car contained seven sticks of dynamite that could be detonated by the simple closing of a switch. Pavlick's intention was to wait until Kennedy entered his car, then drive his own forward into Kennedy's, blowing himself and the President-elect up. Pavlick watched the house and knew Kennedy would be going to Sunday mass at 10:00 a.m. Kennedy opened the door of the house surrounded by agents and accompanied by his wife and children. In an instant, to Pavlick, he changed his mind about killing Kennedy because he did not wish to harm Jackie or the children. Pavlick drove off in the opposite direction. On Thursday December 15th, he was arrested for reckless driving and admitted the dynamite found in the car was to assassinate Kennedy. He was eventually handed over to Secret Service agents who charged him with attempted murder and unlawful possession of explosives. He subsequently spent six years in various federal prisons and mental institutions.[3]

Like Abraham Lincoln, Kennedy had a premonition he would not live out his term in office. In June 1961, Kennedy asked his secretary, Evelyn Lincoln, to come to his cabin aboard Air Force One. Lincoln later recalled that as she cleared the President's papers from his desk, a small slip of paper fell to the floor. It was in JFK's own handwriting and bore the words, "I know that there is a God and I see a storm coming. If He has a place for me, I am ready."[4]

Two years later, in September 1963, on the Labor Day weekend and only two months before his death, Kennedy appeared in a home movie which fictionalized his own death. Whilst cameras rolled, Kennedy disembarked from the family yacht, the 'Honey Fitz', and walked down a pier at the Rhode Island estate of his wife's parents. Suddenly he grasped at his chest and fell to the boards. Jackie and a friend stepped over the 'body'. Undersecretary of the Navy, Paul Fay, then fell on Kennedy's body forcing 'blood' to fall from the president's mouth.[5]

The next stop on the Presidential itinerary was Dallas, where Kennedy was to be driven through the city in a motorcade. The motorcade route has been endlessly speculated upon by conspiracy theorists. It was agreed by all parties concerned, including Kennedy's advisers, that the President should be seen by as many people as possible and a motorcade was proposed by Kenneth O'Donnell. The actual route was selected by Secret Service agents Forrest V. Sorrels and Winston G. Lawson to traverse the distance between the Dallas airport and the site of the luncheon where the President was to speak to business and political leaders.

There were three potential sites for the luncheon. One building, known as Market Hall, was unavailable for the day of Kennedy's Dallas visit. The second building, located at the state fair grounds and known as the Women's Building, had the practical advantage that it was a one – story building with few entrances and it was easy to make secure. However, it lacked food facilities. This left a third possibility – the Trade Mart. The Secret Service was very concerned about security at this venue as there were several entrances and a balcony. The President's advisers overruled them and the Trade Mart was selected.

BEYOND REASONABLE DOUBT

Once the luncheon venue was selected, the motorcade route was easy to determine. Most people would congregate in downtown Dallas. From downtown, the motorcade would then have to head north on to Stemmons Freeway to get to the Trade Mart. But there was a problem. Main Street did not have a direct access on to Stemmons Freeway. To get around this problem, the motorcade would have to make a 90-degree turn onto Houston Street and then another sharp turn onto Elm Street which would lead to Stemmons Freeway. This would take the motorcade past the Texas School Book Depository.

Secret Service agents scanned crowds in buildings to anticipate trouble. Dallas police lined the route, keeping crowds away from the limousine. Although the Presidential limousine's 'bubbletop' was not bulletproof, it would have provided some protection for JFK. Kenneth O'Donnell made the decision to remove the bubbletop protective covering from the car because the weather had changed and it had stopped raining.

On the drive into Dallas from Love Field, Kennedy twice directed the car to come to a halt, once to respond to a sign asking him to shake hands, the second time to talk to a Catholic nun and a small group of children. Along the route, Jackie Kennedy would occasionally put on her sunglasses. Almost under his breath, JFK would say 'Take off your glasses'.

As the Presidential motorcade was about to leave downtown Dallas and drive to the luncheon venue on Stemmons Freeway, a large crowd of people at the triangular Dealey Plaza came into view as JFK's car turned right at the corner of Main and Houston Streets. From Houston, the car slowed to navigate the sharp turn onto Elm Street before it drove on to the freeway. The motorcade slowed to 11.2 mph and moved past the Texas Book Depository building, a warehouse housing textbooks for schools in Dallas and surrounding areas. Inside the Lincoln limousine, Nellie Connally, who was sitting directly in front of Jackie Kennedy, turned to the President and smiled, "Mr. President, you can't say that Dallas doesn't love you." Kennedy replied, "That is very obvious."[6]

At 12:30 p.m., Jackie Kennedy heard a sound similar to a motorcycle noise and a cry from Governor Connally, which caused her to look to her right. On turning, she saw a quizzical look on President Kennedy's face. Jacqueline Kennedy told author Theodore H. White: "They were gunning the motorcycles. There were these little backfires. There was one noise like that. I thought it was a backfire. Then next I saw Connally grabbing his arms and saying no, no, no, no with his fist beating. Then Jack turned and I turned. All I remember was a blue-grey building up ahead. Then Jack turned back so neatly, his last expression was so neat... you know that wonderful expression he had when they'd ask him a question about one of the ten million pieces they have in a rocket, just before he'd answer. He looked puzzled, and then he slumped forward. He was holding out his hand... I could see a piece of his skull coming off. It was flesh-colored, not white. He was holding out his hand... I can see this perfectly clean piece detaching itself from his head. Then he slumped in my lap, his blood and his brains were in my lap... Then (Secret Service agent)

Clint Hill, he loved us, he made my life so easy, he was the first man in the car... We all lay down in the car... And I kept saying, Jack, Jack, Jack, and someone yelling he's dead, he's dead. All the way to the hospital I kept bending over him, saying Jack, Jack, can you hear me? I love you, Jack. I kept holding the top of his head down, trying to keep the brains in."[7]

Governor Connally said the first noise was a rifle shot and he immediately thought of an assassination attempt. He was seated in the right jump seat immediately in front of the President and "instinctively turned to his right because the shot appeared to come from over his right shoulder". Connally was unable to see JFK when he started to turn around and at that instant he "felt something strike him in the back". Connally was still conscious when he fell into his wife's lap. A second or two later he heard a shot and both he and his wife saw brain tissue splattered over the interior of the car.[8]

Two cars to the rear, in the Lincoln carrying the Johnsons and Texas Senator Ralph Yarborough, Secret Service agent Rufus Youngblood heard an "explosive noise". In the second car behind Johnson, Mrs. Earl Cabell, wife of the Mayor of Dallas, saw a "projection" sticking out of a window of the Book Depository. From a press car at the rear of the motorcade, Robert Jackson, a *Dallas Times Herald* photographer, saw a rifle being slowly drawn back through an open window. Directly across from the building, Amos Euins, a 15-year-old schoolboy, saw a man shoot twice from a window. Euins then hid behind a bench.[9] Arnold Rowland had seen a figure silhouetted in a window, holding what appeared to be a high-powered rifle, like 'a Marine on a rifle range'. He assumed that the figure must be a Secret Service agent protecting the President and said to his wife, "Do you want to see a Secret Service agent?" "Where?" she asked, "In that building there", he said, pointing.[10]

The most important witness to the shooting, however, was Howard L. Brennan. Sitting atop a concrete wall across from the Book Depository building, he had noticed a man at the 6th floor corner window. While waiting for the motorcade to arrive, he had watched him leave the window "a couple of times". After Brennan had heard a shot, he looked up again: "And this man that I saw previous was aiming for his last shot. Well, as it appeared to me, he was standing up and resting against the left window sill, taking positive aim, and fired his last shot. As I calculate, a couple of seconds. He drew the gun back from the window as though he was drawing it back to assure hisself (sic) that he hit his mark, and then he disappeared."[11]

Brennan stopped a policeman, Herbert Sawyer, gave a description of the man: slender, about 5 feet, 10 inches tall, in his early 30s. Brennan later wrote of his experience: "What I saw made my blood run cold. Poised in the corner window of the 6th floor was the same young man I had noticed several times before the motorcade arrived. There was one difference – this time he held a rifle in his hands, pointing towards the Presidential car. He steadied the rifle against the cornice and while he moved quickly, he didn't seem to be in any kind of panic.... Then came the sickening sound of the second shot... I wanted to cry, I wanted to scream, but I couldn't utter a sound... He was aiming again

BEYOND REASONABLE DOUBT

and I wanted to pray, to beg God to somehow make him miss the target... The sight became fixed in my mind that I'll never forget it as long as I live... Then another shot rang out. To my amazement, the man still stood there at the window. He didn't appear to be rushed. There was no particular emotion visible on his face except for a slight smirk. It was a look of satisfaction, as if he had accomplished what he set out to do."[12]

The description was flashed to all Dallas patrol cars. After the assassination, Brennan would not positively identify Oswald as the gunman and conspiracy theorists have made much of this fact. However, Brennan reacted this way because he feared for his own safety, believing initial reports of a communist conspiracy, a natural assumption in right-wing Texas.

Another witness, Ronald Fischer, sitting near Brennan, saw a man in the window for 10 or 15 seconds. He said that the man held his attention until the motorcade came because the man: "...appeared uncomfortable for one, and secondly, he wasn't watching....he didn't look like he was watching for the parade. He looked like he was looking down towards the Trinity River and the Triple Underpass down at the end – toward the end of Elm Street. And...all the time I watched him, he never moved his head, he never – he never moved anything. Just was there transfixed." [13]

According to the Warren Report, Fischer could see the man: "from the middle of his chest to the top of his head, and that as he was facing the window, the man was in the lower right-hand portion of the window and

THE WARREN COMMISSION AND THE HSCA

'seemed to be sitting a little forward'. The man was dressed in a light-colored, open-necked shirt which could have been either a sports shirt or a T-shirt, and he had brown hair, a slender face and neck with light complexion, and looked to be 22 or 24 years old. The person in the window was a white man and 'looked to me like he was looking straight at the Triple Underpass' down Elm Street. Boxes and cases were stacked behind him."[14]

The only place where witnesses conclusively saw a gunman and a rifle at the time of the assassination was in the southeast corner of the 6th floor window of the Book Depository. Harold Norman even heard the action of the rifle bolt and the sounds of the cartridges as they hit the floor. Norman was sitting in the southeast corner of the 5th floor. He heard three shots. He told the Warren Commission: "....and I can't remember what the exact time was but I know I heard a shot, and then after I heard the shot, well, it seems as though the President, you know, slumped or something, and then another shot and I believe Jarman or someone told me, he said, 'I believe someone is shooting at the President,' and I think I made a statement 'It is someone shooting at the President, and I believe it came from up above us.' Well, I couldn't see at all during the time, but I know I heard a third shot fired, and I could also hear something sounded like the shell hulls hitting the floor and the ejecting of the rifle."[15]

Following the shots there was a mass of confusion, in part because Dealey Plaza is surrounded on all three sides by tall buildings, which acted as an echo chamber. This led many witnesses to look to a 'grassy knoll', the

BEYOND REASONABLE DOUBT

railway overpass and other places for the origin of the shots. Experienced police officers, however, have always recognized that when you get two or more witnesses to a sudden event you generally get two or more stories as to what exactly happened and the stories are often conflicting. In the case of Dealey Plaza, there were hundreds of witnesses milling around in a state of excitement.

Five minutes after the shooting, the Presidential limousine swept into the driveway of the Parkland Memorial Hospital. Vice President Johnson's car and two cars loaded with Secret Service agents arrived almost simultaneously. Agent Clint Hill removed his suit jacket and covered the President's head wound to prevent photographs. On arrival, President Kennedy was in an 'agonal state' – no blood pressure and a slight heart flutter. He was clinically dead.

The braking of the car jolted Governor Connally back to consciousness. Despite his grave wounds, he bravely tried to stand up and get out so that doctors could reach the President. But he collapsed again. Mrs. Kennedy held the President in her lap, and for a moment refused to release him. Then three Secret Service agents lifted him onto a stretcher and pushed it into Trauma Room One. Nellie Connally bristled at the way the Secret Service agents ignored her husband in favor of the President.

Twelve doctors had rushed into the emergency room. Surgeon Charles Carrico was the first to examine Kennedy and found only slight signs of life. His condition, however, was hopeless. One bullet had hit near the base of the neck, slightly to the right, causing damage to the President's spine. The bullet had shot out the front of his neck, nicking the knot on his tie. This wound was not necessarily lethal. The second bullet that hit President Kennedy bored into the rear of his skull and exited the right side of his head, causing a massive and fatal wound. So extensive was the damage that doctors were unsure whether the bullets had entered from the front or the rear. They did not discover the wound in the back (lower neck/right shoulder) because they did not roll him over to examine him, concentrating instead on the right side of his head where the damage was most extensive.

Dr. Malcolm Perry performed a tracheotomy, making an incision that cut away the wound in the front of the throat. It was a futile effort and President Kennedy was pronounced dead at 1:00 p.m. Central Standard Time.

THE WARREN COMMISSION

The Warren Commission was appointed by President Johnson to investigate the circumstances surrounding the assassination and was headed by the Chief Justice of the Supreme Court, Earl Warren. The other members of the Commission were distinguished Americans, but the actual investigative work was carried out by lower ranking staff members like Arlen Specter and David Belin, experienced lawyers who were noted for their integrity. However, they had little contact with the Commission members and they had to rely largely on FBI reports since the Warren Commission had no criminal investigators of its own.

BEYOND REASONABLE DOUBT

President Johnson urged the Commission on to get the report out to stop rumors of conspiracy and members did not fully investigate many aspects of the case. As Philip Shenon wrote, "Warren has to be faulted...for denying key evidence and witnesses to the commission's staff. Those monumental errors included his refusal to allow the commission to review the president's autopsy photos and X-rays – a decision that all but guaranteed the medical evidence would remain hopelessly muddled today ..."[16]

It was later disclosed that President Johnson had intimated to one insider that Kennedy had indeed been assassinated as the result of a conspiracy. As Philip Shenon observed, "What does it say about this presidential commission that its findings were ultimately rejected by the president himself?"[17]

Johnson stated that the United States had been running a "damn Murder Incorporated" in the Caribbean (CIA murder plots against Castro) and Castro had taken revenge. It was also revealed that Johnson told Senator Richard Russell, a Commission member, that he did not believe in the 'Single-Bullet Theory' (President Kennedy and Governor Connally had been hit by the same bullet). However, according to his wife Lady Bird, Johnson accepted the findings of the Warren Commission.[18]

Notwithstanding these facts, the Warren Report was impressive – 27 volumes of witness testimony, exhibits and reports. The Warren Commission heard 552 witnesses and received more than 3000 reports from law enforcement agencies which had conducted 26,000 interviews. It is this fact that many conspiracy theorists fail to comprehend – the inevitability of imperfection given the volume of evidence.

The Commission's first conclusion was that the shots that killed President Kennedy came from the Texas School Book Depository. This conclusion was based on medical evidence which showed that at least two of the shots came from the general direction of the Depository; on the testimony of eyewitnesses who saw a rifle in the sixth-floor window of the Depository; and on the fact that the murder weapon and three cartridges were found on the 6th floor of the Depository. The Warren Commission stated:

"Based on the evidence analyzed...the Commission has concluded that the shots which killed President Kennedy and wounded Governor Connally were fired from the sixth-floor window at the southeast corner of the Texas School Book Depository Building. Two bullets probably caused all the wounds suffered by President Kennedy and Governor Connally. Since the preponderance of the evidence indicated that three shots were fired, the Commission concluded that one shot probably missed the Presidential limousine and its occupants, and that the three shots were fired in a time period ranging from approximately 4.8 to in excess of 7 seconds."[19]

The second conclusion concerned the sequence of events. The clearest movie of the assassination was taken by Abraham Zapruder. It showed the President and Governor Connally were hit less than two seconds apart. The rifle tests showed it was physically impossible for the murder weapon to be accurately fired twice within this period of time. Thus, either both men were hit by the same bullet or there had to be two assassins. The Warren Commission decided on the single-bullet theory.[20]

Thirdly, the Commission concluded that the assassin was Lee Harvey Oswald. This conclusion was based on 8 sub-conclusions:

1. The murder weapon was Oswald's.
2. Oswald carried the weapon into the Book Depository building.
3. At the time of the assassination, Oswald was at the window from which the shots were fired.
4. Oswald killed Dallas policeman J.D. Tippit in an apparent attempt to escape.
5. Oswald resisted arrest in the Texas Theater by drawing a loaded pistol and fighting violently with the police.
6. Oswald lied to the police.
7. Oswald had attempted to kill General Edwin Walker, a right-wing public figure living in Dallas.
8. Oswald possessed enough proficiency with a rifle to have committed the assassination.[21]

The Commission's fourth conclusion concerned Oswald's motive. Although the Commission could not make any definite determination of Oswald's motives, it listed 5 factors which might have influenced Oswald's decision to assassinate President Kennedy:

1. Oswald's resentment of all authority.

2. His inability to enter into meaningful relationships with people.
3. His urge to find a place in history.
4. His capacity for violence.
5. His commitment to Marxism and Communism.

Finally, there were the conclusions concerning whether or not Oswald acted alone. The report stated that because of the difficulty of proving a negative to a certainty, the possibility of others being involved with either Oswald or Ruby in a conspiracy could not be rejected categorically. They concluded that if there was any such evidence it had been beyond the reach of "all investigative agencies and resources of the United States and has not come to the attention of this Commission."[22]

However, it soon became evident that the Warren Report was flawed and inadequate in many ways. As Philip Shenon writes, the Warren Commission investigation was "flawed from the start" because of bureaucratic infighting, political manipulation, destruction of evidence, tight deadlines, understaffing, deception by intelligence agencies and a host of other ills. It was also flawed because Earl Warren refused to provide a motive for the assassination. He believed that if the Warren Commission stated that a violent Marxist had killed the president it would cause diplomatic problems with the Soviet Union and Cuba.

Some of the mistakes Earl Warren made were shocking. He buckled to the pressure he was under from President Johnson and the Kennedy family to wrap up the

BEYOND REASONABLE DOUBT

investigation as quickly as possible. After reviewing the autopsy photographs he decided not to show them to his fellow commissioners on the grounds that they were too grisly. "We don't want to use them in our record," he said, "It would make it a morbid thing for all time to come."[23] Apparently, it did not occur to him that it would fuel rumors of a cover-up. More importantly he was reluctant to press witnesses too hard or allow much time to follow up leads. In one instance he refused to allow his staff to interview Mexico Cuban consulate employee Silvia Duran who had met Oswald on his visit to the Cuban embassy weeks before the assassination as she was a proclaimed 'communist' and Warren said such people could not be believed.[24]

As Shenon points out, the commission's flawed final report has ended up fueling rather than suppressing public suspicions of a high-level conspiracy — precisely the opposite of what Johnson and Warren intended. However, in the "jittery, even apocalyptic" atmosphere of 1963, Shenon writes, it seemed entirely possible that an accusation of Soviet or Cuban involvement could spark a full-blown foreign-policy crisis or even a nuclear war. Given these facts it is entirely understandable that President Johnson's efforts to limit the commission's work was done for the nation's safety.

Critics seized on a variety of issues in the Report:

- Witnesses differed on identifying Lee Harvey Oswald, a 24-year-old ex-Marine and former defector to the Soviet Union, as the man firing a rifle from the Texas School Book Depository building. The only one who claimed to have seen him positively did not identify Oswald later in a police line-up.

- Many witnesses thought the first shot came from the railway overpass, or a grassy knoll, ahead of the Presidential car, instead of from "above and behind", as the Commission found. Three railway workers standing on the overpass bridge thought they saw smoke rising from behind the fenced-in grassy knoll area just after the shots. Within minutes, dozens of people followed a police officer up the grassy embankment and behind the fence. Three witnesses who rushed up the knoll spoke of encountering mysterious 'government agents', although government agencies denied they had any agents in that vicinity. A few ear witnesses believed one shot came from behind the picket fence at the top of the knoll.

- There was a wide difference among eye and ear witnesses as to how many shots were actually fired: some thought they heard only 2 shots, others up to 5 or 6.

- The murder weapon originally was identified by a Deputy Sheriff as a 7.65 Mauser, rather than a 6.5 Mannlicher-Carcano, indicating that there might have been more than one weapon, or a switch of weapons.

- Oswald was said to be a poor shot, using a secondhand rifle with a defective gun sight, and he could not possibly have fired three shots with such accuracy. Oswald was not known to be a 'Marksman'. He had no criminal record and

BEYOND REASONABLE DOUBT

>
> he allegedly used a cheap rifle to shoot a moving target two or more times.

- It was alleged that a paper bag the Commission concluded Oswald used to bring a rifle into the building showed no chemical or physical evidence of ever having contained a rifle, and was of a different size than witnesses remembered.

- The single bullet – Commission Exhibit No. 399 – which the Commission said hit both President Kennedy and Governor Connally, was so clean and apparently undamaged it seemed impossible that it could have gone through two bodies.

- This same bullet, found on a stretcher at Parkland Hospital in Dallas, originally was thought to have come from the President's body during heart massage, but later was identified as having fallen from Governor Connally's stretcher – one of several apparent discrepancies in testimony that critics used to infer conspiracy. The bullet found on the hospital stretcher could have been 'planted' there, and certain other evidence 'faked' to implicate Oswald, while the real killer escaped.

- The weight of fragments found in Governor Connally's wrist, when added to the weight of the bullet found at the hospital, was alleged to add up to more than the weight of a complete bullet – indicating that more shots were fired than the Warren Commission Report indicated.

- The Commission was accused of dismissing the testimonies of some witnesses and failing to call others who claimed to have pertinent information.

- The Dallas police allegedly failed to keep a record of their interrogations of Oswald while he was alive and in their custody.

- The Commission allegedly failed to reckon with testimony of witnesses who claimed to have seen Oswald, or persons resembling Oswald or giving his name, at times when the Commission found he was elsewhere.

- The Commission allegedly failed to examine the X-rays and photographs taken at the time of the autopsy at Bethesda Naval Hospital, which might have cleared up any doubt about the number and position of the wounds in the President's body.

- Many critics said Oswald's guilt was not established by due process of law under legal rules of evidence. Oswald repeatedly insisted on his innocence, unusual for political assassins. Had he lived, the critics believe, and if there had been a trial, a good lawyer could have established such a case of 'reasonable doubt' as to enable Oswald to go free.

However, David Belin, former Assistant Counsel to the Warren Commission, testifying in 1996 to the Assassination Records Review Board chaired by Judge John Tunheim, defended the integrity of the Warren Commission and its staff. Belin told the Board: "I was one of two lawyers concentrating on...the determination of who killed President Kennedy, which was expanded to who killed Officer Tippit. We interviewed the witnesses at the time shortly after the event when their recollections were the freshest and therefore the best. In undertaking our investigation, we followed but one standard, a standard that was established by Chief Justice Earl Warren in our very first meeting – Truth is our only goal – It was the standard Lee Rankin followed. It was the standard that Professor (Wesley J.) Liebeler followed. It was the standard that all of us followed....The evidence beyond a reasonable doubt was Oswald was the lone gunman. Jack Ruby was in no way conspiratorially involved. As a matter of fact, unbeknownst to most people, he offered to take lie-detector tests which confirmed that everything he told the Warren Commission was true."[25]

Throughout the decades since the Warren Commission released its report, Commission members have sought to defend the report's conclusions. In 1992, Ford said "I've never changed my opinion. I feel as strongly today... on the two basic fundamental issues. Number one, Lee Harvey Oswald was the assassin. Number two, the Commission found no evidence of a conspiracy, foreign or domestic...I am a totally devoted person to the (Commission's) conclusions. But seventy-five percent of the people don't believe the Warren Commssion anymore. It just makes me sad and unhappy."[26]

However, there is a consensus amongst historians that the Warren Commission was inadequate in the manner in which it investigated the assassination:

- The Commission did not demand to see all the CIA files on Oswald, who had been 'tracked' by the CIA and FBI from the time he defected to the Soviet Union to the time he made his trip to the Soviet and Cuban embassies in Mexico City in September of 1963. The CIA had uncovered evidence that during the Mexican trip Oswald had told several people he intended to assassinate the President. The CIA also uncovered evidence that Oswald may have had a sexual relationship with a notary at the Cuban Embassy, Silvia Duran, on this trip who introduced him to some Cuban intelligence officers, but this was withheld from the commission.

- The Commission did not do a thorough job in investigating Oswald's killer, Jack Ruby, and his alleged links to the Mafia.

- The Commission did not investigate Kennedy's natural enemies – Teamsters Union boss James R. Hoffa, New Orleans Mafia boss Carlos Marcello, Chicago mob boss Sam Giancana, Florida mob boss Santos Trafficante, and the various Anti-Castro organizations who had been angry at the President for abandoning their comrades during the 'Bay of Pigs' debacle.

- The Commission did not investigate fully the possibility that Cuban leader Fidel Castro hired Oswald to kill Kennedy as a reprisal for CIA attempts to kill him. The Warren Commission was not told about CIA attempts to kill Castro, even though ex-CIA Director Allen Dulles was a Commission member and knew about the plots. The Commission failed to discover that Castro, in the months prior to the assassination, had made threats against Kennedy.

BEYOND REASONABLE DOUBT

THE HOUSE OF REPRESENTATIVES SELECT COMMITTEE ON ASSASSINATIONS (HSCA) 1977-1979

> *"Because the (HSCA) Committee did not spend nearly enough time to determine if there was a conspiracy, the acoustical findings, which were arrived at in the last month of its existence, forced its hand. The Committee therefore concluded that the acoustical analysis proved a conspiracy, and that its best guess was that some 'individual members' of organized crime may have been involved. The Committee, however, had no names or hard proof to support that conclusion."*
>
> —JFK Researcher and author Gus Russo

The major failings of the Warren Commission were rightly criticized by assassination researchers. And in the 1970s, the FBI was also legitimately criticized when it was revealed that Oswald had delivered a threatening note to the FBI office in Dallas in the weeks prior to the assassination and that FBI agent James Hosty was ordered to destroy it.

Following the Watergate scandal and further Congressional revelations about CIA, FBI, and other government malfeasance, public distrust of governmental agencies forced the United States Congress to investigate the assassination of President Kennedy. The result was the House of Representatives Select Committee on Assassinations (HSCA) investigation. The Committee reopened the JFK assassination case and its investigation lasted three years culminating in their 1979 Final Report.

The HSCA report supported many of the conclusions of the Warren Commission but eventually decided, on the

THE WARREN COMMISSION AND THE HSCA

basis of acoustical evidence found in Dallas Police Department archives, that a conspiracy was likely.

- The major findings of the House Committee's investigation were set out in its 1979 report.[27]

- Lee Harvey Oswald fired three shots at President Kennedy. The second and third shots struck the President. The third shot killed the President. President Kennedy was struck by two rifle shots fired from behind him. The Committee stated:

"The forensic pathology panel concluded that President Kennedy was struck by two, and only two, bullets, each of which entered from the rear. The panel further concluded that the President was struck by one bullet that entered in the upper right of the back and exited from the front of the throat, and one bullet that entered in the right rear of the head near the cowlick area and exited from the right side of the head, toward the front. ... There is no medical evidence that the President was struck by a bullet entering the front of the head, and the possibility that a bullet could have struck the President and yet left no evidence is extremely remote."[28]

- The shots that struck President Kennedy from behind him were fired from the 6th floor window of the southeast corner of the Texas School Book Depository Building.

- Lee Harvey Oswald owned the rifle that was used to fire shots from the 6th floor window of the building.

- Lee Harvey Oswald, shortly before the assassination, had access to and was present on the 6th floor.

- Lee Harvey Oswald's other actions tend to support the conclusion that he assassinated President Kennedy.

- Scientific acoustical evidence established a high probability that two gunmen fired at President Kennedy. This conclusion was based on an examination of a police recording purportedly containing the sounds of four shots. Other scientific evidence did not preclude the possibility of two gunmen firing at the President.

- Scientific evidence negated some specific conspiracy theories.

- The Committee believed, on the basis of the available evidence, that President Kennedy was probably assassinated as the result of a conspiracy.

- The Committee was unable to identify the other gunman or the extent of the conspiracy.

- The Committee believed, on the basis of the available evidence, that the Soviet and Cuban governments, anti-Castro groups (as groups), the Mafia (as a group), the Secret Service, the FBI, and the CIA were not involved in the assassination.

- The HSCA criticized agencies and departments of government in the fulfillment of their duties, especially the Secret Service which did not give President Kennedy adequate protection. The investigation into the possibility of conspiracy in the assassination was inadequate. The conclusions of the Warren Commission investigation were arrived at in good faith, but presented in a fashion that was too definitive.

- The HSCA also criticized the doctors who carried out the autopsy on the President. Dr Michael Baden, the chairman of the medical panel, said the autopsy was deficient because of the "qualification of the pathologists....the failure to inspect the clothing...the inadequate documentation of injuries, lack of proper preservation of evidence, and incompleteness of the autopsy."[29]

- The FBI performed with varying degrees of competency in the fulfillment of its duties; the investigation of Lee Harvey Oswald as responsible for the assassination was thorough and professional but it failed to investigate adequately the possibility of a conspiracy.

- The CIA was deficient in its collection and sharing of information both prior to and subsequent to the assassination.

The Committee, however, was not unanimous in its conclusions that the acoustics evidence that was presented to the committee proved conspiracy. Congressman Robert Edgar issued a dissenting statement which said in part, "I believe the members of the Congress did not have sufficient time or expertise to ask the tough questions. I believe the Committee failed to properly consider how much weight to assign this (acoustics) evidence due to our own limitations of time and familiarity with the science. I believe we rushed to our conclusions and in doing so, overshadowed many important contributions which other aspects of our investigation will have on history. We did a great job up to the last moment when in our focus on the acoustics, we failed to give proper weight to other findings of the investigation."[30]

The Committee was unable to supply any concrete evidence to support its claims of a 'probable' conspiracy (aside from its newly discovered 'acoustical evidence', which will be discussed later). Staff who worked on the investigation spoke of subtle techniques by the CIA to stall the delivery of CIA files the committee requested. The Committee majority believed that, on balance, elements of the Mafia were responsible for the assassination, but there was insufficient evidence with which to bring anyone to justice. However, since the HSCA investigation, many of the anomalies and supposed discrepancies in the evidence have been re-investigated by numerous government and independent investigators.

THE 1998 ASSASSINATION RECORDS REVIEW BOARD (ARRB) REPORT

New information about the circumstances surrounding the assassination was gathered by the ARRB, which was instituted by a 1992 Act of Congress and designed to ensure the release of all government files related to the Dallas tragedy. In executing their responsibilities, they took the advice of David Belin, who told the Board, "....I think you've seen everything...or are getting access to see everything in the CIA files...I would urge that you not let them (CIA) stonewall you with this protection of sources and methods. The CIA really has unclean hands and they will learn something by not being able to protect this. So learn this so that the next time there's any kind of a Presidential commission which says that agencies will cooperate and do everything possible, they will do it. They will say, remember what happened to us when we didn't do it with the Warren Commission. We eventually, because of the ARRB had to disclose everything. So that would be my advice to you people...."[31]

The ARRB became, in effect, another government investigation. Their work was thorough. The Board's major accomplishments were as follows:

- The Board reviewed and voted on over 27,000 previously redacted (censored) assassination records.

- The Board obtained agencies' consent to release an additional 33,000 plus assassination records.

- The Board ensured that the famous Zapruder film of the assassination belonged to the American people and arranged for the first known authenticity of the film.

- The Board opened previously redacted CIA records from the Directorate of Operations.

- The Board released 99% of the 'Hardway/Lopez Report' documenting the CIA's records on Lee Harvey Oswald's trip to Mexico City shortly before the assassination.

- The Board conducted a thorough interview with former FBI agent James P. Hosty, one of two agents who were responsible for the FBI's cases on Lee and Marina Oswald prior to the assassination.

- The Board acquired for public release original notes of Lee Harvey Oswald's interrogation made after his arrest on November 22, 1963.

- The Board deposed 10 Bethesda autopsy participants, 5 Parkland Hospital treating doctors and clarified the medical record of JFK's wounds.

- The Board secured records relating to Jim Garrison's New Orleans investigation of 1967-1969.

- The Board obtained the full release of FBI documents that described the FBI's attempts to track Oswald in Europe at the time he attempted to defect to the Soviet Union.

- The Board instituted new ballistics and forensics tests to determine the origins of a bullet fragment (Warren Commission Exhibit No. 567) found in the front seat of the Presidential limousine, but never previously tested.

*The Board conducted sophisticated digital enhancements of the autopsy photographs.

The ARRB stipulated that their conclusions would not contain any judgment as to the existence or otherwise of a conspiracy to kill the President. However, the results of their work show there is no evidence which would indicate a conspiracy, nor was there evidence to point the finger at government involvement in the assassination.

OTHER GOVERNMENT INVESTIGATIONS

Other government investigations provided answers to one of the most important questions surrounding the JFK assassination – How many bullets struck President Kennedy? All conspiracy theories hinged on this important fact, because if the wounds and ear witness testimony suggested more than three shots, then there must have been a second shooter in Dealey Plaza that day.

We have the same identical conclusion being reached by all five of the following groups and Government organizations:

1. The three doctors who performed the autopsy on President Kennedy's body at Bethesda Naval Hospital on the night of November 22, 1963 (Dr. James J. Humes, Dr. J. Thornton Boswell, and Dr. Pierre A. Finck), all of whom affixed their individual signatures to the official autopsy report on 11/24/63.
2. The Warren Commission.
3. The House Select Committee on Assassinations.
4. The Clark Panel.
5. The Rockefeller Commission.

Despite some discrepancies and disagreements concerning the exact location of the entry wound on the back of JFK's head, all five of the above groups came to

BEYOND REASONABLE DOUBT

the same identical conclusion regarding the total number of bullets that struck the President and the general direction from which those bullets came – i.e., John F. Kennedy was struck by only two bullets, with both of those bullets coming from above and behind the President.

And two of the above groups (the Warren Commission and the HSCA) totally agreed on another important fact regarding the assassination — Lee Harvey Oswald was the one and only gunman who fired any shots that hit any victims in the President's limousine.[32]

CHAPTER THREE

DAMNING EVIDENCE

> *"I would love to be able to say that Lee was not involved in any way whatsoever, but the facts are there. ... What do you do with his rifle? What do you do with his pistol? What do you do with his general opportunity? What do you do with his actions? ... You can't reach but one conclusion...We know he owned a rifle. You've got all kinds of documented evidence. They've gone to the extreme measures to prove that he owned that rifle. You've got the backyard picture. They've got the original negative. They've got the camera. You've got all the physical evidence that ties together. If it was any other murder case other than the President of the United States, it would have been resolved right then."*
>
> —Robert Oswald, brother of Lee Harvey Oswald

Dozens of witnesses pointed to the Texas School Book Depository as the source of the shots. Oswald had been working there as a clerk for five weeks and was the only member of staff found to be missing. That morning he had arrived for work with something long wrapped up. He said it was curtain rods. Later that day, four residents of the Dallas suburb of Oak Cliff saw a man—later identified as Oswald—approach a Dallas police car on Tenth Street. Oswald drew a handgun and shot the officer dead. Thirty-five minutes later, Oswald, still armed, was arrested in the nearby Texas Theater.

Conspiracy theorists have a difficult time in challenging the fact that Oswald had been seen in the sixth-floor corner window of the Book Depository. The most

BEYOND REASONABLE DOUBT

important witness to the shooting who saw him there was

Howard Brennan, a man who prided himself on perfect eyesight and who could read car number plates from 200 feet. "What I saw made my blood run cold," Brennan wrote.

(Author's Note: Conspiracy theorists are wrong when they claim that Brennan's eyesight was poor on November 22, 1963. It was only AFTER the assassination, in January 1964, that Brennan suffered an accident that impaired his vision.[1] Brennan later identified Lee Harvey Oswald as the shooter.)

As the Presidential limousine left Elm Street and rushed to Parkland Memorial Hospital, policemen were rushing to the Texas School Book Depository, alerted by the sounds of the shots and a scattering of pigeons. Marrion L. Baker was the first police officer to reach the building. Baker, who heard three shots and was in the Presidential motorcade, parked his bike at the entrance to the Depository where he met the building manager Roy Truly. Together they raced up the stairs toward the upper floors, where people had reported shots fired. In the second-floor lunchroom, Baker encountered Oswald, but after Truly indicated the man was a Depository employee, they continued climbing the stairs. Less than two minutes had elapsed since the final shot had been fired.[2]

Conspiracy theorists still maintain that Oswald, if he had really shot Kennedy from the sixth floor, could not have made it down to the second floor in time for his encounter with Officer Baker. However, the Warren Commission in 1964 re-enacted Oswald's alleged trip to the second floor[3], and it was easily accomplished multiple times in less than 80 seconds.

The Commission timed Baker's journey at 90 seconds between the time he left his motorcycle and the time he encountered Oswald. Secret Service Agent John J. Howlett performed two separate re-creations of Oswald's probable post-shooting movements, taking 78 seconds on his first try and 74 seconds on the second. And Howlett was not out of breath upon reaching the second-floor lunchroom at the completion of either one of the test runs, which were conducted at a "normal walking pace" and a "fast walk", respectively[4]. Oswald was likely moving faster on November 22 than Howlett was moving during the re-enactments in 1964. The conspiracists who continue to believe that Oswald's 90-second, 4-flight trip to the second floor was a virtual impossibility are simply wrong. It was easily accomplished.

These timings were not only confirmed by the HSCA, but by many assassination researchers over the years. The re-enactments also included taking the time to hide the rifle in the place where Oswald hid it (near the stairwell).

Oswald wasn't surprised when Baker confronted him for one simple reason. He expected the police to be entering the building quickly and he had no reason to ask the officer what was going on. Any innocent bystander in that same situation would probably be a little bit scared, and at the very least ask – What's going on? or What did I do? But Oswald never uttered a word.

THE RIFLE

Shortly after the assassination, Dallas police started a floor-by-floor search of the School Book Depository. When police came to the southeast corner, 6th-floor window, they found stacked boxes that had been used as a rifle perch. Officer Luke Mooney found three cartridge shells scattered on the floor. Minutes later, in the northwest corner of the sixth floor, a bolt-action Mannlicher-Carcano 6.5-millimeter rifle was found by Deputy Sheriff Eugene Boone. It had been placed between boxes of books. Boone did not touch the rifle, but called Captain Will Fritz of the Dallas Police Homicide Bureau, who arrived with Lieutenant J.C. Day of the Crime Scene Search Section of the Identification Bureau. Day photographed it and scratched his initials on the stock. Boone commented that it looked like a 7.65 Mauser because 'Mauser' was a generic term used at that time for a bolt-action rifle. It was later learned that the rifle was really an Italian-made Mannlicher-Carcano, bearing the serial number C2766.[5]

This mis-identification of the weapon used to shoot President Kennedy was seized upon by conspiracy theorists who claimed that another rifle was involved in the assassination. Deputy Sheriff Boone repeated the testimony he gave to the Warren Commission many times as the years passed, but his explanations were simply rejected out of hand by conspiracy theorists. In a 1986 television docu-trial, "On Trial: Lee Harvey Oswald", Boone said he thought the rifle was a Mauser because it had a bolt action and there were a lot of Mausers around at the time. He said he was not an expert on firearms. However, as late as 1996, Ray and Mary La Fontaine, in their conspiracy book, *Oswald Talked*, were using this honest mistake to imply that a Mauser and a Mannlicher-Carcano were found in the Book Depository.[6]

The FBI later learned that the rifle found in the Depository had been mailed in March 1963 from a Chicago mail-order house to "A. Hidell, P.O. Box 2915, Dallas, Texas". Handwriting experts told the Warren Commission that the coupon ordering the $21.45 rifle, the signature on a money order to pay for it, and the address on the envelope were all written in Oswald's hand.[7]

Oswald's wallet contained fake identification cards for "Alek James Hidell"; one such card carried Oswald's photograph. "Alek" had been Oswald's nickname in Russia because his Russian friends thought that 'Lee' sounded 'too Chinese'. "Hidell", however, most probably came from several sources. When Oswald was in the Marine Corps in the late 1950s, he was sent to Atsugi, Japan, where he met a fellow Marine who came from New Orleans and whose name was John Rene Heindell, nicknamed "Hidell". If the name is pronounced "Heedell", the connection with Oswald's hero "Fidel" becomes evident. It was Marina Oswald who spotted the similarity. The name "James" may have been taken from "James Bond". Oswald was an avid reader of Ian Fleming's novels and he frequently commented that he would have liked to have been a spy.[8]

As the handwriting on all of the documents connected with the Klein's Sporting Goods transaction is that of Oswald's, it proves beyond all doubt that it was Oswald (and no other person) who ordered and paid for Carcano rifle #C2766 that was shipped to Oswald/Hidell by Klein's in March 1963.

One of the myths propagated by conspiracy theorists over the years has been the allegation that Oswald never ordered any rifle at all from Klein's in 1963. In one of the first books ever written on the JFK assassination in 1966, *Rush To Judgment*, lawyer and first-generation Warren Commission critic Mark Lane strongly suggested that there could have been something sinister going on with respect to the rifle and the way it was ordered through the mail. Lane also seemed to suggest the possibility that Oswald and A.J. Hidell (Oswald's alias) just might have been two different persons. Lane wrote, "It is of course possible that Oswald or Hidell or someone else ordered a rifle from the February issue of The American Rifleman and that Klein's sent a different but similar weapon by mistake. Without a suitable explanation, however, the chain of evidence relating Oswald, or Hidell, to the weapon appears damaged. The Commission failed to explore this possibility and thereby closed its mind to an important aspect of the investigation."[9]

But, in reality, the "chain of evidence relating Oswald to the weapon" is not "damaged" at all, because the trail of evidence that tells any reasonable person that Mannlicher-Carcano rifle #C2766 (Commission Exhibit 139) was ordered, paid for, and possessed by Lee Harvey Oswald (aka "A. Hidell") is extensive and ironclad. And regardless of the fact that Oswald technically did order a 36-inch Italian carbine, per the words written in the February 1963 American Rifleman magazine ad that Oswald used to order the rifle, Klein's Sporting Goods in Chicago shipped a 40-inch rifle with serial number C2766 on it to "A. Hidell" on March 20, 1963. The internal paperwork generated by Klein's at the time—in March of '63—confirms that Oswald/"Hidell" was shipped an Italian 6.5mm rifle with that exact serial number on it—C2766.[10]

Some conspiracy theorists have said Oswald was not sent the rifle he ordered; therefore, it is proof that someone had a hand in faking the provenance of the weapon. But the likely explanation for why Oswald received a 40-inch rifle instead of the 36-inch model that he ordered via the Klein's mail-order coupon is pretty simple and logical, and it is this: Klein's very likely ran out of the 36-inch model shortly before receiving Oswald's order, and hence shipped a very similar (but slightly lengthier) gun instead.

In August 2010, Gary Mack of the Sixth Floor Museum at Dealey Plaza provided information concerning the advertisements that Klein's was running in American Rifleman magazine throughout the calendar year of 1963. Mack's research revealed the fact that the February '63 Klein's ad was very likely the last time during the year 1963 that Klein's advertised the 36-inch Italian carbine. All other ads for that year that Mack was able to find indicate that the 40-inch rifle was being advertised.[11]

Mack said, "Oswald ordered the 36-inch rifle but, probably due to Klein's running out of stock, he received the 40-inch model instead. The price remained the same, so Klein's may have just sent him the newly available model instead. They would certainly accept a return if he didn't want it. The [Sixth Floor] Museum's copy of the May 1963 issue is missing four pages and, since Klein's ads normally ran in the back half of the magazine, it was likely on one of those pages. But...the ad for the months before and after May showed the exact same 40-inch rifle. I don't know when the American Rifleman normally went to press, but I would think they'd want the new issue to appear on the newsstands and in subscriber's mailboxes at or shortly before the beginning of each month. That would mean all ad copy must be ready and in the hands of the publisher at least 30 days ahead of time, maybe more. If Klein's ran out of 36-inch rifles in January, they might not even have enough time to get a corrected ad in by the March deadline. Maybe that's why there was no ad in the March issue. Perhaps Klein's sold out of the Carcano and other weapons and just couldn't update their new ad before the deadline."[12]

Regarding the way conspiracy theorists have treated the incontrovertible fact that Oswald owned the assassination weapon (and the way conspiracists, in general, treat the evidence in the JFK case), Vincent Bugliosi wrote, "The conspiracy community regularly seizes on one slip of the tongue, misunderstanding, or slight discrepancy to defeat twenty pieces of solid evidence; ...treats rumors, even questions, as the equivalent of proof; leaps from the most minuscule of discoveries to the grandest of conclusions; and insists that the failure to explain everything perfectly negates all that is explained."

Logically, a much better argument for conspiracy theorists would be to just accept the truth—that Oswald did, in fact, order, pay for, and take possession of the Carcano rifle. The conspiracy believers could then pretend that some person or group framed Oswald with Oswald's own rifle, instead of believing in the complicated cloak-and-dagger theory that some conspiracists endorse, which has a band of unknown conspirators faking Oswald's handwriting and also manufacturing all kinds of Klein's Sporting Goods and U.S. Money Order documents pertaining to the mail-order purchase of the rifle, all in an effort to make it look as though Lee Oswald purchased Mannlicher-Carcano rifle #C2766. Conspiracy theorists often overlook other damning evidence when it comes to matching the rifle used in the assassination to Oswald. The FBI also found a tuft of cotton fibers—blue, grey-black and orange-yellow—clinging to the rifle butt. Under microscopic examination, the fibers matched those in the shirt worn by Oswald the day of the assassination. And the rifle was linked to Oswald by a fingerprint and palm print found on the paper sack used to carry the rifle. The spent shells found under the sixth-floor corner window were conclusively proven by firearms identification experts to have been fired in Mannlicher-Carcano rifle #C2766—Oswald's rifle—to the exclusion of every other rifle on Earth.

Oswald had kept his rifle wrapped in an old brown and green blanket in a garage at the Irving, Texas, home of Ruth Paine, where Marina Oswald stayed the previous eight weeks. Ruth felt some compassion for the Oswalds and offered to look after Marina and her baby while Lee Oswald looked for work in Dallas.

When Dallas Police turned up at the Paine house after Oswald's arrest, they asked Marina, through Ruth Paine, who interpreted for her, if her husband had a rifle. She told them the rifle owned by Lee was kept in the Paine garage wrapped in a blanket. When she accompanied the police officers to the garage, the blanket looked exactly as it always had, as if there was something bulky still inside. It was carefully tied with string. As an officer picked it up, it hung limp over his arm. A fiber which had been found in the paper bag Oswald had used to carry the rifle to the Book Depository was forensically, but not conclusively, matched to this blanket.

Oswald was living in a Dallas rooming house and rarely visited the Paine home on weeknights. But on Thursday evening, November 21, 1963, the day before the assassination, he hitched a ride to Irving with fellow worker Buell Wesley Frazier. Oswald told Frazier he wanted to pick up some curtain rods. Later investigations indicated that his room was already supplied with them.

Oswald stayed overnight in the Paine home but never mentioned the curtain rods. He departed in the morning with his package and walked to the Frazier residence. Oswald placed the package in the car before Frazier left the house. When Frazier got into the car, Oswald casually explained that it contained curtain rods and when they arrived at the Book Depository parking lot, Oswald hurried to the building 50 feet ahead of his co-worker. He was carrying the package. Oswald had never previously walked ahead of Frazier to the building. But Friday, November 22nd was different.

Conspiracy theorists criticized the lack of a positive identification of the parcel Oswald carried to work that morning. Both Frazier and his sister, Linnie Mae Randle, made mistakes in describing the parcel's length, and conspiracists maintain that the disassembled rifle was too long to be the package described by these witnesses. However, in 1986, Frazier confirmed via lawyer Vincent Bugliosi's questions that he (Frazier) had only glanced at the package, and that Oswald carried the package parallel to his body. Frazier further said that the package could have extended beyond Oswald's body and he might not have noticed it.[13]

The question of whether or not Oswald took his rifle into work that morning, however, is a moot point. Oswald had plenty of opportunities to hide his rifle in the Book Depository on other occasions.

Conspiracy theorists have also seized on the idea that Oswald's rifle could not fire accurately, therefore the shooting had to be done by others. The Warren Commission and the HSCA determined otherwise. Oswald's 1940-manufactured Mannlicher-Carcano rifle was the weapon of choice at the beginning of the last century for 1,000-yard shooting contests. Travelling at 2,000 feet per second, its bullets are extremely stable. And with a metal jacket, a bullet fired from the rifle can penetrate four feet of pine. During the Second World War, it was frequently observed to travel through two or more soldiers. According to ballistics expert Larry Sturdivan, "... the rifle that Lee Oswald obtained from Klein's Sporting Goods...was accurate, lethal, and well suited for the job. There was no 'better weapon' available..."[14]

The rifle fired a heavy bullet weighing approximately 160 grains, twice the weight of today's bullets of the same caliber. It was a crude weapon, which shot a heavy bullet quite accurately enough to hit someone at 100 yards. And some non-experts, using the iron sights, have fired the weapon with only 1.6 seconds between shots, much less time than was actually needed in the Kennedy assassination.

Scientific tests and expert opinion, therefore, have established that the Mannlicher-Carcano was a powerful and accurate rifle – accurate enough to allow Oswald to fire three shots, of which at least two found their mark, in the time allowed by the Zapruder film of the assassination. Furthermore, the use of a four-power telescopic sight was a substantial aid, although the accuracy of Oswald's firing could be accomplished by using the rifle's standard iron sights. It can be argued that the iron sights would have been much easier to use, as firing time takes longer if you use a scope. Professional hunters who hunt moving game prefer iron sights.

At the time of the first shot, the limousine was approximately 135 feet from the window of the Book Depository. Oswald's scope made the actual distance appear to be only about 33 feet (11 yards). This shot could have been fired through the foliage of the oak tree and the bullet split. It is easy to assume that Oswald suffered from what hunters call 'buck fever', the excitement of seeing the 'trophy' through his line of sight and firing the gun before it is properly aimed.

The second shot struck Kennedy and Connally when the limousine was about 190 feet from Oswald's window, and the third shot (the fatal head shot that killed the President) was fired when the car was precisely 265.3 feet (88 yards) from the window. Not a long distance at all for someone like Oswald, who was trained to fire a rifle in the U.S. Marine Corps.[15]

There has also been much speculation as to Oswald's skill with a rifle. Nelson Delgado's name appears in many conspiracy books, mainly because he testified to the Warren Commission that Oswald was a poor rifle shot when he was in the Marines. He testified that Oswald's shooting was a "big joke" because he got a lot of "Maggie's drawers" – a red flag indicating the shots had missed their target – and that he had barely qualified. He had scored just one point above the score necessary to qualify. As a young recruit, however, he had done better. His rifle score book showed him making 48 and 49 points out of a possible 50 in rapid fire at 200 yards from a sitting position, without a telescopic sight.[16]

Sergeant Zahn, one of Oswald's trainers, has confirmed Oswald's ability with a rifle and described him as an excellent shot. In December 1956, at the end of his training, Oswald was tested and scored 212 — two points above the minimum for 'sharpshooter' on a scale of expertise ranging in ascending order from 'Marksman' to 'Sharpshooter' to 'Expert'. By civilian standards, he was an excellent shot. Moreover, Oswald now had a 4-power scope.[17]

Many conspiracy theorists maintain the shooting has never been duplicated. Of the three professional marksmen used by the Warren Commission to try to duplicate Oswald's performance, only one was able to fire three shots in the time stipulated by the Commission (they were later found to be mistaken about the timing— the time Oswald had to shoot the rifle was eight seconds or more and not six as the Commission believed, because the original timing was based on the assumption that Oswald would not have fired the first shot as the limousine passed under the foliage of an oak tree).

FINGERPRINT AND PALM PRINT EVIDENCE

When Dallas Police Lieutenant J.C. Day took the rifle apart, he found and lifted a palm print from under the rifle barrel which he sent to the FBI laboratories in Washington. It was later identified as "the palm print of Lee Harvey Oswald".

Palm prints are just as unique as fingerprints. Three different fingerprint experts identified two prints lifted from the paper bag as those of Lee Harvey Oswald. Sebastian F. Latona of the FBI identified the prints as positively being Oswald's.[18] And in separate independent examinations of the prints found on the bag, two other experts (Ronald G. Wittmus of the FBI and Arthur

Mandella of the New York City Police Department) came back with the very same results—the prints were Oswald's.[19]

Wesley Liebeler of the Warren Commission staff sought further confirmation as to whether it could be proven that the palm print had really come from Oswald's rifle. And such additional proof was obtained in early September of 1964 when the FBI's fingerprint expert, Sebastian Latona, re-examined the palm print more closely and found rust spots and other marks within the lifted print itself that perfectly matched the same type of marks that could also be seen on Oswald's rifle in exactly the same place on the barrel where Lt. Day said he lifted the print.[20]

In Oliver Stone's movie *JFK*, 'conspirators' imprinted the rifle with the dead Oswald's palm print. There is absolutely no credible evidence to suggest this ever happened. However, the fingerprints which were found on the trigger guard of the rifle were too blurred to make any conclusive opinion as to who had handled the weapon.[21]

The question of fingerprints on the rifle, or supposed lack of them, was finally resolved in 1993 by one of America's leading fingerprint experts, Vincent Scalice, during the making of a PBS 'Frontline' documentary. In 1963, the latent fingerprints on the trigger guard were initially ignored by investigating agencies because they were less defined than the palm print. "The FBI examined these latent prints," Scalice said, "and determined that they were worthless for identification purposes. I re-examined the photo of these latent prints again in 1978 for the Select Committee on Assassinations and came to the same conclusion, due to the faintness of the prints. I determined that they were of no value for identification purposes."[22]

However, Rusty Livingstone, who worked in the Dallas Crime Lab in 1963, found a second set of photographs of the prints which he took for himself and stored. This long neglected evidence was re-examined by Scalice in 1993. On examination, the prints on the trigger guard were found to have three positive and three possible points of identity, though not enough for an 'absolute' identity.

Using a new technique, Scalice was prepared to go much further. "I took the photographs; there were a total of four photographs in all," he said, "Then I began to examine them, and as I did I saw two faint prints which had been taken at different exposures and it was necessary for me to utilize all of the photographs to compare against the ink prints. As I examined them, I found that by maneuvering the photographs in different positions, I was able to pick up some details on one photograph and some details on another photograph. Using all of the photographs at different contrasts, I was able to find in the neighborhood of about 18 points of identity (he would later continue his work and increase the total to 24 points of identity; 10 points of identification are usually required for a positive identification) between the two prints. I feel that this is a major breakthrough in this investigation because we're able, for the first time, to actually say that these are definitely the fingerprints of Lee Harvey Oswald and that they are on the rifle. There is no doubt about it."

DAMNING EVIDENCE

Other experts pointed to the fact that the prints were 'fresh' because they would not last long on an oily metal surface such as the trigger guard housing.[23]

THE TIMING OF THE SHOTS

In 1964, the Warren Commission relied on hundreds of photographs and a number of home movies of the assassination in order to determine how President Kennedy and Governor John Connally sustained their wounds. The Commission also re-enacted the assassination using the photographic evidence as a starting point. Home movies were shot by Orville O. Nix, Marie Muchmore, Charles Bronson, and Robert Hughes.

However, it was Abraham Zapruder's home movie which became the most important visual record of the assassination. Unlike the other movies, Zapruder's 26-second film captured the full range of events from the time the Presidential limousine turned the corner from Houston Street onto Elm Street until the limousine went out of view under the railway overpass (sometimes referred to as the 'triple underpass', as three roads converge in downtown Dallas). It represents a time 'clock' of the assassination, as it was determined that the camera filmed at 18.3 frames per second. It also recorded the exact moments when President Kennedy and Governor Connally were hit. Zapruder had been filming from atop a concrete pedestal on the grassy knoll to the west of the motorcade on Elm Street.

The Warren Commission marked the frames in the Zapruder film, with No. 1 given to the first frame when the motorcycles leading the motorcade came into view on Elm Street. The frames continue in sequence to the time the limousine proceeds down Elm Street and disappears under the railway overpass. From the perspective of the sixth floor of the Texas School Book Depository, JFK passes beneath the foliage of a large oak tree, situated in front of the Depository, at frame 166. For a fleeting moment, President Kennedy comes back into view at frame 186. From the perspective of Abraham Zapruder, the view of President Kennedy is blocked by a road sign at frame 205. When Kennedy comes into view at frame 225, he can be seen to be reacting to a wound in his neck as his hands move towards his throat. At frame 313, Kennedy's head explodes, spraying brain tissue and blood in the vicinity around him.

For nearly five decades, conspiracy theorists have used the Warren Commission's sequence of shots to claim that Oswald could not have fired in the time available. The Warren Commission did not make a definitive judgment as to which shots caused which wounds (other than the fatal head shot at Z313, which is obvious). It did imply, however, that the first shot could not have been fired until frames 193-198 of the Zapruder film, as the oak tree would have obscured Oswald's view. As we shall see later when examinations of the computer models are discussed, this idea was wrong. The Warren Commission's claims are now redundant with the new time sequence of the shots – 3 shots fired – the first shot which missed at frame 157 of the Zapruder film – the second shot at frames 223/224 and the third shot at frame 313 (the head shot). Oswald had 8 to 8.4 seconds to fire his shots and not 5.6 seconds as conspiracy theorists have supposed.

It was the third shot that was fatal. The second shot was probably not fatal. It is entirely feasible that Kennedy could have recovered from this wound to the neck, although his recovery would have been difficult and he may have been paralyzed, the spine having suffered severe trauma. The time between the first bullet to strike JFK and Governor Connally and the head shot to President Kennedy was between 4.8 and 5.6 seconds. Connally was hit at the instant the second bullet exited President Kennedy's throat. The bullet had entered into Connally's back, tore across a rib and out his chest, shattered his right wrist and entered his left thigh.

Most conspiracy theorists have also incorrectly asserted over the years that the Warren Commission was pigeonholed into accepting a 5.6-second timeframe for the three shots that the Commission determined were fired at President Kennedy's limousine in Dallas. But is this really accurate? There are multiple places in the Warren Final Report which convey the Commission's own uncertainty as to which of the three shots missed the President's limousine entirely. For example:

"The evidence is inconclusive as to whether it was the first, second, or third shot which missed." — Warren Report, page 111

"The wide range of possibilities and the existence of conflicting testimony, when coupled with the impossibility of scientific verification, precludes a conclusive finding by the Commission as to which shot missed." – Warren Report, page 117

"If the second shot missed, then 4.8 to 5.6 seconds was the total time span of the shots. If either the first or third shots missed, then a minimum of 2.3 seconds (necessary to operate the rifle) must be added to the time span of the shots which hit, giving a minimum time of 7.1 to 7.9 seconds for the three shots. If more than 2.3 seconds elapsed between a shot that missed and one that hit, then the time span would be correspondingly increased. ... The three shots were fired in a time period ranging from approximately 4.8 to in excess of 7 seconds." – Warren Report, page 117

So, as can be easily seen, the Warren Commission was not limiting itself to only a 5.6-second time span for Lee Harvey Oswald's three rifle shots. The Commission, on page 117 of its Final Report, fully allows for the possibility of up to 7.9 seconds for the three shots, and fully acknowledges the possibility that either the first or the third shot missed the President's car.

THE EAR WITNESS EVIDENCE

Because of the confusion and horror that followed the shooting, no one in the vicinity of Dealey Plaza was quite sure whether there were three or four or more shots fired at the limousine, and some witnesses believed shots came from the area to the right and in front of the limousine – not surprising, as the area around the Book Depository acted as an 'echo chamber'.

Witnesses to gunshots are frequently confused by the direction of the shots because a bullet travels faster than the speed of sound. The acoustics are such that a witness who is standing at right angles to the path of the bullet may perceive the shot to have been fired from a position opposite to him. It is for these reasons that witnesses in Dealey Plaza varied enormously as to the number of shots fired and the direction of the shots.

With respect to the ear witnesses who heard the gunfire in Dealey Plaza, there can be no question that there were varied accounts of exactly where in that park-like Plaza the gunshots came from.[24]

Many witnesses thought the shots had come from the now-famous grassy knoll in front of the President's limousine, while many other witnesses said they heard shots from the direction of the Texas School Book Depository to the rear of the car (a building from where Lee Harvey Oswald was physically seen firing a rifle at the President, and a building where Oswald's own rifle was discovered 52 minutes after the assassination).

The reason that both camps of ear witnesses ("front" vs. "rear") cannot each be accurate when it comes to what they heard is due to an often ignored, overlooked, or buried statistic concerning these same ear witnesses — i.e., the number of them who heard shots coming from more than one direction. Less than 5% of the witnesses who gave an opinion as to the source of the gunfire claimed to have heard shots coming from more than one single direction (be it front or rear), which is an incredibly low percentage if conspiracy theorists like filmmaker Oliver Stone are to be believed—with Stone contending that there were three different gunmen taking aim at President Kennedy in Dealey Plaza that day, two in the rear and one on the grassy knoll. And yet more than 95 percent of the witnesses said that shots had come from just one location in the Plaza.

THE BACKYARD PHOTOS

Lee Harvey Oswald's wife, Marina, identified the rifle in testimony to the Warren Commission during its 1964 hearings. She described it as "the fateful rifle of Lee Oswald". She also said she had taken some photographs of her husband with the rifle and his pistol in the backyard of their Neely Street apartment in Dallas. Lee arranged for Marina to take the photographs with Lee's Imperial Reflex Duo Lens camera on Sunday, March 31, 1963, just days after Oswald had acquired the two weapons. This was damning evidence.[25]

After his arrest, Oswald told Captain Will Fritz of the Dallas Police Department that the Neely Street backyard photographs were fakes – a claim promoted by conspiracy theorists ever since. Oswald claimed the photograph shown to him by detectives was a composite made by superimposing his head on someone else's body – a claim also made by Oliver Stone in the movie "JFK".

During his work for the Warren Commission, photographic expert Lyndal Shaneyfelt of the FBI concluded beyond all doubt that the negative to the backyard photo known as CE133-B (which is a negative that was recovered from Ruth Paine's garage along with two of the backyard photos themselves, CE133-A and CE133-B) was positively a negative that came from Lee Oswald's very own Imperial Reflex camera to the exclusion of all other cameras ever made: "I reached the conclusion that the negative, which is Commission Exhibit 749, was exposed in the camera, Commission Exhibit 750, and no other camera."[26]

HSCA members questioned Marina about the photographs in 1978. Dressed in black, Oswald wore a pistol on his belt, holding the rifle in one hand and recent copies of left-wing newspapers, 'The Militant' and 'The Worker', in the other. Lee told her he wanted photographs to send to 'The Militant'.

Additionally, Marina Oswald, many times since 1963, has verified (in books, interviews, and in her Warren Commission and HSCA testimony) that she definitely *did* take pictures of her husband in the backyard of their Neely Street home in Dallas in early 1963.[27]

"I was very nervous that day when I took the pictures," Marina told author Gerald Posner. "I can't remember how many I took, but I know I took them and that is what is important. It would be easier if I said I never took them, but that is not the truth."[28]

Many years after the Warren Commission concluded its investigation, the photographic panel for the HSCA conducted a detailed study of the backyard photographs. Using sophisticated analytical techniques, the panel of experts hired by the committee uncovered a unique mark of wear and tear on the rifle in the photographs that corresponded to a mark on the weapon found in the Depository, and concluded that the two weapons were identical. The HSCA experts proved that the photographs were genuine by making reference to the unique grain within the photographs. The HSCA panel of experts also rejected a former Scotland Yard detective's interpretation that the photographs had been forged. The HSCA determined, therefore, that the rifle being held by Lee Harvey Oswald in the backyard photographs was, in fact, the very same rifle that was determined to be the weapon used to assassinate John F. Kennedy: "A comparison of identifying marks that exist on the rifle as shown in photographs today with marks shown on the rifle in photographs taken in 1963 indicates both that the rifle in the Archives is the same weapon that Oswald is shown holding in the backyard picture and the same weapon, found by Dallas police, that appears in various post assassination photographs."[29]

The HSCA concluded: "The panel detects no evidence of fakery in any of the backyard picture materials."[30]

This did not prevent Anthony Summers, in his 1980 book *Conspiracy*, and Robert Groden, in his 1995 book, *The Search for Lee Harvey Oswald*, from using these photographs to infer conspiracy and using a Scotland Yard expert to support their conclusions. Missing from their accounts is the fact their 'expert' later deferred to the analysis of the photos by the HSCA team.

In 1997, however, Groden was discredited as a photographic expert during the O.J. Simpson civil trial. G. Robert Blakey, a top University of Notre Dame law professor who was

Chief Counsel and director of the HSCA, told the *National Enquirer* that Groden had lied about his credentials: "Groden's ability to interpret photographs is nil," Blakey said. "Groden's theory (that the backyard photos were fakes) produced smiles on the faces of those people who know better. The pictures were sent to the best people in the world, bar none, to check them for authenticity – top labs at Stanford University, the University of Southern California and the Rochester Institute of Technology... (who verified the photos were genuine)."[31]

Furthermore, the photos were seen by someone other than Marina Oswald prior to the assassination. Michael Paine, a friend of the Oswalds, declared that he had seen one of the photos as early as April 1963. This severely damages conspiracy scenarios based on the photos.[32]

Additionally, the idea that just *one* of the photos is legitimate while others were manufactured by a group of photo-faking conspirators, which is what some conspiracy theorists actually believe, is risible. Because if one photo is legitimate, then why would anyone have had any desire to create additional *fake* pictures showing the *exact same thing* – Lee Oswald in his backyard holding guns and Communist newspapers? A re-creation of the backyard photos was simulated by CBS News in 1967 for the four-part CBS-TV special, *A CBS News Inquiry: The Warren Report*. During the photo re-creation, a man went to the location where Marina Oswald took the backyard pictures (214 Neely Street in Dallas, Texas) to see if an exact replica of the original photos could be achieved. On March 31, 1967, the recreation revealed that the shadows that appear in the 1967 photo were *exactly the same* as they appear in the 1963 Oswald backyard photographs, right down to the *angled* body shadow and the *straight* nose shadow. The 1967 photo reconstruction verifies beyond all possible doubt that the shadow patterns exhibited in the 1963 Oswald backyard photos are perfectly consistent with shadows that exist in a photo that was taken in 1967 for comparison purposes.

Perhaps the best proof of the authenticity of the backyard pictures is a signature and inscription that exist on the back of a copy of one of the photos that was found among the possessions of Oswald's friend, George DeMohrenschildt, in 1977. The words that appear on the back of that picture — *"To my friend George from Lee Oswald"* — were determined by the HSCA to be in the handwriting of Lee Harvey Oswald.[33] All the solid evidence (such as the evidence discussed above) indicates beyond all reasonable doubt that the backyard photographs of Lee Harvey Oswald have not been tampered with.

CHAPTER FOUR

THE SINGLE-BULLET THEORY, THE HEAD SHOT, AND THE GRASSY KNOLL

> *"As experienced trial lawyers, we knew that when there are two or more witnesses to a sudden event, you generally get two or more different stories about what happened. Often the stories are conflicting. After all, our eyes are not perfect cameras that can recall exactly what took place in a matter of seconds. If you get two conflicting stories with two witnesses, you can imagine how many arise when there are hundreds of witnesses to a sudden event as there were in Dealey Plaza on November 22, 1963."*
>
> — David Belin
>
> *"The fact that (JFK and Governor Connally) both react at the same time clinches it. So it's not a magic bullet at all. It's not even a single bullet theory, in my opinion. It's a single bullet fact."*
>
> — JFK Assassination researcher Dale Myers

The circumstances surrounding the shots fired at President Kennedy have led conspiracists to claim that there was more than one shooter firing at the President. According to conspiracy theorists, the Kennedy assassination was a brilliant conspiracy including a throw-down bullet placed on a stretcher at Parkland Hospital. There were backup snipers everywhere in Dealey Plaza, in case the primary sniper in the 6th floor window missed. At last count there were three snipers behind the wooden fence on the grassy knoll, one in front of the wooden fence, one in the storm drain on Elm Street, three in the Book Depository, one on the roof of the Depository, one inside a closet in the Dal-Tex Building, and perhaps one more on the roof of the Dal-Tex.

If Oswald took at least one shot, that makes a dozen snipers firing on the motorcade as it passed through Dealey Plaza. All these snipers were able to set up and shoot at the motorcade then leave these various locations completely unseen, except for the patsy. The odds of that happening are astronomical.

JFK's neck wound and Governor Connally's body wounds occurred at virtually the same time. Thus, it was claimed, a second shooter would have to be present. And conspiracists claimed that a wound to the President's head was one of entry and not exit. If this was so, conspiracists claimed, a shot had been fired from the grassy knoll, which was in front and to the right of the Presidential limousine when Kennedy was hit. If a second shooter was firing from the grassy knoll, then Oswald had accomplices or the alleged assassin had been framed.

The *Single-Bullet Theory* was originally advanced by the Warren Commission in 1964. For decades, conspiracy theorists have criticized the "SBT", claiming it's impossible for one bullet to have struck both JFK and Texas Governor John Connally, with many of those same conspiracists also contending that the SBT was merely a convenient fabrication on the part of Arlen Specter and the Warren Commission, a theory that was invented in order to prop up the conclusion that Lee Harvey Oswald,

THE SINGLE BULLET THEORY

by himself, shot and killed President Kennedy. But where does the physical evidence (and common sense) really lead us when discussing the Single-Bullet Theory? Based on the official evidence in the John F. Kennedy murder case, all of the following facts about the assassination are true:

1. President John F. Kennedy and Texas Governor John B. Connally were shot by rifle bullets in Dallas' Dealey Plaza on Friday, November 22, 1963.

2. Lee Harvey Oswald's Mannlicher-Carcano rifle (Serial Number C2766) was located inside a building (the Texas School Book Depository) which overlooked the assassination site when Kennedy and Connally were being wounded by gunfire.[1]

3. A nearly whole bullet (Warren Commission Exhibit 399) was found inside the hospital where JFK and Connally were taken after the shooting.[2] And CE399 was found in a location within the hospital where President Kennedy was never located prior to the bullet being found by Darrell Tomlinson. Nor was JFK's stretcher ever in the area of the hospital where Tomlinson discovered the bullet.[3]

4. Bullet CE399 was positively fired from Lee Harvey Oswald's rifle.[4]

5. Bullet CE399, based on the above points in total, had to have been inside Governor Connally's body on 11/22/63.

6. A man who looked like Lee Harvey Oswald was seen firing a rifle at the President's limousine from a southeast corner window on the sixth

BEYOND REASONABLE DOUBT

floor of the Book Depository Building. No other gunmen were seen firing any weapons in Dealey Plaza on November 22nd.

7. No bullets (or large bullet fragments) were found in the upper back or neck of John Kennedy's body. And no significant damage was found inside these areas of JFK's body either.

8. No bullets (or large bullet fragments) were found inside the body of Governor Connally after the shooting. The only bullet, anywhere, that can possibly be connected with Connally's wounds is Bullet CE399.

9. Given the point in time when both Kennedy and Connally were first hit by rifle fire (based on the Abraham Zapruder Film), and given the known location of Governor Connally's back (entrance) wound, and also taking into account the individual points made above — Bullet CE399 had no choice but to have gone through the body of President Kennedy prior to entering the back of John B. Connally.

Numbers 1 through 9 above add up to a logical, commonsense short explanation of the events in Dealey Plaza on November 22, 1963 (excluding the head shot that killed President Kennedy). The nine points above make the Single-Bullet Theory more than just a "theory" — it's almost certainly the only conceivable way that Kennedy and Connally were wounded. Any alternative theory that must replace the SBT would be a theory that is replete with far more guesswork and unexplainable occurrences than the Single-Bullet Theory possesses. If the Single-Bullet Theory is incorrect, and if JFK's upper-back and throat wounds were caused by two separate

THE SINGLE BULLET THEORY

bullets (as many conspiracy theorists firmly believe), then we are forced to believe that two separate rifle bullets failed to penetrate all the way through the neck and back of JFK. Is this a logical conclusion to reach, especially when factoring in the very minimal damage that was done to these areas of President Kennedy's body? If conspiracy theorists wish to argue that perhaps one of the shots was a "dum-dum" of some type, or that one shot was a misfire and therefore the velocity entering Kennedy was severely reduced, then this is plausible. But two such shots of this kind that do not transit the soft flesh of the President in the throat and upper back regions is not. Two non-lethal missiles that pierce his body only a little bit, and fail to kill him or to completely transit the soft tissues of his neck and upper back is simply not credible.

Even if conspiracists want to argue that the angles are not very accurate for the SBT to work or align properly back to the Oswald window in the Book Depository, any theory that we're forced to substitute for the official SBT falls apart on many different levels. For example, if we're to believe the conspiracy theorists, here's what certainly must have occurred instead of the SBT:

1. The bullet that struck JFK did go all the way through him but somehow missed the man sitting in front of him who was in direct line to receive this bullet. The bullet was then scooped up from inside the limousine by plotters after the fact and disposed of and the damage to the inside of the limousine that was no doubt caused by this bullet was completely eradicated in very short order after the event. This is unlikely, especially in light of the FBI's Robert

BEYOND REASONABLE DOUBT

>Frazier who gave testimony to the Warren Commission[5] : ARLEN SPECTER – "Did your examination of the President's limousine disclose any other holes or markings which could have conceivably been caused by a bullet striking the automobile or any part of the automobile?" ROBERT A. FRAZIER – "No, sir."

2. Lacking a bullet that transits JFK, we're left to accept a three-bullet scenario to explain the wounds sustained by the two victims — fired by three separate gunmen as well (two from the rear and one from the front). Given the very tight timeline per the Zapruder Film, there could not possibly have been fewer than three gunmen utilized to inflict all of the wounds on the two victims in the allowable timeframe via such a "three-bullet" scenario.

3. All three of these (supposedly) entry wounds on JFK and Connally line themselves up in such a fashion on the bodies to give the general appearance that they could have all been caused by just a single missile passing through both men simultaneously. No reasonable and/or believable conspiracy-oriented explanation that logically rationalizes and defends this amazing "wound placement" occurrence on two different victims has been provided. The likelihood of these wounds aligning in such a fashion on two victims is pretty remote if the Single-Bullet Theory is untrue. If three gunmen managed to pull off that shooting feat with three different bullets, it would have represented a truly miraculous marksmanship accomplishment.

4. The two or three bullets that allegedly replace the SBT have never been recovered or they

THE SINGLE BULLET THEORY

have been disposed of by conspirators. In either instance, none of these bullets that conspiracists think peppered Kennedy and Connally are entered into any kind of official record representing this murder case.

Is it logical to conclude that all of the bullets that entered JFK and John Connally on 11/22/63 really did vanish immediately after the shooting? Logic dictates otherwise, especially when this particular conspiracy theory has *two* different bullets going into JFK's body *but not exiting his body at all*. The corollary of this theory means that those two bullets would have still been inside the President's body at his autopsy on the night of November 22.

How could the so-called "plotters" or conspirators have pulled it off – so that all of the whole bullets, in the bodies of two different men, were never recovered by anyone at Parkland Hospital, and so lucky to not have even one of those bullets enter the official record at any time? This applies especially with regard to the Connally bullet – a bullet that enters a man who *lived* through the ordeal, and whose body could not be "controlled" later at a phony autopsy (as some conspiracy theorists think occurred with JFK's autopsy). The odds that the plotters could have controlled all of the trace evidence located inside *two* different victims, one of whom survived the shooting, is essentially implausible.

Any such multi-shooter theory is also very unlikely from the popular "Oswald was framed as the patsy" perspective. Would any conspirators have deliberately been so foolhardy and utterly reckless as to fire several bullets into JFK's body (including the head shot), from

91

varying angles, and yet still expect every last scrap of ballistics evidence to get traced back to *only* Lee Harvey Oswald's rifle and get traced back to *only* Oswald's Sniper's Nest window in the Book Depository? Why would *anyone* deliberately be so reckless? Alternatively, the lone-assassin scenario rests, at least in part, on the very sound and logical shoulders of the Single-Bullet Theory — a theory in which all of the following is thoroughly explained:

1. Every bullet (totaling *one* in number) is recovered and enters the official record (Bullet #CE399). There are no mysteries as to any missing missiles.

2. The fact that no bullets were found inside JFK or Governor Connally (particularly the President) is perfectly logical and to be expected via the SBT. Plus the very important fact that no bullet holes or similar missile damage was done to the limousine's interior in the back seat or jump seat areas of the automobile.

3. All wounds to both men are perfectly consistent with the Single-Bullet Theory.

4. Via the Zapruder Film, the single-bullet conclusion holds up under intense scrutiny as well, with both victims reacting to external (bullet) stimulus at virtually an identical time on the film (see Zapruder frames 224-230).

There is also another logical dimension to the single-bullet *fact*. Kennedy's body would not have stopped a bullet travelling at 2,000 feet per second. Such bullets that can bring down elephants would not have stopped travelling 1 to 2 inches into Kennedy's back.

THE SINGLE BULLET THEORY

The critics have done little to disprove the SBT in any kind of meaningful way. However, there have been true-to-life and animated tests performed over the years that have concretely backed up the validity of the Single-Bullet Theory, beginning with the detailed reconstruction of the shooting done by the Warren Commission at the scene of the crime in Dallas' Dealey Plaza in May of 1964. Plus, there's also the simulation done by Failure Analysis Associates, along with Dale Myers' computer animation project, and the SBT re-creation performed in the 2004 Discovery Channel program, *JFK: Beyond The Magic Bullet*.

All of these re-creations are as close to being accurate as humanly possible, especially given the unknowns regarding some measurements — such as the exact positioning of Connally's wrist at the moment the bullet hit him and the exact positioning of JFK and Connally to each other in the car during the shooting. No such tests have been performed by conspiracists that would undermine the single-bullet conclusions reached by the Warren Commission, Dale Myers, Failure Analysis, and the Discovery Channel.

In 1978, The HSCA convened a medical panel, headed by Chief forensic pathologist Dr. Michael Baden, then the medical examiner of New York City. The members of the nine-man panel collectively had participated in 100,000 autopsies. The panel looked at the Zapruder film and concluded that the Single-Bullet Theory was correct.[6]

When Baden was interviewed by author Gerald Posner he confirmed the validity of the single-bullet 'fact'. Baden said, "One of the silliest arguments critics made over the years is that the bullet came out of Kennedy's neck, made a right turn to hit Connally's shoulder, then made another right when it left his chest in order to strike his wrist and then completely changed direction and made a left to enter his thigh. Some people still believe that, even though photo enhancements long ago showed the Governor was in such a position that his wounds were clearly the result of one bullet passing straight through him."[7]

THE HEAD SHOT

The fatal JFK head shot entered the rear of the President's skull and exited on the right side. The Warren Commission and the HSCA concluded the wound on the right side of Kennedy's head was an 'exit wound'. Conspiracists insist it was an entry wound from a bullet that had been fired from the grassy knoll and they reference the Zapruder home movie film footage which shows Kennedy's head snapping backwards, which to the lay person indicates a shot had been fired from the front. They also allege that the back of Kennedy's head was 'blown away'.

At the time of the shooting, there were scores of people running in the direction of the knoll. There were also many who were running in the direction of the Book Depository. Most of the grassy knoll runners had no explanation of why they ran in that direction. Some said it was the logical place to go. Some saw police motorcyclist Bobby Hargis run to the area to inspect it; he had deduced there could only be two places where the shots originated, and as he was nearest to the grassy knoll, he headed in that direction. He saw

THE SINGLE BULLET THEORY

nothing suspicious. Hargis was soon followed by curious onlookers.

Perhaps one of the biggest mistakes made by the Warren Commission was in not releasing to the public the X-rays and photographs of President Kennedy's body taken during the autopsy. Instead of submitting the X-rays and photographs, the Warren Commission directed the doctors, who were clinical pathologists—not forensic pathologists—to furnish their own drawings. As the doctors themselves were to say – they were doctors, not artists. Consequently, their misplacing of wounds contributed to the popularizing of false theories – many of which could have been demolished had the X-rays and photographs been available. There was no sinister motive blocking their release, as some conspiracy theorists have claimed; the decision was made in the interests of good taste and the feelings of the Kennedy family.

Dr. Lundberg, the editor of the Journal of the American Medical Association asked Dr. Humes and Dr. Boswell to clear up the anomalies arising out of the autopsy report. Dr. Humes, although admitting his own errors, called the conspiracy theorists 'supremely ignorant'. Humes concluded, "In 1963, we proved at the autopsy table that President Kennedy was struck from above and behind by the fatal shot. The pattern of the entrance and exit wounds in the skull proves it, and if we stayed here until hell freezes over, nothing will change this proof. It happens 100 times out of 100, and I will defend it until I die. This is the essence of our autopsy, and it is supreme ignorance to argue any other scenario. This is the law of physics and it is foolproof-absolutely, unequivocally, and without question. The conspiracy buffs have totally ignored this scientific fact, and everything else is hogwash. There was no interference with our autopsy, and there was no conspiracy to suppress our findings."[8]

Conspiracists have also used the 'Harper fragment' of bone from Kennedy's skull as proof that the area that was blown out was 'occipital' (rear), thus indicating that the autopsy photographs and X-rays were fake. On November 23, 1963, William Allen Harper found a piece of John Kennedy's skull in Dealey Plaza. The HSCA forensic panel accepted the Harper fragment as 'parietal', meaning it came from the side of Kennedy's head, which would be consistent with an exit wound from a bullet fired from behind and consistent with the X-rays and autopsy photographs. The anatomical features of the Harper fragment are consistent with it being parietal bone, and this finding has been confirmed by a number of medical experts.

For decades, conspiracists have used the movie film footage to try and prove JFK was shot from the grassy knoll. The Zapruder film revealed how Kennedy's head snapped backwards, indicating he had been shot from the right front. However, two logical alternative explanations have been given to explain why President Kennedy's head jerks backwards when he is struck by the fatal bullet. Neuropathology doctor Richard Lindenberg told the Rockefeller Commission (investigating CIA activities and tangentially the possible conspiracy to assassinate President Kennedy) that the movement could have been caused by a violent neuromuscular reaction resulting from "major damage

THE SINGLE BULLET THEORY

inflicted to the nerve centers in the brain" thus causing a 'jet effect'.[9]

Physicist Luis Alvarez experimented by firing a rifle into watermelons wrapped with tape. Each time, the melon was propelled backward in the direction of the rifle. Alvarez cited the laws of conservation of momentum – as the contents of the melon were driven forward and out by the force of the bullet, an opposite force was created, similar to the thrust of a jet engine, propelling the melon in the opposite direction. The dynamics of a bullet hitting a skull cannot be compared to billiard balls. A bullet that enters a pressurized human skull produces minimal resistance, therefore minimal forward movement. The bullet which traverses a brain causes a pressure cavity to form behind the bullet. The greatest mass of brain exits in the area of least resistance. In Kennedy's case, it was the side of the head, causing a jet effect which pushed the head in the opposite direction, in this case to the left and backwards.[10]

Conspiracists have also alleged that the rear ('occipital') area of Kennedy's head had been blown out, indicating the fatal bullet had entered the front/right portion of the president's head then exited from the rear. However, they have ignored vital evidence. When a bullet penetrates the skull bone, it will leave a small hole on the side from which it enters, and a larger dished-out crater on the side that it exits. The existence of 'beveling' of the bone of Kennedy's skull allowed the autopsy doctors and later a panel of forensic pathologists appointed by the HSCA to establish that the bullet that hit Kennedy in the head entered from behind, with at least one large fragment exiting toward the front.

In addition, contrary to the claims of conspiracy theorists, the back of Kennedy's head, as shown in the autopsy photographs and X-rays, is intact, with a large gaping wound in the parietal area (right side/front/top). One X-ray, in particular, vividly demonstrates that the theorists who continue to believe that the back of President Kennedy's head was blown out are wrong. It's a lateral X-ray depicting the right side of JFK's head, which shows the back of the head to have no bone missing whatsoever. There's a radiating fracture line visible at the right-rear of Kennedy's head, but there is no missing skull bone. This is consistent with a shot from the rear and is also totally consistent with what can be seen in Abraham Zapruder's film of the assassination. The Zapruder film also clearly shows the President's head bursting open in the *front* and the *right*. It is also obvious that a large flap of scalp hangs down from the large exit wound.

Also of extreme importance is a key point that is often overlooked or downplayed by conspiracy theorists, and that is the fact that when JFK is struck in the head with a bullet at frame 313 of the Zapruder home movie, the President's head initially moves *forward*, not backward, at the very same instant the bullet hits his skull, which is consistent with the head shot coming from behind the President.[11]

Furthermore, Mary Moorman's Polaroid photograph also shows the rear of the head to be intact. Therefore, the photographs and X-rays taken during the autopsy are

THE SINGLE BULLET THEORY

consistent with photographs and films taken in Dealey Plaza. Contrary to the claims of many conspiracy believers, there is no credible evidence that the autopsy X-rays and photos of Kennedy's wounds were faked. And, of course, if the autopsy materials were faked, why leave the 'head snap' in the Zapruder movie – a vital piece of evidence which was also handled by government agencies? If the Zapruder movie was tampered with, as some people claim, why leave in movie frames which were guaranteed to cause controversy? Ironically, this reasoning that the Zapruder film was altered surfaced years after conspiracy theorists began using the Zapruder film to *prove* there was a conspiracy.

The most compelling evidence in the controversy, however, comes from an examination of the autopsy X-rays of Kennedy's skull. The dispersal of bullet fragments comes from the back to the front. And, as HSCA pathologists testified, the particulate matter (brain tissue) from the President's head, after the head shot, is spraying *forwards*, as can be seen from a high-contrast photo of frame 313 of the Zapruder film. Dr. Lundberg of JAMA confirms that the 52 photos and X-rays of the President's body support Dr. Humes' and Dr. Boswell's findings, and the HSCA panel of forensic pathologists concur.

THE PHOTOS OF GRASSY KNOLL GUNMEN

Conspiracy theorists have alleged that photographic proof had been uncovered revealing a gunman on the grassy knoll. They have used stills from Orville Nix's movie of the assassination, taken from a position directly opposite Abraham Zapruder, with the grassy knoll in the background. Nix's film clearly shows what looks like a gunman leaning on a motor vehicle and firing a rifle. However, photo analysis has revealed it was only light and shadows. Moreover, a viewing the actual movie film clearly reveals that the "gunman" does not move even when the shots were supposedly fired and the Presidential limousine is speeding away. The 'figure' does not move. A conspiratorial gunman, one would assume, would feel the necessity for a quick exit.

Robert Groden claims in his 1993 book, *The Killing of a President,* and in his 1995 book, *The Search for Lee Harvey Oswald*, that conspirators were caught in many photographs taken in Dealey Plaza. Groden also maintains that Oswald had assistance within the Texas School Book Depository and he pointed to the Hughes film, which he alleged indicated figures moving around the 6th floor minutes before the assassination. The movie, however, was examined by Frances Corbett, an image processing analyst, and the claims were found to be erroneous.[12]

Furthermore, consider the scenario. The Depository building was occupied by dozens of employees who had free run. From the Warren Commission's witness testimonies, it is clear some employees only decided on their motorcade viewing position minutes before the assassination. How could conspirators depend upon employees staying clear of their snipers' positions? Obviously they could not. Oswald did not appear suspicious in his movements around the building. Other conspirators would have looked very conspicuous.

Groden's analyses of photographs and movie footage were convincingly shown to be in error by experts appointed by the Rockefeller Commission. For example, Groden claims there were rifles and conspirators in the Zapruder movie film of the assassination. He claimed that in frame 413 the shape of a rifle could be seen, when in fact it showed nothing of the kind. He also claimed that in frames 412 to 414 a human head secreted behind a tree and the outline of a rifle were visible. However, in television documentaries and lectures around colleges throughout the United States, he does not tell his audiences that the head of the 'gunman' appears and then disappears within a quarter of a second or that a shape of a rifle appears then disappears within an eighteenth of a second. His computer enhancements and colorization are simply wishful thinking. An assassin stationed where Groden purported him to be would be unlikely to hide himself in a tree five feet away from Abraham Zapruder and expose himself to hundreds of people. In Groden's books, conspirators are everywhere in photographs of Dealey Plaza. His photos reveal nothing but lumps of bush, trees, and shadows, and only with a lot of imagination could they possibly be interpreted as 'gunmen'.[13]

Another photograph, taken by Mary Ann Moorman, purported to show 'the gunman' behind the grassy knoll at the instant the head shot was fired. It was investigated by researchers at the Polaroid Company and the Rochester Institute of Technology. They concluded that it could be a man, but the 'rifle' was light filtering through trees.[14] Additionally, the only place where a gunman could have fired the alleged grassy knoll shot, according to computer expert Dale Myers, is 30 feet in the air, hovering above the fence.

A number of conspiracy theorists have also used other photographs to allege that conspirators had been stationed on the grassy knoll and made their escape via the railway yards. They have claimed that three tramps, arrested in the railway yards behind the grassy knoll, were in fact not tramps, but ex-CIA agents E. Howard Hunt and Frank Sturgis of Watergate fame. In later conspiracy books, the tramps were identified as supposed hired killers Chauncey Holt, Charles Harrelson, and Charles Rogers. However, the photographs were examined by FBI photo analyst Lyndal Shaneyfelt for the Rockefeller Commission, who concluded the men arrested were not Hunt or Sturgis. In 1992, the Dallas Police finally put an end to speculation surrounding the photographs by releasing all their files for this period. The three tramps were revealed to be – three tramps, all of whom were identified.[15]

Marilyn Sitzman, who accompanied Abraham Zapruder to Dealey Plaza and watched as her boss filmed the assassination heard shots coming from the Book Depository. "We kept our attention on what was happening exactly in front of us and if you look at his film there's very little jumping. It's very steady considering what was going on, and that's why I'm saying the sound we heard...the third sound still sounded a distance (away) because if it had been as close as everybody's trying to tell us, you know, twenty feet behind us (over the picket fence)....we would have jumped sky high".[16]

THE SINGLE BULLET THEORY

The Warren Commission failed to take evidence from important grassy knoll witnesses Jim and Patricia Towner and Carl Desroe were in a position to give evidence about activity in the grassy knoll and railroad areas. As the motorcade passed by them as they were standing in Dealey Plaza the Towners began walking towards the railroad tracks where their car was parked nearby. Jim Towner, a former military man immediately recognized what his wife described as 'firecrackers' as gunshots. He heard three shots which he thought came from the Book Depository. He followed a crowd of spectators to the picket fence and spoke to a black man wearing a white uniform standing on the back of a Pullman dining car. It was Carl Desroe. Desroe responded to questions from the crowd asking if he had observed anyone in the vicinity. "No sir" Desroe said, "I haven't seen anybody back here and I've been back here watching the whole thing."[17]

In one of the most historic photographs of the assassination, Kennedy is seen to grasp at his throat as the first bullet that hits him goes through his neck. In the background can be seen the entrance to the Texas School Book Depository, and in the doorway stands a figure curiously like Lee Harvey Oswald. If this really is Oswald, of course, then he cannot be the assassin. The picture was taken by Associated Press photographer Jim Altgens, who was standing on the south side of Elm Street between the Triple Underpass and the Book Depository. As the motorcade started its descent down Elm Street, Altgens took the picture approximately five seconds after the firing of the first shot. It has been determined that the figure is a Book Depository employee, Billy Lovelady, and was so established by the Warren Commission, yet is still speculated upon by conspiracy theorists.[18]

These facts were corroborated by Depository worker Buell Wesley Frazier in his testimony during the 1986 television docu-trial, *On Trial: Lee Harvey Oswald*, when Frazier verified that the man in the doorway was Billy Lovelady, and not Oswald. Additionally, Lee Harvey Oswald never told his interrogators he was standing in the doorway of the Depository at the time of the shooting. In fact, just prior to uttering his famous "I'm just a patsy" declaration on live television at approximately 7:55 PM CST on November 22, 1963, Oswald specifically confirmed that he was "inside" the Depository building at the time JFK was shot, not outside on the front steps watching the motorcade.

THE ACOUSTICS EVIDENCE

As we have seen, compelling evidence shows that three bullets were fired, all of them from behind. The HSCA agreed that the bullets which hit President Kennedy and Governor Connally were fired from Oswald's rifle. But they did say a fourth shot was fired from the 'grassy knoll' and missed, basing many of their conclusions on acoustics evidence from a police audio tape recording.

The HSCA examined the audio recording of police messages in Dealey Plaza made at the time of the assassination. It was believed that motorcycle police officer H.B. McLain's radio transmitter was stuck in the 'on' position at the time of the assassination, recording the sounds of four shots in Dealey Plaza. The Committee

THE SINGLE BULLET THEORY

re-enacted the shooting in Dealey Plaza on August 20, 1978. However, it was immediately apparent to a number of observers that the re-enactment was flawed. There were no boxes on the 6th floor and two types of ammunition were used. It was evident that these flaws would inevitably affect the scientific results.

Acoustics experts working for the committee said initially there was a fifty-fifty chance of a second gunman. The committee decided to draft a report that indicated no conspiracy until G. Robert Blakey stepped in and asked two additional acoustics experts to review the findings. They said there was a 95 percent probability that one of the 'shots' came from the grassy knoll, specifically at a 'point along the east-west line of the wooden fence on the Grassy Knoll, about eight feet west of the corner of the fence'. This persuaded the committee there was evidence of a second gunman. It concluded that this second gunman had fired a shot that missed the motorcade completely.[19]

The Justice Department conducted two scientific studies to evaluate the acoustics evidence. The FBI concluded that the shots which were apparently identified on the police tape were not fired in Dealey Plaza. And in 1982, a new panel of acoustical experts (dubbed the Ramsey Panel after its chairman, Professor Norman F. Ramsey of Harvard University) re-examined the tape after an assassination researcher, Steve Barber, listened to a published recording of the tape recording and identified a number of anomalies. The Ramsey Panel issued its report in 1982 and concluded that the noise impulses on the audio recording occurred around 60 seconds *after* the assassination. The sounds therefore did not originate with any weapon that was used in Dealey Plaza and that there was therefore no evidence for a second gunman.[20]

And in 1997, researcher Greg Jaynes published a study in which he concluded that the sounds of the shots could not have originated from Dallas Police Officer H.B. McLain's motorcycle radio as the HSCA stipulated. He concluded, "Therefore, since the microphone was not in Dealey Plaza, it did not record the sounds of the shots."[21]

Conspiracy theorists reacted to these results by claiming the 'hold everything secure' message could have been the result of an 'over recording' which may have occurred if the audio recording head was knocked backward by about one minute in the first minute after the assassination, or if a new Dictabelt copy, made by audio coupling while a Channel 2 recording was playing in the background, was substituted for the original. However, the Ramsey Panel concluded that this was not the case. The panel concluded that the Dictabelt had been recorded in another location after the assassination.[22]

These conclusions were confirmed by recent research carried out in 2013 by Michael O'Dell (See: Appendix 2: Replication of the HSCA Weiss & Aschkenasy Acoustic Analysis (2013) by Michael O'Dell) and University of Virginia political scientist Larry Sabato. Sabato commissioned a scientific analysis of the Dallas Police Department's Dictabelt recording of scanner traffic from Nov. 22, 1963, as part of his research for *The Kennedy Half Century: The Presidency, Assassination, and Lasting Legacy of John F. Kennedy.* Working with a team of

THE SINGLE BULLET THEORY

researchers, Sabato used new technology to analyze the audio from a police radio transmission that appeared to show four shots being fired when the president was killed. However, Sabato and his team re-examined the audio and concluded that the alleged gunshots were only the sounds of an idling motorcycle and the rattling of a microphone. Moreover, they said, the motorcycle was two miles from Dealey Plaza when the president was shot. "There is simply no evidence for that fourth shot," Sabato said.

The firm he hired, Sonalysts, concluded that some of the sound impressions on the recordings that were interpreted as gunfire a generation ago are nearly identical to other sound impressions earlier on the tape that are definitively not gunshots." In fact, there are no less than twelve similar impulses in a period spanning just over a three-minute segment of the open microphone audio," Sabato writes, guessing that they are probably "of a mechanical origin associated with the motorcycle."[23]

As conspiracy theorists still maintain that the original acoustics evidence is reliable and a second gunman was firing, this raises two questions: If someone did fire from the knoll, where did the bullet go? – and – What kind of 'hit man' would miss a relatively easy target from a little over 100 feet away? This so-called grassy knoll bullet did not go into Kennedy's body. As we have seen, the characteristics of both the President's neck wound and the head wound ruled that out. Therefore, the shot must have missed, yet none of the spectators in the line of fire along Elm Street was hit by an errant bullet, nor did they hear any impact.

Nor was the side of the car struck. If a stray bullet coming in from the front and to the right did somehow manage to miss the President, Mrs. Kennedy, the car, and nearby spectators, it may have hit the curbstone or lawn. It is logical to assume that spectators, police, and federal agents who were swarming all over this area after the shooting would have found something. They did not. So-called 'evidence' that police detective Buddy Walthers found a bullet in Dealey Plaza and handed it over to an FBI agent is typical of how conspiracy theorists manipulate the truth. Walthers was in fact retrieving a piece of the President's skull from the scene of the crime.

The Ramsey Panel's report on the HSCA's acoustics evidence, which is backed up by further studies, conclusively demonstrates that the HSCA's conspiracy conclusion was wrong.

THE SEQUENCE OF SHOTS

The Warren Commission held that the "preponderance of evidence" indicated three shots were fired at the President, but there was no real certainty as to which bullets caused which wounds. However, five investigations of the shooting in Dealey Plaza have been carried out by leading experts in the fields of forensics, ballistics, and bullet trajectory science and have determined a precise sequence of events. The highly qualified and authoritative experts used computer modeling and laser technology equipment to simulate the assassination. Using a computer-enhanced version of Abraham Zapruder's 8mm. film of the assassination,

THE SINGLE BULLET THEORY

they set about the task of settling the issue once and for all.

The first attempt to use computer modeling began with PBS Television's 'Nova' team in 1988. However, this model was simple by today's standards. It was unable to simulate an overhead view of the positions of President Kennedy and Governor Connally at the time of the shots. But Nova's model did conclude that contrary to the contentions of the conspiracy theorists, President Kennedy and Governor Connally had been hit by the same bullet and all the shots came from the rear of the limousine.

By comparison, Failure Analysis Inc.'s 1992 computer model was more sophisticated. However, as Dale Myers wrote in explaining his own advanced computer model, "It is important to note the distinction between (our) computer study and other similar work done in this area. (The Nova and Failure Analysis models)...were illustrative renderings of various theories about the assassination. In other words, they demonstrate what might have happened in Dealey Plaza."[24]

In 1994, Dr. John K. Lattimer duplicated the assassination conditions by using identical weaponry as Oswald. The bullets were slowed by firing through pork muscle with the same dimensions as President Kennedy's neck. 24 inches to the front, Lattimer placed a rack of pork ribs, clothed like Governor Connally, and a radius bone the size of Connally's. The recovered bullet was identical to the so-called 'magic bullet' (CE399). Later he used human cadavers and came up with the same result.[25]

In 1998, a laser-assisted trajectory investigation was carried out in Dealey Plaza by a team of experts led by Anthony Larry Paul, a ballistics expert who had 30 years of experience in crime scene reconstruction and served as ballistics instructor for the FBI and the Philadelphia and Los Angeles Police Departments. The team was comprised of: laser expert Heinz Thummel of Laser Devices Inc., who had originated the idea of using laser technology with weapons; Dr. Vincent DiMaio, an acclaimed forensic pathologist who had authored textbooks and papers which have set the standard for his field; Ronald L. Singer, chief criminalist for Tarrant County, Texas, who had a lot of experience in crime scene reconstructions and criminalistics; Kerry M. Hoefner, a land surveyor; and conspiracist Robert Groden, who provided 'balance' to the team as a committed conspiracy theorist. The team decided that, in all medical probability and in all scientific probability a) the Single Bullet Theory was correct b) everything pointed to the 6th floor of the Texas School Book Depository as the position where all the shots had been fired c) the grassy knoll was eliminated as a possible source of any of the shots. With the exception of Robert Groden, the team decided there was good scientific evidence that a shot from the grassy knoll was impossible.[26]

Computer animator Dale Myers' computer model was the most sophisticated of all the models and differed from the others as it was the first computer study to examine Abraham Zapruder's film in three dimensions. Myers generated a computer simulation of every frame in the Zapruder film. He began by constructing a three-

THE SINGLE BULLET THEORY

dimensional scale model of Dealey Plaza. His model revealed that around frame 160 the first shot was fired and apparently missed. The next shot struck both Kennedy and Connally in frames 223-224. JFK comes out from behind a sign and his hands immediately go up toward his throat. Both men react simultaneously.[27]

Myers said, "Kennedy and Connally were hit by the same bullet," which hit Kennedy first and then wounded Connally in the back. With his computer model he demonstrates that, because of the way Connally was sitting – in a small jump seat, lower than Kennedy and leaning out to the right trying to see where the gunshot came from – the trajectory of one single, high-velocity bullet fired from the window of the Texas Book Depository entered Kennedy from behind, blew out his throat, then hit Connally. As Myers puts it: "The fact that they both react at the same time clinches it. So it's not a magic bullet at all. It's not even a single bullet theory, in my opinion. It's a single bullet fact."[28]

The sequence of shots can now be established as follows:

SHOT 1

The preponderance of evidence and witness testimony suggests that the first shot was fired shortly after the Presidential limousine turned the corner from Houston Street on to Elm Street (frame 157 of the Zapruder film). Ear witnesses Buell Frazier, Howard Brennan, Barbara Rowland, Royce Skelton, Geneva Hine, and Secret Service Agents William Greer and Paul Landis all testified towards this. This bullet probably struck the branch of the oak tree, splitting the metal jacket from the lead core. The lead core part of the bullet then continued diagonally beneath the limousine to the area of the overpass and struck the pavement on Main Street, throwing up a piece of concrete which struck James Tague on the cheek. The concrete near Tague was examined and found to have traces of lead with a trace of antimony. No copper was discovered; therefore a part of a bullet without the full copper jacket was responsible for the damage. We can conclude that the Warren Commission was wrong on this point – Tague's injury was probably not caused by the fragments emanating from the head shot, the energy to carry them would have been too spent, although the Commission also considered the possibility that the Main Street curb damage and, hence, Tague's slight cheek injury, "might have been a product of the fragmentation of the missed shot upon hitting some other object in the area."[29]

Concurrently, the metal jacket part of the bullet struck an area on Elm Street near the Presidential limousine. Virgie Rachley and four other witnesses saw the bullet strike; Rachley said, "You could see the sparks from it." Mr. and Mrs. Jack Franzen both noticed small fragments flying about inside the limousine. Postal Inspector Harry Holmes saw the bullet strike the road through binoculars from his office across Dealey Plaza. Royce Skelton, who was stationed on the triple overpass, saw pieces of concrete fly up at the rear of the limousine. Pearl Harbor veteran Phil Willis snapped his first photo at the exact time of this first shot. It is therefore easy to imagine a nervous Oswald firing prematurely as the limousine turned the corner of Elm Street and missing his target. Friends of Oswald's in the Soviet Union said that he had acted impulsively during hunting trips they took together. When the metal jacket part of the bullet hit the ground near the limousine, it is possible that fragments peppered Kennedy and there is some indication he may have responded to being slightly struck. It is also entirely possible that one of the fragments from the first shot travelled to the area of the grassy knoll near the picket fence, throwing up dirt which was mistaken for 'puffs of smoke'.

Governor Connally responded to this first shot at frame 157 by turning to see if the President was alright. Connally told the Warren Commission, "I heard this noise which I immediately took to be a rifle shot. I instinctively turned to my right because the sound appeared to come from over my right shoulder, so I turned to look back over my right shoulder, and I saw nothing unusual except just people in the crowd."[30]

In 1979, David Lui was the first researcher to identify a telling clue as to when the first shot was fired. Whilst watching the Zapruder film, Lui noticed a young girl running to keep pace with the Presidential limousine. She stopped abruptly and turned towards the Texas School Book Depository – before any shots were supposed to have been fired. Many years later, Lui asked the girl (Rosemary Willis) why she had stopped running with the limousine and she replied she had heard a shot.[31]

SHOT 2

The second bullet was fired at Zapruder frames 223-224 and the President was hit in the right side upper back/base of neck. As the limousine emerges from behind the road sign (from the viewpoint of the Zapruder film), Kennedy's elbows rise. A second later, his fists are directed towards his torn windpipe. The second bullet fired has entered Kennedy's back.

It is possible, some experts aver, that Kennedy was exhibiting an immediate response to the bullet passing through the base of his right neck; as the bullet enters the pressure cavity, it causes an immediate stimulation of all the nerves in the surrounding area, the 'brachial plexus', the nerves that supply motor function to the arms. Neural impulses travel very fast, therefore Kennedy would have been expected to react within one frame of the Zapruder film. According to the Zapruder film, Kennedy can be seen to be reacting on the right side just before the left side – proof that the bullet passed through the right side of the upper back/neck. It confirms the upper location of the back wound. If the wound had been any lower, it would have entered the chest cavity and we would not have seen the peculiar arm movements of Kennedy.

The bullet now exits and there is nowhere for it to go except through Governor Connally who is seated almost directly in front of the President, especially when we consider that the bullet had been travelling at 2,000 feet per second. Connally was seated slightly to the left of Kennedy and about three inches lower than the President. Conspiracy theorists have maintained that the bullet could not zigzag. It is evident they have been confused about the alignments of Kennedy and

THE SINGLE BULLET THEORY

Connally. Computer simulations have posited a direct line in which the bullet travels. The bullet enters Connally's back sideways as it tumbles – this accounts for the large wound in Connally's back. Exiting his body, the bullet pushes Connally's jacket lapel outward, as can be seen in the Zapruder film. Emerging from his right nipple, it travels through his right wrist backwards and hits his left thigh, slightly puncturing the skin. The bullet stays in his trouser leg until he arrives at the hospital, where it falls onto his stretcher. It is intact and pristine at the nose end only – but the bottom of the bullet is damaged. The bullet is also flattened on its side.

SHOT 3

In response to the second shot, Secret Service agent Bill Greer, the driver of the limousine, turns around to observe what was happening. He slams his foot on the brakes and the limousine nearly comes to a halt. Following his second shot, Oswald now has a nearly perfect target. He tracks the back of Kennedy's head for more than four seconds. The third shot (Zapruder frame 313) enters the top of Kennedy's head and exits to the right temporal side, blowing part of his skull away. (The body part was later found on Elm Street.) Although the movement of Kennedy to the left and backwards was proof to some that Kennedy was shot from the front, his jerking reaction is entirely consistent with the dynamics of a bullet entering a human skull from behind.

Two large fragments from the head-shot bullet were later found in the limousine, a quarter and an eighth of a whole bullet. Smaller lead fragments were found under the seat occupied by Nellie Connally. The two fragments

BEYOND REASONABLE DOUBT

found in the front seat (CE567 and CE569) were responsible for the damage to the windshield and the chrome strip above the windshield.

To summarize, strong and substantial evidence indicates that Lee Harvey Oswald acted alone when he fired three shots at the presidential limousine in Dealey Plaza. No credible evidence exists that indicates Oswald had been assisted by fellow conspirators.

CHAPTER FIVE

CONSCIOUSNESS OF GUILT

> "When he was interrogated, Oswald, from his own lips, he told us he was guilty....he told us he was guilty....almost the same as if he had said 'I murdered President Kennedy'....he told us. How did he tell us? Well, the lies he told, one after another, showed an unmistakable consciousness of guilt. If Oswald were innocent, why did he find it necessary to deny purchasing that Carcano rifle from the Klein's store in Chicago? Why did he even deny owning any rifle at all? Why did he find it necessary to do that if he's innocent?"
>
> — Vincent Bugliosi; *1986*

> "(Priscilla Johnson McMillan's Marina and Lee) wasn't what the conspiracy-minded American public was in the mood to buy. McMillan's book forces readers to confront something more vexing than a conspiracy: an absence of conspiracy. .... Only if you haven't read Marina and Lee can you take Oswald's famous jailhouse remark—"I'm just a patsy!"— at face value"
>
> — Joseph Finder, *The Daily Beast, February 2013*

> "(Reasonable doubt) is not a mere or imaginary or possible doubt but a fair doubt based on reason and common sense. It is such a doubt as to leave your minds, after a careful examination of the evidence, in the condition that you cannot say you have an abiding conviction amounting to a moral certainty of the truth of the charge made against the defendant."
>
> — William J. Coughlin, *Shadow of a Doubt (1995)*

BEYOND REASONABLE DOUBT

Reasonable doubt is not "doubt with a reason", as many lawyers define it. The true meaning of the term is not simply "possible doubt", because everything relating to human affairs is open to some possible or imaginary doubt. If the preponderance of evidence points to the guilt of the accused, it is not reasonable to say a particular anomalous piece of evidence shows innocence. Even when more than one anomaly arises, as it certainly does with respect to the JFK assassination, it is still not 'reasonable' to assume innocence if the preponderance of evidence shows guilt.

The fact that Oswald did not stay in the Texas School Book Depository after the shooting clearly indicates he had something to hide. For if he was truly innocent, why did he leave his place of employment without telling anyone, including his supervisor, take a taxi to his rooming house on North Beckley Avenue, collect his gun, and then shoot a police officer?

Within a minute after Police Officer Marrion L. Baker and Depository Superintendent Roy S. Truly left Oswald in the second-floor lunchroom, Mrs. R.A. Reid, clerical supervisor for the Book Depository, ran into the building after hearing shots and saw and spoke to Oswald, who mumbled a reply and proceeded in the direction of the front entrance to the building. From the Depository building, Oswald moved on foot looking for a bus. Oswald boarded a bus within minutes. But the assassination on Elm Street had tied up traffic. The Marsalis Street bus was hopelessly stalled.

During the short bus ride, Oswald was recognized by his former landlady Mary Bledsoe. She said Oswald, "... got

CONSCIOUSNESS OF GUILT

on (the bus). He looks like a maniac. His sleeve was out here. His shirt was undone....he looked so bad in his face and his face was so distorted....hole in his sleeve right here." The Warren Commission reported that as Mrs. Bledsoe said these words "she pointed to her right elbow." When Oswald was arrested in the Texas Theater, he was wearing a brown sport shirt with a hole in the right sleeve at the elbow. Bledsoe identified the shirt as the one Oswald was wearing. She said she was certain that it was Oswald who boarded the bus. Oswald sat halfway to the rear of the bus, which moved slowly as traffic became heavy. She heard a passing motorist tell the driver that the President had been shot. People on the bus began talking about it. As the bus neared Lamar Street, Oswald left the bus and disappeared into the crowd. Cecil J. McWatters, the bus driver, testified that he gave Oswald a bus transfer ticket before he disembarked. At the time of his arrest, Oswald had the ticket on him.

Oswald's method of escape is central to an understanding of how the assassin could not have been in league with others in committing the crime. Would it be rational, for example, for a group of conspirators, who had carried out the most complex and elaborate conspiracy in history, to allow one of its participants to escape in this manner? This rationale, however, is contradicted by those theorists who claim Oswald had been a 'patsy'. We must then address the other issues which show Oswald's guilty actions that day. If Oswald was indeed a 'patsy', why didn't he stay in the building if he did not have any knowledge of the 'conspiracy'? And, if he was innocent— why did he shoot a Dallas police officer?

As the bus became ensnarled in traffic, Oswald disembarked, walked to the nearby Greyhound bus terminal, and approached an empty waiting cab. Oswald saw that an elderly woman was waiting for a cab too. He graciously offered his cab to her. However, the lady declined the offer when the cab driver informed her that another taxi was pulling in right behind his. Oswald got in the cab and headed off toward the Oak Cliff area of Dallas. Oswald told the taxi driver to take him not to the front door of 1026 North Beckley (his residence), but instead to a point three blocks beyond his rooming house[1]. He actually passes his house first in the cab, which is clearly an obvious attempt to see if any police officers are waiting for him there and also so that cab driver William Whaley will not know exactly where his passenger lives. Oswald returned to his rooming house shortly before 1:00 p.m., picked up his mail-order Smith and Wesson .38 caliber revolver, and left at about 1:00[2].

Nearly every conspiracy author has used the statements made by Oswald's Oak Cliff housekeeper to introduce conspiratorial elements into Oswald's appearance at his boarding house. The housekeeper, Earlene Roberts, was interviewed at least four times in the weeks and months after the assassination, each time adding a new dimension to her story. Shortly before Oswald left the rooming house, she later claimed, a police car pulled up outside the house and honked its horn twice. To conspiracists, this act suggested a rendezvous had been arranged between Oswald and the Dallas police, possibly Officer J.D. Tippit.

However, in her Warren Commission testimony, Mrs. Roberts stated that the police car had two officers in it, whereas Tippit was alone in Car No. 10 on November 22nd. And two witnesses placed Tippit at the 'Top Ten Record Shop' at this time. Furthermore, Mrs. Roberts suffered from cataracts and her eyesight was very poor. It would also have been impossible to observe a police car from where she said she was positioned – as I noted when I visited the rooming house in 1972. And Assistant Dallas District Attorney Bill Alexander and former Dallas reporter Hugh Aynesworth said they spoke to Roberts on the afternoon of the assassination and she did not mention the honking of the police car horn. The owner of the rooming house at 1026 North Beckley Avenue, Roberts' employer, Gladys Johnson, told the Warren Commission that Roberts had some "bad habits". On being asked to elaborate, Johnson said that Roberts had a custom of "making up tales ... just a creative mind, there's nothing to it, and just make up and keep talking until she makes a lie out of it ... she is a person who doesn't mean to do it but she just does it automatically ... I don't understand it myself."[3]

Oswald's final act of violence occurred shortly before he was apprehended. It revealed he had no compunction in snuffing out the life of an innocent person and revealed a definite 'consciousness of guilt'.

Less than a half-hour after shooting President Kennedy, Oswald had arrived at his rooming house at 1026 North Beckley Avenue across the Trinity River. After leaving his rooming house, he was next seen about nine-tenths of a mile away at the southeast corner of 10th Street and

BEYOND REASONABLE DOUBT

Patton Avenue, moments before Police Officer J.D. Tippit was shot and killed.

The controversy concerning the manner of Tippit's death has raged for nearly 50 years. Some of the criticisms of the investigation have been reasonable, others have involved the manipulation of facts to 'prove' that others committed the crime and that more than one person was involved in the shooting. Conspiracy theorists have claimed:

- Police Officer J.D. Tippit was a conspirator with Lee Harvey Oswald in the assassination. Some have said that Officer Tippit may have been captured on film in Dealey Plaza at the time of the assassination of President Kennedy. Author Robert Groden purportedly identified a man on the grassy knoll wearing a 'badge', claiming it could have been Officer Tippit. Expert photo analysts, however, dismissed these claims. Tippit's presence in Dealey Plaza at the time of the assassination would have been impossible, as it is beyond doubt that witnesses place Tippit at 4100 Bonnie View Road between 12:17 and 12:30 p.m. on November 22nd. The original time for President Kennedy's motorcade to have arrived at Dealey Plaza was between 12:15 and 12:20 p.m., if the planned times had been adhered to. It would therefore have been impossible for Tippit to have gone to Dealey Plaza and returned to the Oak Cliff area in the timespan available.

- Tippit pulled his patrol car up to Oswald's apartment house and honked a warning as Oswald was fleeing.

- Oswald, Tippit, and Jack Ruby knew each other.

- Oswald and Tippit did not meet by chance prior to the shooting.

- Sinister reasons account for Tippit stopping Oswald. Claims have been made that Tippit had been nominated by conspirators to kill Oswald, but that the assassin 'got the jump on the police officer'.

- Oswald could not have fired the shots which killed Tippit, as the weapon used was an automatic pistol.

Dale Myers researched and analyzed all of these conspiracy claims in his 1998 book, *With Malice*. Myers sought out every conceivable source that had knowledge of the Tippit killing, interviewed hundreds of people and studied Tippit's life from boyhood. He dug deep into the Warren Commission and HSCA files and discovered documents never previously made public. Myers successfully debunked the many myths that had been propagated by conspiracy theorists arguing Lee Oswald's innocence in the shooting.

Officer Tippit had been alerted about the assassination at 12:45 p.m. and was told to be on the lookout for a suspect with a description based upon a report made by an eyewitness to the assassination, Howard Brennan. Brennan had given the description to a police officer shortly after he observed the assassin firing from the sixth-floor window of the Book Depository.

At 1:15 p.m., Tippit saw Oswald walking briskly on the sidewalk on Tenth Street in Oak Cliff and called him over to his patrol car. Oswald spoke to the Dallas officer briefly through a window vent before Tippit exited his car and began walking towards the suspect. Within seconds, Oswald had drawn his pistol and began firing, hitting the police officer four times. Tippit was dead before he hit the ground. One bullet had entered the chest. Another bullet had been fired at his chest and struck a metal button on his shirt, driving it deep into his body. Oswald stood over the slain policeman, looked down, and administered the *coup de grace* – a shot to Tippit's head.

Conspiracy theorists have used this murder to prove that the assassination of President Kennedy and the murder of Officer Tippit were conspiratorially connected. They have also insisted that the eyewitness testimony was contradictory and that there is no reliable evidence which points to a certain identification of Oswald as the shooter. Eyewitnesses were not totally in agreement in their descriptions of Oswald's clothing, his facial features, and the direction in which he was heading.

There will always be inconsistencies in any eyewitness testimony to a shooting. This is especially so when the criminal involved is less than 15 feet in proximity and the primary concern is one of safety. Although William Scoggins, Helen Markham, Barbara Davis, Virginia Davis, Ted Callaway, and Sam Guinyard differed in the details of what they saw at the scene of the Tippit murder, they all agreed on the major issue – Lee Harvey Oswald was the gunman.[4]

Most conspiracy theorists fail to mention that there were six witnesses who were at the scene of the murder of

CONSCIOUSNESS OF GUILT

Officer Tippit or saw the gunman running from the scene, gun in hand. At least 12 persons saw the man with the revolver in the vicinity of the Tippit crime scene at the time of the murder or immediately after the shooting. Five of them — Helen Markham, Barbara Davis, Virginia Davis, Ted Callaway, and Sam Guinyard — had identified Lee Harvey Oswald in a police line-up the night of the killing. A sixth, William Scoggins, did so the next day. Four others — Warren Reynolds, Harold Russell, B.M. 'Pat' Patterson, and L.J. Lewis — subsequently identified Oswald from photographs. Two witnesses testified that Oswald resembled the man they had seen. One witness felt he was too distant from the gunman to make a positive identification.

Witness Jack Tatum was so positive of his identification, he was struck by Oswald's 'smirk' which can be seen in most film footage of Oswald after his arrest. "The one characteristic about Oswald that I saw and will never forget," Tatum said, "was his mouth seemed to curl up as if he was smiling. I saw that when he was looking into the squad car before the shots. I noticed that same characteristic when I saw him on T.V." Tatum is the only witness who saw Oswald walk over to Tippit and fire a bullet into his head at point-blank range, a detail confirmed by Tippit's autopsy.[5]

William Scoggins was also convinced that Oswald was the man he saw. According to Scoggins, he had been eating lunch in his cab, which was parked on Patton facing the southeast corner of 10th Street and Patton Avenue, a few feet to the north, when he observed a police car. It was moving east on 10th at about 10 or 12 miles an hour, and passed in front of his cab. About 100 feet from the corner, the police car pulled up alongside a man on the sidewalk. The man, Scoggins said, was dressed in a light-colored jacket and approached Tippit's car. Scoggins lost sight of him behind some shrubbery on the southeast corner lot, but he saw Tippit leave the car, heard 3 or 4 shots, and then saw the officer fall. Scoggins hurriedly jumped out of his seat and hid behind his cab as the suspect came towards him, cutting across a yard through some bushes. The gunman passed within 12 feet of Scoggins, running south on Patton Avenue. Scoggins was so close to the killer he heard him mutter "Poor damn cop" or "Poor dumb cop". The day after the Tippit shooting, Scoggins viewed a lineup of four persons and identified Oswald as the man he had seen the day before at 10th and Patton.[6]

Later, Oswald's brother, Robert, would remember a time in their past when he heard Lee utter similar words. In 1957, Robert had noticed a car which was 'tailgating' them. Robert avoided a collision by going through a traffic light and was immediately pulled in by a police car. The police officer was unsympathetic and as they pulled away, Oswald looked over his shoulder and muttered 'That damn cop!' Robert gave it no thought until many years later when he heard Scoggins' statement.[7]

Most conspiracy theorists ignore witnesses like Scoggins and instead concentrate on those who were inconsistent in their recall of the shooting. Frequently, conspiracists use the testimonies of Acquilla Clemmons and Helen Markham to bolster their claims of Oswald's purported innocence. Clemmons told investigators she saw two men at the scene of the Tippit shooting. However, every

CONSCIOUSNESS OF GUILT

other witness disagrees and rejects Clemmons' version of the shooting. Her account is simply not credible.[8]

Conspiracy promoters differ in the importance they place on various discrepancies in eyewitness testimony, but they all make the same mistake of ignoring important witnesses like Barbara Davis, Virginia Davis, Sam Guinyard, and Ted Callaway.

Witnesses Domingo Benavides, Barbara Davis, and Virginia Davis found the spent cartridge cases (bullet shells) at the Tippit murder scene and turned them over to the police. The bullets in Tippit's body were too mutilated to be identifiable, according to FBI experts. However, one independent firearms expert retained by the Warren Commission, Joseph D. Nicol of Illinois, believed that he could identify one of those bullets as having been fired from Oswald's pistol. The cartridge cases were identified as having come from Oswald's pistol to the exclusion of all other weapons in the world. This is irrefutable ballistics evidence.[9]

The conspiracy buffs also like to point to the mismatch of the brands of bullets and shells in the Tippit murder case. Of the four bullet shells that were recovered at the scene of Tippit's murder, two of them were Winchester-Western shells and two were manufactured by Remington-Peters. But the four bullets that were taken out of Officer Tippit's body were not an even '2 and 2' division of those two brands. Three of the bullets were one brand, while only one was the other.

But, as Dale Myers wrote, "Considering the record, the discrepancy between the Tippit shells and slugs isn't that unusual. The number of shots fired could easily have been more than four, and the possibility that some cartridges went undiscovered is not beyond reason...Further, the suggestion that two types of ammunition...means that two people cut down Tippit, ignores the fact that Oswald had a mix of both types of ammo in his revolver when he was arrested...In retrospect, the critics' assertion that an Oswald frame-up is the best explanation of the ballistic evidence is simply not accurate. The bullets pulled from Tippit's body are consistent with having been fired from a .38 caliber revolver that had been re-chambered to fire .38 Specials. Oswald's revolver was such a weapon. Two of the four shells recovered at the scene have a clear, unbroken chain of custody and were proven to have been fired in Oswald's revolver to the exclusion of all other weapons... In the final analysis, the ballistic evidence consistently and repeatedly points to Lee Harvey Oswald."[10]

One of the most intriguing parts of the Tippit murder has never been satisfactorily answered. Why did Oswald shoot the Dallas police officer? Researchers have generally assumed Oswald panicked and became frightened when Tippit got out of his patrol car and approached the man whose general description matched the profile of the fugitive. But Oswald could very well have bluffed his way out of the encounter. However, it is unlikely Tippit would have allowed Oswald to continue on his journey if the officer had found Oswald's concealed weapon. Concealing a weapon was a crime in Texas at the time of the assassination.

Former FBI agent James Hosty has provided an alternative theory of why Oswald shot Tippit. When the report that a police officer had been shot came over the radio, Hosty said, FBI Agent Bob Barrett rushed to the scene of the crime. Barrett maintains that the police officer in charge of the scene, Captain W.R. Westbrook, had found a man's wallet lying near a pool of blood. In it he discovered identification for Lee Harvey Oswald as well as identification for Alek J. Hidell. Westbrook showed the IDs to Barrett, then took the wallet so that it could be listed with other crime scene materials.

In the confusion which reigned that day, Hosty believes, it is likely that the wallet somehow managed to be itemized as being on Oswald's person at the time he was arrested at the Texas Theater. It is unlikely that FBI Agent Barrett would have made the story up, therefore an understanding of why Oswald panicked and shot Tippit becomes clearer. Oswald would definitely have been arrested if Tippit had read the two I.D.'s.[11]

Although Barrett was a very credible witness, Dale Myers maintains that it is likely he was mistaken, as the preponderance of evidence shows that Oswald's wallet was retrieved following his arrest. Furthermore, Myers' investigation has revealed that the alleged wallet which was captured on television footage was not the same wallet listed amongst Oswald's possessions at the Dallas Police Department.[12]

The circumstances surrounding each and every rumor about alleged connections between Oswald, Tippit, and Jack Ruby were thoroughly examined and investigated by Dale Myers. In each and every instance, the author was able to prove that the allegations were unsubstantiated and uncorroborated. Nearly everyone who knew Tippit throughout his 39-year life testified to the police officer's dedication to his job and his love for his family (although Myers found the allegations of a short-term affair with a waitress to be true). The only time the Dallas officer frequented night clubs, he was accompanied by his wife, and allegations that he visited Jack Ruby's night club are baseless. Nearly every friend and acquaintance, including his fellow police officers, reject any of the claims made by conspiracists that Tippit was in some way involved in the assassination.[13]

In fact, Myers' portrait of J.D. Tippit confirms the truth of what I was told by one of Tippit's colleagues when I visited Dallas in 1972. "The allegations that Tippit was tied in to the assassination are nothing short of outrageous lies", Officer Jim High Jr. told me. "J.D. Tippit was a good officer and conspiracy writers who make these allegations should be ashamed."

Following Oswald's coup de grace shot to Tippit's head, he fled, eventually arriving at the Texas Theater, which was located eight blocks from where Tippit was murdered.

Johnny Brewer was the manager of Hardy's Shoe Shop on West Jefferson Boulevard, a few doors east of the Texas Theater. On the afternoon of November 22nd, Brewer was in his shop listening to reports on the radio about the assassination. Suddenly a news report stated that a police officer had been shot nearby. At that moment, he heard police sirens and looked out onto the street. He saw Oswald duck into his doorway. His

CONSCIOUSNESS OF GUILT

nervous state made Brewer suspicious. He thought Oswald looked "funny". As the police sirens died away, Oswald walked away from Brewer's shop and towards the Texas Theater. Brewer saw him walk inside without paying. Brewer became highly suspicious. Oswald's shirt was untucked and his hair was disheveled. He looked "scared". For Brewer, entering the theater without paying confirmed his suspicions, so he informed the ticket attendant, Julia Postal, who called the police.[14]

Meanwhile, Brewer walked inside the theater, told his story to an employee, and they both proceeded to check the exits. None appeared to have been used. A dozen or so people were in the theater. Brewer could not pick out the man, but by this time the police had arrived. As the house lights went on, Brewer met Officer M.N. McDonald and the other policemen at the alley exit door, stepped out onto the stage with them, and pointed out the man who was sitting at the rear of the theater.

Several conspiracy theorists have said that Oswald was "fingered" by a mysterious person who was sitting at the front of the theater, thus leading to speculation that Oswald was framed. Oswald, they say, went to the movie house to rendezvous with another conspirator. However, they ignore the testimony of Officer McDonald, who confirmed that the man who pointed out Oswald was Johnny Brewer. At the time of the arrest, McDonald did not know the shoe store manager's name, leading to press reports about an unidentified witness.

Undoubtedly Oswald knew his time was up when he saw police officers inside the theater. He knows multiple witnesses saw him kill Tippit and he also knows that an even larger number of additional witnesses saw him flee the scene of Tippit's murder with a gun in his hand. But he's only got so much ammunition with him, so he very likely can't eliminate all of these witnesses (although Oswald does have eleven unfired bullets at his disposal — six rounds in his revolver and another five live rounds in his pants pockets). It is credible to assume Oswald wanted to save his last bullets for when it really counted — on more police officers. Which is exactly what he attempted to do once he was cornered in the Texas Theater at approximately 1:50 p.m. on November 22.

In the theater, Oswald tried to kill police officer M.N. (Nick) McDonald with the same gun he used on Tippit a half-hour earlier. Luckily, McDonald and other officers were able to wrest the gun away from their suspect before it could be successfully fired, saving Oswald from yet another possible murder charge that day.

Officer McDonald had first searched two men near the front. When he reached the row where Oswald was sitting, McDonald stopped abruptly and told the man to get on his feet. Oswald rose from his seat, bringing up both of his hands. As McDonald started to search him, Oswald said, "Well, it's all over now." Oswald struck McDonald in the face and reached down for his revolver. McDonald and Oswald grappled for the gun. Oswald pulled the trigger, but there was only a click; the hammer of the gun had pinched a portion of Officer McDonald's hand, preventing the bullet from being fired. By now, the other policemen had surrounded Oswald. Detective Bob Carroll, who was standing beside McDonald, grabbed the gun. Although Oswald's attempt to shoot a police officer in the theater reveals the

CONSCIOUSNESS OF GUILT

assassin's willingness to commit murder, it is often overlooked by conspiracy theorists.

As Oswald was taken through the theater's lobby, he was heard to shout, "I protest this police brutality," and "I am not resisting arrest." A large crowd had gathered outside. Rumors spread that the incident was somehow connected to President Kennedy's assassination. When the crowd saw the policemen emerge with Oswald, some of them shouted, "Kill the son of a bitch" and "Let us have him." Oswald was hustled into a police car and was driven to police headquarters.

Many conspiracy writers believe Lee Harvey Oswald was nothing but an innocent "patsy". Oswald, according to conspiracy theorists like Oliver Stone, Jim Garrison, and many others, never even fired a shot at President Kennedy.

Did the clandestine assassins who made Oswald into a patsy really not consider the potential eyewitness accounts of the literally hundreds of witnesses who were scattered throughout Dealey Plaza to watch the President pass by? (Many of them possessed cameras, potentially acquiring the filmed proof of conspiracy.)

One of the other things that makes such a plot so transparently foolish stems from the idea, as presented in Oliver Stone's 1991 movie, that these behind-the-scenes plotters (who were supposedly manipulating Oswald like a puppet on a string) couldn't have cared less about the precise whereabouts of their one and only patsy at the time JFK was being murdered.

Stone evidently took assassin Lee Oswald at his word when Oswald shouted "I'm just a patsy!" to the waiting press in the hallways of the Dallas Police Department. Of course, just exactly why this known liar (Oswald), who told one falsehood after another to both the police and the anxious press at the police station, would suddenly be looked upon by the conspiracy theorists as a *truthful* person when he uttered his famous "I'm just a patsy" declaration after his arrest is a real mystery. When Oswald's "patsy" statement (which was uttered by Oswald at 7:55 p.m., Dallas time, on 11/22/63, per reporter Seth Kantor's notes [Kantor Exhibit No. 3, at 20 H 366]) isn't broken up into smaller sections (which it usually is, so that people don't get to hear Oswald's lie about being "taken in" because of his once having lived in Russia), it becomes fairly clear that the patsy statement is nothing more than a whitewash and a desperate lie being spoken by Lee Oswald in an obvious attempt to divert suspicion away from the man who killed two people in Dallas on November 22.

The full "patsy" declaration is rarely cited in conspiracy books: *"They've taken me in because of the fact that I lived in the Soviet Union. I'm just a patsy!"* It was clearly a lie when he said that he had been taken in because of previously residing in the USSR – a lie which no rational person could ever accept.

Additionally, we can deduce Oswald's "Soviet Union" declaration is a lie because Oswald was told in the police car on his way to Dallas Police Headquarters the real reason why he was being "taken in". In the Warren Commission testimony of Dallas Police Officer C.T. Walker, Walker said that Oswald had been told point-blank by police officers that he had been arrested on suspicion of killing a policeman: "Oswald said, 'What is this all about?', he was relating this all the time. He said, 'I know my rights'. And we told him that he was under arrest because...he was suspected in the murder of a police officer. And he said, 'Police officer been killed?'; and nobody said nothing. He said, 'I hear they burn for murder'. And I said, 'You might find out'. And he said, 'Well, they say it just takes a second to die'."[15] Now, can anyone imagine an *innocent* person saying these words right after being arrested for a murder he did not commit? — *"Well, they say it just takes a second to die."* That statement, all by itself, reeks with guilt.

Also, if Oswald had really been an innocent "patsy", then why didn't he reveal some names for the police to check out? It is inconceivable that Oswald was involved in a highly sophisticated plan to assassinate the President and yet he had not one shred of an idea as to what any of his co-conspirators looked like or what any of their names (even fake names) might have been.

When Oswald was arrested in the Texas Theater, his first words when cornered are also indicative of guilt — "It's all over now" and/or "This is it" are the quotes that have been attributed to Lee Harvey Oswald within the movie theater. (Dallas Police Detective Paul Bentley was interviewed on live television on November 23, 1963, with Bentley telling the reporters in the DPD corridor that Oswald made *both* of those statements inside the theater.) When he was bundled into a police car, one of Oswald's statements was, "I haven't done anything to be ashamed of." This remark is revealing. He did not say, "I didn't shoot anyone." He may have committed murder – but within the fantasies of his own mind, Oswald's crime was "an act of war" (supporting Castro's revolution), which put him outside the norms of lawful behavior and moral culpability.

OSWALD'S INTERROGATION

The evidence concerning Oswald's interrogation is vital to understanding Lee Harvey Oswald, for if he was truly innocent of any involvement in the assassination, as many conspiracy theorists claim, then why did he repeatedly lie after his arrest?

Lee Oswald had a history of lying and often astounded his wife by lying about even the slightest things. He lied on job applications, and all through their marriage it was Oswald's lying and Marina's telling off that led to the bitter quarrels between them.

Lee apparently inherited this trait from his mother, according to Priscilla Johnson McMillan, who had spent a year with Marina Oswald after the assassination. Lee's mother, Marguerite, "apparently had enough contact with reality to control her abuse of it. This was not true of Lee." McMillan concluded, "Neither Lee nor his mother could open up or allow themselves to be vulnerable to anyone. They had to keep others from glimpsing what was inside their minds. And, since they were holding together a view of the world that was not in accordance with reality, they spent a great deal of energy tuning out signals that did not fit."[16]

Marina recognized how her husband lied "pointlessly, to no purpose and all the time, even when he had nothing to hide." Marina says Lee told three kinds of lies –

CONSCIOUSNESS OF GUILT

'vranyo', an exaggerated "wild Russian cock-and-bull lying that has a certain imaginative joy to it." Another type of lie hid his "secretiveness". The third type was lying "calculated", because he had something to hide.

Following his arrest, Oswald was interrogated for 12 hours during the period between his arrival at Police Headquarters and his murder on Sunday morning, November 24th. At all times during these interrogation sessions, a combination of police officers, Secret Service agents, and FBI agents were present, as well as Postal Inspector Holmes, who was there because the rifle and pistol used in the murders of the President and Officer Tippit had been ordered by mail.

Oswald's chief interrogator was Captain J. Will Fritz of the Dallas Police Homicide Department. Fritz recalled that Oswald would talk to him readily "until I asked him a question that meant something, that would produce evidence," and then Oswald would immediately tell him he wouldn't answer. Fritz thought he seemed to anticipate what he was going to ask. Others who were there also got the impression that Oswald was quick with his answers and that he appeared to have planned what he was going to say.

The fact that there were no recordings or written statements made at the time of the interrogations has led many conspiracy theorists to suspect that the Dallas Police, FBI, and Secret Service were trying to cover up. They see sinister reasons in not tape recording the conversations between Oswald and the authorities. Oswald's interviews were not recorded, they speculate, because there was a lot to hide and the police did not want any record of the interrogations.

However, there were less dramatic reasons which prevented the interrogation from being recorded. Captain Will Fritz had been trying for months to obtain a tape recorder for the Homicide and Robbery Bureau, without success. As a result, the only record of Oswald's 12 hours of interrogation during the period from Friday afternoon to Sunday morning comes from the notes of those who happened to be present.

There were seven or eight men moving in and out of the Police Homicide Office and no person was there the entire time the interrogations took place. Fritz admits he was violating every principle of interrogation, but excuses it on the grounds that numerous federal and local agencies were involved; there was an atmosphere of chaos within Dallas Police headquarters. On one occasion, Fritz asked reporter Lonnie Hudkins to sit in on an interrogation session. According to Hudkins, he asked Oswald about his black eye and "The next question – why did you kill Officer Tippit? — and he threw the question right back at me. He said, 'Someone get killed, policeman get killed?' At that point he had this little smirk on him and I could have hit him but I didn't, and then all of a sudden it dawned on me. He wasn't sweating, not a drop of sweat on him."[17]

On Friday afternoon, Fritz had just begun asking some general questions about Oswald's background when FBI agents James P. Hosty and James Bookhout entered the Homicide office. When Hosty introduced himself, Oswald reacted angrily, accusing Hosty of harassing his wife – a reference to Hosty's calling at the Paine home in Irving to keep tabs on the former Soviet defector. Hosty and Bookhout left it up to Fritz to continue the interrogation as they did not wish to incite Oswald any further.

During his stay in New Orleans the previous summer, Oswald had been questioned by FBI agents Fain and Quigley and Lieutenant Martello of the New Orleans Police Department. He had told many blatant lies. Now Oswald was engaging in the same type of behavior. When Fritz asked Oswald if he owned a rifle, he replied that he had seen his Depository supervisor, Roy Truly, showing a rifle to some other people in his office on November 20th, but he denied owning a rifle himself. He maintained that he had been eating his lunch when the motorcade passed by and that afterward he assumed there would be no more work that day, so he went home and decided to go to a movie. When he was asked why he took the pistol with him, he said it was because he just wanted to. "Well, you know about a pistol," Oswald replied, "I just carried it."[18]

As the interrogation continued, Oswald denied that he had told Wesley Frazier he was going to Irving to pick up curtain rods. He said the package he brought to work contained his lunch, which was clearly ridiculous, considering the size of the package. Oswald said he had gone to Irving on Thursday (something he had not done before) because Ruth Paine, the person with whom Marina Oswald was staying, was planning to give a party for the children and he didn't want to be there then. In fact, the party had been held the week before. When told that Wesley Frazier and Mrs. Randle had seen him carrying a long heavy package, Oswald replied, "Well, they was (sic) mistaken."[19]

The "curtain rod" lie told by Lee Oswald was a very important lie. We know, through Marina Oswald's testimony, that on November 21, 1963, Lee was trying to make up with Marina after they had quarreled earlier in the week. Lee told Marina that he was lonely and that he was tired of living by himself. He wanted to get back together with her and start living together again after having been separated for more than five weeks, except on most weekends. Lee also told Marina that he would start looking for an apartment in Dallas for the four of them (Lee, Marina, and their two infant daughters).

Marina's exact words to the Warren Commission on this subject were: "He said that he was lonely because he hadn't come the preceding weekend, and he wanted to make his peace with me. ... On that day [November 21, 1963], he suggested that we rent an apartment in Dallas. He said that he was tired of living alone and perhaps the reason for my being so angry was the fact that we were not living together. That if I want to, he would rent an apartment in Dallas tomorrow—that he didn't want me to remain with Ruth any longer, but wanted me to live with him in Dallas. He repeated this not once but several times, but I refused. And he said that once again I was preferring my friends to him, and that I didn't need him."[20]

It's safe to assume that Lee had no intention of bringing his family back to live with him at his closet-sized room on Beckley Avenue in the Dallas suburb of Oak Cliff. And it's also interesting to note that Lee told Marina he would rent an apartment "tomorrow" (November 22). Marina turned down Lee's offer to rent an apartment the very next day, with Marina telling the Warren Commission: "I said it would be better if I remained with Ruth until the holidays."

Therefore, even though Marina had said no to Lee about renting an apartment right away, it was quite clear that Marina was willing to rejoin her husband in Dallas sometime after "the holidays". This would mean that Lee would probably be vacating his Beckley room within a short time period.

Therefore, given all of the above information, the logical question to ask next is: Why would Lee Oswald want to put up new curtain rods at his Beckley room if he had every intention of moving to a new residence very soon thereafter?

Oswald's curtain rod story was clearly a lie. A brief review of why:

1. Oswald's rented room on Beckley Avenue in Oak Cliff already had curtain rods and curtains (and blinds) in place, as can be seen in the photographs taken on the afternoon of the assassination.

2. Oswald's unusual Thursday trip to Irving on November 21, if it were to only retrieve curtain rods, doesn't make much sense, since he'd probably be going there the very next day anyway to visit his wife at the Paine house.

3. Oswald said absolutely nothing to his wife or to Ruth Paine about wanting to get some curtain

BEYOND REASONABLE DOUBT

rods at any time on November 21, or at any other time for that matter.

4. Oswald lied to the police after his arrest when he told them he never said anything to Wesley Frazier about curtain rods; and he also lied when he said he had not carried a bulky package into work with him on November 22. (It is more logical to believe that Frazier was being truthful in this regard rather than to believe the man who had just been arrested and wanted to distance himself from the mysterious brown paper package.)

5. No curtain rods were found in the Book Depository in the days and weeks after the assassination. Warren Commission Exhibit No. 2640 verifies this fact, via a statement made by TSBD Superintendent Roy Truly in a September 2, 1964, FBI report.

6. Oswald did not take any curtain rods out of the TSBD when he left that building on 11/22/63. If he did, he disposed of them somewhere between the Depository Building on Elm Street and his rooming house at 1026 North Beckley Avenue in Oak Cliff, because he definitely did not enter the rooming house with any sort of package. If he had, the package would have been discovered by police. Plus, there's also the fact that the housekeeper at Oswald's rooming house, Earlene Roberts, who saw Oswald hurriedly enter and leave the rooming house at about 1:00 p.m. on the day of the assassination, didn't say anything about Oswald entering the house or leaving the house with any kind of package[21].

7. From comments he made to his wife on 11/21/63, there is at least some indication that Lee Oswald was planning to move away from his Beckley room soon after 11/21/63. If this was in Oswald's mind on the evening of November 21, then the act of obtaining curtain rods for a room he would soon be vacating makes no sense whatsoever.

8. The two lightweight curtain rods that Mrs. Ruth Paine had stored in her garage in Irving were still in her garage in the days following President Kennedy's assassination. Mrs. Paine verified this fact in 1986 during a television docu-trial held in London, *On Trial: Lee Harvey Oswald.*

VINCENT BUGLIOSI — "Now you, in fact, did have some curtain rods in the garage, is that correct?"

RUTH PAINE — "In the garage...yes."

MR. BUGLIOSI — "After the assassination, they were still there."

MRS. PAINE — "Yes, that's right."[22]

Lee Harvey Oswald's curtain rod story was a complete fabrication, used as a device to avoid suspicion when he carried his dismantled Mannlicher-Carcano rifle into the Book Depository Building on the morning of Friday, November 22, 1963. The "curtain rod" lies were, in essence, "bookend lies", which served Oswald's purposes very nicely. The first lie (on November 21, prior to Oswald visiting his wife, Marina, at Ruth Paine's house in Irving) gave Lee a nice excuse for wanting to drive out to Irving with Frazier on a Thursday night, instead of his customary Friday visit. And the second "curtain rod" lie provided Lee with the perfect explanation for why he was hauling a lengthy paper package into work on the morning of November 22.

Frazier had no reason whatsoever to think that Oswald was doing anything illegal (or that he was about to do something illegal), so when Lee told Frazier that the package contained curtain rods, Buell didn't think anything more about it.[23]

Oswald continued with his lies when he told his interrogators that when the motorcade passed the Book Depository, he had been on the first floor or in the second-floor lunchroom of the TSBD (his story changed at different times) and had seen some of his fellow workers, notably "Junior" Jarman. Jarman, however, testified that he had not seen Oswald in the lunchroom at any time that day.[24]

Jarman had finished his lunch before noon and went up to the fifth floor to watch the motorcade with co-workers Harold Norman and Bonnie Ray Williams. They heard the shots going off over their heads and Norman even said he heard the sound of the cartridge cases hitting the floor above them.

Later in the day, FBI agent Manning C. Clements asked Oswald for some information concerning his residences. Oswald told the truth about every address he had lived at since his return from Russia, with one exception—the Neely Street address. Oswald was fearful the 'backyard rifle photographs' would be matched to his Neely Street residence. Captain Fritz also asked Oswald about the

CONSCIOUSNESS OF GUILT

Neely Street address and found that he was "very evasive about this location."[25]

Oswald also lied about owning the rifle found at the Book Depository. During Saturday's interrogation session, Captain Fritz told Oswald of the evidence that he had purchased the rifle under the name "Hidell". Oswald said it was untrue. Contrary to his wife's statements to the police, he said he had never owned a rifle and that since leaving the Marine Corps he had only fired a .22 rifle. When confronted with the photographs showing him holding the rifle and pistol, Oswald claimed they were fakes.[26]

Throughout his interrogations, then, Oswald made many statements about his actions on November 22nd that were known lies. He lied about his whereabouts at the time of the assassination, the rifle and pistol, his flight from the Book Depository, using an alias at his rooming house, using the name Hidell, his trip to Mexico City, membership in the Fair Play for Cuba Committee, and having an undesirable discharge from the Marines. At every opportunity, Oswald stonewalled when his interrogators raised matters which he could not deny. It was evident to the interrogators that there was a pattern in Oswald's lies. Each and every lie he told were about facts that could link him to the assassination.

Conspiracists fail to grasp the motive behind Oswald's denials. Denying guilt furthered Oswald's self-image as one of the persecuted martyrs of America's anti-establishment left. Denying guilt and accusing the police of having arrested an innocent man would have exaggerated the image of himself as a martyr for a political cause. It is plausible Oswald had been emulating other famous leftists of the past, including the Rosenberg spies, with whom he became enamored during his teenage years. The Rosenbergs were found guilty of espionage and protested their innocence even as they were sent to the execution chamber. However, for the past six decades, historians have established the Rosenbergs' incontrovertible guilt.

Oswald's wife Marina and his brother Robert, who knew him better than anyone, sensed his guilt when they visited him at the Dallas jail. Marina could see it in Lee's eyes. She knew that if Oswald were truly innocent, he would be "screaming for his rights" and demanding to see officials at the highest levels. Oswald's compliance was, to Marina, proof of his guilt. Robert believed his brother's demeanor in jail was telling. As he told author Priscilla Johnson McMillan, "(Lee) seemed at first to me to be very mechanical. He was making sense, but it was all mechanical. I interrupted him and tried to get him to answer my questions rather than listening to what he had to say. And then the really astounding thought dawned on me. I realized that he was really unconcerned, I was looking into his eyes, but they were blank, like Orphan Annie's, and he knew, I guess from the amazement on my face, that I saw that. He knew what was happening because as I searched his eyes he said to me, 'Brother, you won't find anything there.'"[27]

In 1993, Robert was insistent that the evidence pointed towards his brother's guilt. He told PBS' Frontline, "There's hard physical evidence there. True, no one saw him actually pull the trigger on the President [which is not correct, because Howard Brennan did see him pull that trigger], but...his presence in the building was there. What he did after he left the building is known: bus ride, taxi ride, boarding house, pick up the pistol, leave, shoot the police officer. Five or six eyewitnesses there. You can't set that aside just because he is saying 'I'm a patsy'. I'd love to do that, but you cannot. ... He did not and would not talk to any of the interrogators about anything of substance. Anytime they brought anything up that pertained to the assassination of the President and the shooting of the police officer, he knew nothing about it. He would talk about anything else. He had the presence of mind then to do that. ... It's good that people raise questions and say, 'Wait a minute, let's take a second look at this.' But when you take the second look and the third and the 40th and the 50th, hey, enough's enough. It's there; put it to rest."[28]

The Secret Service agents, FBI agents, and Dallas police who interrogated Oswald have all testified, under oath, to the Warren Commission and the HSCA. No one has yet discredited their testimony. To say they lied would be tantamount to believing in an incredible and vast conspiracy involving thousands of people, none of whom have come forward in the intervening years. The truth of the matter is quite different. Oswald lied repeatedly during the interrogation. He had a history of lying. And the preponderance of evidence related to the Tippit shooting and his arrest and interrogation clearly points to Oswald's "consciousness of guilt".

BEYOND REASONABLE DOUBT

CHAPTER SIX

AN INCONVENIENT TRUTH

> "Oswald wanted to decapitate capitalism as he, almost literally, decapitated the president of the United States. Seen in this light, an observation by Marina, the person closest to him at this period of his life, makes perfect sense. Had her husband survived to be tried for the president's murder, Marina believed, not only would he have confessed—he would have boasted about what he had done and proclaimed that it was all for the Socialist cause."
>
> — Priscilla Johnson McMillan
>
> "Everything in Oswald's life proclaims that this was a man prepared to take dangerous and dramatic action for the sake of his political beliefs." — Priscilla Johnson McMillan
>
> "Far from being a confused loner in search of meaning, Oswald was politicized to a lethal degree..."
>
> — James Pierson

Lee Harvey Oswald's potential for violence to promote his revolutionary agenda is often overlooked by most conspiracy theorists. Some seven months before Oswald shot President Kennedy, he tried to assassinate a right-wing political leader in Dallas. On April 10, 1963, Oswald planned and executed a bold plan to eliminate former Army General Edwin A. Walker, a leader of ultra-conservative groups. It is the most compelling pre-assassination evidence for Oswald's propensity to meticulously plan and carry out an act of political assassination, alone and unaided. For conspiracists, especially those on the left who blame right wing groups and the CIA for the assassination, it is an inconvenient truth.

From the time Lee was 11 years old he constructed a world based in intrigue and drama, according to his brother Robert. His favorite television program had been "I Led Three Lives", based on the career of an FBI informant who posed as a Communist spy. At the time of the assassination his favorite television program was "The Fugitive", the story of a man falsely accused of murdering his wife and hounded by the authorities.

It is apparent that Oswald inherited some of the flaws in his personality from his mother. "Our mother was Lee's most important person in his life", Robert Oswald said, ". ... That influence was just tremendous on him. But at the same time, he always was trying to get away from her. ... She had certain characteristics that were so much like Lee: the time and circumstances always seemed to be against her; the world owed her a living; she wanted to be somebody. I think this was passed on to Lee….[she did] a lousy job, a lousy job."[1]

Oswald had harbored violent thoughts since his teenage years. In the mid-1950s, he had spoken about shooting an American President. Palmer McBride testified to the Warren Commission that, in 1956, he befriended Oswald and they often discussed politics. McBride said that one central theme in their discussions was the 'exploitation of the working class' and on one occasion, after they began discussing President Eisenhower, Oswald made a statement to the effect that he would like to kill the

President because he was exploiting the working class. McBride said that the statement was not made in jest.

In an interview with the FBI on November 23, 1963, Palmer McBride told agents: "During his first visit to my home in late 1957 or early 1958 the discussion turned to politics and to the possibility of war. At this time I made a statement to the effect that President Dwight Eisenhower was doing a pretty good job for a man of his...background but that I did feel more emphasis should be placed on the space program in view of Russian successes. Oswald was very anti-Eisenhower, and stated that President Eisenhower was exploiting the working people. He then made a statement to the effect that he would like to kill President Eisenhower because he was exploiting the working class. This statement was not made in jest and Oswald was in a serious frame of mind when this statement was made. Lee Oswald was very serious about the virtues of communism, and discussed those virtues at every opportunity. He would say that the capitalists were exploiting the working class and his central theme seemed to be that the workers in the world would one day rise up and throw off their chains...In early 1958 I took Oswald with me to a meeting of the New Orleans Amateur Astronomy Association at the home of Walter Geherke...This meeting was presided over by the Association president William Eugene Wulf Jr....At this meeting I recall that Mr. Wulf told Oswald that if he liked Russia so damn much why didn't he go over there. I do not know what Oswald had said to bring forth this remark from Wulf."[2]

McBride also told the FBI, "During the period I knew Oswald he resided with his mother in the Senator Hotel or a rooming house next door...I went with him to his room on one occasion, and he showed me copies of Das Kapital and the Communist Manifesto. Oswald stated he had received these books from the public library, and he seemed quite proud to have them."[3]

An incident from Oswald's time in the Marine Corps testifies to Oswald's revolutionary fervor. Fellow Marine Kerry Thornley testified to the Warren Commission about an incident "which grew out of a combination of Oswald's known Marxist sympathies and George Orwell's book *1984*." After Thornley finished reading the book, Thornley and Oswald both took part in a parade they were assigned to. Whilst waiting for the parade to start, they talked briefly about '1984', even though Oswald "seemed to be lost in his own thoughts." Oswald remarked on the stupidity of the parade and on how angry it made him, to which Thornley replied: 'Well, come the revolution you will change all that." Thornley said, "At which time he looked at me like a betrayed Caesar and screamed, screamed definitely, 'Not you, too, Thornley.' And I remember his voice cracked as he said this. He was definitely disturbed at what I had said and I didn't really think I had said that much...I never said anything to him again and he never said anything to me again."[4]

Nelson Delgado, another friend of Oswald's in the Marine Corps, said that one of Oswald's heroes was William Morgan, a former sergeant in the U.S. Army who became a major in Castro's army. In August 1959, Morgan received considerable press coverage when he lured some anti-Castro rebels into a trap by pretending to be a counter-revolutionary. Oswald emulated Morgan by acting as a counter-revolutionary in New Orleans when he visited Carlos Bringuier, an anti-Castroite, offering his services as a trained ex-Marine.[5]

When Oswald defected to Russia following a stint in the U.S. Marines, he told Aline Mosby, a reporter who interviewed him in Moscow after his defection, about how he became interested in Communist ideology when "an old lady handed me a pamphlet about saving the Rosenbergs." The pamphlet led Oswald to change the direction of his life, for it was from this period he became enamored with left-wing politics. After a controversial trial in 1951, Julius and Ethel Rosenberg were convicted of conspiracy to commit wartime espionage and sentenced to death. They had been accused of transmitting atomic bomb secrets to the Russians. After several legal appeals, President Eisenhower refused to commute the death sentence and they were executed in New York's Sing Sing prison on June 19, 1953. During their final months, campaigns were mounted to save the Rosenbergs and pamphlets were distributed around New York City when Oswald was living there with his mother.[6]

The memory of the Rosenberg case lasted until his incarceration in the Dallas police jail, accused of killing the President. Oswald had made repeated requests the weekend of the assassination for John Abt to defend him. Abt was a left-wing New York lawyer who had defended Communists, and a newspaper story about Abt had appeared on the same page as the President's visit to Dallas. In attempting to contact Abt, Oswald was revealing something about himself – he was already preparing for his appearance on the political stage, emulating the Rosenbergs by becoming a 'cause célèbre'.

Oswald turned to radical politics for the purpose of ego-building, according to his wife Marina. She also believed that learning Russian gave Oswald a reputation for being intelligent, making up for the fact that he had a reading disability which gave him feelings of inadequacy. He believed he was an important man and Marina often ridiculed him for this 'unfounded' belief. "At least his imagination," Marina said, "his fantasy, which was quite unfounded, as to the fact that he was an outstanding man. (I) always tried to point out to him that he was a man like any others who were around us. But he simply could not understand that."[7]

Disillusioned by the Soviet Union, Oswald still had a desperate desire to act in a political way to further the cause of his commitment to Communism. He decided that having some kind of connection to the Cuban Revolution would give him some status as an important 'revolutionary'. He needed a cause to belong to; to inflate his self-image and sustain it. Marina testified to Oswald's hero worship of Castro. She even said Oswald had wanted to call their second child Fidel if it had been a boy.

By 1963 Oswald realized he hated the American way of life and could never settle in a country that kept him at the bottom of the pile. Years earlier he had come to detest his beloved Russia. Cuba became the answer to all his problems. As Robert Oswald said, " I think I've come to an understanding of Lee that I have now that I didn't, of course ... I mean, I watched the deterioration of a human being. You look at that last year — his work, and his family, trying to go to Cuba, trying to go back to Russia. ... Everything is deteriorating. It was a terrible thing to look at."[8] Marina eventually came to believe that Lee had no sense of right and wrong; no moral sense at all; only egotism, anger at others because of his failed life and he was unable to understand his mistakes.

The circumstances in the final weeks of Oswald's life accumulated into a 'perfect storm'. He had been rejected by his beloved revolutionaries; he had been rejected by American society and finally he had been rejected by his wife Marina. As Dr Roy Baumeister of the University of Florida discovered in his research into 'spree killers', people like Oswald who are inclined to violence often respond to 'social exclusion' with acts of extreme violence.[9]

Cuba was Oswald's last chance to fulfill his political fantasies. As Marina testified to the Warren Commission, "I only know that his basic desire was to get to Cuba by any means and all the rest of it was window dressing for that purpose."[10] According to Cuban expert Arnaldo M. Fernandez, "Oswald wanted to go to Cuba — and stay there — (this) was supported by the Warren Commission in its report that said Oswald most likely 'intended to remain in Cuba'...Oswald had earlier defected to the USSR and also tried to get a visa to go back, but Cuba was Oswald's passion and destination in 1963".[11]

According to Michael Paine, Oswald "...wanted to be a guerrilla in the revolution which should come...he wanted to be a guerrilla showing (photos of Oswald with his rifle) that he was ready to go active, able – 'call me' – ...."[12] Paine also had "...no doubt in my mind (Oswald) believed violence was the only effective tool. He didn't want to mess around with trying to change the system." They talked about right-wing groups in Dallas and Oswald described his activities to Paine as "spying on them."[13]

One month before Kennedy was assassinated, two movies Oswald watched may have contributed to his passionate yearning to be a fighter for the Cuban cause. His wife Marina told Secret Service agents that on Friday, October 18, 1963, Oswald had watched two movies on television and he had been "greatly excited." The first movie was *Suddenly*, in which Frank Sinatra plays an ex-soldier who plans to shoot an American President. Sinatra's character was to use a high-powered rifle to shoot from a window overlooking a small town's railway station where the president is due to arrive. The second movie, *We Were Strangers,* was based on the overthrow of Cuba's Machado regime in 1933. John Garfield had played an American who had gone to Cuba to help a group of rebels assassinate the Cuba leader. Oswald's reactions to these movies made a strong impression on his wife, according to the Secret Service report.[14]

Early in 1963, a supper was arranged at the Paine household so Michael Paine could get acquainted with Oswald. During the conversation that night, the subject of General Walker, a well-known extreme right politician in Dallas, was discussed and at the mention of Walker's name, a "peculiar smile" crossed Oswald's face.[15]

Oswald had wanted to kill Walker close up with his pistol but it had not arrived at his PO Box address yet. The retired general had planned a speaking tour with right-wing evangelist Billy James Hargis. As he would not return until after April 3rd, Oswald's plans would have to be put on hold. On March 10th, Oswald rode a bus to Walker's home and took photographs. It gave him an idea for a new plan. He would not shoot Walker up close but from a distance using a sniper rifle, which he would order on March 12th. He picked the rifle up at the Post Office on March 25th.[16]

On March 28th, Oswald filled a loose leaf folder, which included photos he had taken of Walker's house since January and a description of the route he planned to use for his escape on foot. He also included in his folder an autobiography and an historical rationale for his act of murder. He was acting, he wrote, out of a belief in a "separate, democratic pure communist society." He would later add to the folder the backyard rifle and pistol photos which were taken on March 31st.[17]

In his revolutionary state of mind, Oswald needed a catalyst to spur him on. And it came in the form of an aristocratic member of the Dallas émigré community, George DeMohrenschildt. DeMohrenschildt had an important influence on Oswald in the year before the assassination. He befriended the Oswalds and the older man became Lee's mentor. Unlike the other members of the community, DeMohrenschildt had a soft spot for Oswald and sympathized with his left-wing views. In reality, DeMohrenschildt thought Oswald was a pathetic individual who pretentiously believed he was a left-wing intellectual.[18]

Marina has testified as to DeMohrenschildt's influence on Lee and how Lee looked up to him as a 'father figure'. Most members of the émigré community were rabid anti-communists, except for George, who sympathized with Lee's world view. George had always been a rebellious figure who had expressed unconventional views. Marina said that in a conversation between the two men, "...they began to speak in English, a sign that George and Lee were talking politics". Marina could not follow what they were saying but she has always felt that this evening was a turning point in Lee's life. She believes that Lee pounced on some remark that affected his later actions. She suspects that George said something that inadvertently, in her words, 'influenced Lee's sick fantasy', and that Lee, having seized the idea, squirreled it away out of sight so that neither she nor George would guess where it came from.[19]

It is possible DeMohrenschildt's statements had influenced Oswald in his decision to assassinate General Walker. Oswald's "mentor" referred to the right wing politician as the "Hitler of tomorrow". Lee Oswald, according to Marina, often repeated unoriginal things which she believed may have come from DeMohrenschildt. One of Oswald's oft-repeated sayings was that if Hitler had been assassinated it would have benefitted the world. It is therefore possible that the anti-fascist DeMohrenschildt unintentionally provoked Oswald to kill Walker. Oswald may have wanted to impress his "surrogate father". According to Samuel

Ballen, a close friend of DeMohrenschildt's, "(In DeMohrenschildt's conversations with Lee) his unconventional, shocking, humorous and irreverent ideas would have been coming out of George all the time." Ballen also believed that DeMohrenschildt could have influenced Oswald to shoot General Walker.[20]

During the first week of April 1963, Oswald learned that Walker had been calling for Castro's overthrow. "Lee Oswald considered [General Edwin] Walker to be a leader of a fascist organization," Gus Russo and Stephen Molton wrote, "and Lee now considered himself a hunter of fascists." (Oswald's attempt to kill Walker came only days after the retired General called for Castro's death.) As Russo and Molton described the Walker shooting, "In preparing himself to kill Walker, Lee was auditioning for the Cubans."[21]

On the evening of April 10, 1963, Oswald left his apartment after dinner and headed for Walker's Dallas suburban home. He had chosen this night because he had heard there was to be a gathering at the church next door to Walker's house on that evening. Oswald wanted more people in the vicinity at the time of the attempt so that his arrival and departure would not attract great attention.

At about 11:00 p.m., Marina found a note Lee had left for her. Written in Russian, the note told her what to do if he was arrested:

1. This is the key to the mailbox which is located in the main post office in the city on Ervay Street. This is the same street where the drugstore, in which you always waited is

located. You will find the mailbox in the post office which is located 4 blocks from the drugstore on that street. I paid for the box so don't worry about it...

2. Send the information as to what has happened to me to the Embassy and include newspaper clippings (should there be anything about me in the newspapers). I believe that the Embassy will come quickly to your assistance on learning everything.

3. I paid the house rent on the 2nd. So don't worry about it.

4. Recently I also paid for water and gas.

5. The money from work will possibly be coming. The money will be sent to our post office box. Go to the bank and cash the check.

6. You can either throw out or give my clothing, etc., away. Do not keep these. However, I prefer that you hold on to my personal papers (military, civil, etc.).

7. Certain of my documents are in the small blue valise.

8. The address book can be found on my table in the study should need same.

9. We have friends here. The Red Cross also will help you.

10. I left you as much money as I could, 60 dollars on the second of the month. You and the baby (apparently) can live for another 2 months using 10 dollars per week.

11. If I am alive and taken prisoner, the city jail is located at the end of the bridge through which we always passed on going to the city (right in the beginning of the city after crossing the bridge).

When Oswald arrived at Walker's house, he stood behind a stockade fence, 120 feet away from Walker who had been sitting at his desk facing out. Using his telescopic sights, Walker appeared to Oswald to be only 30 feet away. However, his aim was thrown off by poor lighting. Oswald fired one shot. The bullet barely missed Walker and had been deflected by strips of window casing.

When Oswald returned home, he told Marina that he had attempted to kill General Walker. Marina asked him why he had done such a foolish act, and Oswald responded by telling her Walker was an extremist like Hitler and he deserved to die. Marina secreted the 'Walker note' in a cookbook and warned him that she would show it to the police if he ever tried to do anything like that again.[22]

Marina believed her husband "wanted to be caught". Her discovery that he was capable of committing murder was "shock...like all the shocks in the world put together, a volcano." According to Priscilla Johnson McMillan, Marina became afraid of Oswald "for months...to kill someone you did not know...to (Marina) that was unbelievable. It was sick."[23]

The following day, newspaper reports which Oswald read erroneously implied that the shooter had escaped by car. Lee showed contempt for the police. "Americans are so spoiled," he said, "It never occurs to them that you might use your own two legs. They always think you have a car. They chased a car. And here I am sitting here!" Lee also laughed at the police for making mistakes in identifying the gun used in the shooting. "They got the bullet-found it in the chimney," he said, "They say I had a .30-caliber bullet when I didn't at all. They've got the bullet and the rifle all wrong. Can't even figure that out. What fools!"[24]

Eleven days after he took a shot at Walker, Oswald heard that Nixon was arriving in Dallas. He had read a newspaper story that morning which carried the headline, "*Nixon Calls For Decision To Force Reds Out Of Cuba.*" Oswald's plan was to assassinate former Vice President Richard Nixon, even though Nixon was not in Dallas at the time when Oswald planned to shoot him. Oswald had probably confused Lyndon Johnson with Nixon as the title "Vice President" was still used in media references to Nixon.[25]

The lead story, accompanied by a front-page photograph of Nixon, reported Nixon's comments in a speech he made in Washington, accusing President Kennedy of being too soft on Castro and demanding a 'command decision' to force the Russians out of Cuba. The speech has been interpreted as a call for a new invasion of Cuba. "(Oswald) got dressed and put on a new suit," Marina said. "I saw that he took a pistol. I asked him where he was going, and why he was getting dressed. He answered 'Nixon is coming. I want to go and have a look'. I said, 'I know how you look'." She did not know who Nixon was, but she knew his life was in danger and that was enough. After Marina attempted to lock Lee in the bathroom, Lee finally relented.[26]

For decades, conspiracy theorists have insisted Oswald was innocent of firing the rifle shot at General Walker. But, like the JFK and Tippit cases, the evidence of Oswald's guilt in the Walker assassination attempt is overwhelming. The note that Oswald left for Marina telling her what she should do in case he was captured or killed was proven to have been in Oswald's own handwriting.[27] There were also pictures of Walker's house found among Oswald's possessions and Marina Oswald has never retracted her account of how she was told—by Lee himself—that he had taken a shot at the right wing general.

The Warren Commission concluded that Oswald had committed the attempted murder. The Report stated, "Although the Commission recognizes that neither expert was able to state that the bullet which missed General Walker was fired from Oswald's rifle to the exclusion of all others, this testimony was considered probative when combined with the other testimony linking Oswald to the shooting...The admission made to Marina Oswald by her husband [is] an important element in the evidence that Lee Harvey Oswald fired the shot at General Walker...the note and the photographs of Walker's house and of the nearby railroad tracks provide important corroboration for her account of the incident. Other details described by Marina Oswald coincide with facts developed independently of her statements. She testified that her husband had postponed his attempt to kill Walker until that Wednesday because he had heard that there was to be a gathering at the church next door to Walker's house on that evening. He indicated that he wanted more people in the vicinity at the time of the attempt so that his arrival and departure would not attract great attention."[28]

The bullet recovered inside General Walker's house (CE573) had the same general physical characteristics as bullets that are known to have been fired in Lee Oswald's Mannlicher-Carcano rifle, although an exact match to Oswald's gun could not be obtained by the firearms experts who examined the Walker bullet. However, a side-by-side comparison of CE573 (the Walker bullet) and CE399 (the "stretcher" bullet connected to the JFK case, which was ballistically linked, beyond all doubt, to Oswald's rifle), shows how very similar they are. The FBI's firearms expert, Robert A. Frazier, testified to the Warren Commission: "Placing (the two bullets) side by side, the cannelure, which is really the only physical characteristic apparent, comes to exactly the same place on both 399 and 573, indicating that this bullet was loaded to exactly the same depth in the cartridge—the two bullets, both 399 and 573."[29]

If conspiracy theorists reject the proof that Oswald tried to shoot General Walker, they will have to accept the following preposterous 'facts':

1. Somebody faked the note that Oswald left for his wife.

2. The photographs of Walker's house were faked and/or planted among Oswald's possessions.

3. Marina Oswald lied repeatedly for decades whenever she spoke of the Walker shooting and her husband's guilt in the Walker crime.

4. The bullet that ended up in General Walker's house just happened (by sheer coincidence) to look almost exactly like a Mannlicher-Carcano bullet. Or, as an alternative here, the real Walker bullet was destroyed or swept under the carpet by conspirators after JFK's assassination, and a bullet from Oswald's rifle was inserted into the official record of the case, in order to implicate Lee Harvey Oswald in the Walker shooting.

But if that latter situation had actually occurred, then why would the conspirators be so foolish as to insert a Carcano bullet into the record that the FBI couldn't positively say had come from Oswald's rifle to the exclusion of all other weapons? Surely the plotters would have been smart enough to plant a bullet into the record that could be linked *conclusively* to their 'patsy'.

The attempted murder of General Walker is an exceedingly important event that is too often overlooked or distorted by conspiracy theorists. When Oswald took that shot at Edwin Walker seven months before President Kennedy was killed, it revealed a very important thing about Oswald — it revealed the fact that he had murder running through his veins, and it also revealed he had it within himself to take a gun and aim it at another human being.

And the fact that Oswald was willing to fire a bullet at the head of a retired U.S. General makes it much easier to believe that he could have also had a desire to take that same Mannlicher-Carcano rifle to work with him on the morning of November 22, 1963, and fire some shots at the United States President who was passing slowly beneath the Texas School Book Depository.

Following the Walker shooting, Oswald continued to believe he could be a one-man revolutionary unit, a 'hunter of fascists'. And he had already proved his worth by trying to kill General Walker. He travelled to New Orleans to look for work and escape the scrutiny of the Dallas police. His plans included compiling a dossier detailing his political activism.

In New Orleans, he played the role of an anti-Castroite whilst actively promoting his own chapter of the Fair Play for Cuba Committee, a chapter that had only one member – Oswald. On one occasion, he attempted to infiltrate an anti-Castro group and visited one of its leading members who had a store in New Orleans. His name was Carlos Bringuier. Oswald offered to pass on to Bringuier information about his military training and how he could be useful in training anti-Castro Cubans. Bringuier later saw Oswald passing out pro-Castro literature on the streets of the city and confronted him. It led to an altercation with other Cuban exiles and the police were called. Oswald was arrested along with others, but he got what he wanted – publicity to persuade others he was a worthy individual who could help with the Cuban cause.

During the third week in August of 1963, Oswald became desperate to go to Cuba. He told his wife he wanted to teach Castro's army how to repel an American invasion and that he had a plan to hijack a plane. He asked Marina to help him. He would hijack an airplane headed to Florida and redirect it to Cuba. While he was in the cockpit, Marina would stand at the rear of the plane holding their baby daughter with one hand and pointing Lee's pistol at the passengers with the other.

Marina refused to go along with her husband's deranged scheme and laughed at him, asking how she could possibly do what he asked when she could not speak English[30] A few days later he arrived home and told her he had found a legal way to go to Cuba. He would go to Mexico. As Americans could only get a visa for Cuba if they were in transit to the Soviet Union, Oswald said he would go to Cuba then meet her in Leningrad.[31]

Although Oswald's assassination attempt on General Walker had failed, he did not become disillusioned with his plans to impress the Cubans. On September 26th, 1963, he was on his way to Mexico City. Oswald checked into a cheap hotel, not far from the bus station.

On Friday, September 27, Oswald walked into the Cuban embassy and requested an in-transit visa to Cuba for a journey that would eventually take him, he said, to the Soviet Union. Oswald lied. His real goal was to stay in Cuba and help the revolution and if that quixotic trip did not turn out to be what he was looking for, he was going to join his wife in Russia. He took a file with him which detailed his political activities in New Orleans, the distribution of pro-Castro leaflets, and publicity about his arrest and appearances on radio and television. He also described himself to the Cuban embassy staff as a Marxist, political organizer and street agitator who had infiltrated Carlos Bringuier's anti-Castro group. When he told the secretary, Silvia Duran, that he was a member of the Communist Party, she asked why the Party had not arranged for his visa. He replied he had not time to do that but implied that the Cubans should accept him based on his commitment to the revolution. Unimpressed, Duran told Oswald the situation was more complex than he had figured and suggested he walk a few blocks to the Soviet embassy to have the necessary photos taken while she checked with her Soviet counterparts.

Oswald walked to the Soviet embassy, but when he returned an hour or so later with the photographs, he was told he must first have a Soviet visa before an in-transit visa to Cuba could be arranged. Oswald left a second time and again walked to the Soviet embassy.

Oswald was met by three consular officials, in reality KGB officers acting under diplomatic cover. They said it would take three or four months to arrange a visa. They observed that Oswald's hands were shaking and he was in a nervous condition, at one time taking out a pistol and placing it on the table in front of him, saying he was afraid of the FBI. He claimed the FBI had been harassing him because he was a former defector to Russia. KGB Colonel Oleg Nechiporenko said, "We all thought the man had an unstable nervous system. He was extremely agitated." Valeriy Kostikov said Oswald kept feeling in his pockets and taking out all sorts of papers during their discussion. "Then he took out a gun and put it in front of him" Kostikov said, "I took the gun away and put it on Pavel's desk. Pavel (Yatskov) asked him, 'Why did you come here with a gun? What do you need a gun for?' He said 'I'm afraid of the FBI. I'm being persecuted. I need a gun to protect myself, for my personal safety.' That's what he said". When Oswald left the embassy he, "wrapped himself tighter like somebody who was hiding from someone."[32]

It was going to take months to get the Soviet visa; his entry to Cuba was barred. When he returned to the Cuban embassy he lied, saying he had been granted the Russian visa. Duran did not believe him and phoned the Soviet embassy and learned the truth. Oswald became enraged. Angrily waving his file, he shouted that he had been jailed for his activities in behalf of the Cuban revolution. He added that his credentials were beyond question and demanded the visa.

"I explained and (Oswald) couldn't believe what I was saying," she said. "He said 'That's impossible because I have to go to Cuba right now because I only have...3 or 4 days in Mexico City so I have to go'...I thought he would cry because he was red and excited. His eyes were shining like he was in tears. He didn't want to understand." Duran called for the consulate, Eusebio Azcue, and Oswald was once more told to leave. Oswald screamed that he deserved better treatment for all he had done for Cuba and called Azcue a petty bureaucrat. Azcue was offended and told Oswald that the revolution did not need people like him. Azcue said, "Listen, get out, get out" before walking to the door and threatening to "kick" Oswald out if he saw him again. Oswald left the embassy devastated by the insult.[33]

When Oswald returned from his trip to Mexico City he continued to keep abreast of events in Cuba, listening to Radio Havana and scanning the newspapers for any information about Fidel Castro. Castro's opposition to President Kennedy's policies was reported in the October 1, 1963, issue of "The Worker", to which Oswald also subscribed. Oswald spoke to Michael Paine about "The Worker", saying "you could tell what they wanted you to do . . . by reading between the lines, reading the thing and doing a little reading between the lines."[34]

And even after his arrest, Oswald's political ideals remained with him. There is convincing evidence to support this. It was inevitable that someone as politically motivated as Oswald would eventually reveal his political self.

A committed political activist like Oswald needed a stage to show the world he was a true revolutionary. But he did not do this by confessing. Instead, he showed his commitment to his ideals with a clenched-fist salute, a gesture of left-wing radicalism that had been in vogue since the 1930s, as he was paraded around the Dallas police station.

A photo showing Oswald's clenched-fist salute appeared in the UPI/American Heritage book, *Four Days* (1964). The caption for the UPI photo reads, "Oswald shakes his fist at reporters inside police headquarters." Most JFK conspiracy advocates have assumed that Oswald was merely showing the photographers his manacled hands. However, a clearer portrayal of Oswald's gesture can be seen in two television news broadcasts of Oswald being escorted into the Dallas Police Department's Homicide and Robbery Bureau. In the first film footage, which appeared in the 1993 television documentary *The Mysterious Career of Lee Harvey Oswald,* the assassin raises his clenched fist to news reporters. In the second film clip, which appears in the Robert Stone documentary *Oswald's Ghost* (2007), a raised clenched fist is clearly visible as Oswald is escorted by police officers through the corridors of the police building. There is a definite clenched-fist salute portrayed on both occasions.

And Oswald repeated this gesture as he lay dying, after being shot by Jack Ruby in the Dallas police basement. According to Dallas policeman Billy Combest, he made a "definite clenched fist."[35] Some conspiracists have dismissed this vital piece of evidence, claiming that a clenched-fist salute did not come into vogue until the late 1960s. However, Communists and left-wing militant groups have used the salute since the 1930s – in the political elections in Germany in 1930 and in Spain during that period.

By killing Kennedy, Oswald demonstrated he was a true revolutionary hero and a great Communist. Acting on impulse, Lee Harvey Oswald killed not John F. Kennedy, the man. He killed the most important human symbol of America – the President.

PHOTOS

BEYOND REASONABLE DOUBT

November 22, 1963. President Kennedy outside his hotel in the Fort Worth parking lot - with Vice President Lyndon B Johnson, Senator Ralph W. Yarborough, and Texas Governor John B. Connally. (JFK Presidential Library)

President and Mrs Kennedy arrive at Love Field airport for their motorcade through the streets of Dallas. (JFK Presidential Library)

PHOTOS

November 1963. Presidential motorcade on Main Street at Griffin Street, Dallas, Texas. (JFK Presidential Library)

The Texas School Book Depository. When the JFK limousine reached the corner of Houston Street, shown above, it slowed down to make a sharp turn into Elm Street to the left. (Copyright Mel Ayton)

175

Elm Street, Dealey Plaza, Dallas. The fatal shot came as the presidential limousine was in the approximate position of the grey car in the centre of the photo. (Copyright Mel Ayton)

A clip from Abraham Zapruder's movie film showing JFK clutching at his throat as Oswald's bullet enters his back and exits his throat. (National Archives)

President Kennedy is shown clutching his throat as a bullet tears through his upper back and exits his throat, travelling through Governor Connally's chest and embedding in the Governor's leg. (National Archives)

Spectators dive for cover on the Dealey Plaza 'Grassy Knoll' when three shots rang out. (National Archives)

BEYOND REASONABLE DOUBT

At the top right section of the photo is the south-east corner of the 6th floor window of the Texas School Book Depository. Harold Norman was sitting in the south-east corner of the 5th floor, below. He heard the action of the rifle bolt and the sounds of the cartridges as they hit the floor. Norman heard three shots. (National Archives)

Dallas Police Officer Jim High Jr, friend of Officer J.D. Tippit, at the entrance to the Texas School Book Depository. Following the assassination, Oswald left the building here, then caught a downtown taxi to his rooming house in the Oak Cliff area of Dallas before shooting Tippit. (Copyright Mel Ayton)

PHOTOS

Vice President Lyndon Johnson is sworn into office aboard Air Force One at Love Field Airport, Dallas, before his flight to Washington DC. President Kennedy's widow Jacqueline Kennedy stands next to Johnson. (Library of Congress)

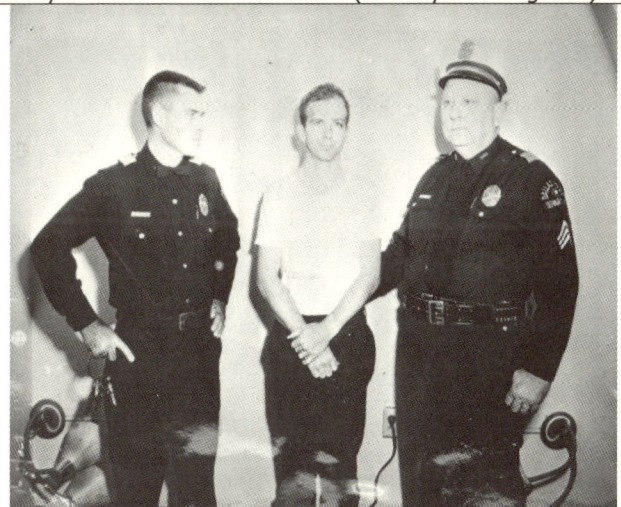

Lee Harvey Oswald and Dallas Police arresting officers. (Dallas Police photo, National Archives)

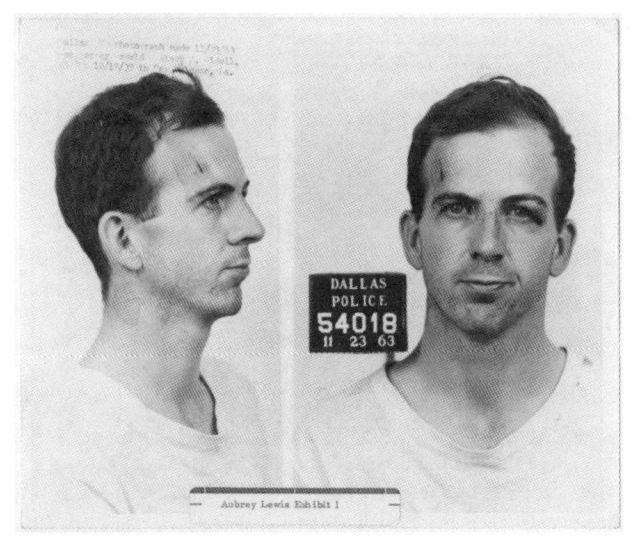

Dallas Police mugshot of Lee Harvey Oswald (Dallas Police Department, National Archives)

The infamous "back yard photo" of Lee Harvey Oswald. The photo was taken by his wife, Marina, in their Dallas home. Oswald holds the Mannlicher-Carcano rifle he used to murder John F Kennedy and the pistol he used to kill Dallas police officer J.D. Tippit. (National Archives)

Oswald's 1940-manufactured Mannlicher-Carcano rifle was the weapon of choice at the beginning of the last century for 1,000-yard shooting contests. Travelling at 2,000 feet per second, its bullets are extremely stable. And with a metal jacket, a bullet fired from the rifle can penetrate four feet of pine. During the Second World War, it was frequently observed to travel through two or more soldiers. According to ballistics expert Larry Sturdivan, "...the rifle that Lee Oswald obtained from Klein's Sporting Goods...was accurate, lethal, and well suited for the job. There was no 'better weapon' available...". (National Archives)

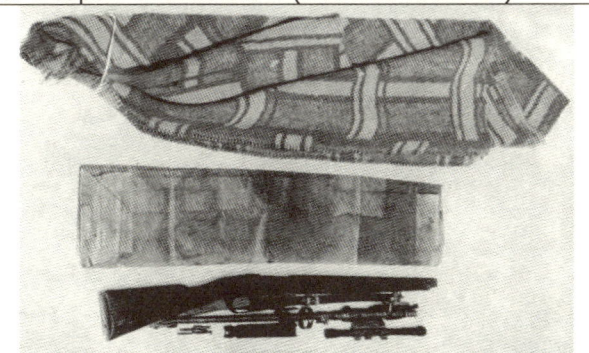

Blanket found in Oswald's Garage, wrapping paper bag found on 6th floor of Texas School Book Depository Building near 6.5 millimeter Mannlicher-Carcano rifle (Rifle shown disassembled) showing relative size of the three objects. (National Archives)

BEYOND REASONABLE DOUBT

As Oswald is transferred from Dallas Police Headquarters to the Dallas County Jail on November 24, 1963, he is shot by Dallas night club owner Jack Ruby. Robert Jackson of the *Dallas Times Herald* won a Pulitzer Prize for this famous photo showing Jack Ruby murdering Lee Harvey Oswald in the basement of Dallas City Hall at 11:21 AM (CST) on Sunday, November 24, 1963. Oswald died at Parkland Hospital at 1:07 PM that day. (Library of Congress)

PHOTOS

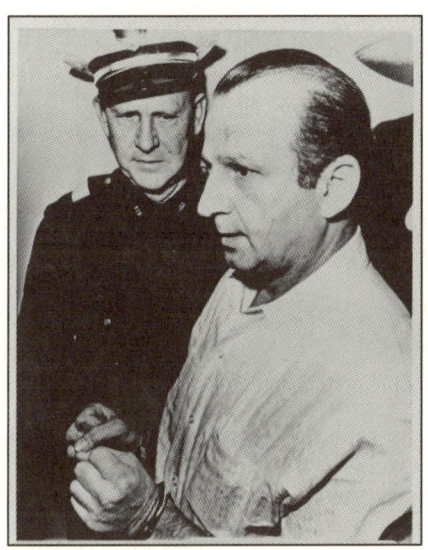

Jack Ruby following his arrest for the shooting of Oswald

November 25, 1963. The Funeral procession proceeds from the North Front of the White House to St. Matthew's Cathedral in Washington DC. "Black Jack", the riderless horse follows behind. (National Park Service)

Earl Warren and commission members present their report to President Johnson, September 1964. The Warren Commission members were Representative Gerald R. Ford, Representative Hale Boggs, Senator Richard Russell, Earl Warren, Senator John Sherman Cooper, John J. McCloy, Allen W. Dulles - and General Counsel J. Lee Rankin. (LBJ Library)

The author with Senator Arlen Specter, former Assistant Counsel to the Warren Commission, and author of the *Single Bullet Theory*. Specter said he believed conspiracy writers had distorted the evidence in the case and had used many Warren Commission witness statements out of context, particularly the testimony of Jack Ruby. (Copyright Mel Ayton)

Senator Edward M. Kennedy, brother of President Kennedy, with the author in 1994. In his 2009 memoirs Kennedy said that after a four-hour conversation with Warren Commission Chairman Earl Warren, he "accepted the commission's report". He also said his brother Robert F. Kennedy had also accepted the report's conclusions. (Copyright Mel Ayton)

CHAPTER SEVEN

THE USUAL SUSPECTS

> "(Prsicilla Johnson) McMillan's book undermines all the conspiracy theories so successfully because it doesn't set out to do so. Marina and Lee doesn't polemicize; it portrays. It's alive to the small crevices of character—and to the vast and irreducible role of chance".
>
> — Joseph Finder, *The Daily Beast* February 2013

THE KGB

The idea that Lee Harvey Oswald had been working for the KGB was first popularized by Edward J. Epstein in his 1977 book, *Legend – The Secret World Of Lee Harvey Oswald*. Epstein's scenario, implied rather than stated, went something like this: Oswald became disaffected with America and capitalism while serving with the Marine Corps in Japan, where he was in a position to learn details of U2 spy flights, radar-jamming codes and other sensitive matters; he started to learn Russian, possibly with the assistance of a Soviet contact, and laid intricate plans for his defection to Russia as soon as he was discharged from the Marines. He had assistance, financial and otherwise, in making the journey to Russia and, once in Moscow, was thoroughly coached in all his actions, statements and letters, by the KGB. Oswald was being debriefed – possibly providing the information that enabled the Soviets to shoot down the hitherto inviolable U2 – and then trained for later use as a KGB agent inside the United States. There was also the possibility that Oswald returned to America with a Soviet agent for a wife. Thus, Lee and Marina Oswald became 'sleepers' – undercover agents who could be reactivated at any time to serve the purposes of the Soviet authorities.

Shortly after Oswald joined the Marines, colleagues were referring to him as Oswaldskovitch. Oswald, in turn, was addressing them as 'comrade'. Oswald was clearly infatuated with the Soviet Union. Some conspiracy theorists claim there was a sea change after his period in the Marine Corps, hinting that Oswald may have been recruited as an intelligence agent for future espionage activities in the Soviet Union. They ignore the fact that Oswald had been attracted to Communism from the time he was a teenage boy and had been acquiring knowledge of Soviet affairs and ideology since that time.

After requesting to leave the Marine Corps, Oswald left for the Soviet Union. He arrived in Moscow around the time of his 20th birthday in October 1959. Shortly thereafter he told his government guide that he wanted to become a Soviet citizen. Turned down, he made a dramatic attempt at suicide. The ploy worked, at least for a while. After his release from the hospital, Oswald was transferred to another hotel, although his tourist visa had expired. His diary claims he was interviewed by a new set of Soviet officials the same afternoon. They, too, denied Oswald's request to remain in the Soviet Union, considering him to be unstable. However, a member of the Soviet politburo decided that Oswald's expulsion could cause embarrassment for the 'socialist state', and the authorities relented. Oswald got what he

THE USUAL SUSPECTS

wanted and was allowed to stay, securing employment at a factory in Minsk.

The Warren Commission explained why Oswald was allowed to stay in Russia, "When compared to five other defector cases, this procedure seems unexceptional. Two defectors from US Army intelligence units in West Germany appear to have been given citizenship immediately, but both had prior KGB connections and fled as a result of Army security checks. Of the other three cases, one was accepted after not more than 5 weeks and given a stateless passport (like Oswald) apparently at about the same time. The second was immediately given permission to stay for a while, and his subsequent request for citizenship was granted three months later. The third was allowed to stay after he made his citizenship request, but almost two months had passed before he was told that he had been accepted. Although the Soviet Ministry of Foreign Affairs soon after told the US Embassy that he was a Soviet citizen, he did not receive his document until five or six months after initial application. We know of only one case in which an American asked for Soviet citizenship but did not take up residence in the USSR. In that instance, the American changed his mind and voluntarily returned to the United States less than three weeks after he had requested Soviet citizenship."[1]

The KGB has always claimed they had never interrogated Oswald, but now after the end of the Cold War, KGB agents have spoken the truth about those events. According to the head of the KGB at the time, Vladimir Semichastny, the KGB moved Oswald from the hospital where he had been treated for the injuries sustained in the suicide attempt, to a hotel while they considered his fate. They did indeed question Oswald about his military service. Semichastny said, "Counter intelligence and Intelligence both looked him over to see what he was capable of, but unfortunately neither could find any ability at all...We were not convinced this would be his last act of blackmail (Oswald's suicide attempt). We expected he would try again, which would be difficult to deal with in Moscow, so we decided to send him to Minsk."[2]

Oleg M. Nechiporenko, a KGB agent who read the Soviet secret service's file on Oswald, wrote that the KGB found Oswald to be bizarre and unstable. The KGB wondered if Oswald was a spy and kept tabs on him throughout his stay in Russia. Nechiporenko maintains that when Oswald defected in 1959, an agent cover-named 'Andrei Nikolayevich' interviewed Oswald and was unimpressed. According to Nechiporenko, Oswald was a resentful person whose vainglory and pent-up capacity for violence made him unsuitable for almost any group that would have wanted JFK dead. Oswald was simply too undependable to have been a likely cog in a conspiracy.[3]

And two and a half years of KGB surveillance had revealed nothing which would suggest Oswald had been planted by American Intelligence. Semichastny said, "We concluded that he was not working for U.S. intelligence. His intellectual training and capabilities were such that it would not show the FBI. and the CIA in a good light if they used people like him."[4]

The HSCA decided that the Soviets had no part in the President's murder. One of the difficult tasks they faced

THE USUAL SUSPECTS

was to assess the bona fides of KGB defector Yuri Nosenko. The Warren Commission knew about him, but did not make his defection public in 1964. Nosenko claimed to have been Oswald's case officer and stated that the Soviets had no real interest in the defector and they did not recruit him as a Soviet spy. Nosenko met secretly with the House Assassinations Committee at CIA headquarters in Langley, Virginia. They decided that Nosenko had actually been sent by the KGB to assure the United States government of Soviet innocence in the assassination and were unable to resolve the matter. This decision sparked numerous conspiracy theories which centered on the 'fact' that Oswald had been recruited by the Soviets.[5]

However, as Tom Mangold has made clear in his excellent biography of CIA counter espionage chief, James Jesus Angleton, published in 1991, that assessment by the HSCA was wrong. Nosenko was a bona fide defector who was correct when he said there was no Soviet involvement in the assassination and Oswald was not a KGB agent. The details of Mangold's investigation are complex and far too detailed for a book this size. However, Nosenko's legitimacy is now accepted by most writers on intelligence activities (e.g., Christopher Andrew, Evan Thomas, and Peter Grose). Furthermore, Nosenko's credentials were confirmed by a top KGB defector to the U.K., Oleg Gordievskiy, who corroborated Nosenko's story (that Oswald was not recruited by the KGB) after his own defection in the 1980s.[6]

Oswald was never recruited as an agent, Gordievskiy has explained, "Oswald was, of course, known to the

KGB, but he was never recruited as an agent. It appears that our people deemed him useless." Gordievskiy's observations about Oswald were recognized as likely true by Oswald's friend in Dallas, George DeMohrenschildt. DeMohrenschildt told the Warren Commission: "I would never believe that any government would be stupid enough to trust Lee with anything important. An unstable individual, mixed-up individual, uneducated individual, without background. What government would give him any confidential work? No government would. Even the government of Ghana would not give him any job of any type...knowing what kind of brains he had, and what kind of education, I was not interested in listening to him (talking about his Marxist principles) because it was nothing; it was zero."[7]

There is little doubt that Oswald was questioned by representatives of the KGB, butthiswas normal procedure. There is also evidence that Oswald was secretly 'bugged' and followed by security police during his stay in the Soviet Union, and fellow factory workers were requested by the KGB to inform on Oswald. However, since the end of the Cold War, former KGB agents have revealed the truth behind their interest in Oswald. They initially thought he was a spy and they didn't know what to make of the 'arrogant' 20-year-old who offered to tell them everything he had learned in the Marines.

"He had no contacts we were interested in, no information we did not have already," former KGB chief Vladimir Semichastny said in a 1993 interview. "There were conversations, but this was such outdated information. The kind who say the sparrows have already chirped to the entire world and now Oswald tells us about it" Semichastny said, "Not the kind of information that would interest such a high level organization like ours...We concluded that he was not working for U.S. Intelligence. His intellectual training and capabilities were such that it would not show the FBI and CIA in a good light if they used people like him."[8]

Oswald soon became disillusioned with the Soviet system, which he saw as a perversion of Marxism. He made two makeshift grenades – possibly to blackmail the Russians into letting him leave. That wasn't necessary. When Semichastny heard of his request, he said, "Thank God...Let him go."[9]

It is reasonable to assume Semichastny is telling the truth. He gave his observations long after the Cold War ended and, since that time, ex-KGB agents have not been restricted by totalitarian state secrecy acts. It would have been in Semichastny's interest had there been a KGB conspiracy to kill Kennedy, as the world rights to his revelations would have netted millions of dollars.

It is extremely unlikely that Kennedy was the victim of a Russian state-sponsored assassination. Soviet Premier Nikita Khrushchev was trying to make peace with Kennedy in 1963, not kill him. The KGB regarded Oswald, as we have seen, as a neurotic nuisance and was happy to see him go when he re-defected to the United States in 1962. Moreover, in the rules of the Cold War, his character traits were questionable; his life was loose and undisciplined and he stood out from his environment, unlike those KGB 'moles' who adapted to American society. Oswald's strange lifestyle and Russian wife only invited examination by the people and government agencies in every place he lived in the year prior to the assassination. Oswald was not the sort of person that spying agencies build intelligence networks around.

One of the most compelling reasons why the KGB did not assassinate President Kennedy was that Kennedy's successor, Lyndon Johnson, was anathema to the Russians. As Johnson was a southerner, he was considered to be a racist, anti-Soviet, and anti-Communist to the core; a reactionary right-winger who was associated in their minds with belligerent and militaristic solutions to the growing Soviet arsenal.

In 1999, the idea that Oswald had been a KGB agent was further damaged by the release of Soviet Government files which were given to President Clinton by Russian leader Boris Yeltsin. The 80 pages of Russian language documents showed Oswald to be a nuisance to the Soviets and reveal the Soviet Government found attempts by the American press to link him to a Soviet conspiracy insulting. The files revealed that Oswald's three-year stay in the Soviet Union was innocuous.

In 2012 former British diplomat Robert Holmes alleged there had been KGB involvement in the assassination. Holmes said, "Yes, (Oswald) had spent a couple of years in the Soviet Union but he wasn't anybody special. He had applied on the Saturday morning for a visa that was going to take four months to come through. The answer would have been, 'Come back on Monday.' But no, three of them stayed behind to talk to Oswald for up to two hours. For that to happen, he had to be somebody. Immediately after the meeting with Oswald, they sent a classified telegram to Moscow. You don't do that for someone who walks in for a visa. There was something special going on there." Unfortunately for Holmes this is the sum total of his evidence against the Russian spy agency.[10]

THE MAFIA

If the idea that Oswald was working for an intelligence agency did not persuade Warren Commission and HSCA investigators, there were, at least, suspicions of Mafia involvement in the assassination of President Kennedy. In 1979, the House Assassinations Committee gave the Mafia theory a boost with its conclusion that Kennedy's death was "probably" the result of a conspiracy and that Mafia leaders had the "means, motive and opportunity to kill the President." In all, 116 indictments were handed out between 1960 and 1964 against Mafia members throughout the United States. It was this volatile climate of hostility which persuaded many researchers that the Mafia was behind the assassination of President Kennedy. The criminal organization had the motive, the means, and the will to carry out the crime.

Both John H. Davis and David Scheim popularized the Mafia theory in their books, respectively, Mafia Kingfish: Carlos Marcello and the Assassination of John F. Kennedy (1989) and Contract on America: The Mafia Murder of John F. Kennedy (1988). These two books helped make the 'Mafia Did It' school of assassination theories grow all the more persuasive in the 1980s. In the 1990s, the American public became convinced of Mafia involvement with the publication of Double Cross: The Story of the Man Who Controlled America (1992). It was written by Sam Giancana's younger brother, Chuck, and Chuck's son, Sam Jr. In the book, they revealed the confessions of Sam Giancana, who supposedly said the Mafia killed Kennedy. True to form, the 'conspirators' are now dead; therefore, the story cannot be corroborated. As the Giancanas tell it, Dealey Plaza was filled with conspirators shooting at the President. In the first printing of their book, they named one of the assassins as Jack Lawrence, a Christian Minister who was totally innocent of any involvement in the assassination, merely a Dealey Plaza witness. Realizing their mistake, his name was eventually omitted in reprints of the book.

The HSCA believed the motive for the assassination was the need to stop Attorney General Robert F. Kennedy from pursuing the Mafia and their ally, Teamsters Union President Jimmy Hoffa. As the HSCA stated, "The zeal of the Kennedy brothers signified the roughest period for organized crime in Department of Justice history...The Attorney General (Robert Kennedy) focused on targets he had become acquainted with as counsel for the Rackets Committee. He was particularly concerned about the alliance of the top labor leaders and racketeers as personified by Teamster President James R. Hoffa."[11]

The HSCA stated that Chicago boss Sam Giancana's concern could be readily understood. For some time he had been the subject of intense coverage by the FBI and by the spring of 1963 it had become extremely troublesome.

THE USUAL SUSPECTS

Other La Cosa Nostra leaders were experiencing difficulties, including New Orleans mafia boss Carlos Marcello. After Marcello appeared as a witness before the Kefauver Committee in the 1950s, senators were astonished that he had not been deported as an illegal alien. When Robert Kennedy became Attorney General in 1961 he deported Marcello, but Marcello re-entered the United States surreptitiously shortly afterwards.

Unlike the Warren Commission, the HSCA investigated New Orleans Mafia Boss Carlos Marcello, as Oswald spent the summer of 1963 in that city. They interviewed Edward Becker, a speculator in the oil business. He told the HSCA that Marcello, making reference to Robert Kennedy, told him, "Livarsi 'na pietra di la scarpa!" (Sicilian for "Take the stone out of my shoe") and spoke of using a "nut" for an assassination. Becker said Marcello added, "If you want to kill a dog, you don't cut off the tail, you cut off the head." But another man present at the meeting, Carlo Roppolo, denied Marcello ever said anything like that, and was not even sure if there was a meeting with Becker. The HSCA concluded that it was extremely unlikely that Marcello, who knew he was under Federal investigation, would discuss a plot to kill the President with anyone but his close colleagues. The Committee also discovered that Becker had a "questionable reputation for honesty and may not be a credible source of information."[12]

Hubie Badeaux, the former New Orleans police intelligence chief who was personally acquainted with Marcello, told author Gerald Posner, "Carlos doesn't talk like that. He talks with 'dees and dems and dose', just like in Brooklyn. Carlos wouldn't know what the s*** you are talking about. He's not even from Sicily, for God's sake, he's from North Africa, Tripoli. I don't even know if he speaks Sicilian worth a damn. If he was going to talk about Kennedy, there is no way on this earth he would talk to a geologist about that. What the hell is the geologist going to do but get him in trouble? He doesn't need his help. And for Carlos, who hardly ever talks, that would have been a goddamn oration. That story doesn't fit Carlos Marcello. You have to know Marcello and know how he talks to understand how stupid that story is."[13]

Florida Mafia Boss Santos Trafficante also came under suspicion from the HSCA. Trafficante had been the boss of Mafia gambling operations in Cuba before the revolution of 1959. Jailed by Castro shortly afterwards, he had been bailed out by Rolando Cubela, the Cuban military official who later became the CIA's 'AM/LASH' assassin. In the summer of 1963, Trafficante, like Marcello, expressed contempt for the Kennedys, and said that the President was going to be "hit", according to Jose Aleman, a prominent Cuban exile. Giving testimony before the HSCA, however, Aleman offered a more innocent explanation – President Kennedy was going to be hit with a lot more votes from the Republican Party in the 1964 election.

In 1992, the idea that Santos Trafficante had been involved in JFK's assassination received some credence with the publication of Frank Ragano's book, "Mob Lawyer". Ragano was Jimmy Hoffa's and the Florida mob boss's lawyer. Ragano was also a close friend of Carlos Marcello. Based on Ragano's conversations with

THE USUAL SUSPECTS

journalist Jack Newfield, the following critical events led to the assassination of President Kennedy:

In August of 1962, Teamsters Boss Jimmy Hoffa (a corrupt Union Boss who was being pursued by Attorney General Robert Kennedy and who later was convicted and sent to prison) spoke with Ed Partin about possible plans to kill both Robert and John Kennedy. In September of 1962, Carlos Marcello discussed 'killing' Kennedy with Edward Becker (as discussed above). In February of 1963, Jimmy Hoffa sent his lawyer, Frank Ragano, to enlist two friends, Santos Trafficante and Carlos Marcello, in helping Hoffa get rid of the Kennedy brothers.

The way the two Mafia bosses responded led Ragano to believe that Hoffa's request would be granted. In December 1963, the first time Hoffa saw Ragano after the assassination, Hoffa told him, "I'll never forget what Santos did for me." Almost 24 years later, in February 1987, on the occasion of a reunion between the lawyer and his old client, Trafficante told Ragano, "Carlos f***ed up. We shouldn't have gotten rid of Giovanni (John Kennedy). We should have killed Bobby."[14]

The big question is Ragano's credibility. It is interesting to note that Ragano made his claims less than three weeks after the movie *JFK* had created a national frenzy about the assassination. Furthermore, the mob lawyer was, coincidentally, trying to sell his autobiography. There is no corroboration for his tale and no witness to support his allegations. Both Marcello and Trafficante are now dead.

BEYOND REASONABLE DOUBT

Lamar Waldron and Thom Hartmann's book, *Ultimate Sacrifice: John and Robert Kennedy, the Plan for a Coup in Cuba, and the Murder of JFK* points the finger of blame at Santos Trafficante, Carlos Marcello and Johnny Roselli because of Kennedy's attempts to crack down on organized crime. The theory of mob involvement in the assassination isn't new. What is new is the book's main disclosure that the Mafia believed it could get away with the President's assassination because it had inside CIA knowledge of a purported "Kennedy secret" – the alleged December 1, 1963, plan to overthrow Fidel Castro in a violent coup (C-Day, they call it), then replace him with a pro-U.S. puppet regime. The authors argue that killing JFK would leave the Mafia protected because the government could not implicate the mob without revealing the invasion plans. If the plans had been revealed, the United States would have risked another Cuban Missile Crisis.

The allegations that Louisiana mob boss Carlos Marcello had been involved in Kennedy's assassination was resurrected in 2009 when Thom Hartmann and Lamar Waldron published their book *Legacy of Secrecy*. The authors maintain J.F.K.'s assassination was planned by Marcello in retaliation for R.F.K's organized-crime prosecutions. And they say Marcello confessed in 1985 in his prison cell in Texarkana.

However, the idea is logically counterproductive. It would be the end of the Mafia if they went after the Attorney General or the President and anything went wrong. Additionally, Hartmann and Waldron are far from proving their thesis. In *Legacy of Secrecy* the authors provide as 'proof' a statement Marcello allegedly made

THE USUAL SUSPECTS

to a prison informant. Marcello purportedly said in the prison yard, "Yeah, I had the little son of a bitch (JFK) killed. I'm sorry I didn't do it myself." However, as credible evidence the 'proof' runs short. Marcello may have been bragging to impress his fellow convicts and he was apparently in the early stages of Alzheimer's disease. Additionally, the prison informant may have been under some kind of pressure to provide information in return for leniency.[15]

For many of their conclusions, the authors rely on interviews with former Secretary of State Dean Rusk, no friend of Bobby Kennedy's, and Enrique "Harry" Ruiz-Williams, a veteran of the 1961 Bay of Pigs debacle. Mr. Ruiz-Williams was believed to be Robert Kennedy's closest friend and ally in the Cuban exile community. Despite the collaboration of these distinguished "witnesses", the authors fail to convince. Ruiz's statements to the authors can be characterized as wishful thinking, and Rusk has provided no concrete proof that an invasion was pending. All the authors have succeeded in doing is presenting the reader with evidence that a *contingency* plan, not an actual plan, had been presented for JFK's perusal. JFK's Defense Secretary, Robert S. McNamara, for example, has given interviews claiming not to know of any such plot and rejecting the idea that such plans were in the works. It is inconceivable McNamara would have been out-of-the-loop for any such plans.

Another weakness with this book is the contention that the Mafia wanted to return to their lucrative Cuban casinos following Castro's elimination. The coup would have let the purported conspirators, Marcello, Trafficante and Roselli, in on the start to regain control of organized crime in Cuba. But killing Kennedy would guarantee that the purported plans would be dropped.

Additionally, the authors rely on old theories about second shooters and purported photographs of gunmen, which have been thoroughly debunked by the HSCA, ballistics experts, and leading researchers in the scientific community. For example, the authors quote former Kennedy aide Kenneth O'Donnell, who was in the motorcade and who told Tip O'Neill, former Speaker of the House, in 1968 that "he had heard two shots" from the grassy knoll. They also quote former Kennedy aide Dave Powers, who was in the motorcade and who spoke to the authors before his death in 1998, that he felt they were "riding into an ambush" because of shots from the grassy knoll. But this is nothing new – many witnesses were confused as to the direction of the shots, but this does not prove that more than one shooter was present in Dealey Plaza. Ballistics expert Larry Sturdivan decisively relegates those myths about the shooting to the dustbin of history.[16]

Marcello and Trafficante both make prime suspects. But in addition to the lack of credible and corroborative evidence, there are two big problems with these accusations. The two men lasted as dons for decades, in part by running their enterprises without attracting attention, not trying to kill the President of the United States. FBI agent William Roemer insists that if the Mafia planned to kill Kennedy, he would have heard about it as he listened to Chicago Boss Sam Giancana (who helped the CIA plot to kill Castro) and other members of the Mafia's national commission scheme

THE USUAL SUSPECTS

and brag. As Roemer told Gerald Posner, "The mob would never go after someone as high ranking as JFK and RFK. They don't go after judges, they don't go after reporters, they don't go after FBI agents or cops – they will only go after these people when they wrong. It's not the way these businessmen would have acted. The risk would be far too great."[17]

Central to the idea that the mafia killed JFK, a number of questions are crucial. Why would the Mafia decide to kill President Kennedy when, one would assume, they held incriminating knowledge linking the President with the mistress of a mob boss? In the 1970s, President Kennedy and Chicago Mafia boss Sam Giancana shared a mistress, Judith Campbell Exner. There were also statements made by mob-linked figures that Kennedy was having an affair with Marilyn Monroe and the Mafia was aware of it. Secondly – Why would the Mafia kill Kennedy if they could get rid of him in a much 'cleaner' way – blackmail? The information about these scandalous activities would have doomed Kennedy's chances for re-election in 1964. Kennedy's close friend, ex-Washington Post Editor Ben Bradlee, has said the revelations would have led to Kennedy's impeachment by Congress. For the first time in the history of the U.S., Mafia mob bosses had a President who was in their 'hip pocket'. Why on earth would they risk organizing a vast conspiracy, knowing they would be putting their own positions at extreme risk?

Another problem with the 'Mafia Did It' school of thought is Oswald himself. It is hard to think of a more unreliable, unlikely professional hit-man than a paranoid loser like Oswald. If he was working for the Mafia, why did he try to assassinate retired General Edwin A. Walker seven months before he killed Kennedy, thus risking the whole enterprise? His job at the Book Depository was very convenient. But he got the job *before* the motorcade route was selected. There is no trail of phone calls between Oswald and the Mafia in the days before the assassination, nor does any evidence suggest the Mafia placed Oswald in the Book Depository building. Conspiracy theorists might also explain how some of the world's most notorious criminals might allow an incredibly complicated plot to be centered on men like Ruby and Oswald, who were unstable and unreliable individuals. Why would conspirators choose Oswald to participate in their plot, when they could have hired much more experienced assassins? Conspiracy theorists may counter that Oswald was a 'patsy' who was unaware of the plot. We must then look at the many incriminating movements of Oswald which disproves he was innocently led – why did he leave the scene of the crime? – why did he shoot Tippit? – and so on and so forth. Instead, we can realistically conclude that there is no credible evidence of Mafia involvement in the assassination of President Kennedy.

The books linking the Mafia with the murder of JFK provide nothing but second-hand accounts, speculation, and obscure connections between the various and nefarious characters who dot the landscape of assassination literature. The 'Mafia Did It' school of authors need to explain how and why the violent threats against the Kennedy brothers would have been voiced before such low-level figures as Aleman or the Marcello informant if a plot had actually existed. At most, these

THE USUAL SUSPECTS

books have established that the Mafia hated the Kennedys, talked about killing them, and wanted them out of their lives, but the idea that they carried out their wishes simply lacks inherent logic.

It was Ruby's relationships with unsavory mob-linked characters throughout his life that led to a great deal of speculation that he was controlled by crime. The Warren Commission's investigation into his background failed to dispel this notion because the commission – which basically relied on hundreds of FBI interviews of Ruby's known associates – did not fully investigate his alleged Mafia connections and his trips to Cuba.

One of the most intriguing questions surrounding Oswald's assassin concerned Ruby's 1959trip to Cuba. The 1976-1979 House Select Committee on Assassinations investigation determined that he had made at least three trips to Havana that summer and that he had visited a safe deposit box in Dallas in the meantime. However, the trips had nothing to do with the Mafia.[18]

The HSCA eventually decided that, "On the basis of the evidence available to it...the national syndicate of organized crime, as a group, was not involved in the assassination of President Kennedy, but that the available evidence does not preclude the possibility that individual members may have been involved."[19]

JACK RUBY AND THE MAFIA

Following Ruby's death in 1967, discoveries about his activities provided more material for sensationalist speculation by conspiracy advocates. According to the

205

HSCA investigation, the FBI contacted Ruby eight times trying to recruit him as an informant. But J. Edgar Hoover, head of the FBI, withheld the information from the Warren Commission. Later it was disclosed that Ruby, because of his advantageous position as a Dallas nightclub owner, had given FBI agent Charles Flynn information about thefts and similar offenses in the Dallas area. In November of 1959, Flynn recommended that no further attempt be made to develop Ruby as a PCI (Potential Criminal Informant), since his information was useless. Ruby simply had been trying to dish the dirt on his nightclub competitors. Hugh Aynesworth, a *Times Herald* reporter who knew Ruby well, said, "In 1959 the FBI tried eight times to recruit Jack Ruby. They wanted him as an informer on drugs, gambling, and organized crime, but every time they contacted him, Ruby tried to get his competitors in trouble. 'Ol' Abe over at the Colony Club is cheating on his income tax....Ol' Barney at the Theatre Lounge is selling booze after hours." After a while the FBI gave up on the idea." [20]

During the 1970s, the public also learned that the CIA failed to disclose a report that Ruby may have visited Santos Trafficante, mob boss of Florida, during the time Trafficante was in a Cuban jail. The HSCA later investigated these reports but did not place any credence upon them.[21]

Ruby's lawyer, Melvin Belli, had explained Ruby's Cuba trips as far back as 1964. Belli said, "It came out in one of our earliest interviews that he had tried to arrange some sort of deal with Cuba soon after Fidel Castro overthrew the Batista regime. But that, Ruby would

THE USUAL SUSPECTS

insist, was when Castro was considered something of a hero in the United States. Now Castro was considered a Russian-supported Communist, and Ruby was mortified to think that anyone might get the wrong impression of the deal. 'When Castro first came in he was considered a hero,' Ruby said, 'and I thought maybe I could make a deal in selling jeeps to Cuba. He was still a hero at the time; his brother was the first one to turn. Steve Allen and Jack Paar (television entertainers) and Jake Arvey's son were all interested then in making deals with him. I had been associated with a very high type of person, but a gambler, Mack Willie, who ran a club in Cuba, so I went there for eight or ten days.' People would say he had planned to give guns to Cuba, Ruby fretted; they would think he wasn't a good American. He insisted that we telephone all over the place to try to set the record straight on this, although I got the impression, frankly, that the deal had been primarily the figment of his imagination."[22]

Ruby's telephone records have also been the subject of numerous investigations and some conspiracists have alleged they provide proof of Mafia involvement in the assassination of President Kennedy. While it is true that Ruby made many telephone calls to his underworld contacts in the months before the Kennedy assassination, the calls had nothing to do with any arrangements to kill the President. There is no evidence the calls were conspiratorial in nature. In fact, the calls centered around the fact that Ruby had wanted assistance from the strippers' labor union to dissuade rival clubs from using amateur talent.

Furthermore, most of the calls were made before the President's trip to Dallas was even announced, much less before the motorcade route was set. Journalist Seth Kantor speculated that Ruby borrowed money from the mob and that the mob later called in the debt by asking him to silence Oswald. Kantor, however, provides no proof of his allegations.[23] Conspiracy advocates rightly point to Ruby's association with Dallas mob bosses Joe Civello and Joe Campisi as evidence that Ruby was mob-linked, but they fail to put the connection in the right context. Ruby's world consisted of nightclubs and socializing with people who were in the same business. As the McClellan Committee recognized in the 1950s, no city in the United States was immune to Mafia control of off-track betting, gambling, and nightclub entertainment. It was the milieu in which Ruby operated. Ruby also entertained many Dallas police officers at his club. None of them testified to any sinister connection with the Dallas bosses. One police officer, Joe Cody, said that Ruby was often seen with Joe and Sam Campisi because they were part of Ruby's social scene. Ruby ate at the Egyptian Lounge and Cody often joined Ruby and the Campisi brothers. Cody said there were no criminal reasons for the meetings.[24]

It was inevitable that Ruby would associate with characters that could be linked in some way with the underworld. But it is illogical to assume mob involvement in Ruby's actions that tragic weekend. The evidence indicates otherwise. "It is so ludicrous to believe that Ruby was part of the mob," Tony Zoppi, a close friend of Ruby's, said. ''The conspiracy theorists want to believe everybody but those who really knew

THE USUAL SUSPECTS

him. People in Dallas, in those circles, knew Ruby was a snitch. The word on the street was that you couldn't trust him because he was telling the cops everything. He was a real talker, a fellow who would talk your ear off if he had the chance. You have to be crazy to think anyone would have trusted Ruby to be part of the mob. He couldn't keep a secret for five minutes. He was just a hanger-on, somebody who would have liked some of the action but was never going to get any."[25]

Former Dallas Assistant D.A. Bill Alexander said, "It's hard to believe...that I, who prosecuted Ruby for killing Oswald, am almost in the position of defending his honor. Ruby was not in the Mafia. He was not a gangster. We knew who the criminals were in Dallas back then, and to say Ruby was part of organized crime is just bullshit. There's no way he was connected. It's guilt by association, that A knew B, and Ruby knew B back in 1950, so he must have known A, and that must be the link to the conspiracy. It's crap written by people who don't know the facts."[26]

Conspiracy advocates have alleged that Ruby had been involved in the nightclub business in Chicago and was sent to Dallas by the Chicago Mafia. However, many years later, Ruby's brother Earl said, "That's absolutely false. I worked with Jack during that time, and he never had anything to do with nightclubs in Chicago. When you were actually there and know what went on, it drives you crazy to hear charges like that, which are just completely wrong."[27]

Bill Roemer, the FBI agent in charge of investigating the Chicago Mafia in the 1960s, agrees. "Ruby was absolutely nothing in terms of the Chicago mob," Roemer said. "We had thousands and thousands of hours of tape recordings of the top mobsters in Chicago, including Sam Giancana (the Chicago godfather), and Ruby just didn't exist as far as they were concerned. We talked to every hoodlum in Chicago after the assassination, and some of the top guys in the mob, my informants, I had a close relationship with them – they didn't know who Ruby was. He was not a front for them in Dallas." Roemer knew how the Mafia operated. He arrested many members of the Mafia and bugged the Armory Lounge, Giancana's headquarters. Roemer was convinced that if the Mafia hired anyone for a hit, they would choose someone who had a track record of killing and who would remain "tight lipped." None of these traits applied to Ruby.[28]

Ruby certainly knew many people who had police records. "It was the nature of his business," said Bill Alexander. "Running those types of nightclubs, he came across plenty of unsavory characters. The police had a pretty good idea of what happened at Ruby's club, and there was no dope and he certainly didn't allow any of the girls to do anything illegal from the club, because that would have cost him his license. Ruby was a small-time operator on the fringe of everything, but he never crossed over to breaking the law big-time."[29]

Despite attempts by conspiracy writers to prove Ruby was part of a conspiracy to kill JFK, there are compelling and persuasive reasons that Ruby was acting alone when he shot Oswald. Despite some claims to the contrary, there is no evidence to suggest Ruby had been hired by the Mafia to silence Oswald. Allegations that

THE USUAL SUSPECTS

Ruby acquiesced to the Mafia's demands because he knew he had cancer have made the rounds for years – and continue to do so – but the allegations are spurious. There are no medical records or statements from his brothers and sister to say that Ruby knew he had cancer prior to killing Oswald. Ruby certainly never claimed he had cancer prior to killing Oswald. It was not until 1966 that Ruby, suffering from paranoia and delusions, would claim that he was being injected with cancer cells. The doctors at Parkland Hospital, who began treating Ruby for cancer in December of 1966, estimated he'd had the disease for only the last 15 months.

THE FBI

There is little doubt amongst historians that the FBI seriously erred in its dealings with Lee Harvey Oswald. In his memoirs, Senator Edward Kennedy wrote that President Johnson confided in him his true feelings about the FBI. "As Johnson saw it", Kennedy wrote, "(the FBI) were aware that Oswald was dangerous and that he had visited Moscow and Mexico. FBI agents had even interviewed Oswald, but they had neglected to warn the Secret Service of their suspicions, and that's why Johnson thought the agency was culpable."[30]

According to many conspiracy theorists, FBI Director J. Edgar Hoover was one of the key people who contributed to a cover-up after the assassination of President Kennedy. And they cite statements made by Hoover when he reported the circumstances of the assassination. But there is a wealth of evidence to show that these suspicions simply arose through bad communication and mistakes in reporting agents' investigations.

President Lyndon B. Johnson was told several incorrect things by the FBI in the days that immediately followed the assassination. Such as when Hoover erroneously told Johnson that the "Stretcher Bullet" connected to the President's murder was found on Kennedy's stretcher, when, in fact, that was impossible, since JFK's stretcher was never in the area of Parkland Hospital where that bullet (Warren Commission Exhibit No. 399) was found by hospital employee Darrell Tomlinson.

In a taped telephone conversation between Hoover and President Johnson on November 29, 1963, several other errors can also be found, including Hoover telling LBJ that the shots from the Texas School Book Depository Building had come from the "fifth" floor, instead of the sixth floor.

However, the mistakes made in the November 29th phone call were later corrected by the Warren Commission during that Commission's nearly ten-month probe into the events of November 22:

LYNDON JOHNSON — "How many shots were fired?"

J. EDGAR HOOVER — "Three."

JOHNSON — "Any of 'em fired at me?"

HOOVER — "No."

JOHNSON — "All three at the President?"

THE USUAL SUSPECTS

HOOVER — "All three at the President...and we have them."

Some conspiracy theorists pounce on the above error, wherein Hoover claims that the FBI had in its possession all three of the rifle bullets fired by Oswald's Carcano rifle during the Presidential shooting. When, of course, in reality, only two of the three bullets were recovered, because one of the shots, as later determined by the Warren Commission, missed the car entirely and was unrecoverable.

It seems fairly obvious that Hoover, as of the date of the November 29 phone call, was under the impression that the two bullet fragments found in the front seat of JFK's limousine represented the remains of two *separate* bullets. Later detailed examination, however, would determine that the two front-seat fragments were almost certainly portions of just one single bullet, not two; with one of the front-seat fragments being a "nose" section of a bullet, while the other fragment was the "base" portion of a 6.5-millimeter Mannlicher-Carcano missile.

Hoover also said in error, "He [JFK] was hit by the first and the third [shots]. The second shot hit the Governor. The third shot is a complete bullet, and wasn't shattered; and that rolled out of the President's head, and tore a large part of the President's head off. And in trying to massage his heart at the hospital, they apparently loosened that, and it fell onto the stretcher."

Hoover also mixed up the bullets and the timing of the shots in his conversation with the new President and said — "Those three shots were fired within three seconds" – which, of course, is totally incorrect (and also impossible). And then we have more inaccuracies coming from the FBI Director:

JOHNSON — "If Connally hadn't been in his way..."

HOOVER — "Oh yes...yes. The President no doubt would have been hit [a third time]."

JOHNSON — "He [JFK] would have been hit three times."

HOOVER — "He would have been hit three times."

As researcher John McAdams demonstrates, Hoover was "clueless" in the first weeks after the assassination. The FBI Director had been kept informed about the direction of the FBI's investigation by his agents on the ground. Inevitably, investigating agents were confronted by contradictory statements made by witnesses at the scene of the assassination and the doctors who attended the President and Governor Connally. The 'less than coherent' data that agents collected in the frenetic circumstances of the time was utilized by Hoover when the Director passed information about the investigation to President Johnson, Bobby Kennedy, and other government leaders.

The FBI eventually cleared up the false data, false leads, and false witness statements. But some conspiracists still were determined to concentrate only on Hoover's obviously inaccurate early comments and statements, with those theorists claiming that (at least in part) those gaffes made by Hoover and his Bureau constituted proof

THE USUAL SUSPECTS

of a conspiracy and proof that the FBI Director was covering up the facts surrounding the death of the President. The conspiracy theorists, bent on implicating the head man at the FBI, refused to put Hoover's remarks in context as the act of a confused person attempting to grasp what exactly had happened in the hours and days following the assassination.

McAdams writes: "So just how does somebody who is so confused on so many points direct a cover-up?" McAdams comes to the logical conclusion that bureaucratic bungling, rather than conspiratorial malfeasance, lay at the heart of the FBI's efforts.[31]

Many conspiracy theorists also contend that Lee Harvey Oswald was unquestionably an informant or agent for Mr. Hoover's FBI. They offer no concrete proof, however, and the FBI assassination files, as examined by the HSCA, show no such link. The allegation that Oswald was an agent or informant stems from two connections Oswald had with the FBI – his surveillance as a pro-Castro, ex – Soviet Union defector by the Dallas office of the FBI, and an interview with FBI agents in New Orleans that Oswald requested after his arrest for his involvement in a scuffle with anti-Castro Cubans on the streets of New Orleans.

The question of whether or not Oswald was an FBI informant plagued the FBI from the start. Shortly after the assassination, a newspaper reporter printed the story that Oswald had been an FBI informant and even gave an informant code number, S172. The reporter, assisted by Dallas Assistant District Attorney Bill Alexander, did it as a way to 'draw out' the FBI on the issue of whether or not Oswald had worked for the Bureau. In 1976, in an 'Esquire' magazine article, the reporter retracted his story.

If Oswald had been an informant, the possibility of his manipulation by a government agency would lend credence to conspiracy theories. Robert Groden (*The Search For Lee Harvey Oswald*, 1995) quoted purported former CIA and FBI agent Harry Dean saying, "The agency is not going to send an agent to talk to an individual who has been thrown into jail for simply disturbing the peace. The FBI knew that Oswald was an agent."

Less sinister motives, however, account for the error in identifying Oswald as an FBI informant. It was likely Oswald knew that sooner or later the New Orleans office of the FBI would learn about his Fair Play for Cuba activities. He had previously lost a number of jobs because, he believed, the FBI informed his employers that he had been a pro-Soviet ex-defector. Contacting the FBI to explain his activities could, in a way, preempt any investigation of his activities, which would involve questions asked at his place of work. Furthermore, no undercover agent would blow his cover by summoning an agent to a police station. It was also FBI procedure to grant interviews to anyone who requested one.

Conspiracy theorists pour suspicion on the fact that Oswald had FBI agent James Hosty's telephone number in his address book – proof, they say, that Oswald was an informant. Oswald obtained Hosty's number from his wife, Marina, whom Hosty had visited when she lived with Ruth Paine in Irving, Texas. Oswald was living in

THE USUAL SUSPECTS

Dallas at the time, and Hosty did not interview him. It was natural for the FBI to track any former defector to the Soviet Union.

In 1993, James Hosty said Jack Ruby was an informant for the FBI only for a short period of time and there was nothing nefarious about Ruby's role. However, conspiracy theorists have questioned the veracity of the FBI and the truthfulness of Hosty ever since the Warren Report was released. Hosty had been told in the spring of 1963 to investigate Oswald, a former defector to the Soviet Union, as a potential security risk. But he was not allowed to confront Oswald with the fact that later that year Oswald had been secretly filmed by CIA cameras outside the Soviet and Cuban embassies in Mexico City. Letting Oswald know what the CIA and FBI knew about his Mexico trip might reveal that the American government was bugging an embassy, thus causing a scandal. It is not unusual for agencies to protect their sources rather than prevent a crime. But in this instance Hosty had no way of knowing what Oswald was up to, so he questioned his wife about Oswald's whereabouts.

When Oswald heard about Hosty's visit to the Paine house, he delivered a note to Hosty, care of the Dallas FBI Office, warning the FBI agent to stop harassing his wife. FBI receptionist Nanny Lee Fenner managed to read the note, and she said it contained threats of violence. The note was later destroyed, as J. Edgar Hoover was worried that it may have been construed as FBI ineptitude in not keeping track of an obviously unstable individual during the period of the President's visit to Dallas. Conspiracy theorists claimed that the note may have indicated a deeper relationship between Oswald and the FBI or a threat to the President.

However, the note was a complaint, not a threat and it dealt with the fact that Hosty had interviewed Marina without his permission. The note was unsigned and Hosty wasn't sure who it was from. He only realized it was Oswald when he interviewed the accused assassin at the police station after the assassination.[32]

There is also compelling evidence that Hosty told Dallas Police Officer Lieutenant Revill, shortly after the assassination, that "....we knew Lee Harvey Oswald was capable of assassinating the President of the United States, we didn't dream he would do it". Even though Hosty denied saying this, Warren Commission lawyers concluded that Revill had been telling the truth and Hosty denied it because he knew the revelations would bring the Bureau into serious disrepute.[33] Lee Oswald's brother, Robert, told of how the FBI asked his brother on his return from the Soviet Union if he was an FBI agent. He said: "If they didn't know who worked for them, he could always say he worked for them; he was in control of the FBI then. They didn't know for sure if he was an agent or not. He was toying with them. He toyed with people like that. He toyed with the interrogators down at the Dallas police station, all that weekend [after the assassination]. It was a game to him. He knew something they didn't know, and he would keep it to himself. He was in control."[34]

If the suspicions of the conspiracists are correct and Oswald was indeed an FBI informant, then why was he constantly suffering a shortage of finances? One of

THE USUAL SUSPECTS

Oswald's landladies in New Orleans said that Oswald used to go up and down the street placing his garbage in neighbor's bins. He took a bus to Mexico and he looked for the cheapest accommodation in whatever place he was living.

HSCA Head Counsel, Professor G. Robert Blakey, and Warren Commission Counsel David Belin, who had access to the FBI files relating to the assassination, state there is no 'smoking gun' that would indicate Oswald had worked for the federal agency. Their observations were confirmed by the later release of FBI files by the ARRB.[35]

PRESIDENT LYNDON B JOHNSON

For the past five decades, various conspiracy authors have claimed Kennedy was assassinated on the orders of Vice President Lyndon B. Johnson.

Texas attorney Barr McClellan put the case against LBJ pretty strongly in his 2003 book, *Blood, Money & Power*. McClellan had alleged that Johnson hired a hit man, Malcolm Wallace, to kill Kennedy. He said Wallace put together a three-man hit team – Oswald, Wallace and a third man firing from the grassy knoll. A central piece of evidence, crucial to McClellan's theory, was an unidentified 'fingerprint' found on a box carton on the sixth floor of the Texas School Book Depository. However, Vincent Bugliosi successfully debunked McClellan's claims in his book, *Reclaiming History,* and also demolished his crucial piece of evidence – the alleged fingerprint purportedly belonging to Wallace. In a telephone conversation with 'fingerprint expert'

Nathan Darby, Bugliosi discovered Darby had been fooled by McClellan. As Bugliosi told Darby, "the unidentified latent print found at the sniper's nest was a palm print, not a fingerprint and unless you've come up with something new, I've never heard of anyone matching a palm print to a fingerprint." Darby concurred.[36]

In 2013, Roger Stone published his conspiracy book, *The Man Who Killed Kennedy – The Case Against LBJ*. Stone claimed Johnson "had John F. Kennedy murdered and then as president used those powers to cover up the murder."

Stone also alleged that LBJ was complicit in at least six other murders, including that of a Department of Agriculture official who had been investigating a close Johnson associate and that of his own sister, Josefa Johnson.

"Johnson is facing jail, ruin, and the end of his political career. He is a very desperate man," Stone said. "Johnson knows that he is about to be indicted. He knows that Life magazine is going to publish an exposé regarding his relationship with Bobby Baker [a Johnson protégé accused of bribery]. After Kennedy's death, Life magazine spikes the story. Johnson knows that the source of the story is Bobby Kennedy, then the attorney general desperate to get Johnson off the ticket. Johnson knows that Kennedy has told a number of people, before leaving Washington, that he will dump Johnson and take Terry Sanford, then the governor of North Carolina, for vice president. He's got a set of hearings coming up about his relationship to Billie Sol Estes [a Johnson ally later jailed for fraud]. On top of that, the two Kennedy brothers treat him like dog shit."[37]

However, Stone's work is essentially based on speculation, rumor, and is devoid of any real and credible evidence. As JFK researcher John Kirsch wrote with regard to Stone's work, "I believe much of the effort to pin the assassination on LBJ is politically motivated, an effort by frustrated extremists who want to blacken the memory of a Democratic president who presided over the greatest period of domestic reform since the New Deal. Have any of these extremists ever had a book or article published by a reputable publisher? Do they have any real, solid, actual evidence that LBJ was involved in any way? So far I haven't seen any. All I've seen are dark hints and troubling suggestions that don't amount to anything".[38]

Additionally, Stone's use of Sol Estes's allegations is a central weakness with his Johnson-did-it theory. Billie Sol Estes, a twice-convicted felon and compulsive swindler who spent more than 10 years in federal prison, was incapable of telling the truth. In 1984, when Estes first alleged Johnson's involvement in the assassination, it probably had everything to do with promoting his just published autobiography, and nothing to do with reality. At that time, Walter Jenkins, formerly Johnson's closest aide, noted that Estes's charge "was just so far-fetched, it's sick." And as Estes himself admitted to the federal judge who sentenced him in 1979, "I have a problem. I live in a dream world."[39]

Like all the other LBJ-Did-It authors that came before him, Stone fails to provide convincing evidence. In fact, many of his allegations he makes were debunked by Vincent Bugliosi in 2007. As Bugliosi concluded:

"....If (LBJ) was part of a plot to kill Kennedy, and the Warren Commission thereafter officially concluded there was no plot, wouldn't he be very likely to keep quiet? Would he be likely to say more than once that, as he told the Atlantic in 1973, "I never believed that Oswald acted alone although I can accept he pulled the trigger"? Indeed, if LBJ were complicit in the assassination, why would he appoint a blue ribbon commission to investigate the assassination... consisting of seven men of impeccable reputation and unquestioned probity, five of whom were Republicans? Wouldn't he know that the likelihood he could get such a group to protect him and cover up for him would be substantially diminished?"[40]

Bugliosi's debunking was supported by LBJ biographer and Pulitzer Prize winner Robert Caro in his award-winning biography of Johnson, *The Years of Lyndon Johnson – Passage to Power,* published in 2012. The book was characterized by the *London Times* as "the greatest biography of our era."[41] Caro wrote, "....unless one believes that he planned or in some way was aware in advance of the assassination (and nowhere in the letters, memoranda and other written documents in the Lyndon B. Johnson Library, the John F. Kennedy Library and other public and private collections the author has reviewed – and nowhere in the interviews that the author has conducted – has he found facts to support such a theory), he couldn't have foreseen the unprecedented circumstances under which it actually happened."[42] Caro stated,"....nothing that I have found in my research leads me to believe that whatever the full story of the assassination may be, Lyndon Johnson had anything to do with it".[43]

CHAPTER EIGHT

THE CIA-DID-IT THEORY

> *"I would never believe that any government would be stupid enough to trust Lee with anything important."*
>
> — George De Mohrenschildt, Lee Harvey Oswald's best friend in Dallas

For nearly 50 years, Lee Harvey Oswald's strange life prior to the assassination has provoked numerous allegations that the CIA had to have had some interest in him. The rumor that Oswald had been working for American intelligence was started by his mother, who was obviously embarrassed and could not come to terms with her son's defection. After the assassination, lawyer Mark Lane represented Marguerite Oswald and she repeated the same tales she had told when Oswald defected to the Soviet Union some years earlier.

As revelations about CIA malfeasance became headline news in the 1970s, conspiracists took advantage of the mood of national distrust of the Agency and were able to persuade the American public of CIA involvement in the Kennedy assassination. They were aided by the national media, who were only too willing to give credence to allegations against the CIA and helped fan the flames of an Oswald/CIA connection. But many assassination researchers, ironically, had a reason for being suspicious of the CIA – the Agency had covered up the facts surrounding its surveillance of Oswald during his trips to the Soviet and Cuban embassies in Mexico City. As Tim Weiner wrote, "By early 1962 the CIA, the FBI, the Pentagon, the State Department, and the Immigration and Naturalization Service all had files on Oswald.... an angry defector who admired Castro, whom the CIA had reason to believe might be a recruited communist agent, who was urgently seeking to return to Moscow via Havana, was staking out the route of the president's motorcade in Dallas."[1]

In the aftermath of the assassination, top officials were more concerned with safeguarding their own agendas than they were in discovering all the facts relevant to the investigation. The attitude towards secrecy was different 30 years ago. At the CIA, 'plausible deniability' was the game. Agents, operating with almost limitless funds, were allowed to do as they pleased, as long as their bosses were free to deny it. During the 1950s and 1960s, the FBI and its Director, J. Edgar Hoover, frequently violated the rights of American citizens with illegal wire-taps and break-ins, while the CIA enlisted the help of the Mafia to eliminate Fidel Castro. The top men at the FBI and CIA had worried that their operations would be publicized through the Kennedy assassination investigation. Additionally, the FBI had a great deal to be embarrassed about – by October 1963, the FBI knew Oswald to be a possible deranged Marxist, a supporter of an enemy of the United States, who was capable of violent acts and who had recently been in contact with Soviet intelligence officers. On October 30, 1963, the FBI also learned Oswald was working at the

THE CIA-DID-IT THEORY

Texas School Book Depository in Dallas and they knew questions would be asked.

But these were only the initial considerations for the new President, Lyndon Johnson. As the conspiracy theories grew over the years, many Americans came to believe their own government had been responsible for the assassination. Did Oswald work for an American agency? Did agencies of the American government use Oswald in a conspiracy to eliminate their own leader? And if Oswald did have some connection to intelligence agencies, foreign or domestic, what would the repercussions be? Was Oswald working for the CIA, and if so did the CIA, or a rogue department within the CIA, hire Oswald to kill Kennedy? Or did the CIA assist anti-Castro Cubans to eliminate the president?

The rumors of Oswald's alleged CIA connections were to lead to all kinds of speculation that the truth would never be arrived at because the FBI and the CIA would always lie. These bureaucratic positions could do nothing but feed conspiracy ideas that the agencies were hiding incriminating evidence of CIA involvement in the assassination. The bureaucratic urge to protect sources and methods forced intelligence agencies to ask that

not everything be released. In this sense there was a cover-up. The Warren Commission conclusions were sound, but their manner of investigating all possible leads was, at the very least, inadequate.

As Arthur Schlesinger put it, "The Chief Justice and his colleagues had perforce to depend greatly on the intelligence agencies. They did not know that the agencies had their own secret reasons to fear a thorough inquiry. If it came out that the putative killer might have had intelligence connections, domestic or foreign, that FBI agents should have had him under close surveillance, that CIA assassins might have provoked him to the terrible deed, the agencies would be in the deepest trouble."[2]

At the time of the assassination, relations between President Kennedy and Castro were at an all-time low. Because of the threat to American interests, the Kennedy brothers demanded that the CIA weaken or remove Castro. There were two possible solutions – the assassination of Castro by a hired killer or his removal by a Cuban uprising, initiated and supported by an invasion of the island by anti-communist Cuban émigrés, most of whom were living in the Miami and New Orleans districts.

The CIA set about hiring the Mafia to organize the murder of Castro. Claiming they were representing a group of businessmen who wanted to see Cuba liberated, they approached Mafia member Johnny Roselli, who in turn secured the support of Chicago Mafia Boss Sam Giancana and Florida Mafia Boss Santos Trafficante.

But plans to kill Castro came to nothing and the CIA decided to concentrate on its second plan to assist in the invasion of Cuba. The 'Bay of Pigs' invasion in April 1961 ended in failure. The CIA was blamed for the disaster and its chief, Allen Dulles, was forced to resign along

THE CIA-DID-IT THEORY

with Richard Bissell, his deputy. Immediately afterwards, President Kennedy ordered the CIA to organize a more determined and highly secret operation to overthrow Castro. It was given the code name 'Operation Mongoose'.

Hundreds of CIA agents and contract agents were assigned to the task. It was overseen by Robert Kennedy.

In February 1963, the CIA terminated its contract with Roselli and began negotiations with Rolando Cubella, a Cuban Minister and friend of Castro. He was given the code name 'AMLASH'. On the very day that President Kennedy was killed, a CIA agent handed him a specially designed ballpoint pen that could inject its user with a lethal poison.

However, there is no credible evidence the plots had anything to do with trying to kill JFK, contrary to the claims of some conspiracy theorists who say that a "secret cabal" of renegade CIA agents, the FBI, Mafia, and anti-Castro Cubans hired Oswald to kill Kennedy or set Oswald up to take the fall. There is no corroborated or credible evidence to support the theory that Kennedy was killed as revenge for 'betrayal' in the Bay of Pigs fiasco when the President refused to give air support for the invasion, allowing hundreds of anti-Castro Cubans to be either captured or killed.

Apart from non-corroborated hearsay and 'confessions' by individuals with less than stable backgrounds, there is no reliable evidence which proves the CIA or renegade groups within the CIA conspired to murder the

President. A number of anti-Castro Cubans, like Antonio Veciana, have stated that they saw Oswald with CIA agents, but their stories were investigated by the House Assassinations Committee and were found to be not credible.[3]

Suspicions the CIA had some kind of connection with the President's assassination began when it was learned Oswald had visited the Cuban and Russian embassies in Mexico City a short time before the assassination.

A photo of a second "Oswald" became central to the claims of conspiracy advocates. In the days following the assassination, the CIA searched its files on the surveillance activities of CIA agents who were watching the Soviet and Cuban Mexico City embassies during the time Oswald visited them. Individuals seen entering and leaving the embassy were examined. A photo of a heavyset blond man was mistakenly identified as Oswald. This tentative identification caused the CIA considerable embarrassment in the coming years as conspiracists pounced on the idea that someone may have been impersonating the assassin.

The man in the photograph was never identified, but no connection with Oswald was ever discovered. He may even have been a Russian diplomat. Furthermore, the 'Oswald impersonator' visited the embassy at times when Oswald was known to be in the United States. The circumstance surrounding the mistaken identification of Oswald led to theories that the CIA was covering up. The confusion was based simply on the fact that the CIA

THE CIA-DID-IT THEORY

did not have any pictures of Oswald in its files (other CIA files held newspaper clippings with Oswald's photo) and the teletype it sent to Washington was replete with errors.[4]

Many conspiracy writers allege someone with CIA connections impersonated Oswald as a ploy to incriminate him. However, it is a myth. There is ample evidence to indicate that Lee Harvey Oswald was in Mexico City in late September and early October of 1963.

The most convincing evidence is the fact that Oswald himself signed various documents relating to his Mexico trip, including the guest register at the Hotel del Comercio in Mexico City and the visa application at the Cuban embassy, which also has Oswald's picture on it.[5]

In addition, Oswald wrote a letter to the Soviet embassy in Washington, D.C., dated November 9, 1963 (Commission Exhibit No. 15). In the typewritten letter, which bears the signature "Lee H. Oswald", Oswald talks about his visits to both the Soviet and Cuban embassies in Mexico City: "Dear sirs, This is to inform you of recent events since my meetings with comrade Kostin [sic] in the Embassy Of the Soviet Union, Mexico City, Mexico. ... The Cuban consulate was guilty of a gross breach of regulations."

What would be the purpose of any such Mexico City charade that had an imposter pretending to be Oswald at the Russian and Cuban embassies? And what if it would have backfired on the plotters?

Conspiracy theorists are remiss in omitting a logical examination of the allegations. What if the "imposter" Oswald had actually been granted a visa to go to Cuba right away? Would the imposter have really travelled to Cuba and then on to Russia? And what would that development have done to the plot against the real Oswald? Because if Oswald were to have gotten permission to go to Cuba, he very likely would have gone there, and therefore he would likely have not even been in the city of Dallas on November 22, and hence could not possibly have been utilized by any behind-the-scenes manipulators as the patsy in President Kennedy's murder. Even most lifelong conspiracy advocates will admit that it would have been difficult to frame a person for a murder that occurred in Dallas, Texas, when that person was in Havana, Cuba, when the murder took place.

And if Oswald did not travel to Mexico City during those few days in late 1963, then where was he? No one who came in contact with the prospective assassin has ever claimed to have seen him anywhere except in Mexico City (or on the buses that he took to get there and back) during the week in question in late September and early October of 1963. His wife, Marina, didn't see him during that time period, nor did Ruth Paine. So if he wasn't down in Mexico, then where was he?

Possible CIA involvement in the Kennedy assassination had first been investigated on a government level in 1975, before the HSCA was organized by Congress. The Rockefeller Commission, named after the Commission's chairman, Vice President Nelson Rockefeller, dismissed theories that the CIA was somehow involved in the

THE CIA-DID-IT THEORY

assassination. The report rejected as 'far-fetched' speculation the claim that the agency had connections with either assassin Lee Harvey Oswald or Jack Ruby. Similarly, the Commission dismantled the theory that former CIA agents E. Howard Hunt and Frank Sturgis, both of 'Watergate' fame, had participated in the assassination.

As evidence of E. Howard Hunt's and Frank Sturgis's involvement in the assassination, proponents of the CIA theory cited photographs of the 'three tramps'. At the Commission's request, FBI photo analyst Lyndal Shaneyfelt studied the photographs and determined that they were not of Hunt or Sturgis. Moreover, the panel found no evidence the two men were in Dallas that day. Nor could the Commission find any evidence that Hunt and Sturgis had known each other before 1971. One unidentified witness said that Sturgis, born Frank Fiorini, had taken his name from the fictional character Hank Sturgis in Hunt's 1949 novel *Bimini Run*. But the Commission found court records that Sturgis had changed his name in 1952 at the request of his mother, who had divorced his father and married a man named Ralph Sturgis.

Although the Rockefeller Commission could not assess all the Kennedy assassination records and evidence, the commissioners agreed that Oswald had acted alone and had no assistance from the CIA. However, it is generally accepted that the Commission's work was less than adequate and failed to order the CIA to provide files which it had requested.

Notwithstanding these facts, it is also quite evident that most conspiracy theorists show little understanding of the CIA as an institution and the motivating factors that agents embraced. They see CIA personnel as shadowy figures that are out of control and frequently ignore the instituted chain of command within the organization. To conspiracy theorists, CIA agents are not dedicated and professional men and women but untrustworthy 'spooks'. Evan Thomas, who interviewed more than 66 former CIA agents for his book *The Very Best Men* (1995) wrote that far from the popular notion that CIA agents were reactionary and sinister, they were in fact, in the 1950s and 1960s, very liberal in their views. Thomas wrote, "(Men like Frank Wisner, Richard Bissell, Tracy Barnes, and Desmond Fitzgerald were) patriotic, decent, well-meaning, and brave...they were also uniquely suited to the grubby, necessarily devious world of intelligence. 'They were innocents,' said John Bruce Lockhart, a senior official in the British S.I.S. who knew the four men from his service as...liaison to the CIA in the 1950s and as chief of operations in Europe, the Middle East, and Africa. By 'innocent', Lockhart meant incapable of wickedness and naive about the difficulties and risks of what he called 'a life in secrets'."[6] Thomas, an expert on CIA activities, believed there was no evidence to link the CIA with the Kennedy assassination.

William Colby, an OSS officer during the Second World War and later transferred to the newly created CIA after it was instituted in 1947, was appointed Director of the Agency in the 1970s. Colby was a practicing Catholic, whose probity and moral perspective is unquestioned. He dealt with the rumors of CIA involvement in the

THE CIA-DID-IT THEORY

assassination of President Kennedy in his memoirs. Colby wrote, "I...had no inkling then (November 22, 1963) of the impact it (the assassination) would have on the CIA, forcing it to defend itself against paranoid conspiracy theories that it had a role in the assassination. The intense investigations of later years showed that it had no such role, and I am satisfied from my own knowledge of the CIA and its dedicated American officers that no such activity took place or was even possible. And as for the allegation that CIA's actions against Castro stimulated the Cuban dictator to retaliate in this fashion, I have never seen anything but the most far-fetched circumstantial reasoning that could support such a theory. The fact of the matter is that the CIA could not have had a better friend in a President than John F. Kennedy. He understood the Agency and used it effectively, exploiting its intellectual abilities to help him analyze a complex world and its paramilitary and covert political talents to react to it in a low key."[7]

Although conspiracy theorists dismiss these descriptions of CIA agents, Colby's actions as the head of the organization enhance his reputation as a credible witness – he was the CIA Director who insisted the agency hand over all its files about the Castro assassination attempts to Congress.

After his brother's death in Dallas, Attorney General Robert Kennedy confided his suspicions of CIA involvement to a family friend, CIA Director John McCone. RFK said later, "You know, at the time I asked McCone...if they had killed my brother, and I asked him in a way that he couldn't lie to me, and they hadn't."[8] But Bobby Kennedy did have suspicions that the

Kennedy vendetta against Castro could have backfired, resulting in the President's death. (See Chapter 11)

It can now be established to a virtual certainty that the CIA lied to the Warren Commission. The CIA told the Warren Commission it did not learn about Oswald's visit to the Cuban embassy until after the assassination. This was blatantly untrue and was confirmed by statements made by CIA personnel Winston Scott, Anna Tarasoff, and Russell Holmes, the guardian of Oswald's '201' CIA file. The CIA also deliberately withheld files from the Commission and the HSCA. Such arrogance did nothing but encourage some conspiracy theorists in their attempt to prove that Oswald had had contact with the Agency before, during, or after his defection to the Soviet Union and that the CIA may have encouraged Oswald to kill Kennedy.[9]

The CIA may have been aware that Oswald offered to kill Kennedy during his visits to the Cuban and Russian embassies. On November 27, 1963, Castro allegedly said Oswald made a 'provocative statement' when he visited the Cuban embassy. A few months later, Jack Childs, a member of the American Communist Party, but also a known reliable informer for the FBI (code-named SOLO), asked Castro what he meant by 'provocative statement' and Castro told him of Oswald's announcement he was going to kill Kennedy.

Ex-CIA Director Richard Helms has stated that the reason the CIA lied to various government investigators was to protect their sources within the Cuban embassy. But they lied for another reason – to cover up the fact they had not informed the FBI or Kennedy's security

THE CIA-DID-IT THEORY

detail about this part of Oswald's visits to the Mexico City Soviet and Cuban embassies. The CIA was therefore negligent in its duties. If this was true it would have been a nightmare when the Agency learned of Oswald's arrest for the assassination of the President. Their bureaucratic bungling in not alerting the Secret Service to Oswald's potentially sinister movements when the President's trip to Texas was organized became an awful embarrassment. In this scenario, the CIA became culpable; their fears may have led to a 'cover-up'.

After the movie *JFK* came out in December 1991, there was an outcry for the release of CIA files on the assassination. John Newman, who researched released CIA files after a ruling by the 1992 JFK Records Act, wrote, "...we have yet to find documentary evidence for an institutional plot in the CIA to murder the president. The facts do not compel such a conclusion. If there had been such a plot, many of the documents we are reading – such as CIA cables to Mexico City, the FBI, State (Department), and Navy – would never have been created."[10]

But Newman did find reasons why the CIA was not as forthcoming as they should have been. After researching released CIA files after passage of the 1992 JFK Records Act, Newman believes that the CIA, following Oswald's return from the Soviet Union, possibly entered Oswald on a 'Watch List'. This decision would have prompted the Agency to illegally open Oswald's mail and alert other departments to his activities after his return to the United States. And the CIA erred in not opening a '201' file when Oswald offered to give the Russians radar secrets when he 'defected'. Oswald's CIA file, he believes, is linked to the betrayal of the U2 spy plane by a CIA 'mole' and the handling of Oswald's file was part of an operation to hunt out the 'mole'. This may partly explain the anomalies arriving out of the CIA's unwillingness to present their files to the Warren Commission and the HSCA.

Furthermore, both the CIA and the FBI were engaged in illegal operations against the 'Fair Play For Cuba Committee', seeking to discredit the FPCC in a 'foreign country' at the time of Oswald's visit to Mexico City. The CIA may also have known that Valeriy Kostikov, a Soviet official with whom Oswald spoke during his Mexico City visit, worked for the KGB assassinations department. Such revelations would have severely embarrassed the CIA, exposing their incompetence.

However, outside of the wild and speculative conspiracy books, there have been a number of respected authors (including Bayard Stockton, Vincent Bugliosi, Gus Russo, Evan Thomas, Tim Weiner, and Peter Grose) who have researched the allegation that the CIA had been tied into the assassination and may have been responsible. Most of them discovered curious—but essentially ephemeral— Oswald connections to anti-Castro Cubans and their CIA handlers. Additionally, alleged CIA/Oswald connections were investigated by the Warren Commission, Rockefeller Commission, the Church Committee, and the HSCA. All these investigatory bodies concluded there was no credible evidence to support CIA involvement or culpability in the assassination.

Vincent Bugliosi concluded that conspiracy theorists have been unable to come up with "any evidence

THE CIA-DID-IT THEORY

connecting the CIA to Oswald," and accuses theorists of having little regard for causation and factual analysis, or the application of the rules of evidence and common sense. Bugliosi meticulously researched the JFK/CIA allegations that had been circulating since the sixties and observed that ". . .the only books written that suggest the CIA was behind the assassination are those by conspiracy theorists . . .on the other hand, a considerable number of books have been written about the CIA and its history, warts and all, and not one of their authors, even though they had every ethical, professional (Pulitzer Prize, esteem of peers, etc.) and commercial reason to expose the CIA . . .as being behind the assassination, found the need to devote more than a paragraph or two in their long books to Lee Harvey Oswald and the assassination."[11]

Bayard Stockton, an ex-CIA agent who later worked as a journalist for *Newsweek*, may be the exception, as he devotes a chapter of his 2006 book to the allegations. He researched the possibility of CIA involvement in the JFK assassination for his biography of CIA officer William Harvey. Stockton interviewed many former officials and Harvey's wife, all of whom reacted with "horror and disbelief" about the allegations. Stockton wrote that although a conclusive decision could not be made until the CIA releases all its documents, there was no credible evidence to blame the CIA. "I find it very hard to believe," Stockton wrote, "that sworn officers of the CIA plotted the death of the president of the United States. I think the Agency's top echelon knew more than it has admitted and was embarrassed that it had not yielded its knowledge instantly."[12]

THE MANCHURIAN-CANDIDATE ASSASSIN

Conspiracy writers have also used the 'Manchurian Candidate' theory to imply Oswald was manipulated by the CIA.

In a 2007 documentary, *RFK Must Die*, and a 2008 National Geographic Channel documentary, *CIA Secret Experiments*, a number of conspiracy advocates alleged RFK assassin Sirhan Bishara Sirhan was a Manchurian Candidate-type assassin—an unwitting tool of faceless conspirators in the CIA and the military-industrial complex. The conspiracy writers also alleged Lee Harvey Oswald had also been a brainwashed assassin. Conspiracists also believe RFK was murdered because he was about to end the war in Vietnam, thus he was working against the interests of the military-industrial complex. Jerry Leonard, Lincoln Lawrence, and Kenn Thomas believe that Oswald's bizarre behavior was remarkably consistent with that of an unwitting "hypno-programmed spy". They also believe that Oswald's alleged links to the CIA and the further allegation that George DeMohrenschildt was Oswald's "handler" or "controller" were proof enough that Oswald had been brainwashed to kill President Kennedy.[13]

Dick Russell also alleged Oswald had been a hypnotized assassin in his book, *The Man Who Knew Too Much*, an account of Russell's investigation into the subject of Richard Case Nagell. Nagell stated that during the summer of 1963 he had discovered that Oswald was "undergoing hypnotherapy" from JFK conspirator David Ferrie. The story, however, had originated with a

THE CIA-DID-IT THEORY

notorious fabricator, Jack Martin, who later admitted the story was false.[14]

The only plausible JFK "Manchurian Candidate-type" theory comes from Ion Mahai Pacepa, head of Romania's secret security agency before defecting to the U.S. in 1978. In his book, Pacepa maintains that Soviet Premier Nikita Khrushchev plotted the assassination, only to have a change of heart, but Soviet agents were unable to deprogram Oswald. Pacepa also claims that Carousel Club owner Jack Ruby was working as an intelligence agent for the Cuban DGI.

However, there are fundamental flaws to Pacepa's story. KGB officers who had an interest in Oswald when he was in the Soviet Union have testified that the KGB found him to be unstable and untrustworthy. It is therefore extremely unlikely the Soviets would have wanted to employ someone of Oswald's caliber.[15]

Additionally, Pacepa is on shaky ground when he alleges that Ruby acted at the behest of the Cuban regime, and was later poisoned in order to silence him. That allegation, of course, would have to take into account the implausible notion that Ruby's doctor was part of the conspiracy. Furthermore, Ruby died from a pulmonary embolism and cancer of the lungs and brain more than three years after he murdered Oswald, raising the question of why would an apparently all-powerful intelligence agency wait that long? If Ruby had wanted to spill the beans, he had plenty of opportunity. As it turned out, the only conspiracy Ruby complained about was a conspiracy to "kill the Jews," a product of his mental illness.

Pacepa offers no convincing Soviet motive for the assassination. Furthermore, as Vincent Bugliosi said in his examination of the allegations that the Soviet Union planned and carried out the assassination, "Russia had absolutely nothing to gain but much to lose in killing Kennedy."[16]

And, according to the State Department and counterintelligence officers who debriefed Pacepa, changes to his defection story cast doubt on his veracity. There is nothing in Oswald's background that could remotely infer he was hypnotically controlled by the CIA, despite the speculative accounts by some JFK assassination writers.

The hypnosis research community is split on whether or not a person can be controlled by others. 'State' theorists believe hypnotized subjects have entered a dissociative state and can be controlled by the hypnotist. However, it is the non-state theorists who dominate the research community in the United States and Europe. Non-state theorists agree that the hypnotic state is less like a trance but more like imaginative involvement in a task. A hypnotized subject's abnormal behavior can be explained by normal human abilities, e.g., intense concentration, creative imagination, suggestibility, a willingness to act out inhibitions, and peer-group pressure (insofar as stage performances are concerned). Acts carried out by a hypnotized subject are the result of the subject's positive attitude, motivation, and expectancy. Non-state theorists argue that a subject's responsiveness to suggestions, like "raise an arm," "appear drowsy," etc., cannot be the result of a hypnotic trance, because non-hypnotized subjects in control

THE CIA-DID-IT THEORY

groups will respond to such suggestions in a similar manner.[17]

A number of myths about hypnosis have led most conspiracy writers to make grossly speculative conclusions about Oswald's purported hypnotic state. No one really knows how hypnosis works, and scientists, including psychiatrists and psychologists, disagree about not only a definition, but also how and why people react when in a trance. They do agree, however, that something unusual happens when a subject is put into a hypnotic state. Most psychologists agree that hypnotic techniques give the hypnotist access to the subconscious and have value as a therapeutic technique in the treatment of mental disorders. However, the notion that a hypnotist has control over a subject is, essentially, a myth. A 1979 study by Coe and Ryken indicated that hypnosis is no more bothersome to subjects than other activities, such as taking a college exam, and the subject retains the ultimate decision to comply with or refuse the suggestion.[18]

Although hypnosis is a highly controversial subject and leading experts differ in their opinions and research, the academic scientific community has reached the consensus that the popular press has misled the public regarding the nature of hypnosis. Countless movies and books have populated the idea that a human subject can be controlled. Hypnosis expert Robert Baker claims that what we call "hypnosis" is actually a form of learned social behavior. The hypnotist and subject learn what is expected of them and reinforce each other's behavior with their performances. The hypnotist provides the suggestions, and the subject responds to the

243

suggestions. The rest of the behavior—the hypnotist's repetitious sounds and the subject's trance—are simply window-dressing, part of the drama that makes hypnosis intriguing. Strip away these dramas, Baker argues, and what is left is psyched-up states of suggestibility.[19]

Evidence that North Korean torture, isolation, and sensory deprivation tactics were successfully used to control their captives is nonexistent. Only 22 out of 4,500 (or 0.5%) of those Americans captured by the Chinese defected. It was also unlikely "confessions" by American soldiers could be considered proof of brainwashing, because soldiers had received specific instructions from their superiors to cooperate without giving away secrets if they were captured. Prisoners side with their captors because of their own low morale and the proclivities of a number of left-leaning POWs rather than because they have been effectively brainwashed. It has been argued that the U.S. government knew the Communists did not have any "magical tool", but it allowed the suspicions to remain public to alert U.S. citizens to the dangers of Communism.[20]

According to psychologist Dr. Graham Wagstaff, "hypnotic subjects do not lose consciousness, control of their behavior, or their normal scruples...the recent definition of hypnosis provided by the American Psychological Association clearly rejects the notion of the hypnotic automaton...in a further recent survey of 10 experts on forensic hypnosis . conducted by Vingoe (1995), all rejected the view that, 'during hypnosis the control a person normally has over him or herself is in the hands of the hypnotist'."

THE CIA-DID-IT THEORY

Wagstaff quoted a similar view expressed by the editors of the contributors to what is probably one of the most important academic volumes on hypnosis to be published, *Theories of Hypnosis*, edited by Lynn and Rhue, who concluded, "Since the 'golden age' of hypnotism (the 1880s and 1890s), the view of the hypnotized subject as a passive automaton under the sway of a powerful hypnotist has faded in popularity. In fact, this rather extreme position is not endorsed by any of the theorists whose ideas are represented in this book."[21]

Despite the overwhelming evidence that points to the impossibility that a person can be made to commit murder under hypnosis, conspiracists continue to insist there is evidence that such a crime had been committed in the past. In their RFK assassination books, conspiracy advocates Philip Melanson, Jon Christian, and Lisa Pease, and most recently James DiEugenio and Robert Blair Kaiser, reference Bjorn Nielsen, who purportedly hypnotized Palle Hardrup to commit murder in 1951. They used this case as a proven example of how someone can hypnotize another to commit murder. What these conspiracists do not do, however, is inform their readers that Hardrup, in 1972, confessed to making everything up in an interview with Soren Petersen of the Danish newspaper "BT".[22]

Conspiracy theorists also suggest the CIA had successfully developed drugs and mind-control techniques to manipulate their Cold War adversaries or to get unwitting persons to do their bidding. Many conspiracists also believe the CIA used these techniques to control Oswald and then program him to forget.

However, the Agency abandoned the idea that it was possible to turn men into puppets.[23] CIA scientists were also never able to produce "total amnesia" in a subject. The record shows that the CIA made two attempts to produce a "Manchurian Candidate Assassin". The first involved a hypnotist hired by the Agency to hypnotize a suspected Mexican double agent. The hypnotist's job was to coax the subject to murder a Soviet KGB agent. Eventually, the hypnotist, code-named "Mindbender", decided the idea was unrealistic and decided not to continue. The second attempt occurred in 1966 when the CIA hired a hypnotist to coax a Cuban exile to return to his homeland and assassinate Fidel Castro. The hypnotist tried to coerce three subjects into committing the act — all attempts failed.[24]

According to an ARTICHOKE and MKULTRA operative, "All experiments beyond a certain point always failed because the subject jerked himself back for some reason or the subject got amnesiac or catatonic" and the Agency's methods occasionally turned the subjects into vegetables who could not do anything, especially the Agency's bidding.

A former MKULTRA official told author John Marks that a foolproof way of triggering amnesia could not be found. "You had to accept," he said, "that when someone is caught, they're going to tell some things." David Rhodes, a long-serving MKULTRA official, said, "Creating a Manchurian Candidate is a total psychological impossibility."[25]

THE CIA-DID-IT THEORY

Conspiracy advocates frequently cite experiments conducted by CIA scientist Morse Allen, who they allege was successful in programming an assassin. Allen hypnotized his secretary, who had a fear and loathing of guns, to pick up a pistol and shoot another secretary. The gun, of course, was unloaded. After Allen brought the secretary out of the trance, she had no memory of what she had done.

Those who promoted this experiment as proof of programmed assassins failed to mention that Allen did not give much credibility to it. Allen believed that he had simply convinced an impressionable young woman volunteer to accept orders from a legitimate authority figure to carry out an order she likely knew would not end in tragedy.[26]

Allen also believed there were too many variables in hypnosis for it to be a reliable weapon. And all the participants in such trials knew they were involved in a scientific experiment. An authority figure was always present to remind the subject or some part of the subject's mind that it was only an experiment. The CIA's ARTICHOKE team concluded that it could not effectively hypnotize a subject, even though Allen thought it could be possible.[27]

Following years of research into the subject of possible CIA mind-controlled assassin programs, author John Marks concluded that, "[MKULTRA officials] were not interested in a programmed assassin because they knew in general it would not work and, specifically, that they could not exert total control. The CIA had concluded that there were more reliable ways 'to kill people'."[28]

CIA agent William Buckley, who acted as liaison between the CIA and Ewan Cameron, an MKULTRA psychiatrist who was conducting experiments into the use of hypnosis to build a robotic assassin, said "MK-ULTRA had become a big, bad, black game which men like [CIA Dr.] Gottlieb and Cameron and others like them played because they wanted to believe. Not actually believe, but wanted to." Gottlieb confessed to Buckley, "Nothing worked for me, so why should it work for anyone else?"[29]

A leading hypnosis expert, Dr. Steve Lynn of Binghamton University, concurs. Lynn believes that a "trigger [mechanism] that would move someone into a hypnotic state where they would commit murder...would [not] really work. You do not relinquish your will. You do not become a dupe, a patsy or a mindless automaton despite some public beliefs that this may be the case."[30]

In 2011, conspiracy theorists believed they had found 'proof' that someone like Lee Harvey Oswald or Sirhan Sirhan could be hypnotized against his will. The illusionist Derren Brown purportedly hypnotized a man to kill a 'celebrity' and then forget about it. However, conspiracists have clearly missed the point. As an illusionist, Derren Brown expects that when he is performing that he "lies" about what he does which is mixing magic, suggestion, psychology, misdirection and showmanship for entertainment purposes – fun for the viewer comes from not knowing what's real and what isn't. He's a magician, doing what magicians do. Except he has the decency to say up front he's 'messing' with us.

THE CIA-DID-IT THEORY

During filming of *The Assassin*, Brown asked psychologists from Sussex University and Birmingham University whether they thought it was possible to hypnotically program someone to carry out an assassination, both academics confidently said that they didn't believe so. One of the psychologists, Stuart Derbyshire, said that unless the person is predisposed to killing, it would be impossible to get an ordinary man to commit such a crime.

However, Brown's test was seen to purportedly work. But it only worked because part of his experiment was safe as it was being conducted in a TV studio and participants played along for a variety of reasons. As one of his 'actors' stated, "When it came to the final scene I was supposed to have been 'programmed' to act in a certain way by various subliminal messages and triggers, but that was just part of the misdirection for the benefit of the viewers. The way it actually worked was that Derren was off-camera and giving me directions, telling me what to do....Before the filming had started he'd been through a hypnosis routine with me; although this was never mentioned or shown in the finished item. I never felt hypnotized but I went along with it."[31] Another participant in his program said, "Something which is hard to appreciate, unless you've experienced it for yourself, is the huge pressure you feel under when it comes to filming. Nothing was ever said to me, but it didn't need to be. You just know how much time and effort has gone into setting up something like this. And you know that everything ultimately depends on you to make it work. So you're trying to give them what they want."[32]

Brown was clearly perpetrating a type of 'hoax'. According to James Randi, the famous illusionist who has revealed many secrets behind acts like Brown's, "This man is a highly inventive and very strong performer of mentalism, an illusionist who weaves fascinating stories into his mind-blowing shows."[33] Professor Chris French, a leading skeptic and Professor of Psychology at Goldsmiths College said, "I'm sure many people accept it as entertainment and realize that he often uses science as a form of misdirection for more conventional tricks, but a great many of his viewers don't see this subtlety. They take his explanations at face value and believe that what they're seeing is genuine. The problem, from a science point of view, is that it's muddying the waters and creating a false perception about the way these things actually work."[34]

Additionally, Brown had been caught twice before in misrepresenting what he does. Following his 'russian roulette' show, in which members of the audience actually played the dangerous game, the police had to issue a statement saying that it was fake and that they would have never allowed it to take place.[35] During Brown's lottery game ticket 'hoax', which he swore was real, a number of people noticed he was using TV trickery. Simon Singh, a noted skeptic, wrote an article where he exposed one of Brown's card tricks as a straight-forward magic trick, and objected to Brown claiming that it was done through psychology.[36]

Brown is an illusionist and the 'assassin' show was entertainment. Accordingly, it would behoove conspiracy theorists not to jump to ill-considered conclusions about allegations that Lee Harvey Oswald and Sirhan Sirhan

THE CIA-DID-IT THEORY

were Manchurian Candidate-style assassins, the evidence for which is clearly lacking.

CIA-CONTROLLED ANTI-CASTRO AGENT

Lee Harvey Oswald's whole life had been dedicated to Marxist principles and he became enamored with the Cuban revolution even during his time in the Marine Corps. Yet there were some curious activities during Oswald's stay in New Orleans in the summer of 1963 which would suggest he was playing the role of an anti-Castro agent controlled by the CIA. During this period, he was actively promoting his own chapter of the Fair Play for Cuba Committee on the streets of New Orleans.

On one occasion he was known to attempt to infiltrate an anti-Castro group and visited one of its leading members, Carlos Bringuier, which later led to a fracas in which Oswald had been arrested. So far the story is straightforward – it is likely Oswald had been trying to build up his credentials as a dedicated supporter of Castro and it is also reasonable to assume he intended to use the publicity that was created to impress the Cuban authorities when the time came for him to fulfill his fantasy of joining the Cuban revolution.

Yet someone who had important connections to anti-Castro groups in New Orleans, Miami, and Dallas came forward to say that Oswald had visited her and offered to shoot Kennedy in retaliation for his betrayal of anti-Castro Cubans at the 'Bay of Pigs'. It seemed to be the most compelling piece of evidence linking Oswald to anti-Castro Cubans. The woman who was 'visited' by Oswald was Sylvia Odio, a member of the Cuban

Revolutionary Junta, or JURE, an organization which had a lot of credibility with Cuban émigrés, and her story has been used by just about every conspiracy theorist. She told the HSCA, after they had called her to testify during its hearings, that she had been visited, in late September 1963, by three men who asked for help in preparing a fundraising letter for JURE. The HSCA stated that Mrs. Odio identified two of the men as Cubans or possibly Mexicans.

The two individuals, she remembered, indicated that their 'war' names were 'Leopoldo' and 'Angelo'. The third man was an American called 'Leon Oswald', and she was told he was very much interested in the anti-Castro cause. Mrs. Odio stated that the men told her that they had just come from New Orleans and that they were about to leave on a trip. The next day, one of the Cubans called her on the telephone and told her that it had been his idea to introduce the American into the underground because he had characteristics which suggested instability; meaning he had the ability to commit violent acts.

The Cubans also said that the American had been in the Marine Corps and was an excellent shot, and that the American had said that Cubans were weak and should have assassinated President Kennedy after the Bay of Pigs fiasco. Mrs. Odio claimed the American was Lee Harvey Oswald. Her sister, who was in the apartment at the time of the visit and saw the men briefly in the hallway when answering the door, also believed that the American was Lee Harvey Oswald.

THE CIA-DID-IT THEORY

Back in 1964, the Warren Commission did not believe Sylvia Odio or her sister, claiming that Oswald was on his way to Mexico City by bus when the incident was alleged to occur: "During the course of its investigation... the Commission concluded that Oswald could not have been in Dallas on the evening of either September 26 or 27, 1963. It also developed considerable evidence that he was not in Dallas at any time between the beginning of September and October 3, 1963. On April 24, Oswald left Dallas for New Orleans, where he lived until his trip to Mexico City in late September and his subsequent return to Dallas. Oswald is known to have been in New Orleans as late as September 23, 1963, the date on which Mrs. Paine and Marina Oswald left New Orleans for Dallas. Sometime between 4 p.m. on September 24 and 1 p.m. on September 25, Oswald cashed an unemployment compensation check at a store in New Orleans; under normal procedures this check would not have reached Oswald's postal box in New Orleans until at least 5 a.m. on September 25. The store at which he cashed the check did not open until 8 a.m. Therefore, it appeared that Oswald's presence in New Orleans until sometime between 8 a.m. and 1 p.m. on September 25 was quite firmly established   In spite of the fact that it appeared almost certain that Oswald could not have been in Dallas at the time Mrs. Odio thought he was, the Commission requested the FBI to conduct further investigation to determine the validity of Mrs. Odio's testimony.

"The Commission considered the problems that had arisen by her testimony were important because they presented the Commission with the idea that Oswald may have had companions on his trip to Mexico. The Commission specifically requested the FBI to attempt to locate and identify the two men who Mrs. Odio stated were with the man she thought was Oswald. In an effort to do that the FBI located and interviewed Manual Ray, a leader of JURE who confirmed that Mrs. Odio's parents were political prisoners in Cuba, but stated that he did not know anything about the alleged Oswald visit. The same was true of Rogelio Cisneros, a former anti-Castro leader from Miami who had visited Mrs. Odio in June of 1962 in connection with certain anti-Castro activities. Additional investigation was conducted in Dallas and in other cities in search of the visitors to Mrs. Odio's apartment."[37]

Sylvia Odio was re-interviewed by the HSCA in the 1970s. Her story helped to convince the HSCA that there was a conspiracy to assassinate President Kennedy and found her to be a credible witness when she appeared before them at their hearings in Washington.

Sylvia Odio and her sister came to Dallas after the Castro revolution in Cuba. Her parents had been imprisoned in Cuba for opposing Castro. This incident and the fact that her husband had abandoned her, predisposed Sylvia to a mental illness and she frequently suffered 'fainting spells'. She underwent treatment by a psychiatrist. Odio was still active in the anti-Castro underground, however, and was in contact with the leaders of JURE. She was also active in negotiating arms deals for the organization.

However, it is likely the visitor who allegedly offered to kill Kennedy was not Oswald. In her testimony to the

THE CIA-DID-IT THEORY

Warren Commission, Odio did not positively recognize Oswald and said, "I think this man was the one that was in my apartment. I am not too sure of that picture. He didn't look like that." And Oswald had been visiting Mexico City in the time period she related for the visit.

There is no doubt that three men visited her, as her story is confirmed by her sister. However, Gerald Posner also researched the background to her story and found too many contradictions and a lack of corroboration to render it credible. Odio had been receiving psychiatric treatment during this period and her emotional state made her statements unreliable. He also found evidence from those who knew her that she tended to 'exaggerate' and often did things in order to bring attention to herself.

Her family was split in their judgments of Odio – some believed her 'crazy'. Posner quoted Cuban exile leader Carlos Bringuier, who experienced a confrontation with the pro-Castro Oswald in New Orleans, as a reason for disbelieving Odio. Bringuier told Posner, "I believe it is possible she was visited by someone – there were a lot of people with different organizations out there. But after the assassination, I believe her immediate reaction would have been the same as mine, to have jumped up and called the FBI and say 'hey, that guy visited me!' Instead, she casually told a neighbor, and that neighbor told the FBI, and that's the only reason it came out. That makes me suspicious of her story. It doesn't sound right, and I know from my own personal experience on what I did and how I felt when I realized I had some contact with the man who killed the President of the United States....Maybe with all the news after the assassination she became confused and put Oswald's face and name onto the person she actually met. I have seen this as a lawyer in criminal cases. There is an accident with four witnesses and they give four different versions and they all believe they are telling the truth, and could even pass a lie detector. She thinks she is telling the truth. I hate to say she is lying, but she is mistaken."[38]

FBI agent James Hosty believes that his fellow agent, Wally Heitman, discovered the true identity of one of the trio. Heitman maintained that he was Loran Hall, a half-Indian who frequently passed as a Latin. As described by Odio, he had a marked resemblance to Oswald. The other two men were Laurence Howard and William Seymour, and together with Hall they visited Odio's home to collect money for a JURE rival group, 'Alpha 66'. Hall had described Seymour as an ex-Marine who frequently 'popped off' about President Kennedy. However, in the 1970s, Hall retracted his statement that he and his companions were the men who visited Odio. He refused to testify regarding what he told the FBI back in 1964 about visiting Odio's home. This was entirely understandable, as Hall had committed a grave mistake – identifying another member of this underground terrorist group and saying that Seymour had 'popped off ' about Kennedy, which led to drastic reductions in donations to the movement after the assassination.[39]

Philip Shenon takes issue with Hosty's conclusions and believes the three men who visited Odio were not Hall, Seymour and Howard. Shenon wrote, ""Over time Loran Hall would change his story more than once, eventually insisting – under oath to congressional investigators –

THE CIA-DID-IT THEORY

that the FBI agents who had initially interviewed him might have concocted a false story to appease the commission. Seymour and Howard were also located; both insisted that they did not know Odio and had never been to her apartment. There was evidence to support their denials."[40]

The true story behind the 'Odio affair', according to authors Ray and Mary LaFontaine, is that it was made up. They conclude that Odio did it as a ploy to help her anti-Castro friends avoid blame for the assassination. As the LaFontaines describe it, Oswald may very well have visited her in Dallas when she held her meetings for the émigré anti-Castro community, and Oswald may have joined them at such a meeting proclaiming that the detested Kennedy, who betrayed the anti-Castro Cubans, should be killed when he visited Dallas the next month. This was Oswald's way of acting as a daring 'agent provocateur', as he did in New Orleans the previous summer. This meeting was more likely to have occurred in October when Oswald had returned from his Mexico trip.

Continuing, then, his one-man 'revolutionary' infiltration operations and claiming that Kennedy should be killed, Odio became fearful after the assassination. She suspected that the President's murder would be blamed on anti-Castro Cubans in Dallas. She had to invent an official story declaring herself innocent and by extension her émigré friends, because she believed the story of Oswald's non-conspiratorial visit had leaked out after the assassination. Odio chose to put the Oswald connection in the context of a hallway meeting that occurred in June with three men named Rodriguez,

Cisneros, and Martin. She then 'persuaded' her sister, Annie, that the meeting took place with Oswald and two others. Apparently Odio had tripped herself up when she admitted to a Catholic priest that one of the names of the sinister group was a man called *"Cisneros"*.[41]

This may very well be the most logical answer about 'Oswald imposters'. At the very least, the HSCA erred in accepting Odio's story without full corroborating details. In short, there is no credible evidence for the post-assassination claims that one of the three men who visited Sylvia Odio was 'Lee Harvey Oswald' or 'Leon Oswald'.

CHAPTER NINE

THE NEW ORLEANS DEBACLE

> *"I am still dismayed to find myself charged with the most heinous crime of the century, but I am completely innocent... Aside from any questions of guilt or innocence, anyone who knows me knows that I would have better sense than to plot with two nuts like that."*
>
> — Clay Shaw, charged with the crime of conspiring to assassinate President Kennedy
>
> *"(Oliver Stone) asked me what I thought of Garrison and his investigation. I told him it was the biggest bunch of crap ever to be allowed in a courthouse. And you know what he replied? He said, 'Well we're going to make it anyway.'"*
>
> — Harry Connick – who defeated Jim Garrison for New Orleans Parish District Attorney in 1973
>
> *"(Oliver Stone is) ...an intellectual sociopath, indifferent to truth.... (a man who combined) moral arrogance with historical ignorance....(the movie JFK is)...execrable history and contemptible citizenship."*
>
> — George Will

Ruth Paine visited the Oswalds in Dallas around April 24th, 1963, and saw that Lee's bags were packed. Marina had suggested that Lee go to New Orleans to look for work. She also thought that with Lee in New Orleans he would abandon his preposterous ideas about wanting to be a political assassin and a 'revolutionary' for the Cuban cause. Lee had agreed, but he insisted Marina go back to Russia where he would join her, presumably after his planned trip to Cuba. Ruth felt sorry for Marina and invited her to stay with her in Dallas while Lee tried to find work in New Orleans.

Conspiracy theorists allege that Oswald's sojourn to New Orleans, from July 19th, 1963, to September 25th, 1963, centered on participation in a plot with anti-Castro Cubans, the CIA, FBI, and the Mafia to kill the President. The evidence suggests otherwise. The testimonies of those who met him during this period do not indicate any conspiratorial involvement. Marina's Warren Commission testimony and the testimony of neighbors, librarians, employees of the Louisiana Employment Exchange, prospective employers, staff of a local radio station, people who saw him hand out 'Fair Play for Cuba' leaflets, and most important of all, his relatives – do not indicate any conspiratorial activity.

However, during his time in New Orleans, Oswald was committed to his 'agent provocateur' activities and political interests. He wrote to the Fair Play for Cuba Committee in New York and said he was anxious to become more active. He told the organization about his plans to stir things up with the anti-Castro groups in the city. Oswald approached an exile group leader, Carlos Bringuier, introducing himself as an ex-Marine and saying he had the experience to fight Castro. When Bringuier saw Oswald handing out pro-Castro leaflets, a scuffle ensued between Oswald and the Cuban exiles and a number of participants were arrested, including Oswald.[1]

Oswald's efforts were clearly a ploy. He desperately wanted publicity to shore up his credentials as a

THE NEW ORLEANS DEBACLE

'revolutionary'. And it is likely he intended to report what he had learned of Castro's enemies to Cuban representatives for his planned trip to the Cuban embassy in Mexico City to secure a visa for entry into Cuba. During his visit to the Cuban embassy, he had hopes he could persuade Castro's representatives he had the wherewithal to become a fighter for the Cuban revolution.

In 1967, New Orleans District Attorney Jim Garrison (his given first names were Earling Carothers) announced to the press he had solved the Kennedy assassination and would be making arrests of the conspirators who were involved. Two years later, the one person who had been indicted, a New Orleans businessman, Clay Shaw, was put on trial.

The jury, in the six-week trial, reached a verdict of 'not guilty' in less than an hour, but Garrison held firm, until his death in 1992, to his theory that Clay Shaw was part of a coup engineered by the covert action wing of the CIA. His 1988 book, *On The Trail of the Assassins*, along with Jim Marrs' *Crossfire*, was the basis for Oliver Stone's movie 'JFK'.

Garrison believed that the cast of characters involved in the conspiracy or cover-up ultimately included the CIA, the Secret Service, President Johnson, Earl Warren, the Dallas Police, and just about everybody else except Lee Harvey Oswald, who he claimed was busy that day being framed. Garrison said Oswald was completely innocent of the assassination:

"Lee Oswald was totally, unequivocally, completely innocent of the assassination...and the fact that history, or in the re-writing of history, disinformation has made a villain out of this young man who wanted nothing more than to be a fine Marine...is in some ways the greatest injustice of all." — Jim Garrison[2]

Jim Garrison did indeed take the world by surprise when he revealed that he had proof of a plot to kill Kennedy and the names of culprits who were responsible. Unfortunately, the American public was unaware of how the New Orleans District Attorney came to prominence through corruption and a dangerous lust for publicity.

After serving as an artillery officer and a pilot of an unarmed spotter plane in World War II, 'Big Jim' Garrison joined the FBI. On his application form, he wrongly indicated his father was deceased and failed to inform the Bureau that his sister, Judith, had been placed in a Mississippi state hospital suffering from schizophrenia. After a few months, he resigned from the FBI, purportedly because his army reserve unit had been called to active duty in Korea. However, after the first day with his unit, he called in sick and was treated for 'exhaustion'. His actual medical condition was hypochondriasis and he had a 'severe and disabling psychoneurosis of long duration'. Years later, two leading United States Senators would describe the New Orleans District Attorney as "unstable".[3]

Many years later the full truth about Garrison's state of mind was revealed by author Patricia Lambert (*False Witness: The Real Story of Jim Garrison's Investigation and Oliver Stone's JFK*, 1998) Lambert wrote, "In my conversations with mental health professionals, two of them suggested that Garrison might have been a psychopath, not the homicide variety, obviously, but the other end of the spectrum – the charming con artist – what sets them apart is a lack of conscience."[4]

On discharge from the Army, Garrison returned to New Orleans and began to build a career as a local government lawyer. After a period in private and government practice, he eventually won the election for District Attorney in New Orleans in 1962. In the period after his election, Garrison had conducted a running battle with the city's judicial and legal establishment, a position that only raised him in the estimation of most New Orleans voters. He was loud and reckless, and even before the Kennedy case his exploits had made him famous.

In September 1967, LIFE magazine published the results of its investigation into Mafia activities in New Orleans. The articles revealed a great deal about Garrison's character. "State authorities, for the most part," LIFE said, "take the view that [Carlos] Marcello and his gang aren't there. 'I'm thankful we haven't had any racketeering to speak of in this state,' says Governor John McKeithen."

Garrison responded to the LIFE articles by stating he would resign if any evidence of the Mafia was found in New Orleans. However, he later changed his mind after "federal officials found "overwhelming evidence of Cosa Nostra activities" in the city.[5]

The article went on to point out that three times since 1963 Garrison had his hotel bill at the Sands Club in Las Vegas paid for by Carlos Marcello's lieutenant, Mario Marino, who had moved from New Orleans to Las Vegas ten years earlier. LIFE said that on his last trip to Las Vegas in March of that year, Garrison had also been granted $5,000 credit at the cashier's cage. Garrison told the LIFE reporters that he believed it was customary for casinos to pick up the hotel bills of prominent public officials.[6]

Garrison's denials of New Orleans organized crime came at a time when the scale of Mafia operations ran to over 1 billion dollars a year. The vice arrests in the early sixties that won Garrison his popularity as a 'racket-buster' were all low-level operators of prostitution and gambling. Their removal from the scene helped Carlos Marcello consolidate his hold on the city's vice and narcotics. Garrison enjoyed considerably less success against Marcello. Between 1965 and 1969, Garrison managed just two convictions and five guilty pleas in cases the New Orleans Police Department made against Marcello's organization. He dismissed 84 cases, including 22 gambling charges, one of attempted murder, 3 of kidnapping, and one of manslaughter.[7]

At the time of the Shaw trial, Marcello, a convicted drug dealer and associate of Meyer Lansky and Frank Costello, was regarded by law enforcement officials as one of the most powerful organized crime figures in America, dominating an area that spread across the southern parts of the United States. Garrison, however, told a national television audience that Marcello was a 'respectable businessman'. LIFE magazine also revealed that Garrison "even managed to hush up the fact that last June (1969), a Marcello bagman, Vic Corona, died after suffering a heart attack during a political meeting held in Garrison's own home."[8]

Garrison began investigating the New Orleans connection to a purported Kennedy assassination conspiracy two days after JFK's murder. His efforts were inspired by reports that Lee Harvey Oswald had spent some time in the city the previous summer. His investigation stalled when he found no evidence to support his suspicions.

Garrison's short inquiry might have ended there except for a conversation he had with Senator Russell B. Long and Joseph M. Rault Jr, a wealthy New Orleans oilman. In November 1966, Long remarked that the Warren Commission was in error and it gave Garrison an idea. The District Attorney now had the kind of publicity-generating case every prosecutor dreams of.[9]

Garrison re-opened his investigation immediately and found an alleged getaway pilot in the 'conspiracy' by the name of David William Ferrie. Ferrie had been allegedly fingered by Jack Martin, who was later discovered to be a notorious fabricator. Acting on Martin's stories, Ferrie, a private investigator who had worked for Carlos Marcello, was put under close surveillance by Garrison's team of investigators. Long after the affair had died down did researchers discover Martin's allegations against Ferrie had been founded on a long-standing grudge between the two men. In 1961, Martin had fallen out with Ferrie, claiming he defrauded him over fees for an investigation into 'diploma mill' certificate fraud.[10]

In late 1966 and early 1967, Garrison set about checking old leads. One lead involved a story told by a New Orleans lawyer named Dean Adams Andrews, Jr. Shortly after the assassination, Andrews had informed the Secret Service that Lee Harvey Oswald had visited his office several times during the summer of 1963 looking for help in converting his Marine Corps 'undesirable' discharge to 'honorable'. The day after the JFK assassination, Andrews added, he received a phone call from a man requesting he go to Dallas and defend Oswald. The lawyer's name, Andrews said, was 'Clay Bertrand'.

That was one version of Andrews's story. In another, he told the FBI the whole thing had been a hoax. Garrison chose to believe the first version of the story and decided that 'Clay Bertrand' was an alias for Clay Shaw, the director of the New Orleans Trade Mart. There was no evidence to substantiate such a conclusion, except for a New Orleans police officer's statement that Shaw gave the alias 'Bertrand' during Shaw's booking process following his arrest on March 1, 1967. It was a vital piece of evidence in Garrison's case against Mr. Shaw. However, the police officer's story was discredited by three members of the New Orleans Police Department who were present at the time of Shaw's booking. Later, Andrews admitted that 'Clay Bertrand' was a pseudonym he heard at a 'fag' wedding and that he invented other parts of his story to 'get on the publicity gravy train and ride it to glory...I was just huffing and puffing. I let my mouth run away with my brain.'[11]

In February 1967, David Ferrie was found dead in his apartment. On March 1, without any substantial

THE NEW ORLEANS DEBACLE

evidence to go by, Garrison arrested Shaw for participating in a conspiracy to murder President Kennedy. It was sensational news. "My staff and I solved the assassination weeks ago," the District Attorney claimed. "I wouldn't say this if we didn't have evidence beyond a shadow of a doubt. We know the key individuals, the cities involved, and how it was done."

The more publicity Garrison got, the wilder his charges became. Throughout 1967 and 1968, in the period before Shaw's trial, Garrison's claims were becoming increasingly bizarre. The American press began referring to Garrison's investigation as a farce. In June 1967, an hour-long documentary was broadcast by NBC-TV, charging Garrison with attempting to bribe and intimidate witnesses and using other questionable tactics. When NBC gave Garrison broadcast time to reply on July 15th, Garrison once again asserted that Oswald was without question, "in the employ of intelligence agencies." He did not, however, produce any credible evidence.[12]

The crime Clay Shaw was accused of was not murder—but conspiracy. According to Garrison, who not only leaked details of the case but presented his findings on "The Tonight Show Starring Johnny Carson" on January 31, 1968, the men Shaw supposedly conspired with constituted a fair representation of New Orleans 'lowlife'. The dramatis personae of the plot included not only Ferrie and Oswald, but also a Cuban exile named Carlos Quiroga, W. Guy Banister, a former FBI agent and private detective involved in anti-Castro activities, and Edgar Eugene Bradley, a Californian whose only apparent offense was having a name like Eugene Hale

Brading, the reported organized crime associate who was found in the Dal-Tex building in Dealey Plaza after the assassination. Bradley was financially ruined as a direct result of Garrison's probe.

It was Ferrie, however, who first attracted the attention of Jim Garrison. Under any circumstances, David William Ferrie would have been hard to overlook. He was a character out of a comic strip, with his stuck-on eyebrows and flaming red wig, a victim of alopecia. He was a would-be priest who was thrown out of two seminaries for 'erratic behavior' (Ferrie was a sexual deviant) before making himself a 'bishop' in the Orthodox Old Catholic Church of North America. Ferrie had been employed by Eastern Airlines as a pilot. It was this man, Jim Garrison would say later, who would be remembered as "one of history's most important individuals."

The day of JFK's assassination, Ferrie was in a New Orleans courtroom as Carlos Marcello was being cleared of charges that had resulted in his deportation two years before. Ferrie had been active in anti-Castro activities and had worked as a private investigator. Marcello's lawyers included G. Wray Gill, who had hired Ferrie to help with the immigration case. The conclusion of the case on November 22, 1963, gave Ferrie some free time to take a short vacation he had been planning.[13]

On February 22, 1967, the day after Ferrie's release from questioning, he was found dead in his apartment, the result, the coroner later determined, of a cerebral hemorrhage caused by the rupture of a blood vessel. In the movie "JFK", Ferrie was portrayed as a conspirator

THE NEW ORLEANS DEBACLE

who had been fearful for his life after the media learned he was being questioned by Garrison. Ferrie was certainly frightened in the final five days of his life – but not because he was fearful that fellow conspirators were going to 'eliminate' him. He was frightened that Garrison would wrongfully arrest him – and because of his past scandals involving young boys, he was terrified what fellow prisoners would do to him. This was confirmed by investigative reporter David Snyder, who had been in contact with Ferrie by telephone during this period.[14]

As proof of Ferrie's involvement in the assassination, Garrison pointed to a 'suspicious' trip Ferrie made the day Kennedy was killed. Ferrie and two friends, Alvin Beauboeuf and Melvin Coffey, decided to drive to Baton Rouge to an ice-skating rink, but on hearing that the place was closed decided to drive to Houston instead. "It wasn't even Dave's idea to go to Houston," Alvin Beauboeuf told Gerald Posner. "It was my idea. I used to competitively roller-skate for years, and I had never ice-skated. So I told Dave, 'you are from Ohio, you ice-skate, and I would like to go.' And it was just like Dave to say, 'Let's go.'" They set off, drove all night and arrived at the ice-rink at 4.30 a.m., some 16 hours after Kennedy's death. Conspiracy theorists made much of this event, linking it to the assassination. Ferrie was alleged to be the getaway pilot for the Dallas conspirators and he travelled to Texas on the day of the assassination to 'await further instructions'. They do not explain how a 'getaway pilot', supposedly ready and waiting to fly the assassins to safety, manages to arrive at the 'rendezvous' nearly a full day after the crime has been committed.[15]

269

BEYOND REASONABLE DOUBT

The man who had fingered Ferrie, Jack Martin, in a later interview with the FBI, claimed he had invented the 'getaway pilot' story. He also made a stronger denial to Secret Service agents. The following is an extract from a United States Secret Service report filed by Special Agents Anthony E. Gerrets and John W. Rice, which reveals the true nature of the man who Garrison labeled as an important witness to the 'Kennedy Conspiracy':

"On the night of 11-29-63 SAIC Rice and reporting agent interviewed Jack S. Martin at length in his small run-down apartment located at 1311 N. Prieur Street, New Orleans, which he shares with his wife and 6-year-old son. Martin, who has every appearance of being an alcoholic, admitted during the interview that he suffers from 'telephonitis' when drinking and that it was during one of his drinking sprees that he telephoned Assistant District Attorney Herman S. Kohlman and told him this fantastic story about William David Ferrie [sic] being involved with Lee Harvey Oswald. He said he had heard on television that Oswald had at one time been active in the Civil Air Patrol and had later heard that Ferrie had been his Squadron Commander. Martin stated that Ferrie was well known to him; that he recalled having seen rifles in Ferrie's home and also recalled that Kohlman had written an article on Ferrie and that Ferrie had been a Marine and had been with the Civil Air Patrol. Martin stated that after turning all those thoughts over in his mind, he had telephoned Herman S. Kohlman and told his story as though it was based on facts rather than on his imagination." On the basis of Martin's lies, Jim Garrison decided to arrest Ferrie.[16]

THE NEW ORLEANS DEBACLE

Jack Martin seemed very credible to Garrison, but not only was he an alcoholic, he had received treatment for mental illness. Hubie Badeux, the former chief of the New Orleans police intelligence division told author Gerald Posner, "He was goofy to begin with and lied all the time." The part of Martin was dramatized by the actor Jack Lemmon in Oliver Stone's movie *JFK*, giving credence to the character. Jack Martin later said that Garrison's investigation was based on information he and a friend, David Lewis, "made up".[17]

Nearly every conspiracy theorist has used Jack Martin's story of Ferrie's library card being in the possession of Lee Oswald after Oswald's arrest. The story originated with Ferrie's friend, Layton Martens, and Martens' assertion that he was told about it by Ferrie's lawyer and employer, G. Wray Gill. Gill in turn told the FBI that he had heard about it from a man named Hardy Davis, who in turn had learned about it from Jack Martin, who in turn had simply guessed that Oswald would have used the card, as he believed Ferrie knew Oswald. As Patricia Lambert discovered, "By omitting Martin's role as author of the story, and Davis's as a conduit of it, the Committee (HSCA) created the impression that Gill's knowledge came from some mysterious, authoritative source. This curious presentation, cutting it off from its false roots, made the story sound like an authentic possibility instead of what it actually was – one of the most effective falsehoods Martin ever told."[18]

Conspiracy theorists, including David Kaiser, also promoted the idea that Lee Harvey Oswald knew David Ferrie and that the HSCA turned up five witnesses who confirmed that Oswald was in Ferrie's Civil Air Patrol unit when Oswald was a teenage boy.[19]

However, as JFK researcher John McAdams stated, "What Kaiser fails to mention is that the HSCA witnesses also made it clear that Oswald was not any sort of gung-ho cadet (attending only a few meetings), and he didn't have any sort of special relationship with Ferrie. Yet Kaiser makes a point of asserting that Ferrie lied when he claimed not to know Oswald when questioned a few days after the assassination. But not recalling one cadet who was briefly in his unit 8 years earlier seems plausible enough. Not yet done, Kaiser points to the somewhat famous photo of Ferrie and Oswald together at a CAP picnic as evidence they knew each other. But the two are standing at opposite sides of a small crowd, and it's hardly clear that Ferrie would have personally interacted with Oswald at that picnic, and if he did, hardly obvious that he would remember it."[20]

Conspiracy theorists also single out the alleged role a former FBI agent, private investigator Guy Banister, played in the purported New Orleans conspiracy. Oswald, in his pro-Castro activities on the streets of New Orleans in the summer of 1963, had been passing out handbills with the address "544 Camp Street" stamped on them, which was around the corner from Guy Banister's office address.[21]

But there are several innocent reasons why Oswald was using this address. His weekly visits to the employment exchange took him past that address and he could easily have seen the 'For Rent' signs displayed on the small corner building. There is evidence that Oswald may have attempted to rent an office at this address, but his meager income prevented it. It is also possible that Oswald may have used this address, which was used at one time as an office for an anti-Castro group, as a way to embarrass his anti-Castro opponents. Guy Banister's brother, Ross, believed Oswald had used the 544 Camp Street address on his Fair Play for Cuba Committee (FPCC) literature to embarrass Guy. Ross Banister knew of no direct link between his brother and Oswald.[22]

Conspiracy theorists claim that Oswald's 'pro-Castro' stance in New Orleans was a ruse designed to assist anti-Castroites Ferrie and Banister in their efforts to discredit the Fair Play for Cuba Committee. But Oswald's first pro-Castro demonstration occurred before he arrived in New Orleans. In early April 1963, Oswald staged his first pro-Castro demonstration in Dallas. Around his neck he carried a placard which proclaimed, 'Hands off Cuba! Viva Fidel!' Oswald handed out FPCC leaflets on the streets. Two police officers later reported seeing the demonstration and Oswald himself reported these activities to the New York office of the FPCC.

Anthony Summers, in his book 'Conspiracy' (1980), relates the story of Guy Banister's secretary, Delphine Roberts, 'finally' confessing to seeing Oswald, Ferrie, and Banister together at Banister's office. Evidently Summers did not make any judgment as to Roberts' mental state. She told Gerald Posner: "...read the sacred scrolls that God himself wrote and gave to the ancient Hebrews for placing in the Ark of the Covenant...I think I have been the last person to see them." Roberts also told Posner she gave the story to Summers for "money".[23]

Most conspiracy authors fail to inform their readers that Ferrie, Banister, Martin, and Andrews were not overlooked in the original FBI investigation. The FBI checked Ferrie's plane and found it had not been airworthy since 1962. At the time of the assassination, Ferrie was questioned by the FBI.[24] And during the initial investigation, Ferrie had been cleared not only by the FBI but the Texas Rangers, the Houston Police, and the New Orleans Police Department. Conspiracy theorists also do not tell their readers that Ferrie had told Jim Garrison he was willing to take a lie-detector test and 'truth serum'. Garrison rejected his offer.

Conspiracy writers have attempted to link Clay Shaw with the CIA. The truth, however, is entirely different. Conspiracists had been reporting a simple truth – Shaw's cooperation with the Domestic Contact Service of the CIA, whose job was to seek the assistance of Americans in all walks of life, to learn about the activities of foreign governments and their citizens. From 1948 Shaw founded the New Orleans International Trade Mart. He was an obvious contact for the CIA's New Orleans DCS office. In 1948 until 1956 Shaw volunteered information thirty-three times. It was the type of public assistance the CIA had always received and was common during the Cold War. There is no evidence that Shaw did any more than inform the DCS of statistics pertaining to shipments through the port of New Orleans. This was, of course, consistent with Shaw's job as Director of the International Trade Mart in New Orleans.[25]

The Central Intelligence Agency was dismayed at the antics of Garrison in trying to link the CIA with the assassination of President Kennedy. The Agency did not respond to Garrison's claims during the period of the New Orleans investigation because they were in a difficult position, and their quandary is revealed in a September 29, 1967, CIA memo:

"Shaw himself was a contact of the Domestic Contact Service's New Orleans office from 1948 to 1956 and introduced General Cabell, then Deputy Director of Central Intelligence, when he addressed the New Orleans Foreign Policy Association in May 1961. In view of this dilemma, the Department of Justice has so far taken the position that if any effort is made by either the prosecution (Jim Garrison) or defense (Shaw's lawyers) to involve CIA in the trial, the Government will claim executive privilege. This, too, can be turned by Garrison into a claim that it is part of the whole cover-up by the establishment and particularly CIA...No alternative to the claim of privilege appears to be available, however...To protect the Government's position on privilege, it would appear that the Government cannot take any action publicly to refute Garrison's claims and the testimony of his witnesses, as the Louisiana judge would almost certainly take the position that any such public statement would negate the privilege."[26]

It would seem that secrecy, albeit in most cases benign, took precedence above all other considerations.

Garrison's efforts were directed at making his conspiracy hypothesis stick. Any evidence that led away from Shaw was discarded, while testimony from dubious sources was accepted as fact. Given those ground rules, which are remarkably similar to the methodology many conspiracy theorists adopt, it was not too difficult to turn up leads.

During the Shaw trial, Garrison produced a number of witnesses who claimed to have seen Banister, Ferrie, Oswald, and Shaw together. Most of these witnesses were eventually discovered to be fabricators – with the exception of a few who lived in Clinton, Louisiana, and told the authorities they saw Shaw, (or Banister), Ferrie, and Oswald together in the summer of 1963. The 'Clinton Episode' is cited by most conspiracy authors and many use it as 'proof' that Oswald conspired with others during his time in New Orleans.

The Clinton witnesses were interviewed by Garrison's investigators in 1967 and gave evidence at the 1969 trial of Clay Shaw. They claimed that Shaw, Oswald, Ferrie, and possibly Banister arrived in town at the time of a black voter registration drive. They assumed they were FBI agents. The HSCA found their testimony credible and significant.

Gerald Posner, however, obtained affidavits, handwritten statements, and District Attorney Office memos regarding the initial stories the Clinton residents told and found they contradicted testimony they gave at the Shaw trial. The evidence suggests their disparate stories only became consistent after coaching by Garrison's staff.

Most conspiracy theorists give credence to the Clinton witnesses and ridicule Posner's research. However, Posner's investigation into the witnesses is supported by a contemporary account by Newsweek's Hugh

Aynesworth. According to Aynesworth, "Many people have asked me about the Clinton-Jackson witnesses. Were they mistaken? Who did they see? How could so many be wrong? And so on. I honestly cannot explain how it happened, though I have some small insight into how it could have occurred. First I think John Manchester and a State Policeman...put it all together. I'm certain that there were many out-of-towners – FBI, press, etc. – during that summer of 1963... I feel certain every damn one of them was resented. And remembered. Maybe one of them looked something like Shaw or like Oswald. Funny though that nobody came forth after Oswald's face was plastered all over the world, November 22-24, 1963, when their memories should have been ultra-sharp."[27]

The truth of Aynesworth's contemporary account of the Clinton witnesses was finally corroborated by author Patricia Lambert in her 1998 book False Witness. After a painstaking and thorough investigation involving hundreds of interviews, the resourceful author found people who were closely connected to the District Attorney's Clinton investigation and townspeople who gave a much more truthful version of what exactly happened during September 1963.

Working with old Garrison office files, Lambert discovered during her research that the Clinton witnesses had embellished the truth, conspired to invent stories, and were mistaken in identifying Oswald, Shaw, Banister, and Ferrie. The Machiavellian tale of intrigue and misinformation which led to the witnesses appearing at Clay Shaw's trial is too complex for a book this size, but the reader is directed to Ms. Lambert's account, which proves without a shadow of doubt that the Oswald sightings were bogus. The witnesses' credibility was also called into question because they did not come forward until years after the assassination.[28]

The most important witness, however, in the trial of Clay Shaw was Perry Raymond Russo, and Garrison's case was built around Russo's testimony. Garrison's first contact with Russo had come in a letter Russo wrote to the District Attorney stating that he had known David Ferrie and possessed interesting information about him.

In late February 1967, Garrison sent his chief assistant to Baton Rouge to interview Russo. During the two-hour interview, Russo quoted Ferrie as hinting how easy it would be to shoot a President and flee to Mexico or Brazil, and that one day he would 'get' Kennedy. Russo, however, made no mention of a plot. That came only after Garrison had jogged his memory, first with truth serum, under whose influence he supposedly recalled meeting with a man named 'Bertram', and later under hypnosis, when at long last the details of the 'plot' emerged. During his trance, Russo recalled having attended a party at Ferrie's apartment in September 1963. At the party, three men supposedly discussed the details of the forthcoming assassination, the need for an appropriate scapegoat, and possible means of escape. The three men, according to Russo, were Ferrie, a tall white-haired man named 'Clay Bertrand', and 'Lee Harvey Oswald'.

During his investigation, Garrison failed to see the ridiculous nature of Russo's story. Why would Clay Shaw, David Ferrie, and Lee Harvey Oswald discuss the assassination within earshot of a virtual stranger? Additionally, if Russo were a part of the 'conspiracy', what possible motive would he have in coming forward to testify for Jim Garrison? Ferrie and Oswald were dead and the only two 'co-conspirators' left were Russo and Shaw. Russo was home free; the 'conspiracy' had succeeded. In fingering Shaw, how would he know that Shaw wouldn't finger him? Then they would both go to prison.

James Phelan was the first reporter to see through Russo's story. Phelan discovered the vast discrepancies in Assistant District Attorney Andrew Sciambra's memos about the Russo interviews. It was clear to Phelan that Russo was changing his story about Ferrie and Shaw in each telling.[29]

Author James Kirkwood interviewed Russo against the wishes of Garrison, "Russo said, 'Oh, the hell with it. If we do it (the interview), it'll get back to Garrison and Garrison will clobber me.'...The real reason I didn't want to see Shaw was that I knew if I sat down in a room with him, talked to him, listened to him, that I'd know he's not the guy and then all I could do is go on the run, go to Mexico or go out to California and become a beatnik, but I couldn't run from myself...They asked me a lot of questions (Garrison's staff) and I'm a pretty perceptive guy. I was able to figure what they wanted to know from the questions they asked. And when they got through asking me questions, I asked them a lot of questions, like who is this guy? Who is that guy? Why is this so important?...In addition, I read every scrap of stuff that was in the papers about the case."

Kirkwood said that in the interview, Russo told him he was, "...'Caught up in the middle on this thing', that if he stuck to his story, Shaw and his friends and lawyers would clobber him. If he changed his story, then Garrison would charge him with perjury and chuck! – there would go his job with Equitable Life. He told me all he was concerned about was his own position, that he wished he'd never opened his mouth about it, wished he could go back to the day before he shot off his mouth up in Baton Rouge... He said, 'I no longer know what the truth is. I don't know the difference between reality and fantasy'."[30]

At the time of the Shaw trial, Russo had second thoughts about his testimony and refused to repeat the fabrication about the Ferrie party. He gave Shaw's lawyers a tape recording confessing that Garrison's assistants had told him what to say. Russo confessed, "It was sort of a script and I was playing my part. I guess I played too good one, huh...I never dreamed he (Garrison) only had me. I guess I always knew he (Shaw) had nothing to do with anything... (Garrison said) that after Shaw was convicted we'd all be rich...(Garrison) told me about people who had been convicted of perjury and said mine would be worse because a lot of people had been affected by what I said." In the mid-1990s, shortly before his death from a heart attack, he recanted again, this time to author Patricia Lambert.[31]

By the time Shaw finally came to trial in 1969, the case was in shreds. Garrison himself rarely turned up in the courtroom and the 'secret evidence' that Garrison had promised was not forthcoming. Instead, his assistants

THE NEW ORLEANS DEBACLE

called a parade of witnesses to the stand, many of whom proved more beneficial to the defense. As Vincent Bugliosi wrote, "In view of the fact that Garrison had accused Shaw of conspiring to murder the president of the United States, one would expect Garrison himself to face Shaw in court and cross-examine him during his testimony on February 27, 1969. But instead, he let his assistant, James Alcock, do so.

And even with Alcock, if one wasn't told that Shaw was on trial for Kennedy's murder, one would hardly have known this from Alcock's cross-examination. Not only was it extremely short (consuming exactly fifty pages of transcript)—one would automatically expect the cross-examination of someone accused of conspiring to murder the president of the United States to go on for several days and take up hundreds of pages of transcript—but it couldn't possibly have been more soft and civil. So much so that it could have been Shaw's own lawyer asking the questions. So soft, civil, and non-confrontational, in fact, that when Shaw's lawyer was asked if he had any questions to ask on redirect examination, [Irvin] Dymond said no, seeing no need to explain away or mitigate any damage to his client's cause that came out during cross-examination. It couldn't have been more obvious that Alcock never had his heart in what he was doing, and knew further that there was nothing of any substance to cross-examine Shaw about. (For the record, Shaw denied on direct examination knowing or ever having met Oswald, Ferrie, or Perry Russo, ever having conspired with them or anyone else to murder President Kennedy, and ever having worked for the CIA.)"[32]

The Shaw jury was out only 50 minutes before they returned a 'Not Guilty' verdict. The Garrison investigation into the assassination of President Kennedy and the subsequent trial of businessman Clay Shaw had proved nothing. But Garrison's reckless investigation had far-reaching effects on Shaw. Drained of the experience, he died a few years later. James Kirkwood believed that an innocent man had been hounded to death. Kirkwood interviewed Shaw on a number of occasions whilst Shaw was awaiting trial. Shaw told Kirkwood, "I'm no authority to judge and it's difficult to sift through all that's written about the Warren Commission, the CIA, the FBI, the Attorney General, the Right and the Left, the Cuban situation and so forth. I only know I had no part in any plot. But I do feel many people believe in a conspiracy...I suppose the knowledge of my innocence has been the great sustaining factor...It's gone on too long, the pressures are as great in this limbo I've been in, going on two years now, I want it over with. If I weren't innocent, perhaps...but I am. I'm ready to prove it. I'm ready for the trial."[33]

In November 1997, the Assassination Records Review Board, instituted by Congress as a result of public pressure after the release of the movie 'JFK', released Clay Shaw's secret diary. In it he wrote of being wrongly persecuted, "I am still dismayed to find myself charged with the most heinous crime of the century, but I am completely innocent and the feeling of being a stunned animal seems to have gone now." In another section of Shaw's diary, he wrote about his feelings of being accused of having associated with Lee Harvey Oswald and David Ferrie, "Aside from any questions of guilt or innocence, anyone who knows me knows that I would have better sense than to plot with two nuts like that."[34]

However, there was a moment of victory for Shaw in 1971, three years before his death from lung cancer, when he successfully sued Jim Garrison. Judge Christenberry pulled no punches in his criticisms of the motives and methods employed by the New Orleans District Attorney. Unfortunately, however, Garrison's lies outlived him. Even today, conspiracy theorists still accept the claims of Garrison witnesses Vernon Bundy (a heroin addict who failed a lie-detector test) and Perry Russo who, as we saw, retracted his spurious allegations that Shaw and Oswald knew each other.

Jim Garrison, after surviving trials of his own on charges of income tax evasion and bribery, was driven from office. It was clear to many that Garrison had been seriously lacking in judgment and had not brought the case of Clay Shaw to trial to solve the assassination of President Kennedy, but to further his own ambitions.

Twenty-two years following the bogus trial, Oliver Stone resurrected Garrison's reputation, perpetrating another hoax on the American people. By the time the Stone movie was released on December 20, 1991, the outrageous circumstances of the trial had been forgotten.

To summarize: Even if we were to make the assumption that Lee Harvey Oswald was acquainted with the various New Orleans characters that some conspiracy theorists think were involved in JFK's assassination (Clay Shaw,

BEYOND REASONABLE DOUBT

David Ferrie, and Guy Banister), that would still be many miles away from proving that any of those New Orleans characters had any involvement, in any way, with the assassination of President Kennedy in Dallas on November 22, 1963.

And the reason the above paragraph is the truth is because (once Perry Russo's lie is tossed aside, as it must be) there isn't a shred of evidence that connects any of those New Orleans individuals to the planning and/or carrying out of the murder of John F. Kennedy in Dallas, Texas. No evidence whatsoever.

Everything Lee Harvey Oswald did on November 21st and 22nd indicates that he was a lone assassin in Dallas. And that fact would still be true even if Oswald had been pals with the three previously-named individuals.

In other words, where is the bridge or umbilical cord that allows conspiracy theorists to make the grand leap from this:

Lee Harvey Oswald personally knew Clay Shaw, David Ferrie, and Guy Banister,

to this:

Shaw, Ferrie, and Banister were co-conspirators in the assassination of President Kennedy?

Given the physical and circumstantial evidence that exists of only Oswald's guilt in the assassination of JFK, such a monumental leap of faith like the one suggested above is, to put it bluntly, monumentally ridiculous.

CHAPTER TEN

OSWALD'S DEFENDERS

> "...some of the injury (to American society) can, with justice, be attributed to conspiracy theorists who have gone to superhuman lengths to avoid facing the truth. They have constructed wildly-implausible scenarios, far-out, fictitious 'conspirators,' and have scandalously maligned the motives of Kennedy's successor, rather than take a hard look at the man who actually did it. They have, ironically, done more to poison American political life than Lee Oswald—with the most terrible of intentions—was able to do."
>
> — Priscilla Johnson McMillan
>
> "It is sad to say, yet true, that there never would have been any serious speculation about conspiracies in the Kennedy assassination if the president had been killed by a right-winger whose guilt was confirmed by the same evidence as condemned Lee Harvey Oswald."
>
> — James Pierson

For the past 50 years there have been a number of books that have been influential when it comes to examining the true facts about the JFK assassination. They bristle with common sense and provide rational answers to anomalous pieces of evidence that have been exaggerated beyond belief by bogus historians and academics cashing in on the public's desire for drama and intrigue.

In the 1970s, Priscilla Johnson McMillan's *Marina and Lee*, a book which could be characterized as 'Marina Oswald's Memoirs', gave the American public an insight into the mind and character of JFK's assassin, Lee Harvey Oswald, an enigmatic young man who has remained a puzzle to the American people since the November 1963 assassination.

In the 1980s, Jean Davison's *Oswald's Game* gave readers a logical explanation for the assassination: Oswald, a hero-worshipper of Fidel Castro and a wannabe revolutionary, had political motives, and he likely acted out of a distorted sense of political idealism.

In the 1990s, Gerald Posner's *Case Closed*, a well-written account of the assassination which debunked numerous conspiracy scenarios, provided a refreshing antidote to Oliver Stone's movie about the assassination, *JFK*. Stone's largely fictional drama had been released in theaters in the early 1990s. Its central character was Jim Garrison, the New Orleans District Attorney who accused the CIA of Kennedy's murder. His false history of the assassination had a corrosive effect on a new generation's ability to understand this important event in U.S. history. Fortunately, another corrective to the movie came in 1998 with the publication of Patricia Lambert's excellent book *False Witness*, which decisively exposed Garrison as a charlatan and a fraud.

In recent years, Professor John McAdams' book *JFK Assassination Logic: How To Think About Claims of Conspiracy* (2011) has provided a blueprint for understanding how JFK conspiracy theories have arisen and how anyone interested in the subject should judge the mass of contradictory evidence in the case. Having studied the JFK assassination for the past two decades,

McAdams has developed a sharp intellectual ability at pointing out the illogical nature of virtually all conspiracy theories and helps the reader to separate the wheat from the chaff in Kennedy assassination literature.

In 2007, Vincent Bugliosi's *Reclaiming History*, a mammoth 1600-page book, examined every theory and every conspiracy claim. The former Los Angeles lawyer took the debate about conspiracy allegations a step further by providing a devastating no-nonsense approach to the ridiculous assassination scenarios constructed by conspiracy authors, all of whom, as his book ably demonstrates, deliberately skewed the evidence in the case. His book was a masterwork which decisively helped marginalize JFK conspiracists.

However, despite Bugliosi's best efforts, the JFK conspiracy debate persisted. 50 years on, the misinformation about the Kennedy assassination has spread throughout the Internet and has so distorted the true facts in the case that it is very difficult for future generations to learn the truth about the crime. Although dozens of researchers have toiled as voices in the wilderness in exposing the bogus nature of JFK conspiracy theories, they have been largely ignored by academia and the media. Conspiracy theorists continue to grab the limelight, giving the American public misinformation packaged to look like fact. Most attempt to provide 'proof' that Oswald was an innocent 'patsy'. Their works are packaged so effectively that the 21st century is facing a pandemic of credulous thinking about the JFK assassination and other famous murders. Ideas that, in their original raw form, flourished only on the fringes of society are now being taken seriously by educated people in the west and are circulated by many professional academics.

Two JFK conspiracy books published in the last decade, for example, Mark Lane's *Last Word* (2011) and Joan Mellen's *A Farewell To Justice* (2005) are typical of how some of the trappings of academia are promoted by publishers – but Lane and Mellen's 'academic' books are essentially constructed on clever tinkering with the facts and pure speculation. Both writers accuse the CIA of plotting to kill JFK. However, their CIA assassination scenarios are rooted in wishful thinking, error, deceit, or a mixture of the three. Internal inconsistencies exist throughout their works and they draw heavily on their imaginations.

MARK LANE

The cycle of endless myth-making about the Kennedy assassination began with Lane five decades ago with his advocacy of President Kennedy's assassin, Lee Harvey Oswald. In the weeks following the assassination the New York lawyer was 'hired' by Oswald's mother, a neurotic and unstable woman who shame-facedly told the press her son was a 'patsy' and a 'hero'. Lane began to scavenge any paper trail for another piece of the puzzle – a puzzle which continued with his distortion of Warren Commission testimony. His conclusions, published in a variety of magazines and newspapers, were repeated ad nauseam by conspiracy writers who followed in his wake.

Long before scientists, medical experts and ballistics experts had a chance to clear up the anomalous evidence the Warren Commission failed to address, Lane published *Rush to Judgment* in 1966. It was a book inundated with false stories about Oswald which, for the most part, originated with so-called assassination 'witnesses' telling fanciful tales and clamoring to be part of the story. It was an instant hit with the American public who were fooled by Lane's lawyerly tricks and silver tongue. The strange truth behind Lane's credulity was not intellectual but emotional. The American public simply could not accept that a misfit like Oswald could change the course of history all by himself.

In what judicious frame of mind Lane approached his task of examining the Warren Report can be deduced from an understanding of how he manipulated the evidence contained in the 26 volumes of the Warren Commission Hearings. His book, plausible only to those who do not know their way around the vast mass of material contained in these volumes, is virtually worthless. Lane's technique was to assemble a mass of unconsidered trifles and then by careful selection and arrangement—and no less careful omission of the huge mass of evidence on the other side—make the results look sinister. Lane's technique has been copied by many conspiracy writers – taking perfectly reasonable mistakes and making them appear 'conspiratorial'.

Take, for example, the autopsy notes written by Commander Humes at Bethesda Naval Hospital on the night of JFK's assassination. Conspiracy theorists say the notes were destroyed because they indicated the wounds to President Kennedy were inconsistent with a single shooter. During the HSCA hearings, Humes was asked if the original autopsy notes were still in existence:

DR. HUMES — "The original notes, which were stained with the blood of our late President, I felt, were inappropriate to retain to turn in to anyone in that condition. I felt that people with some particular ideas about the value of that type of material, they might fall into their hands. I sat down and word for word copied what I had on fresh paper."

GARY CORNWELL — "And then you destroyed them?"

DR. HUMES — "Destroyed the ones that were stained with the President's blood."

Evidently, Humes had been upset some years earlier when he had seen the chair that President Abraham Lincoln had sat in the night he was assassinated. The chair had been supposedly covered in Lincoln's blood from the head wound (in fact, it was a type of hair oil). Humes did not want to preserve similar grotesque artifacts.[1]

How Lane handled District Attorney Henry Wade is also insightful. During a press conference (as quoted by Lane): "Wade was unequivocal, stating, 'First, there was a number of witnesses that saw the person with the gun on the sixth floor of the bookstore building, in the window— detailing the window—where he was looking out'."

Lane did not attack this position, as it is correct and truthful. Instead, Lane rebuilt the statement into something else, creating a straw argument, and attacked that. Lane claimed that Wade actually said: "A number of witnesses saw Oswald at the window of the sixth floor of the Texas School Book Depository." That is a misstatement of Wade's position, and it is done for no other reason than to build an apparent rebuttal argument. Wade did not mention Oswald at all, and claimed merely that numerous witnesses "saw the person with the gun on the sixth floor of the bookstore building." Lane redefined it as mentioning Oswald, and attacked a claim Wade did not make.

After Ruby had been convicted of Oswald's murder and sentenced to death, Warren Commission members Earl Warren and Gerald Ford questioned him at the Dallas jail. For many months there had been rumors that Ruby was a hit man whose job had been to silence Oswald. According to Lane and Stone, Ruby seemed eager to disclose his part in a conspiracy. According to Lane, "Ruby made it plain that if the Commission took him from the Dallas jail and permitted him to testify in Washington, he could tell more there; it was impossible for him to tell the whole truth so long as he was in the jail in Dallas...(Ruby said) 'I would like to request that I go to Washington and... take all the tests that I have to take. It is very important... Gentlemen, unless you get me to Washington, you can't get a fair shake out of me'."[2]

However, it is clear from Ruby's Warren Commission testimony that he simply wanted to inform the commissioners of a conspiracy to murder Jews. Earl Warren, the Commission's chairman said, "I went down and took Jack Ruby's testimony myself – he wouldn't talk to anybody but me. And he wanted the FBI to give him a lie detector test, and I think the FBI did, and he cleared it all right. I was satisfied myself that he didn't know Oswald, never had heard of him. But the fellow was clearly delusional when I talked to him. He took me aside and he said, 'Hear those voices, hear those voices'? He thought they were Jewish children and Jewish women who were being put to death in the building there." He told Warren, Gerald Ford, and others, "I am as innocent regarding any conspiracy as any of you gentlemen in the room." Ruby was actually begging the Commission to take him back to Washington so that he could take a polygraph examination and prove that he was telling the truth when he denied any role in a conspiracy.[3]

Before his death in January, 1967 Ruby made a deathbed statement using a tape recorder, secreted in an attaché case, which was smuggled into his hospital room by his brother, Earl Ruby. Ruby was questioned by his lawyers. The tape recording was later incorporated in an L.P. record entitled *The Controversy* (1967).[4] The interview lasted 12 minutes, but was edited down to four minutes for the recording. Ruby said that it was pure chance in meeting Oswald at the Dallas police headquarters, "The ironic part of this is, I had made an illegal turn behind a bus to the parking lot. Had I gone the way I was supposed to go, straight down Main Street, I would never have met this fate, because the difference in meeting this fate was 30 seconds one way or the other...All I did is walk down there, down to the bottom of the ramp and that's when the incident happened – at the bottom of the ramp." In the final recording of Ruby's voice, he was asked if he knew the time Oswald was supposed to have been moved, Ruby replied, "He was supposed to be moved at 10 o'clock."[5]

Other witness testimonies received similar abuse at the hands of Mark Lane. Charles Brehm, an alleged "grassy knoll" witness, said Lane took his statements out of context and added a different meaning to them. Lane also omitted the statements of key witnesses like Johnny Brewer, who observed a nervous Oswald avoid police cars after the shooting of Officer Tippit.[6]

Lane claims that Helen Markham, who witnessed Tippit's murder, described the killer to him in a telephone conversation as "a short man, somewhat on the heavy side, with slightly bushy hair." But if we look at the actual transcript of her description in the relevant volume of the Warren Commission findings, we see not only that Lane put that entire description into her mouth, but she was only with difficulty persuaded to accept any of it from him. And at one point in the conversation, she in fact denied it: "And was he a little bit on the heavy side?" "Uh, not too heavy." "Not too heavy, but slightly heavy?" "Uh, well, he was, no he wasn't, didn't look too heavy, uh-huh."[7]

In another excerpt from his book, witness Julia Ann Mercer's testimony is used by Lane to place a gunman on the grassy knoll before the shooting begins. Mercer said that she observed a green pickup truck blocking a lane on Elm Street near the grassy knoll and triple underpass prior to the motorcade's arrival in Dealey Plaza. She recalled seeing a man "wearing a grey jacket, brown pants and plaid shirt, best as I can remember, get what appeared to be a gun case out of the back of the truck and walk up the grassy knoll." She later identified the gunman as Lee Harvey Oswald and the driver of the truck as Jack Ruby. In his book, Lane imbues this incident with sinister connotations as there were three policemen standing nearby – no doubt in his mind they were part of the conspiracy. What Lane fails to inform his readers is that subsequent investigations identified the truck and the three men, who took tools from their stalled vehicle and waited until another truck came to tow them away.[8] As Lane's book became a best seller around the world, he gave lectures at leading universities both in Europe and the United States. He also debated supporters of the Warren Commission around the world. However, as Commission lawyer Wesley Liebeler observed, Lane's antics during these debates reminded him of "an old legend about frogs jumping from the mouth of a perfidious man every time he speaks . . . If (Lane) talks for five minutes, it takes an hour to straighten out the record." Even the counter-culture Rolling Stone magazine characterized Lane as a "huckster" and "hearse chaser." Vince Bugliosi describes Lane as having "infidelity to the truth" . . . a person who commits "outright fabrications" . . . "a fraud in his preachments about the known assassin" . . . and that he had "deliberately distorted the evidence" and repeatedly omitted "evidence damaging to his side." Critic Dwight MacDonald called Lane a "crude, tireless and demagogic advocate" for his self-aggrandizing and dishonest criticism.[9]

Gus Russo, author of two books about the Kennedy assassination, *Live By The Sword* (1998) and *Brothers In Arms* (2008), described Lane as a "flim-flam artist who almost single-handedly created the conspiracy movement through outright fraud."[10] Hugh Aynesworth who reported the JFK assassination 50 years ago as a journalist for the Washington *Times* and *Newsweek*, accused Lane of making "...almost any assertion about the assassination – even under oath – with impunity...His book *Rush To Judgment* was a mishmash of unproven and unlikely allegations and off-the-wall speculations".[11]

In fact, Lane has built a career of playing fast and loose with the facts. In the early 1970s, he used unreliable testimony to accuse American soldiers of multiple atrocities during the Vietnam War, according to New York *Times* correspondent Neil Sheehan, an anti-Vietnam War advocate. Sheehan investigated the accounts in Lane's book, *Conversations with Americans: Testimony from 32 Vietnam Veterans*, and found most of them to be bogus. Sheehan said Lane's book was "a lesson in what happens when a society shuns the examination of a pressing, emotional issue and leaves the answers to a Mark Lane." James Reston, Jr., in the *Saturday Review*, described Lane's book as "disreputable" in that all the reports contained in the book were "unverified and lean(t) toward the salacious....Lane makes no pretense of distinguishing between fact and a soldier's talent for embellishment".[12]

In the late 1970s, as a lawyer for Martin Luther King Jr.'s assassin, James Earl Ray, Lane appeared before the House Select Committee on Assassinations. The HSCA said of Lane in its report, "Many of the allegations of conspiracy that the committee investigated were first raised by Mark Lane . . . As has been noted, the facts were often at variance with Lane's assertions . . . Lane was willing to advocate conspiracy theories publicly without having checked the factual basis for them . . . Lane's conduct resulted in public misperception about the assassination of Dr. King and must be condemned."[13]

In Lane's latest book, *Last Word*, he has partly built his arguments around preposterous propositions, first expounded in *Rush To Judgment*, including the notion that the witness testimony and physical evidence "proves" a second shooter was involved in the assassination. Lane repeats old canards that have been debunked for years. It is a book designed for a new generation of readers who are unfamiliar with Lane's previous attacks on the truth. For example, the author of the book's introduction resurrects the myth that FBI agents listened to a tape recording of a "Lee Oswald" at the Soviet embassy during the assassin's trip to Mexico City weeks before the assassination. The allegation that such a tape existed was debunked many years ago by the HSCA. The story of the existence of tapes had originated with only one FBI agent out of many who handled the transcripts of the tapes because the tapes had been copied over as per the CIA's usual procedures.[14]

Lane also repeats the false and misleading statements of so-called "JFK assassination witnesses," including Jean Hill, Deputy Sheriff Roger Craig, and disgraced Secret Service agent Abraham Bolden, that were debunked years ago.[15]

In *Last Word*, Lane depends on the public's confusion about the JFK evidence. He manages to resurrect his old theories because he knows that a new generation of Americans will be unable to absorb all the literature on the assassination. There are literally tens of thousands of documents and items of evidence in the JFK case. There are therefore endless opportunities for Lane and others to add a word here or a word there to give a different contextual meaning to either a witness statement or a government document. The vast majority of readers simply do not have the time to wade through the relevant documents, therefore many conspiracy supporters mistake crude manipulation for scholarship. As Victor Navasky observed in a 2010 article in *The Nation*: "... we live in a state of opinion trusteeship. None of us have the time and few of us the ability to do our own research on all the complex, problematic issues of our day."[16]

Lane demonstrates how he can contort language to give a different meaning when he writes, ". . . [former CIA Director Allen] Dulles told the [Warren Commission] members that they need not worry about anyone doubting their false conclusions. Maybe, he suggested, at worst many years will have passed before some professor might study the evidence and by then it would not matter." Was the word "false" Lane's, or did Dulles actually characterize the Warren Commission conclusions as "false?" Lane does not tell us, so it is left to the reader to figure it out. Although Lane does not source the 'top secret' minutes, he is clearly making reference to a Warren Commission document entitled

"Warren Commission Executive Session of April 30, 1964".[17]

As the rational reader will likely agree after reading the document, Dulles' comments are entirely innocuous.

Lane also demonstrates his technique of sowing doubt where none exists when he attempts to tie the RFK assassination in with the alleged shenanigans of the CIA and the JFK assassination. He carefully places suspicion in the mind of the reader by making reference to the alleged sinister circumstances surrounding the shooting of Senator Kennedy. Lane describes how Bobby Kennedy was led out of the Ambassador Hotel pantry by his bodyguard, "FBI agent . . . William Barry." Barry, according to Lane, "changed the route at the last minute." Lane goes on to state that Barry told an onlooker, "No, it's been changed. We're going this way." At the time of the RFK assassination, Bill Barry was an ex-FBI agent and the decision to change the route out of the Embassy Room was made by Barry and RFK aide Fred Dutton to accommodate the realities of running for President—RFK had promised to meet with the print press who were in the Colonial Room, and the simplest route was through the pantry, the scene of the assassination. Additionally, RFK had asked to go the "back way" to the Colonial Room instead of through the crowds in the Embassy Ballroom. Yet via Lane's transparent innuendo, readers will inevitably be left to wonder if a federal agency was responsible for the assassination of JFK's brother. It is therefore ironic that Lane has the gall to criticize Vincent Bugliosi for getting an address wrong in *Reclaiming History*. Lane sarcastically wrote, "Did the publisher never hear of the term shared by the entire [publishing] industry: fact checker?"[18]

Lane also uses wild accusations to silence his critics by denouncing them as "old CIA hand(s)," "CIA assets," "CIA media assets," a "voice for the CIA," "close to the CIA," or they work "on behalf of the CIA." He also uses innuendo to accuse anti-conspiracy writers of working for the Agency in some undefined, but nonetheless sinister, fashion. These phrases will no doubt incite some of his less-than-rational readers. It is essentially McCarthyite in nature. To paraphrase Attorney Joseph Welch at the 1954 Army v McCarthy hearings, "Mr. Lane, you've done enough. Have you no sense of decency, sir? At long last, have you left no sense of decency?"[19]

Lane's omission of important facts about the two Government investigations into the assassination of President Kennedy also leaves his readers with an unenlightened understanding of the inquiries. He tells his readers that the HSCA "concluded that probably a conspiracy was responsible for the murder [of JFK]." What he does not inform his readers about is how the committee toiled for three years to uncover a conspiracy and failed. At the eleventh hour, however, HSCA members were presented with a report from an acoustics firm which examined a Dallas police recording, purportedly of the shots fired in Dealey Plaza. The acoustics experts concluded more than three shots had been fired at the motorcade, therefore there must have been a second shooter. A narrow majority of the HSCA members concurred. In 1982, however, three years after the HSCA dissolved, the National Academy of

Sciences found their acoustics findings to be seriously flawed.[20]

Central to Lane's the-CIA-did-it thesis is his chapter entitled The Indictment – The People of the United States v. the Central Intelligence Agency. It is a regurgitation of his endlessly voiced but unproven vociferations that the CIA was not only at the center of a conspiracy to murder President Kennedy, but that Watergate burglar and former CIA agent E. Howard Hunt, along with others, had been part of the plot.

His publishers promoted the book by proclaiming Lane had successfully persuaded a jury that the CIA killed Kennedy. On the inside book flap they loudly state, "Mark Lane has tried the only case in the history of America . . . in which jurors concluded that the CIA killed President Kennedy." In fact, the jury concluded nothing of the sort. Lane's story about CIA involvement in the assassination begins with a 1976 article published in an anti-Semitic magazine, Spotlight, which alleged that CIA agent E. Howard Hunt, one of the Watergate burglars, was in Dallas on November 22, 1963. The article, written by Victor Marchetti, a former CIA official, alleged Hunt had a role in the Kennedy assassination. The allegation had its origins in a photograph taken at the time of the assassination, which purported to show three mysterious tramps in the railroad yards behind the infamous Book Depository being taken into custody by the Dallas police. One of the tramps bore a resemblance to Hunt. It was not until the 1980s and the release of Dallas Police files that the tramps were identified and they had nothing to do with the assassination.[21]

Hunt won a libel judgment against the magazine in 1981, but it was thrown out on appeal, and the case was re-tried in 1985 in Miami in a civil, not criminal, trial. Hunt lost his case but the jury decision, with the exception of one juror, was based not on their belief that Hunt was a participant in a CIA plot to kill the President, but on the fact there was not "actual malice" (a principle of law established by a 1964 Supreme Court ruling) in the magazine's publication of the article, not that the article was necessarily true. When a "public figure" like E. Howard Hunt is attacked in the media, he cannot win a libel judgment merely by showing that the attack is "untrue and unfair."

Lane claims the jurors accepted his premise that the CIA was responsible for murdering the President. Lane wrote, "The evidence was clear, (jury forewoman Leslie Armstrong) said. The CIA had killed President Kennedy. Hunt had been part of it, and that evidence, so painstakingly presented, should now be examined by the relevant institutions of the United States trial government so that those responsible for the assassination might be brought to justice."[22]

However, two of the jurors told the Miami Herald they did not believe Lane had proven that Hunt was a co-conspirator. Suzanne Reach said that Lane's theory against Hunt was "absolutely not" the reason for the verdict. "We were very disgusted and felt (the article) was trash," she said. "The paper published material that was sloppy – but it wasn't malicious." While Lane avoids literally telling lies in his book, he uses the same convoluted expositions he used before the Miami jury to persuade his readers that Hunt was indeed guilty of conspiring to kill the President.[23]

Lane can be confident that the vast majority of his readers have no way of knowing what he's doing. In the Lane tradition of carefully concealing from his readers any information that might undermine his thesis, he portrays Hunt as having only two alibi witnesses at the trial, and denigrates these because they were CIA employees. But in fact there were three CIA employees who testified at the trial, and three witnesses (two of Hunt's children and a domestic) who swore to the 1975 Rockefeller Commission that Hunt was in the Washington area, and not in Dallas, on the day of the assassination. Lane repeats the story of how Hunt confessed on his deathbed to his alleged knowledge of the conspiracy. He allegedly confessed to his son, Saint John Hunt, and this bogus revelation was published in *Rolling Stone* magazine. In support of his allegations against Hunt, he makes reference to an alleged 'confession' made by the former CIA agent. However, the circumstances of Saint John Hunt's interview with his father are fraught with problems, not least the fact E. Howard Hunt was heavily medicated at the time he 'confessed'. But Lane does not disclose this to his readers. Hunt's memoirs were published posthumously and he vehemently denies any involvement in the JFK assassination. Hunt did "not believe the CIA had anything to do with JFK's death." He even discloses that Lane's irresponsible accusations caused his family great suffering. Additionally, Hunt's 'confession' is nothing more than his own guesswork and ruminations as to who killed JFK. He may even have used this opportunity to vent his spleen over those in government who did not give him any support after he was indicted in the Watergate affair.[24]

A disgraced Secret Service agent, Abraham Bolden, is another bogus witness Lane uses to bolster his misconceived thesis. He is important to Lane because Bolden helps support Lane's view that the Secret Service assisted the CIA in carrying out the assassination. Bolden claimed there had been a plot to kill Kennedy during a planned Presidential trip to Chicago. When Kennedy's trip was cancelled, Bolden alleges, the assassination plans were then adapted to Dallas and Lee Harvey Oswald became the designated patsy. The HSCA, however, said it "was unable to document the existence of the alleged assassination team. Specifically, no agent who had been assigned to Chicago confirmed any aspect of Bolden's version." The HSCA also said that ". . . one agent did state there had been a threat in Chicago during that period . . . but he was unable to recall details." (The existence of a "serious threat" was hardly surprising, as Kennedy received numerous death threats during his Presidency.) The HSCA concluded that Bolden's story was of "questionable authenticity." In 1964, Bolden was prosecuted and convicted of conspiring to sell official information in a counterfeiting case and was sentenced to six years in prison.[25]

Lane also accepts the veracity of Marita Lorenz, even though numerous researchers have proven her stories were not credible or they were constructed on outright lies. Marita Lorenz was the one single witness at the Miami trial who placed Hunt in Dallas on the day of the assassination. She said he was a co-conspirator in the

JFK assassination who went by the name of "Eduardo." Lorenz, a supposed CIA operative and mistress of Fidel Castro, was characterized by Lane as "credible." However, he fails to inform his reader of Lorenz's other claims about the assassination, and Hunt in particular, over the years. In conversations with other writers and investigators for the HSCA, she made a number of allegations which were proven to be false. Lorenz said Oswald was among the conspirators in a "caravan" that drove from Miami to Dallas arriving on November 21, 1963. Numerous witnesses, however, placed Oswald elsewhere. Lorenz also claimed to have seen Oswald participating in training for the Bay of Pigs invasion at a time when Oswald was in the Soviet Union.[26]

During 1977 and 1978, Lorenz's allegations were extensively investigated by the House Select Committee on Assassinations. One of the HSCA's investigators, Edwin Lopez, a conspiracy advocate, told author Gerald Posner, "Oh God, we spent a lot of time with Marita . . . It was hard to ignore her because she gave us so much crap, and we tried to verify it, but let me tell you—she is full of shit. Between her and Frank Sturgis, we must have spent over one hundred hours. They were dead ends . . . Marita is not credible."[27]

Lane is also taken in by the hype surrounding the CIA's efforts in the 1950s and 1960s to find a Manchurian Candidate to do their bidding although he does not make the claim Oswald had been a brainwashed assassin. His chapter, entitled MKULTRA The CIA's Dark Secrets, does the job, though, and successfully demonizes the CIA, leading readers to the inevitable conclusion CIA agents were capable of anything –

including the assassination of a President. However, as unethical as those experiments were that Lane writes of, there is no evidence whatsoever they had anything to do with building a brainwashed assassin to murder JFK.[28]

In the end, the sumptuous appeal of Mark Lane's books, the deliberate falsification of the JFK assassination story without any real proof, doesn't need to make sense. His work nourishes the appetite of a ready-made audience eager for stories that will prop up a belief system they are not willing to abandon.

JOAN MELLEN

The incredible contortions involved in Lane's theses are implicit in most conspiracy books, especially Joan Mellen's *A Farewell To Justice*, an examination of the alleged role the CIA and other government agencies played in JFK's assassination and Jim Garrison's New Orleans investigation.

Mellen points to one suspicious-looking anomaly after another and invents scenarios to explain them, without any credible evidence. She avoids incontrovertible facts which prove Oswald's guilt – Oswald went to Irving to collect 'curtain rods', left his wedding ring behind, fled the scene of the crime, appeared in full view of the Tippit murder witnesses, tried to shoot the arresting officer, owned the rifle and pistol, was seen by a witness shooting the President, palm prints, fingerprints, and so on.

New Orleans District Attorney Jim Garrison began his investigation into the JFK assassination by exposing alleged contradictions in the Warren Report. Joan Mellen asserts that Oswald was no Marxist and was in fact working with both the FBI and the CIA, as well as with U.S. Customs, and that the attempts to discredit Garrison's investigation reached the highest levels of the U.S. Government.

Mellen claims to have uncovered new evidence establishing the intelligence agencies' roles in both a President's assassination and its cover-up. She believes the cover-up began well before the assassination. Oswald, she alleges, was closely connected to CIA-sponsored anti-Castro figures in New Orleans, including Clay Shaw, David Ferrie, Guy Banister, and Jack Martin.

Central to Mellen's thesis is her assertion that the CIA and FBI worked with the conspirators to cover up the assassination. It began, Mellen posits, when Oswald, in the company of Shaw and Ferrie, applied for a job at the mental hospital in Jackson, Louisiana. According to Garrison, conspirators wanted Oswald working at the hospital so they could later switch his records to support a frame-up in which Oswald would be characterized as a mental patient. On the strength of an interview with anti-Cuban exile Angelo Murgado (alias Angelo 'Kennedy'), she also alleges—most strikingly of all—that Robert Kennedy was aware of Oswald and his connection to the FBI before the assassination. RFK purportedly put Oswald under surveillance and had his Cuban associates tracking Oswald's movements during the summer of 1963.

On Black Op Radio, Mellen stated that, in March 1967, it was her husband-to-be, Ralph Schoenman (a JFK conspiracy advocate and committed Marxist) who gave

Jim Garrison the now infamous articles about Clay Shaw that had been published in the Italian newspaper *Paese Sera*. The articles stated that Shaw had been on the board of directors of an organization in Rome which the articles alleged had been a CIA front. As Max Holland revealed, the evidence indicates that these articles convinced Garrison that Shaw was a CIA agent and that the Agency was behind the assassination.[29]

Despite Max Holland's debunking of the Italian newspaper's stories in his article 'The Lie That Linked the CIA to the Kennedy Assassination,' Mellen unashamedly gives credence to their distorted facts. As Holland wrote, *Paese Sera's* successful deception turns out to be a major reason why many Americans believe, to this day, that the CIA was involved in the assassination of President Kennedy."[30]

Mellen's 'proof' of the invalidity of Holland's research centers around the simple denials of the editors of *Paese Sera* who said their reporters were not duped by the KGB and that, "Garrison had focused on the CIA well before the publication of the *Paese Sera* articles." This is a pivotal issue because Garrison, in his memoir, *On The Trail Of The Assassins*, lied about when he received the articles; that lie suggests the true significance of these articles to him. Moreover, the articles were not already in the works long before Shaw's arrest, as Mellen claims, on the basis of interviews conducted by the aforementioned Ralph Schoenman. It was Shaw's arrest that prompted those stories. And Garrison only knew of the alleged CIA/Shaw connection through the newspaper articles. Pertinent to this affair is the fact that the KGB was doing everything in its power to link the JFK

307

assassination with the CIA, and that *Paese Sera* was an outlet for KGB disinformation, as the Mitrokhin Archive proves.[31]

Andrew described the active measures by the KGB against the United States and the promotion of false JFK assassination theories, using writer Mark Lane. (Mark Lane denies the allegations.)

Taking her lead from Mark Lane, Mellen brands authors who reject JFK conspiracy theories as 'CIA assets'. It is her favorite smear tactic in the book. It is a common tool used by JFK conspiracy writers. Don Bohning, a former Miami Herald reporter and author of *The Castro Obsession* (2005), is incensed with references made by Mellen that he was a 'CIA sponsored' reporter. Bohning contacted the book's publishers, suggesting it was libelous. They contacted Mellen and said she agreed to change the description to 'CIA linked.' The reference is still extremely misleading, Bohning said. "(I)...never took a cent from the CIA and was outraged by the implication – along with the terms 'writer asset' and 'utilized'. Top editors at the *Herald* were well aware – and approved – of my contacts with the CIA during the 1960s."[32]

Mellen's theories, which center on a CIA conspiracy, make little sense once examined closely. We do not need an alternative explanation to knock down a false belief – in this case Mellen's unsubstantiated conspiracy allegations – if there are no facts making a claim even slightly probable, then it is false. Her allegations that Clay Shaw was created and supervised by the CIA have been examined time and time again by JFK researchers

OSWALD'S DEFENDERS

and found to be false. In reality, Clay Shaw had simply been one of thousands of businessmen who had once been a source for the CIA through its Domestic Contact Service (DCS). Instead, as Patricia Lambert has proven, in a far superior examination of the Garrison case, *False Witness*, Shaw was a Kennedy supporter, a decorated war veteran, and a gifted intellectual who had rightly been found innocent of the conspiracy charges Garrison made against him.

Mellen's allegations that the CIA wanted to impede Garrison's investigation are true, but not because the Agency had something sinister to hide. The CIA was in a quandary because of its innocuous relationship with Shaw and it monitored Garrison's investigation, alarmed that the New Orleans D.A. was wrongly linking the Agency with the JFK assassination. As Max Holland wrote, "Shaw was not...developed as a covert operative...the relationship (with the CIA) just lapsed. He had never received any remuneration and probably considered the reporting a civic duty that was no longer urgent once the hostility between the two superpowers became frozen in place and a new world war no longer appeared imminent... Garrison's allegations—the 'grossest we have seen from any responsible American official'—gave the Agency fits, just as they did Shaw and Shaw's lawyers."[33]

It is difficult to exaggerate the number of previously debunked myths Mellen resurrects. In fact, her book is no different from Lane's books which promote theories based on gossip, innuendo, and tall tales from unreliable sources. Like Lane, she rehabilitates old shibboleths about the Garrison investigation, including the myth that

BEYOND REASONABLE DOUBT

Oswald was in possession of 'a Minox spy camera' and Ferrie's alleged possession of Oswald's library card, both of which have been examined carefully over the years and found to be false. Mellen's thesis also depends on the veracity of New Orleans 'character' Jack Martin and countless other actors in the New Orleans 'drama' whose stories have been fully researched. There are too many to cover in this book review, but the following are examples as to the lengths to which this author will go in building her conspiracy tale.[34]

Mellen recycles, as if true, the testimony of witnesses who were discredited before the Shaw case came to trial in 1969, or who were never called to testify precisely because they lacked credibility. She apparently assumes that readers will not know that these witnesses were discredited. Her 'new' revelations almost always center around the tales told by anti-Cuban exiles and others on the periphery, like Thomas Edward Beckham, a semi-literate who claims, along with dozens of other fantasists, to have observed Ferrie, Oswald, and Ruby together; Richard Case Nagell and Jules Rico Kimble, known liars and fantasists.[35]

Mellen also plays the conspiracists' game of 'A knows B who knows C who knows D, therefore A must know D'.

One witness who Mellen interviewed is Angelo Murgado, mentioned earlier, who changed his name to 'Angelo Kennedy'. Angelo purports to have known about RFK's pre-assassination knowledge of Oswald. Yet Don Bohning's Cuban exile contacts in Florida have poured scorn on Murgado's credibility.[36] He joins the battalions of 'soldier of fortune' types who have, for 40 years, claimed some knowledge of the JFK assassination – all of them supplying no credible evidence of their participation whatsoever.

The most important witness in the trial of Clay Shaw was Perry Raymond Russo and Garrison's case was built around Russo's testimony. According to Mellen, Russo was truthful – but the facts reveal otherwise. Russo began recanting his conspiracy stories almost immediately, beginning in 1967 to his polygraph examiners. In 1971, Russo recanted to Clay Shaw's attorneys, admitting to them that he was coached, brainwashed, and hypnotized into lying under oath.

A particularly glaring example of the kind of distortions Mellen routinely engaged in concerns a CIA officer named Joseph James Martin. Mellen cited CIA documents about him, and alleged he was identical to the 'Jack Martin' who was an associate of Guy Banister. It is a preposterous claim when the full CIA record on this issue and Jack Martin's FBI biography is examined. Garrison's initial ideas and actions were based on allegations made by Martin, who was frequently characterized by people who knew him as a notorious storyteller. Acting on Martin's stories, David Ferrie, a former airlines pilot who had worked for Carlos Marcello's lawyer, G. Wray Gill, was put under round-the-clock surveillance. It was years before Martin's allegations against Ferrie were discovered to be inspired by a longstanding grudge. The mystery is why Garrison, who knew Martin was alcoholic, fabricated information, and had received treatment for mental illness, took his allegations seriously. Hubie Badeux, the former chief of the New Orleans Police Intelligence Division, told author

311

Gerald Posner, "[Martin] was goofy to begin with and lied all the time." Badeux said Martin had a reputation for "crazy and wild stories."[37]

In constructing her story, Mellen takes many leaps of the imagination. For example, she states that Oswald wanted to name his first child David, if it was a boy. She then links this fact with the ridiculous assertion that the only 'David' in Oswald's life was David Ferrie. Mellen posits this as proof of Oswald's connection to the alleged JFK conspirator. This is not analysis; it is paranoia.

Mellen's book has the facade of scholarship, but it is in fact a hocus-pocus act. Many of her strongest assertions are not footnoted and thus undocumented. Incredibly, she gives credence to an anonymous telephone call to Garrison in which the caller, allegedly a friend of Shaw's, said the DA's suspicions about Shaw were correct. She also ignores documents she doesn't like, i.e., that contradict her inferences. She claims, without backing it up, that the FBI and CIA files are 'papered', which presumably means they contain false documents. She also claims that incriminating documents were destroyed. Yet she also (mis)uses CIA and FBI documents to 'make' her case when it suits her purpose. She has created a researcher's 'perfect universe'. Documents she doesn't like are inserted concoctions, and important documents are missing that would prove her allegations (though she purports to know their contents). One wonders why she bothers with documents at all. The answer is: it gives her book a facade of accuracy.

CHAPTER ELEVEN

THE CASTRO CONNECTION

> *"They will have to find the assassin quickly otherwise you watch and see, they will try to blame us."*
>
> — Fidel Castro

Suspicions of a Cuban connection to the Kennedy assassination were only natural. They were heightened by the activities of Oswald, a lifelong Marxist, supporter of Castro and a former defector to the Soviet Union, where he attempted to renounce his U.S. citizenship.

By 1963, Oswald had returned to the United States. But just a few months before Kennedy's death, at a time when tensions between Havana and Washington were at their height, his outspoken public support for Cuba had come to the attention of the news media in New Orleans, where he was living in the summer of that year. And he had also attracted the attention of the CIA, which had the Mexico City embassies of Cuba and the Soviet Union under tight surveillance. The agency spotted Oswald at both embassies on multiple visits between September 27 and October 2, 1963, as he sought visas to travel to either country.

The rumor of Cuban or Russian involvement in the JFK assassination was problematic. International problems could follow if it were true. Following the assassination,

America's leaders feared that the American people would demand retaliation for the murder of their president. The leadership worried that the Cold War would heat up if it was found that the president had been murdered either by Castro's agents or the KGB or both working in conjunction. If Oswald had been working for the Cubans there would be an outcry from the American people for another invasion of Cuba. If the Russians were responsible for the assassination the world could be on the brink of nuclear war. President Johnson quickly decided that he must convince the country that the president's death was the result of a single madman, not of some vast communist plot.

However, the American government became convinced that Castro's agents did not participate in the assassination of JFK. The National Security Agency, which intercepts communications, went all out to decipher intercepts of conversations, cable traffic, and radio and telephone communications at the highest levels of the Soviet and Cuban governments. Together with information from human sources, the intercepts show clearly that both the Soviet and Cuban leaders were ignorant of the assassination and were frightened of receiving the blame. Many years later it was revealed that Chief Justice Earl Warren had dispatched Warren Commission staff counsel, William Coleman, on a secret mission to Havana to investigate Cuban complicity in the assassination. Coleman has declined to speak about the incident except to say that his trip helped to convince him that Castro had nothing to do with the president's assassination.[1] But in their haste to allay fears of Cuban or Russian involvement in the assassination, the Warren

THE CASTRO CONNECTION

Commission failed to pursue many leads, opening up a large vacuum of unanswered questions which were immediately obvious to many Americans. The Warren Commission was not given full information by the FBI and CIA about possible leads suggesting Oswald had not acted alone. Two of the most important failures were in not looking into the attempts by the CIA to murder Castro and determination that Castro's agents in Mexico City had not assisted Oswald.

Former CIA Director Allen Dulles, a Warren Commission member, failed to tell his colleagues on the commission or staff investigators about the attempts by the CIA to kill Castro using everything from poisoned cigars to exploding sea shells. This knowledge could have given investigators an important lead on Oswald's time in Mexico City in the short period before the assassination. Commission members Richard Russell and Gerald Ford also knew about the CIA's attempts to kill the Cuban leader. However, if no link existed between Oswald and the Soviet or Cuban governments, they reasoned, there was no reason to inform their staff investigators who wrote the Commission's report.

The Mexico City visits to the Cuban and Russian embassies, where Oswald took a scrapbook of newspaper clippings and other documents to demonstrate his support for Castro's revolution in hopes of winning a visa, were among evidence considered by all three major investigations of the plots against Castro in the 1970s – the Church Committee, the Rockefeller Commission and the HSCA. All three rejected the idea of any causal link between Castro and the Kennedy assassination. In the 1990s, the Assassination Records

Review Board (ARRB) spent years making sure that all relevant CIA and other US government records were declassified and open to the public. None of the material released pointed to Castro's involvement in the JFK assassination.

When news came that Oswald had been arrested for the assassination of President Kennedy, Castro believed many Americans would blame him for the assassination because of Oswald's Cuban connections. He denied his government had any contacts with Oswald and said he had never heard of him.

In the following years, the idea that Castro had been involved persisted. The Cuban leader certainly had a strong motive. Castro's Cuba was the target of numerous CIA-led sabotage operations, assassination plots, support for anti-Castro guerrillas, and encouragement of military coup plotters. The Kennedy administration efforts to rid the island of a communist dictatorship began with the attempted invasion of Cuba by Cuban anti-Castro exiles in April 1961. Operations to destabilize the Castro regime continued after the missile crisis in October 1962 and lasted until the end of the Kennedy administration.[2]

Within two years of assuming power in Cuba, Castro came to believe, not without reason, that the United States was unable to accommodate his radical socialist policies and so he looked to the Soviet Union for economic assistance. The United States isolated Cuba by cutting off the sugar markets and oil supplies and enlisted the CIA to train Cuban exiles for an invasion of the island. This resulted in the ill-fated 'Bay of Pigs' invasion. The CIA continued to organize anti-Castro groups after the disaster and financed hundreds of covert operations against Cuba ('Operation Mongoose'). The campaign aimed to destabilize Castro's regime rather than to overthrow it. Every possible tactic would be brought to bear, including hostile diplomacy, a trade embargo, paramilitary sabotage, psychological warfare, and assassination. The Kennedy administration eventually became so frustrated with the CIA's poor results that administration officials badgered the CIA's leadership to get rid of Castro at all costs.

Castro was naturally embittered by the many Cuban exile attempts on his life and in September 1963 gave Associated Press reporter Daniel Harker a warning to pass on that if the United States persisted in "aiding terrorist plans to eliminate Cuban leaders" American leaders would be in danger.[3]

In 1978, Castro explained this speech to the HSCA when the Committee interviewed the Cuban leader in Havana. "So, I said something like those plots start a very bad precedent," Castro said, "a very serious one that could become a boomerang against the authors of those actions but I did not mean to threaten by that. I did not mean even that...not in the least...but rather, like a warning that we knew; that we had news about it; and that to set those precedents of plotting the assassination of leaders of other countries would be a very bad precedent.... something very negative. And, if at present, the same would happen under the same circumstances, I would have no doubt in saying the same as I said (then) because I didn't mean a threat by that. I didn't say it as a threat. I did not mean by that we were going to take measures, similar measures like retaliation for that. We never meant that because we knew that there were plots against us. So the conversation came about very casually, you know; but I would say that all these plots or attempts were part of the everyday life."[4]

Castro also told HSCA investigators that from the ideological point of view, his purported involvement in the assassination was "insane". "And from the political point of view, it was a tremendous insanity," he said, "I am going to tell you here that nobody; nobody ever had the idea of such things. What would it do? We just tried to defend our folks here, within our territory. Anyone who subscribed to that idea would have been judged insane, absolutely sick. Never, in 20 years of revolution, I never heard anyone suggest nor even speculate about a measure of that sort, because who could think of the idea of organizing the death of the President of the United States. That would have been the most perfect pretext for the United States to invade our country which is what I have tried to prevent for all these years, in every possible sense. Since the United States is much more powerful than we are, what would we gain from a war with the United States? The United States would lose nothing. The destruction would have been here." He noted that murdering Kennedy brought to office a man (President Johnson) who would have been expected to be tougher toward Cuba. Richard Helms, Deputy CIA Director, commented, "We would have bombed Cuba back into the middle ages."[5]

There is also compelling evidence that Castro, rather than attempting to eliminate his opponent, was instead trying to bring about an accommodation with Kennedy. According to Jean Daniel, foreign editor of *L'Express*, who was with Castro when Kennedy was shot, the Cuban leader believed that JFK had the opportunity to become the greatest president in the history of the United States and that anyone else would be worse. He even mischievously told the journalist that he would give his support to Kennedy's likely opponent in the 1964 presidential election, Barry Goldwater, if that would help him. He asked the reporter to stay a while longer in Cuba so they could continue their discussions. However, according to Brian Latell, the invitation to stay may well have been a ruse in establishing a Castro cover story when he heard the news of the assassination. Castro could then feign shock, even though he purportedly knew Kennedy was going to be killed and may have organized the assassination.[6]

Castro was having lunch with Daniel when the news came that Kennedy had been shot. Daniel said that, "as Castro put the receiver to his ear, his face clouded over... His voice seemed strained...He listened intently, then returned to the table and sat down." Castro told Daniel it was 'bad news'. Following the report of the president's death, Castro stood up and said, "Well, there is the end of your mission of peace. Everything is changed... I'll tell you one thing....At least Kennedy was an enemy to whom we had become accustomed. This is a serious matter, a very serious matter." He reminded Daniel that in the Sierra Maestra he had always opposed assassinations, even of Batista supporters.[7] However,

BEYOND REASONABLE DOUBT

Rudy Apocada, an author, lawyer, and former appellate judge in New Mexico, believes the idea that Castro expressed 'shock' at the assassination was a 'ruse', is illogical. "Castro couldn't be sure exactly how or where (and even exactly at what time) the shot that killed Kennedy would be fired by Oswald," Apocada said, "Also, he wouldn't need a foreign reporter to witness his "shock" when he received the phone call telling him Kennedy had been killed. He could have set up that "ruse" in an easier way.... Also, I'm not sure that Castro would find it necessary to have a witness to his shock. After all, he seemed willing to take the risk of assumptions and conclusions by third parties that he was involved in the assassination, no matter the lack of evidence. And of course, this turned out to be what actually happened."[8]

The idea that Castro was behind the assassination also never arose through interviews of fleeing refugees from Cuba, including former Cuban DGI agents. Due to the heavy work load at the CIA in Miami, the Chief, Justin Gleichauf, recommended they start a Cuban Processing Center to interview the arriving Cubans. This was started in North Miami in March of 1962 and all agencies assigned interviewers, including: CIA, FBI, the three Military Intelligence agencies, Immigration, and others who may have had an interest. The men were housed in former military barracks and women and children released to relatives in Miami. Had there been any suspicion that Castro or Cubans were involved in the JFK assassination, all of them would have been alerted to include this in their interviews and no information was found at that time. CIA and Military Intelligence officers who interviewed Cubans when they arrived in Miami learned that all were not reliable, according to a source who reported to Edward Lansdale, head of the CIA's 'Operation Mongoose'. "Refugees fleeing their country often tell interviewers what they think they want to hear," the source stated.[9]

In recent years, three important books – Gus Russo's and Stephen Molton's *Brothers in Arms*, Philip Shenon's *A Cruel and Shocking Act* and Brian Latell's *Castro's Secrets* – have suggested Castro's protestations of innocence should not be taken at face value and that the Cuban leader may have been involved in Kennedy's assassination.

In a speech Castro had given on November 27, 1963, he mentioned that Oswald had made a "provocative statement" when the assassin visited the Cuban Embassy in Mexico City the previous September. Castro also related Oswald's visit to Mexico City to FBI spy Jack Childs, who worked as top-level international courier and financial adviser for the Communist Party USA (FBI code name SOLO). The double agent was awarded a posthumous Presidential Medal of Freedom for his quarter-century of spying against Moscow and Havana. Ex-FBI agent James P. Hosty said Childs was historically one of the most important and reliable sources the FBI ever had. Childs met with Castro and confirmed the Cuban leader had known about Oswald's threat to kill Kennedy.[10]

The FBI "Airtel" memo was dated June 12, 1964. It stated, in part, "Fidel Castro was not under the influence of liquor at the time he made the statements. Castro does not drink nor did he partake of any stimulants whatsoever

he treated the question as a very serious matter It was the impression of (SOLO) that Castro received the information about Oswald's appearance at the Cuban Embassy in Mexico in an oral report from 'his people' in the Embassy, because he, Castro, was told about it immediately. (SOLO) does not know the identities of the individuals who told Castro. (SOLO) advised that Castro said, 'I was told this by my people in the Embassy – exactly how he (Oswald) stalked in and walked in and ran out. ....he acted like a real madman and started yelling and shouting and yelled on his way out, 'I'm going to kill that bastard, I'm going to kill Kennedy'.

Castro was neither engaging in dramatics nor oratory but was speaking on the basis of facts given to him by his embassy personnel who dealt with Oswald (SOLO) is of the opinion that Castro had nothing to do with the assassination."[11]

Former Head Counsel and Chief of Staff for the HSCA, G. Robert Blakey, thought that Jack Childs' report was more credible than Castro's denial.[12]

Gus Russo's revelations about the role Castro played in the Kennedy assassination began with his book *Live by the Sword* published in 1998. Later he assisted Wilfried Huismann for the German film maker's 2006 television documentary *Rendezvous with Death*. The documentary included an interview with Cuban G2 agent "Oscar Marino" (a pseudonym, as 'Marino' had been active as an intelligence agent until his death in 2009). 'Marino', who fell out with the Castro regime, said the Cubans were desperate to eliminate Kennedy. Marino claims that Castro got Kennedy before Kennedy could assassinate the Cuban leader. He claims Oswald was pointed out to Cuban Intelligence by the Soviet KGB. "There wasn't anyone else," Marino told Huismann, "You take what you can get. . . Oswald volunteered to kill Kennedy." Cuban agents paid Oswald $6,500 for the job, Marino said.[13]

Huismann's documentary also includes a tape recording made of Luisa Calderon Carralero, a Cuban intelligence officer in her early 20s who had lived in Miami with her parents throughout the 1950s. Barely four hours after the assassination, she received a phone call from a man, also apparently a Cuban spy. He asked if she knew what had happened in Dallas. "Yes, of course," she answered. "I knew of it almost before Kennedy did....Wonderful! What good news!" Calderon laughed. "He was a family man, yes, but also a degenerate aggressor," Calderon added, to which her caller responded, "Three shots in the face!" Replied Calderon: "Perfect!" Her caller noted correctly that Oswald spoke Russian and had written to Castro offering to join his fighting forces in 1959. Huismann believes the DGI maintained a file on Oswald and was well acquainted with him.[14]

Calderon was investigated by the HSCA in the 1970s. The committee concluded that her outburst was based on 'braggadocio' and in writing she denied she had foreknowledge of the JFK assassination. Additionally, her remarks about 'knowing' of the assassination 'almost before Kennedy did' can be interpreted as simply knowledge that the DGI knew about an unstable American who had threatened to kill Kennedy at the Cuban embassy in Mexico City. In their 2008 book *Brothers in Arms* Gus Russo and Stephen Molton provided additional evidence to link Castro to the assassination. Their evidence includes reports from former Castro agents who had defected to the United States. "When Juan Antonio Rodriguez Menier, one of the highest ranked Cuban intelligence officers, and a founding member of Cuba's G2 spy agency, defected to the US in 1987", Russo and Molton wrote, "he brought with him a wealth of information on the history and deepest secrets of Cuban intelligence services".[15]

Russo and Molton also interviewed former Castro agents Ricardo Morales, Vladimir Rodriguez Lahera, Gerardo Peraza, Jesus Raúl Perez Mendez, Major Florentino Aspillaga Lombard, Domingo Amuchastegui, Manuel De Beunza, Rafael del Pino, and Jose Cohen, who "helped... fill in even more details". The authors said that Oswald had contact with Cuban agents when he visited the Soviet and Cuban Mexico City embassies a short time before the assassination. They claim that Castro had been aware of Oswald's desire to murder the American president and Cuban agents, either acting on their own or with Castro's blessing, spurred him on. In short, Russo and Molton's research led them to believe that:

- Oswald came to the attention of the Cubans when the former Marine defected to Russia. The Cubans had spies training in Minsk at the time Oswald lived there. After Oswald's return to Texas in 1962, Cuban intelligence, led by Raúl

THE CASTRO CONNECTION

Castro, kept tabs on him, supporting him with small sums of money and subtle encouragement. He was never an actual operative, the authors maintain, since "he was neither smart enough nor mentally reliable enough to be trusted. What he was, within weeks of his arrival, was a Cuban-aligned sleeper agent, a potential asset who might prove useful to Havana one day."

- According to this theory, Oswald's increasingly erratic behavior stemmed from his desire to "prove his devotion to Fidel's cause."

- Oswald had been in touch with Cuban intelligence since he returned from the USSR, but they kept him at arm's length. He needed to convince them of his sincerity, so he went to Mexico to make them an offer they couldn't refuse – kill Kennedy. The Cubans had decided to egg him on to kill Kennedy with false promises of sanctuary.

- Cuban intelligence officer Fabian Escalante flew secretly to Dallas on the day of the Kennedy assassination. His mission is unexplained by Russo and Molton.

- Rolando Cubela was Oswald's Cuban case officer. They allege that Cubela was the first Cuban to contact Oswald, 11 months before his visit to Mexico City, and he gave Oswald sums of money.

- The assassination was Oswald's idea, and Castro's intelligence agents urged him to do it. It was never Castro's plot, but the Cuban leader was a great opportunist, according to Russo. –

In their words, Oswald "did it with the aid and comfort of Fidel and Raúl Castro."[16]

In 2012, Brian Latell, a CIA expert, published *Castro's Secrets,* a book about Castro's spies in the US. Latell added detail to Russo's and Molton's work. He said Castro played at least an indirect role in the assassination. Latell built on Russo's and Molton's evidence and provided additional details that the most important CIA Cuban asset, Rolando Cubela, was in fact a double agent. Latell has also concluded that Castro knew in advance that Lee Harvey Oswald planned to assassinate President Kennedy during the president's trip to Dallas. "Fidel Castro was running the most important double agent operation in the history of intelligence," Latell said. "He wanted definitive proof that Kennedy was trying to kill him. And he got it." (Author's note: From Rolando Cubela who the three authors say was a double agent)."

However, Latell does not say Fidel Castro ordered the assassination. "I don't say Oswald was under his control," Latell said, "He might have been, but I don't argue that, because I was unable to find any evidence for that".[17]

Latell insists Rolando Cubela's recruitment by the CIA (his code name was AMLASH) to assassinate Castro was questionable from the beginning. Castro's agent appeared to have unlimited time and money to travel, meeting with CIA officers on four different continents. Cubela refused to take a lie-detector test and did not report anything of any consequence about Castro's government.[18]

Latell provides evidence implicating Cubela as a double agent, including a recently declassified lie-detector test administered to Cubela's best friend and frequent co-conspirator in CIA adventures, the late Coral Gables, Florida, jeweler Carlos Tepedino. During a confrontational interrogation by CIA handlers in 1965, Tepedino confessed that Cubela was still "cooperating" with Cuban intelligence and had never tried to organize a military revolt against Castro. (Tepedino's suspicions that Cubela had been working with Cuba's intelligence agency all along were reported by Russo and Molton in their book *Brothers In Arms*, page 294.) Tepedino's story was confirmed by another DGI defector, Miguel Mir, a high official in Castro's personal security office from 1986 to 1992. Mir said he had read files identifying Cubela as a double agent under DGI control.[19]

Latell also discloses that a Cuban intelligence agent defector, Florentino Aspillaga, the most valuable defector ever to flee Cuba's DGI intelligence service, was asked by Castro to drop radio surveillance of the CIA hours before the assassination to focus on signals from Texas. Aspillaga told his CIA debriefers about the change in surveillance when he defected in 1987, but that information remained secret until he repeated the story to Latell in interviews for the book.[20]

Latell argues that Lee Harvey Oswald warned Cuban intelligence officers in advance of his plans to kill the president. Latell writes that Oswald, a belligerent Castro supporter, grew frustrated when officials at the Cuban embassy in Mexico City refused to give him a visa to travel to the island, and promised to shoot Kennedy to prove his revolutionary credentials.[21]

The author also reports how, in 1964, the CIA debriefed another DGI defector, Vladimir Rodriguez Ladera. At the time, Rodriguez Ladera told the CIA that Castro was surely lying when he claimed that Oswald's visit to the Cuban embassy in Mexico had been a minor matter that didn't come to the attention of senior officials in Havana. "It caused much comment concerning the fact that Oswald had been in the Cuban embassy," Ladera said. "But did Fidel want Kennedy dead? Yes. He feared Kennedy. And he knew Kennedy was gunning for him. (Author's note: because Rolando Cubela told him so) In Fidel's mind, he was probably acting in self-defense".[22]

JFK researcher and author Edward Jay Epstein believes a Castro connection to Kennedy's death is not only plausible, but likely. "There is no doubt that Castro knew about the CIA plans to assassinate him, and he warned the American government that he knew by telling a reporter about it," Epstein said. "If a Mafia leader did that same thing, and the next day the other guy was found dead, that would be a prima facie case and he'd be the lead suspect."[23]

And Gerald Posner, author of JFK assassination book *Case Closed*, thinks Latell may be onto something. "If there's an area of the case where something new still could emerge, it's the part connected to the CIA and Castro," he said. "There's always a possibility that the Cubans knew what Oswald was going to do because of his visit to their embassy in Mexico City. And if the Cubans knew, so did the Soviets and so did the CIA, because they were all monitoring each other like crazy. You could have a whole new ballgame."[24]

However, there are numerous problems with Russo's and Molton's notion that Oswald was enlisted by Rolando Cubela to kill Kennedy. According to Brian Latell, the authors have used information provided by a KGB officer, `Nikolai,` who allegedly "memorized, during unauthorized forays into Soviet intelligence archives, links (with) Oswald to Rolando Cubela, a Cuban who was used by the CIA in an assassination plot against Fidel.

The authors had no direct contact with 'Nikolai'. All of his testimony is secondhand, taken by Russo's German filmmaking colleague Wilfried Huismann or someone acting for him. Nothing is revealed about Huismann's investigative methods and the authors do not indicate that they made any effort to meet with "Nikolai" or independently to verify his bona fides... Moreover, "Nikolai" was able, he claimed, to read (it's not clear how) and memorize microfilmed KGB records. Somehow, despite such access, he was never able to use a copying machine or hidden camera to reproduce documents because `the risk would be too high.` Russo and Molton build much of their case on "Nikolai." But he does not ring true. Without anything more tangible to verify his claims, even the most novice intelligence analysts would suspect he is a fabricator."[25]

Latell's thesis, in turn, is challenged by Vincent Bugliosi and Peter Kornbluh, director of the Cuba Documentation Project at the National Security Archive. "The notion of Castro being in any way connected to the assassination is preposterous on its face," Vincent Bugliosi said. Kornbluh concurred. "In the last several months of his life," Kornbluh said, "Kennedy sent several peace feelers to Castro. Kennedy even had a guy in Cuba (French journalist Jean Daniel) talking to Castro about rapprochement at the moment of the assassination. Why would Castro want to do anything that encouraged the murder of the first American president willing to talk about coexistence with the Cuban revolution?"[26] Arnaldo M. Fernandez, a former lecturer in philosophy and history of law at the University of Havana, takes issue with Latell's implication that Castro knew Kennedy was going to be shot in Dallas. Fernandez cites Latell's interview with Florentino Aspillaga in which the former DGI agent said Castro had told him to redirect his radio listening antennas away from Miami and Langley and to listen "to any small detail from Texas" on the morning of November 22nd. Fernandez argues that the incident can, "...be explained by Castro's appetite for information about every Kennedy move or word in Texas, after his speech in Miami on November 18, 1963, in which he dismissed Castro's political group as 'a small band of conspirators [that] has stripped the Cuban people of their freedom and handed over the independence and sovereignty of the Cuban nation to forces beyond the hemisphere'.... Castro couldn't have known in advance that Oswald would be in Dallas on November 22, 1963, just because he had shouted 'I'm going to kill Kennedy' at the Cuban Embassy in Mexico City on September 27, 1963".[27]

Aspillaga did not inform his CIA handlers when he defected. Of the three officers Latell interviewed, two of them had no recollection of Aspillaga's story. Latell did not expound on the third.[28] Additionally, Aspillaga himself did not believe Castro had ordered JFKs assassination. "Fidel wanted to know what was going to happen...if he (Kennedy) was going to be killed or not." The former Cuban agent made no allegation that Oswald was a DGI agent or that Oswald had been in contact with DGI agents in Dallas. The information Aspillaga supplied to Latell can be interpreted in other ways. Castro was clearly interested in what Kennedy had to say about Cuba during the Texas visit, especially as the Cuban leader had recently learned of the president's provocative speech in Miami Beach four days earlier.

Fernandez also takes issue with Latell's reliance on Cuban intelligence officer Vladimir Rodriguez (codenamed AMMUG by the CIA) who, when he defected in 1964, said Castro lied about Oswald. Oswald had been in contact with the Cuban leader's intelligence agents according to Rodriguez. Rodriguez defected in 1964 and told his CIA handler that Castro had lied because "before, during and after" Oswald's visits to the Cuban consulate "he was in contact" with Castro's intelligence agents. However, Rodriguez was debriefed again by the CIA for clarification, and their conclusion about Rodrigez's allegations appears in a memo from March 8, 1964. The memo states Rodriguez "does not claim to have any significant information concerning the assassination of President Kennedy or about the activities of Oswald."[29]

Huismann's documentary was criticized by Vincent Bugliosi in his book, *Reclaiming History*. Bugliosi wrote that the German film maker alleged that Castro's Cuban intelligence agents used Oswald to kill Kennedy after Oswald made the offer to Cuban agents in Mexico City. Oswald was apparently paid $6,500 by a black man with reddish hair identified in the program as a top Cuban G-2 agent in Mexico named Cesar Morales Mesa.

Bugliosi says that the story was based on a proven fabrication originating with a then 23-year-old Nicaraguan secret agent, Gilberto Alvarado Ugarte, who wanted to infiltrate Castro's forces.[30] Even Alvarado admitted he had concocted the story to incite hostilities between the United States and Cuba.

Huismann produces several witnesses – a onetime archivist from Cuban intelligence who saw a dossier (but didn't read it); an ex-FBI man who can only speculate; a Cuban ex-diplomat who won't say how he knows his secrets. If Cuban intelligence was supposed to be as super-professional and as under-estimated as he claims it to be, he would know that only officers directly involved in a plot on Kennedy's life would have heard anything. Diplomats would not have been told.

Bugliosi also criticizes Huisemann because the documentary maker, "... sees nothing preposterous about the discussion to murder the president of the United States and the payment to Oswald taking place right outside the Cuban embassy, when Cuban intelligence (the G-2 agent, Morales, who supposedly made the payment) had to know that the lenses of CIA cameras were focused on that area. Nor does he apparently feel that Alvarado's claim to have actually seen (and apparently diligently counted out) precisely $6,500 in American bills ($1,500 for expense money, Alvarado says) being paid to Oswald is preposterous on its face....Further, Huisemann is not bothered by the

THE CASTRO CONNECTION

fact that if a Cuban G-2 agent gave Oswald $6,500 (at least the equivalent of $20,000 today) to kill Kennedy, what happened to all this money? Why Oswald was virtually broke at the time of his death, he and Marina having a grand total of $183.87 to their name? How did Oswald go through the equivalent of $20,000 (or even $6,500) in less than two months? What did he splurge this amount of money on?"[31]

The figure of $6,500 was also investigated by JFK researcher Anthony Marsh. Marsh wrote of how, on November 25, 1963, Alvarado claimed that on September 18, 1963, he saw a Cuban consulate employee give $6,500 in cash to Oswald to assassinate the President. Marsh wrote , "... because Gilberto's story was so elaborate and because it fit in with the prevailing suspicions in the intelligence community it was widely believed to be true. But under intense questioning by the CIA, Alvarado's story began to unravel. Oswald could not have been at the Cuban Consulate in Mexico on the day that he allegedly received the cash, because he was known to have been in New Orleans applying for unemployment insurance." Marsh stated that Alvarado admitted that he had made up the story in hopes that the US would be prompted to invade Cuba in retaliation. According to Anthony Summers, Alvarado later reverted to his story after the retraction.[32]

Gus Russo and Stephen Molton were told by 'Oscar Marino', a DGI intelligence agent, that Oswald "...was on a list of foreign colleagues....he repeatedly received strategic money. No important sum, a couple of thousand dollars...".[33] Yet the evidence which has been gathered over five decades clearly shows that Oswald had lived on a meager income from the time he returned from the Soviet Union. There is no evidence indicating Oswald ever had anywhere near such a large sum of money and if he had indeed received payment from the Cubans, he would have assuredly bought expensive consumer items for his children who he was devoted to. Oswald's second daughter was born on Sunday, October 20, 1963. Oswald was afraid that Parkland Hospital would present him with a bill, so he had stayed in Irving.[34]

Additionally, Oswald was living hand-to-mouth in the weeks before the assassination and the idea that he had been handed $6,500 in Mexico City by Castro's agents appears ridiculous at the outset. Allegedly, he had just been given the revolutionary role of a lifetime — yet those who knew him well, including his wife, Marina, said Oswald returned from Mexico City feeling dejected. He looked, as the Paines described him, "defeated".[35] He was especially vociferous about the Cubans – 'the same bureaucrats as in Russia,' he said. "Ah, they're such terrible bureaucrats that nothing came of it after all," Oswald told Marina before describing his "shuttling from embassy to embassy, how each one told him he had to wait and wait, and see what the other one did, and how the whole time he had worried about *running out of money* (emphasis added)."[36]

If Cuban agents were actively involved in making sure Oswald carried out his threats when they met with him in Mexico City, then it is inconceivable they would not have given him some form of financial assistance. Providing Oswald with some financial support would

THE CASTRO CONNECTION

have ensured their hired assassin did not at some point abandon his plans to kill Kennedy. Cuban agents would also have considered the possibility of Oswald's arrest and trial. They had no way of knowing Jack Ruby was going to murder the assassin. And if Oswald had revealed his Cuban connections during a trial, the American public would have demanded another invasion of Cuba, this time using overwhelming American military force. It is inconceivable Castro would have been the author of his own demise.

A scenario which had Oswald escape with a handful of dollars then catching a bus makes such involvement by sophisticated Cuban agents unlikely. The Warren Commission investigated Oswald's finances and found that during the 17 months preceding his death, Oswald's pattern of living was consistent with his limited income. The couple had a total of $183.87 to their name.[37] When Oswald visited Mexico City, he was careful with his money, spending between 40 and 48 cents for each meal. According to the Warren Commission, he "... ate the soup of the day, rice, and either meat or eggs, but refused dessert and coffee; the waitress concluded that Oswald did not realize that the items which he refused were included in the price of the lunch".[38]

Before he left for the trip, his wife asked him to buy her some long-playing musical records, but he returned without them. She also said she wanted Mexican silver bracelets as a souvenir, and he brought her a silver bracelet inscribed with her name. However, the bracelet he gave her was most probably of a type commonly sold in 5-and-10-cent stores in Dallas.[39] As Vincent Bugliosi asked, "How did Oswald go through the equivalent of $20,000 (or even $6500) in less than two months?"[40]

From September 24 until November 22, 1963, Marina stayed with Ruth Paine, while Oswald lived in a rooming house in Dallas. During the period Marina Oswald resided with others, neither she nor her husband made any contribution to her support. The Oswald's owned no major household appliances, had no automobile, and resorted to dental and hospital clinics for medical care. Acquaintances purchased baby furniture for them, and paid dental bills in one instance.[41] If Oswald had received $6500 there is no evidence that this sum of money was either left to his wife and children or squirreled away. There is also no evidence that from September to the time of the assassination Oswald spent money outside his normal expenditures. In fact, weaknesses in the Castro-did-it thesis are abundant. The idea that Oswald was carefully controlled by Castro's agents, in particular Rolando Cubela, and planned the Dallas assassination, remains unproven. How could Cuban intelligence, for example, have placed Oswald in the Texas School Book Depository? Ruth Paine and Linnie Mae Randle were the two people responsible for securing the Book Depository job for Oswald. What Russo, Molton, Latell, and others have effectively established is 'probable cause' which is a long way from proving 'beyond a reasonable doubt'.

Additionally, if Oswald had been controlled by other conspirators why would he put the whole enterprise in jeopardy by marching into the FBI offices in Dallas ten days before the assassination and threaten the agent who was assigned to watch him? This would only leave

THE CASTRO CONNECTION

him open to heightened scrutiny. As readers will recall, Oswald had left a threatening note for FBI agent Hosty in which he complained of harassment and, according to an FBI receptionist who was judged by the Warren Commission to be a 'disinterested party', Oswald's note indicated he would blow up the FBI offices. Hosty denied Oswald had written any such thing. Instead, he said, the note's wording was "...come talk to me directly. If you don't cease bothering my wife, I will take appropriate action and report this to the authorities". However, at the very least, the note was caustic in nature and certainly threatening. Fortunately for Oswald, Hosty took no action on the note.

It is also inconceivable that Castro's DGI agents would choose a man they must have known had been watched intensely by America's intelligence and law enforcement agencies. And Castro's agents must have known that had they been observed meeting with the assassin it would have led to war with Cuba.

The idea that Oswald was to flee to Mexico is also based on contradictions. Would Oswald's co-conspirators have allowed the assassin to carry only a few dollars with him when he escaped from the Texas Book Depository? Huisemann, Russo, Molton, and Latell also cannot explain why Cuban agents would risk the possibility of Oswald giving up his co-conspirators in the 48 hours or so between the time he was arrested and his murder by Jack Ruby. If Oswald had revealed who his co-conspirators were, the heavens would have fallen on Castro.

And, if Cuban agents had been assisting him in the assassination plot and had been present in Dealey Plaza on November 22, 1963, where were they? Additionally, if Oswald was to be taken out of Dallas by Cuban agents, they would assuredly have prevented his arrest. Such poor planning is inconceivable for an intelligence agency considered to be one of the most proficient in the Western hemisphere.[42]

There are also problems surrounding Oswald's letter which he wrote to the Russian embassy after his return from Mexico City. The letter read in part, "I was unable to remain in Mexico City indefinitely because of my Mexican visa restrictions which was for 15 days only. I could not take a chance on applying for an extension unless I used my real name so I returned to the US...I had not planned to contact the Mexican City Embassy at all so of course they were unprepared for me. Had I been able to reach Havana as planned the Soviet Embassy there would have had time to assist me, but of course the stuip (sic) Cuban Consule (sic) was at fault here I am glad he has since been replaced by another".[43] Had Oswald been given the task by Castro's agents, of becoming 'a hero of the revolution', would he have written such a letter?

These facts are therefore troublesome for those conspiracy theorists who believe Oswald was a willing co-conspirator of Castro's agents. His fellow conspirators would have surely provided him with the most basic of needs. Similarly, if conspirators had supplied the weapons to be used in the assassination, isn't it logical they would have provided Oswald with a weapon they were certain could do the job instead of giving him a

THE CASTRO CONNECTION

weapon which was certainly able to perform well but which could not be one-hundred percent reliable? Additionally, Cuban agents would have had no way of knowing JFK's travel plans or the route the motorcade took in Dallas, which placed the president in sight of his assassin – unless they formulated the purported plot only days before the presidential campaign trip. And if Oswald was penniless, as investigations of his finances have proven, how could he possibly have embarked on trips across the United States stalking Kennedy?

The idea proposed by some conspiracy theorists that Cuban conspirators may have used Jack Ruby to eliminate Oswald is also seriously flawed. Oswald was scheduled to be transferred from the city jail in the police station to the county jail at 10 am on Sunday, November 24th. Before the transfer of Oswald to the county jail, the alleged assassin was due a further interrogation by Captain Will Fritz and representatives of the Secret Service and FBI. Oswald's interrogation on Sunday morning lasted longer than originally planned because Postal Inspector Harry D. Holmes arrived. The arrival of Holmes delayed the transfer of Oswald because, unexpectedly, Fritz then turned to Holmes and asked whether he wanted to interrogate Oswald. Holmes accepted. It was for this reason the interrogation continued for another half hour or so. Ruby shot Oswald approximately four minutes after Ruby left the Western Union office. If Inspector Holmes had continued on to church with his wife that morning, as he had intended, the length of interrogation would have been shortened and Jack Ruby would never have had the opportunity to kill Oswald.

However, ex-FBI agent James P. Hosty (*Assignment: Oswald*, 1996) and former counsel to the Warren Commission David Belin (*Final Disclosure*, 1988) recognized the strong possibility that Oswald had been encouraged by these Cuban intelligence agents in Mexico City. David Belin wrote, "Were it not for Oswald's lies about his trip to Mexico, I would state unequivocally that there was no conspiratorial complicity between Oswald and anyone else. I would suggest that the actions of Oswald were those of a loner and that he was not conspiratorially involved with any pro-Castro agents in Mexico."[44] James Hosty believed Oswald definitely killed President Kennedy. "...The only issue left unresolved in my mind" Hosty wrote, "is whether the Soviets or Cubans were in any way involved in the assassination. This involvement could range from active involvement to tacit encouragement."[45] Oswald had been sighted in Mexico City not only with Russian embassy personnel, including a KGB agent, but with Cuban embassy staff and other pro-Castro individuals. Law Student Oscar Contreras, for example, saw Oswald with communists at Mexico City's National University.[46] There is a wealth of credible and corroborated evidence to also suggest Oswald had met with Cuban agents in the city, specifically Alfredo Mirabel, Manuel Vega Perez and Rogelio Rodriguez Lopez, the three senior Cuban agents in Mexico (There were rumors that DGI head Fabian Escalante had contact with Oswald but that has yet to be proved). Oswald may have been encouraged by them. There is no doubt that Cuban agents had some kind of interest in Oswald. Castro may have been told Oswald's provocative statements in the Cuban embassy were the ravings of a lunatic and because of the adversarial relationship between the U.S. and Cuba, the Cuban leader did not pass on the information to the American government. Whilst this is morally reprehensible, it does not make Castro culpable of planning an assassination.

There is additional evidence that while Oswald was in Mexico City he attended a "twist party" accompanied by two American 'beatniks'. Oswald had purportedly been invited by Silvia Duran, the Mexican national and committed communist, who worked as a Cuban consulate receptionist and spoke with Oswald about his visa application. The party was attended by Cuban diplomats and spies. Another attendee, Elena Garro, said Oswald was at the party. Duran denies it was Oswald. Duran also denied she had an affair with Oswald. "...That's why I get so mad when I read all this (her affairs)...I only saw him (Oswald) inside the consulate. I never saw him outside the consulate – never, never, never." Others insist, however, like Duran's friend, Lidia Duran Navarro, Duran had a 'date' with Oswald, but the idea she would have had an affair with him was 'absurd'. "She should not have accepted an invitation coming from an American," Lidia said. She added that diplomats at the Cuban Embassy were 'furious' when they found out and 'scolded' Duran.[47]

Whilst this evidence does not necessarily prove or disprove Oswald was hired by Russia or Cuba, it is tantalizing in that it suggests that Oswald may have offered to kill Kennedy as a way of proving his worth to them, but the Soviets and Cubans adopted a 'wait-and-see' attitude. Anthony Summers concurs. Summers believes, ".... the Cubans had no real expectation that Oswald could or would do what he bragged he could do, that whatever mild encouragement they'd given him was more in the form of 'Go for it, if you want' and that their sin, maybe, was not to have said 'No, please don't do that' and to have warned the Americans what he might get up to. This would have been a bit much to ask given that they knew the US was trying repeatedly to kill their guy."[48]

There is, however, one singular argument against the idea that Castro plotted to kill Kennedy. It is the fact that JFK would be replaced by a purportedly right-wing Texan by the name of Lyndon Johnson. The FBI's most important secret agents of the Cold War, Morris and Jack Childs, both members of the Communist Party of the United States, knew the USSR politburo intimately. They told their FBI handlers the Soviet hierarchy considered Johnson to be 'a reactionary'.[49] And if the Soviets held this opinion of Vice President Johnson, Castro would assuredly have agreed. As Richard Helms, Deputy CIA Director, recognized, Johnson and his new administration may have been forced to bomb Cuba 'back into the middle ages' if Soviet or Cuban complicity in the assassination had been discovered.[50]

Until the Cuban government archives are opened up for examination and corroborative proof is found, the idea that Castro inspired Oswald to shoot Kennedy and the assassin was aided in some way by the Cuban leader's intelligence agents must remain essentially speculative in nature.

THE CASTRO CONNECTION

However, the theory that Castro's agents inspired Oswald to go ahead with his already formed plans of assassination remains compelling. Oswald read about Castro's threat to retaliate against CIA attempts to kill the Cuban leader and Cuban agents in Mexico City provoked Oswald by telling him about CIA efforts to murder his hero. Agents could also have told Oswald his assassination plans were 'heroic'. Oswald in turn saw this as an opportune moment to fulfill his revolutionary fantasies by taking unilateral action. The *New Orleans Times – Picayune* article featuring Castro's threat to 'American leaders' was prominently displayed on a day when Oswald was in the city and Oswald was an avid reader of newspapers. A clue to Oswald's thinking can be found in a statement he made to Michael Paine, "You can read between the lines", Oswald said, "and see what they want you to do."[51] No doubt Oswald was also listening in to Radio Havana on his short wave radio and hearing stories of how the American government was trying to topple Castro.

It was also common knowledge in New Orleans – certainly amongst anti-Castro groups – that Castro was a target for elimination. In his deluded state, Oswald may have thought that killing Kennedy was one way to win Castro's appreciation. It is unlikely that Oswald's purported meeting with Castro's Mexico City agents could have resulted in any type of planning for Kennedy's assassination. The agents had no idea where Kennedy would be in the foreseeable future. But the Cuban agents may have implanted in Oswald's mind the idea that he could prove his worth to the revolution by assassinating his hero's nemesis.

343

BEYOND REASONABLE DOUBT

CHAPTER TWELVE

THE JFK ASSASSINATION LEGACY

> "They blamed the assassination not on Oswald the communist but on the American people, and the radical right in particular, accusing them of killing Kennedy for his being too soft in the cold war or too accommodating to civil rights for American blacks".
>
> — Daniel Pipes
>
> "Historical lies are nearly impossible to correct once movies and television have given them credibility...the children of the video age will swallow [Oliver Stone's movie] 'JFK' whole."
>
> — Brent Staples, New York Times
>
> "To suggest that Oswald was a patsy at best or didn't act alone – just as Oliver Stone in his controversial biopic JFK and countless other movie and TV dramas have done – is to continue the myth, like believing in Santa Claus."
>
> — Peter Landesman, Film Director, Parkland
>
> "Once Oswald's mouth had been shut, everyone else's was free to open."
>
> — Christopher Hitchens

The Warren Commission Report was severely flawed because government agencies, who attempted to cover their backs, stonewalled when Commission lawyers requested important information for their investigation. It led to the flourishing of conspiracy theories and denied the American people any real kind of closure.

However, the Commission came to the correct conclusions but for the wrong reasons. The Warren Commission investigation and subsequent government investigations found no evidence that could establish Oswald's innocence or any evidence that indicated a conspiracy to assassinate the President. As this book has attempted to demonstrate, not a 'scintilla' of evidence has been found which would call into question Lee Harvey Oswald's guilt, beyond all reasonable doubt. Nor has any evidence surfaced which would conclusively confirm Oswald had acted with others in the commission of his crime. The only possible connection Oswald may have had with others with regard to the assassination remains the remote possibility that he was encouraged to kill Kennedy by Castro's intelligence agents.

Unfortunately, as there has been plenty of room to maneuver when criticizing the JFK assassination investigations, ideas about 'hidden agendas' flourished. The 'wilderness of mirrors' that the controversial evidence in the JFK case created has entered the culture. From JFK to RFK to Martin Luther King, the idea that hidden powers in the United States would do anything to maintain control has partially succeeded. A hidden right wing hand eliminated popular progressive politicians in the United States and the government is hiding the facts from the American people. However, in reality, skepticism about the official assassination story is a leftist obsession that wishes away the painful truth of Lee Harvey Oswald's political motives.[1]

These insidious ideas have become increasingly widespread with the advent of the Internet. They are permeating and affecting our political discourse. And they began with that tragic day in Dallas.

Although conspiracies – imagined or otherwise – have always been part of American culture, they were previously propagated by the fringe press. Today, complex conspiracy themes are the staple diet of the mainstream media. Stories about 9/11 conspiracies, the Robert Kennedy assassination and the Martin Luther King assassination appear regularly on mainstream television media.

From the 1980s to the present day, the JFK conspiracy debate has been controlled by the left, but it took flight in the 1960s when anti-Americanism merged with left-wing academia. President Kennedy's death was the result of clandestine groups or agencies which had a natural right-wing bias – the CIA, the Pentagon, right-wing Texas oilmen-leftists allege. While the Soviet Union and Castro's Cuba were busy subverting democracies in Latin America, conspiracy theorists in the United States began to look inward to the subversion of democratic institutions by faceless and powerful groups dedicated to the advancement of American corporations and the "military-industrial complex" that President Eisenhower spoke of. These efforts by conspiracy theorists on the left are essentially politically motivated, designed to promote the idea that America is essentially a fascist state with a hidden history.

The idea that government agencies were responsible for the Kennedy assassination are accepted by a large body of the American public, even though books by authors like Vincent Bugliosi, John McAdams, Patricia Lambert, and many others have revealed how ridiculous most of these conspiracy theories are. Their books have revealed how conspiracy advocates, fuelled by a public hooked on conspiracy theories, have continually abused the evidence in the case, misrepresented the facts through selective use of witnesses, offered crude scientific opinion about the physical evidence, and accused government officials of involvement in the assassination without any concrete proof whatsoever.

Conspiracy advocates have also promoted the right wing JFK conspiracy myth by adopting changing tactics in their desire to keep the issue alive. When named conspirators were discovered to have been innocent, or no evidence could be provided to support various allegations, conspiracy theorists simply changed tack and alleged the CIA killed the President and engaged vast legions of workers to cover up the conspiracy. These circumstances led Professor Jacob Cohen to criticize: "the platoons of conspiracists (who) concertedly scavenged the record, floating their appalling and thrilling 'might-have-beens,' unfazed by the contradictions and absurdities in their own wantonly selective accounts, often consciously, cunningly deceitful."[2]

Outside of the mistakes made by government-investigating agencies, it is the conspiracy theorists on the left who have distorted the history of the JFK assassination. They put forward good points and bad alike; mingle discredited testimony with valid evidence and make up for weak links in their hypotheses by making false accusations and unlimited calumny against innocent people. They offer no connected account of what they think occurred and content themselves with issuing a barrage of rhetorical questions and innuendo. And, in the majority of cases, conspiracy theories are too often like the Hydra – cut off one of its heads and a score of others take its place.

The American left was primed from the start. In the 1960s, the country was awash with anti-war and anti-government sentiment and the media had been inundated with speculation about the JFK assassination. Given the mindset of the public during this period, it was inevitable Americans would link the RFK and MLK assassinations to suspicions about the JFK murder. As time passed, these concerns grew into a popular view that not everything had been explained by the government.

During the past five decades, American citizens have been inundated with a constant stream of books, television documentaries, and op-ed newspaper accounts which seemed to suggest that the assassinations of JFK, RFK, and MLK had hidden histories; histories that would reveal secret agendas and powerful government dark forces that controlled American society. When logical answers were provided to explain some of the anomalies that existed in the assassinations and murders, conspiracy advocates fanned the flames by finding patterns and connections where none existed or connected some parts of the story to speculation about hidden plotters and sinister forces who tried to hide the truth.

Conspiracy advocates, however, have never been able to address many logical aspects of the crimes which decisively rebut their conspiracy theories. For example, how could the alleged conspiracies to murder American leaders, which would necessarily need to involve hundreds if not thousands of people, remain a secret in an age when "whistle-blowers" have succeeded in everything from revealing corruption in government to publicizing private information about Presidents that led to their impeachment?

Although assassination theories that were promoted in the 1960s found a large audience, it was the post-Watergate American public which became intensely susceptible to conspiracy arguments. A skeptical public looked back to the 1960s and wondered if the corruption they saw in the Nixon Presidency did not begin earlier, and those organs of their government may have eliminated a democratically-elected President. A new search for answers to questions raised by conspiracists began and the public was primed to look for answers.

However, because of the chaos and turmoil which followed each assassination or assassination attempt, it has always been extremely difficult to reconstruct the event in order to make sense of what happened. The assassinations were also criminal acts involving famous people, therefore the cases demanded the closest scrutiny by investigative bodies. The amount of evidence in these cases was therefore voluminous. A less than perfect explanation for the crimes was inevitable. As a result, the conspiracy-minded were always able to uncover one discrepancy after another from the thousands of pages of documented evidence. Thousands of people followed the cases and were able, through their collective consciousness, to select many pieces of the murder case puzzles to construct numerous arguments rebutting the official conclusions. As William Buckley wrote, "If O.J. (Simpson) was found not guilty, why can't everybody be found not guilty?"[3]

The American public also came to believe that conspiracy theories were far more coherent than reality because they leave no room for mistakes, ambiguities, and failures which are a prevalent feature in any human system. Allard Lowenstein echoed these sentiments when he said, "Robert Kennedy's death, like the President's (JFK), was mourned as an extension of the evils of senseless violence...a whimsical fate inconveniently interfering in the workings of democracy. What is odd is not that some people thought it was all random, but that so many intelligent people refused to believe that it might be anything else. Nothing can measure more graphically how limited was the general understanding of what is possible in America."[4]

Some answers about the political assassinations of the 1960s were never found, many mistakes were made by investigators, and there were unrealistic expectations that the public would be presented with 'perfect' criminal cases with orderly, pristine, and conclusive evidence. For example, in the chaos of those crucial moments, many JFK assassination, Martin Luther King assassination, and Robert F. Kennedy assassination eyewitnesses gave conflicting stories as to what occurred during the shootings. The Dallas Police were less than competent in not only securing the physical evidence in the case but also in providing sufficient protection for Lee Harvey Oswald. The area around the MLK murder scene was not secured by Memphis Police in the moments after the shooting. The LAPD did not secure the crime scene very well in the RFK case.

However, instead of concluding that all bureaucracies are fraught with imperfect methods, conspiracy advocates pointed the finger of suspicion at unknown 'conspirators' and accused the LAPD, the Dallas Police, the Memphis Police, the FBI and the CIA of deliberate cover-ups.

Reconstructing the JFK, RFK, and MLK assassinations was like fitting jigsaw pieces together. Some fell into place immediately whilst others did not fit quite exactly. There were bad joints here and there in much the same way that eyewitnesses have faulty memories. Human beings are programmed to see patterns and conspiracies and this tendency increases when we see danger. The notion goes back to primitive man, who learned to spot danger signs in a bush and thus became programmed to avoid dangerous animals. It was not unusual for 'witnesses' to see 'second shooters' in Dealey Plaza, the area around the Lorraine Motel, and the pantry of the Ambassador Hotel. In the chaos and confusion that resulted when Oswald, Sirhan, and Ray fired their weapons, some observers reacted by trying to impose some sense of order. It was like a shooter firing his pistol and then drawing a target around the bullet hole. We give it meaning because it does mean something – but only to us.

It would therefore be surprising had no witnesses come forward to relate the existence of 'second shooters'. If a stream of bullets were ricocheting off Elm Street and bouncing off ceiling tiles in the Ambassador pantry – if the echoes of the shots were reverberating throughout – it would have been a natural inclination, in the periods following the shootings and before the shock of the events had worn off, to believe more than one gunman had been present at each event. In the cases of JFK, RFK, and MLK, the only 'credible' witnesses to 'second shooters' were later discovered to be not credible at all, but only after researchers spent years investigating their claims.

The truths about 'eyewitness' testimony in the midst of chaos and turmoil was first recognized by the United States Army. Many of their reports about battles, based on combat experienced veterans, have shown that it is extraordinarily difficult to make sense out of a battle until the following day, when soldiers have had a chance to experience a good night's sleep. Information from 'shell-shocked' soldiers immediately after combat, the Army discovered, was notoriously poor. Following an intensely traumatic event, the information may still be in the brain but it has not been processed in such a manner that it can be retrieved. Many 'witnesses' in the JFK, RFK, and MLK murders who gave reports about the shooting immediately after the event, later formulated better 'pictures' of what occurred in subsequent interviews.

Other witnesses discovered their memories of events connected with the assassinations were not as reliable as they initially thought. Some came forward to give detailed information about Sirhan Sirhan's activities in the weeks and months preceding the RFK assassination and of how Sirhan had been accompanied by unidentified accomplices. Some witnesses, like gun salesman Larry Arnot, were eventually given polygraph tests which showed their stories were suspect and not believable. Arnot failed his test and admitted he could not remember selling Sirhan bullets at a time the young Arab visited the gun shop where he worked. Arnot eventually realized he had confused the Sirhan sale with another sale after the gun shop owner's wife mentioned to him that Sirhan had been in the shop with others. Mrs. Herrick, too, withdrew her story after she said she could not be sure. Mrs. Herrick's polygraph test revealed she could not honestly remember the alleged incident.

Similarly, MLK conspiracy author William Pepper believed in the conspiracy claims made by Memphis restaurant owner Loyd Jowers, even after several of Jowers' relatives and friends came forward to tell the Memphis District Attorney that Jowers had been lying and had invented his stories to 'make some money'.[5]

William Pepper became the 'Mark Lane' of the Martin Luther King assassination and in later years the leading advocate for Sirhan Sirhan's alleged innocence. Like Lane, Pepper has willfully distorted the evidence in both the RFK and Martin Luther King assassination cases and has persuaded many Americans that both leaders were eliminated by the American government because of their progressive policies. Despite overwhelming evidence to the contrary, Pepper has managed to persuade many liberal-biased US media outlets that both James Earl Ray and Sirhan Sirhan were innocent and he continues to shamelessly point the finger of guilt at innocent people.

For example, Pepper accused an innocent man of involvement in the Martin Luther King assassination. The lawyer had accepted uncorroborated allegations from many sources for his conspiracy books, but his worst mistake was to name a former soldier as one of the alleged King assassination back-up team without verifying if the facts were true. As Pepper told it, the commando of the sniper team, Billy Ray Eidson, was then killed off to keep the plot secret. However, Eidson was found to be alive and well and furious at the allegations that he was involved in the assassination. He was supported by General William Yarborough, the father of the Green Berets and his chief aide, Rudi Gresham. Members of the 'team' were invited to meet Pepper during the filming of an ABC television documentary. When they refused to shake Pepper's hand, the lawyer became visibly shaken. The former army personnel showed contempt for Pepper. Eidson said, "I just want to look at you."

Eidson brought a $15 million lawsuit against Pepper and his publishers and received an out of court settlement and a published retraction. Pepper's publishers, Carroll and Graf, said, "Some statements by the author about Billy Ray Eidson were not accurate. Carroll and Graf regrets that Mr. Eidson was identified as the leader of a military team of snipers assigned as back-up for the assassination of Dr. Martin Luther King. In view of the information received since publication, Carroll and Graf no longer believes that Mr. Eidson was involved in any such assassination team."[6]

Playing a highly selective 'shell game,' Pepper changed the Martin Luther King assassination scenarios to suit his purposes. Over time, his accusation of who the alleged shooter really was has changed, transferring guilt to people who have died during the course of his inquiries. He also manipulated facts to suit new realities. For example, Ray always maintained he had heard the news about the assassination from the Mustang's radio. In a Department of Justice inquiry, investigators discovered the car radio did not actually work. Therefore, Pepper, in his 2003 book, wrote, "He headed south through Mississippi to Atlanta. On the way, he heard on his car or some other radio (emphasis added) when he stopped that Dr. King had been shot and they were looking for a white man in a white Mustang."

Pepper, now working in London as a lawyer, has appeared in numerous television documentaries and news programs yet not one journalist has challenged him to explain the suspicious nature of his past life in the United States. According to Gerald Posner, "....Pepper had moved to England in 1980, claiming in *Orders To Kill* that he was forced to move because the mafia in New England had made him a 'marked man' after he led a successful effort at reorganizing a school system 'rife with corruption'. Actually, a company of which Pepper was the president had received more than $200,000 from the state of Rhode Island to run a foster-care program for troubled youths. On July 6, 1978, Pepper was charged with four felony counts of transporting two teenage boys 'to engage in lewd and indecent activities.' The local police also learned that in 1969 a US Senate subcommittee heard statements from two young boys who said Pepper had sexual contact with them when they were eight. No charges were filed against him then. Shortly after his arrest a state audit charged that more than half of the money given to

Pepper's firm could not be accounted for. His legal problems worsened when a real estate company sued him civilly, claiming he had reneged on a deal to sell his $350,000 Westchester, New York, home. Eventually the felony morals charges were dropped to misdemeanor charges. He left for England, and finally in 1990 the morals charges were dismissed for lack of prosecution. Pepper denied the charges and claimed that his legal problems were part of a conspiracy to punish him for his anti-Vietnam stance in the late 1960's and his friendship with King."[7] Pepper never challenged these allegations in his 2003 book, *An Act Of State,* in which he blamed the American government for King's death.

As visiting scholar at the American Academy of Arts & Sciences, David Greenburg, wrote, "Despite multiple debunking, these (conspiracy) fantasies endure...a crackpot named William F. Pepper has convinced King's entire family that the U.S. Government, including President Lyndon Johnson, was responsible for his death...Conspiracists adopt the trappings of scholarship, touting irrelevant titles and credentials. They burrow into the arcana of their topics and inundate potential acolytes with a barrage of pedantic detail. Rather than build a case from evidence, conspiracists deny the available evidence, maintaining that appearances deceive. Rather than admit to inconvenient facts, they dismiss them as lies, making their own theories irrefutable."[8]

Conspiracy theorists like Pepper have seized upon numerous anomalies in the investigative reports of the JFK, RFK, and King assassinations – they expected all the pieces would fit together exactly, witnesses would give truthful stories, and all the evidence collected without any mistakes having been made. Above all, investigations into political assassinations which go beyond the brief of a simple murder require informed judgments about the way police departments and American government investigative agencies work and also the ability to comprehend complex reports about ballistics, forensic pathology, and crime scenes. But the public cannot form such judgments. They can glimpse only fragments of the covert picture – and since the world of conspiracy is essentially one of duplicity, carefully selecting evidence, and relying on the testimonies of known liars and conmen, they have no way of knowing who is telling the truth or who or what to believe. Furthermore, how can the government 'disprove' the FBI and the CIA had been involved in the JFK, MLK, and RFK assassinations when the public did not believe any claims the agencies made? The outcome has been a lethal open season of claim and counter-claim, in which partial out-of-context or otherwise misleadingly presented portions of 'facts' have been put before a bemused public which is in no position to judge their veracity. Thus a majority of the American public are led into believing there had been conspiratorial involvement in the three assassinations.

In this alternatively constructed world, conspiracy advocates claim they are the only people who can be judged to be reliable sources – 'lone assassin' proponents, they allege, are 'tools' of the government. But as the conspiracists probe deeper into the complexities of the cases, they also connect together pieces of the puzzle that don't necessarily need to fit or are the result of mere chance. Conspiracy advocates also fail to apply logical and rational answers to many of their conclusions about what really happened. Because the LAPD had made a number of mistakes in the collection and handling of the physical evidence in the RFK shooting and had difficulties in reconstructing the crime (due to the chaotic circumstances of the shooting), it was automatically assumed there were sinister reasons for the anomalies in the collection of the physical evidence – someone had been 'covering up'. But, as Police Chief Daryl Gates reasoned, conspiracy advocates seek the least plausible explanation. As Gates reasoned, "In my mind, only one question remains unanswered...That is, how could you possibly get the police, the FBI, the Secret Service, prosecutors, courts and special commissions ALL to engage in this cover-up conspiracy?"[9]

The way the LAPD had mishandled particular pieces of evidence was not at all unusual. Expert forensic scientist Michael Baden insisted it was simply because people wanted to collect memorabilia. As Baden explained, "Memorabilia of the famous have a way of vanishing into doctors' private collections. This is what happened to Einstein's brain. In the 1950s, Martin Luther King was treated at Harlem Hospital for a stab wound in the chest. In 1978, when we tried to get his medical records and X-rays for the House Assassinations Committee (HSCA), they were missing. The administrator had put them in a safe, but somehow they had disappeared . . . [Missing evidence]...happens all the time; people take X-rays, brain tissue, microscopic slides – almost anything – as collectibles."[10]

JFK, RFK, and MLK conspiracy advocates began with the premise that conspirators would organize the assassinations in a certain way. Yet the most basic examination of their 'assassination scenarios' can only leave the reader with the conclusion that the purported 'conspiracy plans' were altogether ridiculous. For example, why would sophisticated conspirators have allowed a 'hypnotized Sirhan' to outspokenly utter contempt for Robert Kennedy when the young Palestinian visited the Ambassador Hotel on June 2nd and June 4th, 1968? If they had the resources to hypnotize Sirhan to murder, then they would surely have been able to make sure the assassin did not act in a way which would bring attention to himself. Behaving in this way is not the modus operandi for conspirators needing to act 'secretively'. Had Ambassador Hotel witnesses Cordero and Rabago, amongst others, told police about Sirhan's hatred for Kennedy, Sirhan would likely have been detained and searched, thus putting the conspiracy in jeopardy.[11]

Furthermore, it would be entirely irrational had conspirators risked their enterprise by enlisting a 'patsy' who owned an illegal weapon and who could have been arrested at any time in the weeks leading up to the shooting. Had Sirhan been challenged at the police shooting range he visited on the day of the assassination and asked to show documentation for the weapon, the whole conspiracy would have collapsed. And, of course, conspirators could never have been certain they would have been able to avoid being photographed by the dozens of television reporters and photo-journalists. Although photographers failed to catch Sirhan on film firing his gun, the possibility of capturing a second assassin on film would always have been a problem.

In the case of James Earl Ray and the assassination of Dr. Martin Luther King Jr. in April 1968, it would have been simply too risky to employ an escaped convict to commit the murder of a famous public figure which would decisively bring all leading law enforcement agencies into play. And, as FBI, DEA and AFT agents, and local police departments know too well – in the 1960s hired killers with no direct links to any criminal or extremist group could be bought for as little as $3000. Furthermore, if Ray had indeed been aided by co-conspirators, they would have spirited him away and placed him in hiding as soon as the murder had been carried out. They would not have allowed him to be exposed so many times during his months on the run. Conspirators would not have put themselves in jeopardy by allowing Ray the opportunity to identify fellow conspirators. And, if Ray had been an unwilling patsy, conspirators could not have been certain that Ray would flee the scene of the crime. Under these circumstances, had Ray stayed put, the whole conspiracy would have collapsed. Additionally, Ray lived until he was 70 years old – why would co-conspirators have allowed that if they knew he could 'spill the beans'?

These were no sophisticated murders, as conspiracy advocates maintain. JFK was riding in an open limousine and his motorcade route had been well-publicized. King was an easy target for any killer bent on eliminating the Civil Rights leader, and so was RFK. King and Bobby Kennedy did not have armed bodyguards; they frequently walked in the midst of crowds; and their travel arrangements were well known in advance.

Conspiracy advocates also expose themselves to central weaknesses in their 'scenarios'. Why would the government, for example, employ so many people in the conspiracies when the risk of 'leakage' would have been so much greater. Had President Johnson wanted to eliminate King, all that was required was for him to request the CIA Director to arrange a 'contract' and that would have been the end of it. The government could also have destroyed King by simply arranging for all the 'scandal-filled' surveillance tapes of the Civil Rights leader to be released and then 'hire' a journalist to publicize them. This would not have been all that unusual. In the 1960s, the CIA enlisted the assistance of journalists and student groups to promote the government's policies.

In the case of RFK, his elimination by the CIA did not require an elaborate plot involving hypnotized assassins and the corruption of the LAPD and FBI. At any point in such a sophisticated conspiracy, a government 'insider' could have given the game away. Such a purported government agent would have been endowed with far more credibility than the fantasists quoted by conspiracy writers.

Conspiracy theorists did not simply use non-linear logic to argue their theses. They also cleverly misinterpreted statements made by witnesses in order to create an aura of suspicion. Lisa Pease, for example, quoted Ambassador Hotel witness Rosey Grier – "Well, first of all, we were up on the stage, and they said they was

[sic] going off to the right of the stage, and at the last minute...Bill Barry decided to change and go a different direction."[12] However, Wayne Rogers, Fred Dutton, and Bill Barry, close aides or friends of the Kennedy family, organized the change in RFK's route through the hotel. It is preposterous to claim they had a hand in the alleged 'conspiracy'.

As the decades passed, conspiracy advocates began to insist that Lee Harvey Oswald, Sirhan Sirhan, and James Earl Ray had not fired any of the fatal shots at all. To 'prove' their claims they managed to bring doubt on the numerous pieces of circumstantial evidence which pointed the finger of guilt at the true assassins.

For example, conspiracy writers have attempted to 'prove' James Earl Ray was innocent of killing Martin Luther King by enlisting bogus 'experts' to cast doubt on the provenance of the assassin's rifle. They also invented scenarios in which Ray had been led step by step into the 'conspiracy' unaware he was being used as a 'patsy'. Yet the evidence proving his guilt is overwhelming. Every decision and every action taken by James Earl Ray in the year leading up to the assassination was taken by Ray. No credible evidence exists that would indicate he was used as a 'patsy' or was instructed to participate in the crime. Ray researched the rifle, the ammunition, and the telescopic sight. Ray bought the Mustang, had it serviced, rented the rooms on his journeys, made his own telephone calls, bought his own clothes and had them laundered. Ray was identified as the person who rented Room 5b of the South Main Street rooming house and he was also identified as the lodger who left the rooming house following the shooting. Ray's fingerprints proved that he owned the bundle that was dropped in the doorway of Canipe's Amusement store shortly after the shooting. The bundle contained the rifle used to shoot King. Ray had expressed hatred for African-Americans; he was responsible for robberies before and following the assassination and he also applied for his false passport, picked up his passport photographs and collected his travel documents. Incontrovertible and overwhelming evidence exists to prove these facts.

The evidence for James Earl Ray's guilt is clear. He was an avowed racist who expressed his opinions on racial matters numerous times in the years preceding the assassination. His selection of lawyers underscored the racial motive for the crime. He told fellow inmates he was looking for the 'big score', aware that his burglaries, bank robberies, and petty crimes had amounted to little. During his time spent in the Missouri State Penitentiary, Ray had associated with known racist groups, was known to harbor ideas about a 'bounty' on King's head, and evidently believed he could beat any murder case brought against him if he could kill King in the Deep South.

However, the assassin fed the public his own conspiracy line, taking every opportunity to build a smokescreen which allowed critics of the government to speculate that the case against Ray was flimsy. Mistakes in the investigation, particularly the rushed autopsy by Dr. Jerry Francisco, and the FBI's failure to pursue many leads promoted the idea that the government may have had a hand in King's death. Critics pounced, using mistakes in the investigation to spin tales of an elaborate plot involving the police, the military, the FBI, the Mafia, and the CIA. However, the Memphis Police Department and the FBI made fewer mistakes in the King case than in a typical murder case. In most criminal investigations, even routine techniques like dusting for fingerprints are frequently overlooked. Moreover, there are very real limits regarding the extent of full investigation and forensics and ballistics testing that can be performed in a case. If the American public demanded 100% certitude in order to convict, very few cases would ever come to trial.

Conspiracy advocates similarly claim that anomalies in the RFK murder investigation pointed to Sirhan having been used as a 'patsy'; he was set up to take the blame for the murder of Senator Kennedy. Conspiracists allege Sirhan had fired blanks and the real killer, security guard Thane Eugene Cesar, who had been standing behind RFK, fired the fatal bullet. However, their thesis is logically flawed. Why would conspirators have Sirhan firing blanks when they could have done a more thorough job by allowing him to fire real bullets? If there had been a conspiracy to kill Robert Kennedy, the conspirators would have wanted to draw as little suspicion to themselves as possible. To that end, having multiple assassins in a crowded room, along with a visible assassin who was shooting blanks, would simply increase the chances that someone would suspect sinister forces at work. And how would the 'team of assassins have had foreknowledge of RFK's route to the Colonial Room? Conspiracy advocates can only fall back on the theory that either someone in Kennedy's retinue had planned the route with the conspirators or multiple teams of assassins had been stationed at various vantage points in the hotel.

In order for the conspiracy writers to make their 'patsy' arguments plausible, they had to rid Sirhan of a motive for the crime. Philosophers reason that any belief can be argued if enough assumptions are present and pertinent facts are forgotten. This is the modus operandi of conspiracy promoters who argued that Sirhan had no motive for killing Robert F. Kennedy. Philip Melanson's and William Klaber's assassination research is typical of how this can be easily accomplished. To prove the assassin did not have a political motive, they selected portions of testimony and evidence from police files and ignored statements made by the many people who knew Sirhan throughout his life. According to Melanson and Klaber, Sirhan had said he heard on the radio that Kennedy had promised to send jet bombers to Israel, "... but (RFK's) statements there (at the Zionist club in Beverly Hills) were anything but inflammatory. He spoke mostly about a negotiated settlement between Israel and her Arab neighbors." Klaber and Melanson imply that Sirhan did not have any political motive in killing Kennedy, as the Senator spoke mostly of peace and only mentioned arms aid in the context of a Soviet build-up in the Middle East. This was important because conspiracy advocates needed to show that a motiveless Sirhan was more likely to have been a pawn in the hands of others. Yet there is a wealth of evidence to show that Sirhan, from a young age, had been fascinated with radical Arab nationalism, left-wing politics, and assassination.[13]

There was always inevitability in the linking of the assassinations to alleged 'conspirators'. America is obsessed with conspiracy theories and a large proportion of the population believes there are conspiratorial answers to everything. This has occurred because there is a general psychological tendency for people to think that a major or significant event must have been caused by something similarly major, significant, or powerful. As historian Henry Steele Commager observed in the late 1960s, "There has come in recent years something that might be called a conspiracy psychology: a feeling that great events can't be explained by ordinary processes... We are on the road to a paranoid explanation of things... The conspiracy theory, the conspiracy mentality, will not accept ordinary evidence...there's some psychological requirement that forces them to reject the ordinary and find refuge in the extraordinary."[14]

An article in the *American Journal of Psychology* explains this phenomena as, "Humans naturally respond[ing] to events or situations which have had an emotional impact upon them by trying to make sense of those events, typically in values-laden spiritual, moral or political terms, though occasionally in scientific terms. Events which resist such interpretation—for example, because they are, in fact, senseless—can provoke the inquirer to have recourse to ever more extreme speculations, until one is reached that is capable of offering the inquirer the required emotional satisfaction. Once cognized, confirmation bias and avoidance of cognitive dissonance may reinforce the belief. In a context where conspiracy theory has become popular within a social group, communal reinforcement may equally play a part. And as sociological historian Holger Herwig found in studying German explanations of World War I: 'Those events that are most important are hardest to understand, because they attract the greatest attention from mythmakers and charlatans'." Dr. Patrick Leman of the Royal Holloway University of London also conducted research into the phenomenon. Leman said that conspiracy theories flower because people feel distanced from institutions of power, so are more likely to distrust official accounts. Furthermore, he observed, the rise of the Internet allows new theories to spread quickly and widely.[15]

The idea that the American Government covered up the truth about the three assassinations has gained powerful political currency in the United States. Conspiracy theories have been given respectability by the electronic and print media and the most powerful arbiter of cultural consensus – Hollywood. The level of debate is not enhanced when Hollywood celebrities, many of whom do not know their way around the vast volumes of evidence, side with the conspiracy theorists. In 2010, film director Oliver Stone, whose 1991 movie *JFK* convinced millions of people that a conspiracy was responsible for the death of President Kennedy, said, "To this day, many key Americans in power are in total denial about this story. They don't even want to know about the possibility that he was killed by someone other than Lee Harvey Oswald. It is a national fairy tale."[16]

Additionally, the mainstream media have skewered the truth about the assassinations of JFK, RFK, and Martin

Luther King by willingly allowing conspiracists to pedal their conspiracy theories. Not so long ago, the mainstream media dismissed far-fetched tales of conspiracy and marginalized conspiracy theorists to the outer reaches of news-land. News organizations knew that every now and then bogus 'witnesses' would appear claiming to reveal low skullduggery in high places. Their stories nearly always lacked substance and corroborative proof and were rightly dismissed. Now, major news organizations appear to be leading the charge. In 2003, the History Channel broadcast a documentary film, "The Guilty Men", in which lawyer Barr McClellan repeated allegations he first made in his book Blood, Money & Power that LBJ was behind Kennedy's murder. It precipitated a flood of protests from American citizens including Presidents Ford and Carter. Ford called McClellan's charges, "...the most damaging accusations ever made against a former vice president and president in American history." In 2004, the History Channel issued an apology and said McClellan's allegations were "entirely unfounded". In response, President Ford said the allegations were "...despicable...trash" and that "...a reputable media organization, which the public trusts to give accurate and unbiased information (was) swept into this frenzy. Who or what is next?...America needs to get a grip on this hysteria."[17]

On November 6, 2006, "Newsnight," the BBC's flagship news program, broadcast a 12-minute segment about a forthcoming "documentary" on the assassination, written by Shane O'Sullivan, an Irish screenwriter. Though not previously known for his investigative prowess or non-fiction writing, O'Sullivan claimed to have uncovered new video and photographic evidence that proved "three senior CIA operatives were behind the [RFK] killing." In the BBC segment, and a companion article published in The Guardian on the same day, O'Sullivan even named names: David Sanchez Morales, Gordon Campbell, and George Joannides, all three of whom were involved in anti-Castro activities out of the CIA's station in Miami in the early '60s.[18]

There was only one problem with O'Sullivan's allegation. These CIA officers he claimed were the real sponsors of the assassination were not at the Ambassador Hotel on the night in question. And it took more than a year (following multiple emails to Newsnight by this author) for the BBC's Newsnight editors and producers to acknowledge O'Sullivan's errors.[19]

In June 2007, the Discovery Times Channel broadcast a documentary, "Conspiracy Test – The RFK Assassination", on unscientific practices to sensationalize their story of how a second gunman acted with Sirhan Sirhan to murder Senator Robert F. Kennedy. The documentary challenged the Pruszynski Tape acoustics research carried out by two teams of experts — Philip Harrison and Professor Peter French of J P French Associates in the UK and Steve Barber, Dr. Chad Zimmerman and Michael O'Dell in the US – which revealed that Sirhan Sirhan did not fire more bullets than his pistol could hold. The documentary also falsely alleged that JFK was assassinated by the CIA.[20]

On April 30, 2012, CNN published a story about claims made by an RFK assassination "witness," Nina Rhodes-Hughes. The article was co-authored by Brad Johnson and Michael Martinez. The article stated that, "...a long overlooked witness to the murder is telling her story: She heard two guns firing during the 1968 shooting and authorities altered her account of the crime." However, the CNN reporters ignored the overwhelming evidence in the case which indicated no more than eight shots were fired and there was no credible evidence to suggest a second gunman. Additionally, the reporters never questioned why a fading Hollywood starlet had waited over 40 years to tell her story.[21]

The CNN story also cited RFK assassin Sirhan Sirhan's attorney, William Pepper, who said Rhodes-Hughes, "... actually had heard a total of twelve to fourteen shots fired". Johnson and Martinez provided readers with additional statements from pro-conspiracy advocates who alleged more than thirteen shots were fired in the Ambassador Hotel pantry the night RFK was assassinated in Los Angeles. Aside from the fact that Rhodes-Hughes's story has never been "overlooked" and was examined in The Forgotten Terrorist, Johnson and Martinez further muddied the waters by claiming "at least four other people told authorities in 1968 that they heard what could have been more than eight shots".

Ear-witness testimony has never established a scenario in which thirteen shots were even possible. FBI files show all the pantry witnesses, with the exception of only a few, never heard more than eight shots and those few who guessed they heard further shots did not put the number beyond ten. The FBI files, furthermore, show that no one who had been in the pantry when Robert Kennedy was shot told the FBI or LAPD that anywhere near thirteen shots had been fired. Only one alleged pantry witness gave this number, Nina Rhodes-Hughes, but she never said this at the time she made her original statement in 1968. In 1968, she said she heard "eight distinct shots." In 1992, Rhodes told conspiracy writers that she heard from ten to fourteen shots.

Rhodes-Hughes also made the allegation that the FBI had altered her 1968 statement, but the CNN reporters never questioned why the agency would alter her statement but leave intact the statements provided by a handful of other witnesses who guessed more than eight shots had been fired.

The 'conspiracy debate' is further distorted when conspiracy writers like Mark Lane and William Pepper slander innocent people in their campaigns to propagate the myth that dark forces were responsible for the political assassinations of the 1960s. Conspiracy theorists show no sense of responsibility when they accuse various 'suspects' in their books, speeches, and Internet ranting.

William Pepper shamefacedly maligned innocent participants who had been caught up in his quest to prove a non-existent and far-fetched conspiracy organized by the U.S. government. He disgracefully pointed the finger of guilt at not only Rev. Kyles but also accused the widow of a Memphis Police Department "conspirator" of having lied about her husband's role in the conspiracy. Raul, an innocent Portuguese immigrant, had his life turned upside down by Pepper's desire to implicate him in a plot. Pepper displayed no shame in accusing each of his targets of criminal acts, perjury in the first instance and murder in the second. He also accused King assassination authors Gerold Frank and George McMillan of having sinister ties to the FBI and/or CIA, implying they conspired with the government to hide the truth or simply were duped when they investigated the King murder. He even gave credence to one of his star witnesses, Glenda Grabow, a JFK conspiracy fantasist who maligned the character of LBJ aide Jack Valenti by describing him as a pornographer. Instead of showing her the door, he enlisted her as a witness in the bogus 1999 MLK assassination trial. As Pepper's former investigator, Ken Herman, told BBC documentary makers, "Pepper is the most gullible person I have ever met in my life".[22]

Don Bohning, a retired Miami Herald Latin America Editor and author of The Castro Obsession, knew personally three victims of the "more egregious peddlers of misinformation and slander" – David Atlee Phillips, a former CIA operative, Rafael Quintero, a Cuban exile CIA recruit, and Carl Jenkins, who also worked for the CIA. After Phillips won a libel suit against a London newspaper, no mention of it was made in future claims that Phillips had been involved with Lee Harvey Oswald. Bohning investigated the claims of conspiracy theorists that both Jenkins and Quintero had also been involved in the Kennedy assassination and found them to be false. However, this also did not prevent conspiracists from continually presenting bogus allegations they were somehow culpable of aiding plotters in the death of the President.[23]

The response of African-Americans to the official government investigations of the King and Kennedy murders has been somewhat unsettling. The conspiracy idea amongst African-Americans is traceable to dynamics rather than the merits of the case against James Earl Ray. From the start, African-Americans believed that King was the victim of the white establishment. Statements by Coretta Scott King and Martin Luther King's aides fuelled this idea. The Memphis prosecutors had contacted Coretta King for her approval of the plea bargain they had worked out with Ray's lawyers, to which she agreed. However, after Ray had been sentenced to a 99-year term in prison, Coretta King released a statement calling on the government to do all it could to find anyone who may have conspired with Ray. She did not believe that Ray had acted alone.

Conspiracy ideas from the left emerged to explain why African-Americans could still not attain social and economic equality in spite of new legislation. Because the existing order did not make African-Americans truly equal with white Americans, theories flourished which sought to lay the blame on powerful forces outside the democratic/ political structure. From the idea that the United States Government must have had a hand in the deaths of black leaders like Malcolm X and Martin Luther King, theories spread that perhaps other sinister plots against African-American communities existed. African-American leaders across America began to promote these sinister ideas, including the notion that African-Americans were being used as medical guinea pigs, the U.S. government was behind the AIDS epidemic, and African-American communities were being deliberately sabotaged. Jesse Jackson, for example, endorsed the idea that the CIA had conspired to flood African-American communities with crack cocaine in order to suppress the black population. His allegations were supported by polls which stated that 60% of African-Americans believed that it was possible that crack cocaine had been deliberately introduced into their communities by the CIA.

In his 1996 testimony to the ARRB, Warren Commission Assistant Counsel David Belin sought to explain the irrational thinking behind notions of JFK conspiracies. "I want you to know," Belin said, "that for me as I speak today, the ultimate issue is not who killed President Kennedy, wounded Governor Connally, and killed Officer Tippit. I already know the answer to that, it was Lee Harvey Oswald. For me, the ultimate issue is whether there will be any change in the present course and direction of the electronic media as profit-seeking corporations and individuals if priority to misrepresentations and deceit over truth going so far as to infiltrate our school system with the virus of lies, the present course of the electronic media poses a clear and present danger for the future of democracy in America. If I leave any legacy on this earth, beyond my five wonderful children, it will not be that historians will ever remember the name of David Belin, but what I have done for more than 25 years in standing up for the truth, and defending Earl Warren might in some small way be a tiny beacon of light that will point the way to people of vision and idealism who will recognize that truth is the foundation of civilization. They will understand how important it is for Americans to understand the truth about the assassination of President John F. Kennedy. They will understand how important it is to expose the misrepresentations of assassination revisionists and the electronic downpour of deceit in movies like JFK and television programs like The Men Who Killed Kennedy. They will help resurrect the reputation of Earl Warren, who has been the victim of libel and slander...And above all, they will help restore trust and confidence in government, the mortar which builds a free society."[24]

NOTES & SOURCES

ABBREVIATIONS

- WR, Warren Report
- WC, Warren Commission
- WCT, Warren Commission testimony
- CD, Warren Commission document
- CE, Warren Commission exhibit
- H, Warren Commission hearings and exhibits (volumes 1–15 are testimony; volumes 16–26 are exhibits)
- HSCA, House Select Committee on Assassinations
- ARRB, Assassination Records Review Board

CHAPTER 1: A NATIONAL OBSESSION

1. The Mail On Sunday, Evenet, "The Day That Changed The World" by Martiyn Palmer, 17 November 2013
2. HSCA Final Report, page 3
3. Write It When I'm Gone – Remarkable Off-the-Record Conversations With Gerald R. *Ford* by Thomas M. DeFrank, 2007, page 197

4. *False Witness*, page 42

5. The Atlantic, The Kennedy Assassination, 47 years later – what do we really know? by Jefferson Morley, 22 November 2010, http://www.theatlantic.com/national/archive/2010/11/ the-kennedy-assassination-47-years-later-what-do-we-really-know/66722/)

6. *False Witness*, page 41

7. The Kennedy Assassination by John McAdams – Eyewitness Testimony, http://mcadams.posc.mu.edu/witnesses.htm)

8. The Kennedy Assassination by John McAdams, Beverly Oliver: Babushka Babe? Or Bamboozling the Buffs?, http://mcadams.posc.mu.edu/oliver. htm

9. Implausible Assertions – Did Mark Lane Convince a Jury that E. Howard Hunt was a Kennedy Assassination Conspirator? by John McAdams, Ed Dolan, and Jean Davison, http://mcadams.posc. mu.edu/denial.htm

10. The Kennedy Assassination by John McAdams, Nowhere Man: The Strange Story of Gordon Arnold by Dave Reitzes, http://mcadams.posc.mu.edu/ arnold1.htm

11. *A Cruel And Shocking Act* by Philip Shenon, page 415

12. *A Cruel And Shocking Act*, page 427

13. New York Review of Books, JFK's Assassination, Norman Mailer, Jefferson Morley, G. Robert Blakey, Gerald Posner, and Anthony Summers, et al., 18 December 2003

14. Washington Decoded, McCone's Telcon Gaffe by David M. Barrett & Max Holland, http://www.washingtondecoded.com/site/2012/08/mccone.html#more

15. Associated Press Poll: Belief In JFK Conspiracy Slipping Slightly, May 9, 2013, http://www.mauiweekly.com/page/content.detail/id/314664/ Poll—Belief-in-JFK-conspiracy-slipping-slightly-. html?isap=1&nav=5045

CHAPTER 2: GOVERNMENT INVESTIGATIONS

1. Warren Report, 42

2. *Secret Service Chief* by U.E. Baughman, 11-12

3. Baughman, 11-12

4. *Los Angeles Times*, JFK Foresaw His Death, Note Suggests, July 24, 1998 http://articles.latimes.com/1998/jul/24/news/mn-6811

5. *Live By The Sword* by Gus Russo, 277

6. Warren Commission Report, 48

7. *In Search Of History*, Theodore H. White, 1978, 521

8. Warren Report, 49-50

9. Warren Report, 64-65

10. Warren Commission Hearings, Testimony of Arnold Louis Rowland http://www.history-matters.com/

archive/jfk/wc/wcvols/wh2/pdf/WH2 Rowland.pdf

11. Warren Report, 63

12. *Eyewitness To History* by Howard Brennan, 1987, 13

13. Warren Report, 146

14. Warren Report, 146

15. Warren Report, 70

16. *A Cruel and Shocking Act*, 549

17. *A Cruel and Shocking Act*, 549

18. *The Assassination Tapes* by Max Holland, *The Atlantic Monthly*, June 2004, http://www.theatlantic.com/past/docs/issues/2004/06/holland.htm

19. Warren Report, 117

20. Warren Report, 117

21. Warren Report, 195

22. Warren Report, 423

23. *A Cruel and Shocking Act*

24. *A Cruel and Shocking Act*, 311

25. ARRB Records, Testimony of David Belin, 17 September 1996, http://mcadams.posc.mu.edu/arrb/index36.htm

26. Write It When I'm Gone – Remarkable Off-the-Record Conversations With Gerald R. Ford by Thomas M. DeFrank, 2007, 195, 197

NOTES & SOURCES

27. HSCA Final Report, 41-256

28. HSCA Final Report

29. JFK Assassination Net

30. http://jfkassassination.net/russ/m_1_russ/hsca badn.htn

31. HSCA Final Report, 41 – 256, http://www.maryferrell.org/mffweb/archive/viewer/showDoc.do?docId=800&relPageId=523

32. ARRB Records, Testimony of David Belin, 17 September 1996, http://mcadams.posc.mu.edu/arrb/index36.htm

CHAPTER 3: DAMNING EVIDENCE

1. *Eyewitness to History: The Kennedy Assassination as seen by Howard L. Brennan* with J. Edward Cherryholmes, Texian Press, 1987, 13

2. Warren Commission Vol 3 page 252

3. Warren Report, 152

4. Warren Report, 152

5. Warren Report, 118-124

6. *Oswald Talked*, 372-375

7. *Warren Report*, 118-122

8. *Marina and Lee*, 329

9. *Rush To Judgment*, 138

10. See Waldman Exhibit No. 7 and the Warren Commission testimony of William J. Waldman, beginning at Warren Commission Hearings Vol 7 page 360

11. E-mail to David Von Pein from Gary Mack, August 18, 2010

12. E-mail to David Von Pein from Gary Mack, August 18, 2010

13. On Trial: Lee Harvey Oswald, http://on-trial-lho. blogspot.com

14. The JFK Myths, 102

15. Warren Commission Volume 18, 86-95

16. Warren Report, 191

17. Warren Report, 192

18. Warren Commission Vol 4 pages 8,19

19. Warren Commission Vol 7 page 590 and Vol 4 page 50,51See CE2637 and 11 HSCA 254-255

20. Warren Report, Chapter IV and Appendix X

21. PBS, Frontline, Who Was Lee Harvey Oswald? http://www.pbs.org/wgbh/pages/frontline/shows/ oswald/etc/credits.html

22. PBS, Frontline, Who Was Lee Harvey Oswald? http://www.pbs.org/wgbh/pages/frontline/shows/ oswald/etc/credits.html and JFK: First Day Evidence, by Gary Savage, The Shoppe Press, http://karws. gso.uri.edu/marsh/jfk-conspiracy/1stDayEvidence. txt (UK title, The Mysterious Career of Lee Harvey Oswald, Written and Produced by William Cran and Ben

Loeterman, Invasion Productions for the BBC, 1993)

23. PBS, Frontline, Who Was Lee Harvey Oswald? http://www.pbs.org/wgbh/pages/frontline/shows/ oswald/etc/credits.html and JFK: First Day Evidence, by Gary Savage, The Shoppe Press, http://karws. gso.uri.edu/marsh/jfk-conspiracy/1stDayEvidence. txt (UK title, The Mysterious Career of Lee Harvey Oswald, Written and Produced by William Cran and Ben Loeterman, Invasion Productions for the BBC, 1993)

24. See: Dealey Plaza Earwitnesses – http://mcadams. posc.mu.edu/shots.htm and Earwitness Tabulation – http://mcadams.posc.mu.edu/earwitnesses.htm

25. Warren Commission vol 1 page 15-16 Testimony of Lyndal L. Shaneyfelt

26. Warren Commission vol 4 page 284 Testimony of Lyndal L. Shaneyfelt

27. Warren Commission Volume 1, 5-16; HSCA Volume 2, 239; Reclaiming History, 1487

28. *Case Closed*, 106

29. HSCA Vol 6 page 66

30. HSCA Volume 6, page 146; also see "Photograph Authentication: The Oswald Backyard Photographs" in HSCA Volume 6, beginning on page 138

31. National Enquirer, July 1997, Vol.71 No. 25 "O.J.'s Photo Expert is a Phony", 34

32. The Kennedy Assassination, Marina and Ruth: The Assassin's Wife and the Quaker Woman Who Took Her In by Thomas Mallon, http://mcadams.posc. mu.edu/garage.htm

33. HSCA Volume 2, 372-377; HSCA Volume 6, 151

CHAPTER 4: THE SINGLE BULLET THEORY

1. Warren Report, 81

2. Warren Report, 79

3. Warren Report, 81

4. Warren Commission vol 3 page 429, Testimony of Robert A. Frazier

5. H 70

6. *Case Closed,* 334-335

7. *Los Angeles Times*, Autopsy Doctors Say One Gunman Killed Kennedy, May 20, 1992, John J Goldman, http://articles.latimes.com/1992-05-20/ news/mn-240 1 gunman-killed-kennedy

8. Report to the President by the Commission on CIA Activities Within the United States, Vice President Nelson A. Rockefeller, Chairman. Washington, D.C.:

9. U.S. Government Printing Office, June, 1975, 262, http://www.history-matters.com/archive/church/ rockcomm/html/Rockefeller_0137b.htm

10. History Matters, HSCA Hearings – Volume I http:// history-

NOTES & SOURCES

matters.com/archive/contents/hsca/ contents hsca vol1.htm

11. DVP's JFK Archives, http://JFK-Archives.blogspot. com/2013/02/headshot.html

12. PBS Frontline, *The Sixth Floor of the Book Depository: Some witnesses thought they saw two men,* November 20 2003, http://www.pbs.org/wgbh/pages/frontline/shows/oswald/conspiracy/

13. The Kennedy Assassination, John McAdams, *Bogus Conspiracy Photo Experts,* http://mcadams.posc. mu.edu/experts.htm

14. The Kennedy Assassination, John McAdams, *Evidence of Fakery in the Zapruder Film? Was Mary Moorman Standing In Elm Street?* http://mcadams. posc.mu.edu/moorman1.htm

15. *Reclaiming History,* 932

16. *The Kennedy Half Century – The Presidency, Assassination, And Lasting Legacy Of John F Kennedy* by Larry Sabato, 143

17. *The Kennedy Half Century,* 145

18. See Warren Commission Exhibit No. 369 and the testimony of Billy Nolan Lovelady

19. The Kennedy Assassination, John McAdams, The Acoustic Evidence in the Kennedy Assassination by Michael O'Dell, http://mcadams.posc.mu.edu/ odell/

20. The Kennedy Assassination, John McAdams, The Acoustic Evidence – A personal Memoir by

Steve Barber,
http://mcadams.posc.mu.edu/barber.htm

21. *Fair Play Magazine*, Better Late than Never by JohnKelin http://www.acorn.net/jfkplace/09/fp.back issues/21st Issue/lancer.html

22. The Kennedy Assassination, John McAdams, The Acoustic Evidence in the Kennedy Assassination by Michael O'Dell, http://mcadams.posc.mu.edu/ odell/

23. *The Kennedy Half-Century*, pages 241-248

24. Secrets of a Homicide – JFK Assassination website, Dale Myers –_http://www.jfkfiles.com/

25. The Kennedy Assassination, Dealey Plaza, http:// mcadams.posc.mu.edu/dealey.htm

26. The KGB Secret JFK Assassination Files, directed by David McKenzie, 1998

27. Secrets of a Homicide – JFK Assassination website, Dale Myers –_http://www.jfkfiles.com/

28. Peter Jennings Reporting —The Kennedy Assassination: Beyond Conspiracy, ABC-TV, 2003

29. Warren Report, 117

30. Warren Commission Vol 4 pages 132-133, Testimony of John B. Connally

31. JFK.hood.edu, Teenager Proves Experts Wrong Over John Kennedy Assassination by Philip Finn, http://jfk.hood.edu/Collection/Weisberg%20Subject%20Index%20Files/L%20Disk/Lui%20David/Item%2004.pdf

CHAPTER 5: CONSCIOUSNESS OF GUILT

1. Warren Commission Vol 6 page 429
2. Warren Commission Vol 6 Pages, 438 – 439
3. Vectors, *The Assassination – Oswald's Flight,* http://www.vectorsite.net/twjfk_05.html
4. See Warren Commission Report, 157
5. Dale K. Myers, *With Malice*, Oak Cliff Press, 1998, 71-72
6. *With Malice,* 75
7. *Lee: A Portrait of Lee Harvey Oswald* by Robert L. Oswald, Myrick Land, Barbara Land, Coward-McCann, 1967, 85
8. *With Malice,* 72-73
9. *With Malice,* 250
10. *With Malice,* 273
11. *Assignment: Oswald* by James Hosty, 1996, 62
12. *With Malice,* 303-304
13. *With Malice,* 26-37
14. *With Malice,* 141-142
15. Warren Commission Volume 7, pages 40-41, Testimony of DPD Officer C.T. Walker
16. *Marina and Lee,* 171
17. *The Mysterious Career of Lee Harvey Oswald,* Written and Produced by William Cran and Ben

Loeterman, Invasion Productions for the BBC, 1993

18. Warren Report, 181
19. Warren Report, 182
20. Warren Commission Volume 1, Testimony of Marina Oswald, 65-66
21. Warren Commission Vol 6 pages 438-440
22. Warren Commission Volume 9, 424
23. Warren Commission Vol 2 page 226
24. Warren Report, 182
25. Warren Report, Appendix XI – Reports Relating to the Interrogation of Lee Harvey Oswald at the Dallas Police Department, http://jfkassassination.net/russ/jfkinfo/app11.htm
26. Warren Report, 181
27. *Marina and Lee*, 436
28. PBS, Frontline, *Interview With Robert Oswald*, 1993, http://www.pbs.org/wgbh/pages/frontline/shows/oswald/interviews/oswald.html

CHAPTER 6: AN INCONVENIENT TRUTH

1. PBS Frontline, An Interview With Robert Oswald, 1993, http://www.pbs.org/wgbh/pages/frontline/biographies/oswald/interview-robert-oswald/

NOTES & SOURCES

2. Warren Commission Volume 22, 251-252, Exhibit 1386
3. Ibid
4. Warren Commission Volume 11, 107, Testimony of Kerry W. Thornley
5. Warren Commission Vol 11 page 95, Testimony of Nelson Delgado
6. *Oswald's Game* by Jean Davison, 34
7. Warren Report, 418
8. PBS, Frontline, Interview with Robert Oswald, 1993, http://www.pbs.org/wgbh/pages/frontline/shows/ oswald/interviews/oswald.html
9. The Independent, Insight: Dr Roy Baumeister, *psychologist* by Will Dean, 23 February 2012, http://www.independent.co.uk/arts-entertainment/ books/features/insight-roy-baum e ister-psychologist-7321338.html
10. Warren Commission Hearings Volume 5, Testimony of Marina Oswald
11. *The Miami Herald*,What did Castro know? – an opposing view by Arnaldo M. Fernandez,June 30, 2012, http://www.miamiherald.com/2012/06/30/v-fullstory/2876687/what-did-castro-know-an-opposing.html
12. *Mrs. Paine's Garage* by Thomas Mallon, 187
13. *The Mysterious Career Of Lee Harvey Oswald*, 1993
14. *Marina and Lee*, 380

15. *Mrs. Paine's Garage*, 29
16. *Marina and Lee*, 261
17. *Marina and Lee*, 271
18. *Marina and Lee*, 214-223
19. *Marina and Lee*, 259
20. *Marina and Lee*, 259
21. Russo & Molton, *Brothers In Arms: The Kennedys, The Castros, and the Politics of Murder,* 2008, 250 – 254
22. *Marina and Lee*, 284
23. *Marina and Lee*, 298
24. *Marina and Lee*, 287
25. *Brothers In Arms*, 258
26. *Washington Decoded, A Word About Lee Harvey Oswald* by Priscilla Johnson McMillan, June 11, 2007, http://www.washingtondecoded.com/site/2007/06/lho.html
27. Warren Commission Volume 7, 438
28. Warren Report, 183-187, CE573
29. Warren Commission Volume 3, 440, Testimony of Robert A. Frazier
30. *A Word About Lee Harvey Oswald*, by Priscilla Johnson McMillan, June 11, 2007, http://www.washingtondecoded.com/site/2007/06/lho.html
31. *The Mysterious Career Of Lee Harvey Oswald*, 1993

NOTES & SOURCES

32. *The Mysterious Career Of Lee Harvey Oswald*, 1993

33. *The Mysterious Career Of Lee Harvey Oswald*, 1993

34. PBS, Frontline, Interview with Robert Oswald, 1993, http://www.pbs.org/wgbh/pages/frontline/shows/ oswald/interviews/oswald.html

35. *Oswald's Game*, 254

CHAPTER 7: THE USUAL SUSPECTS

1. Warren Report, 266

2. ABC-TV and BBC Timewatch, The Kennedy Assassination – Beyond Conspiracy, http://jfk.timewatch.org.uk/BBC/bbc-beyond-conspiracy.html

3. *Passport To Assassination* by Oleg M. Nechiporenko, page 38

4. ABC-TV and BBC Timewatch, The Kennedy Assassination – Beyond Conspiracy, http://jfk.timewatch.org.uk/BBC/bbc-beyond-conspiracy.html, 2004

5. HSCA Report, 102

6. Tom Mangold, *Cold Warrior: James Jesus Angleton : The CIA's Master Spy Hunter*, 356

7. Warren Commission, Testimony Of George S. De Mohrenschildt Resumed, http://jfkassassination.net/russ/testimony/demohr g.htm

8. ABC-TV and BBC Timewatch, The Kennedy Assassination – Beyond Conspiracy, http://jfk.timewatch.org.uk/BBC/bbc-beyond-conspiracy.html

9. ABC-TV and BBC Timewatch, The Kennedy Assassination – Beyond Conspiracy, http://jfk.timewatch.org.uk/BBC/bbc-beyond-conspiracy.html

10. *The Telegraph*, The Assassination of President John F Kennedy: the finger points to the KGB by Neil Tweedie, 24 October 2012, http://www.telegraph.co.uk/history/9628028/The-assassination-of-President-John-F-Kennedy-the-finger-points-to-the-KGB.html

11. HSCA Report Narration by G Robert Blakey, Chief Counsel and Staff Director, 9 http://www.aarclibrary.org/publib/jfk/hsca/reportvols/vol1/pdf/HSCA Vol1 0906 2 Narration.pdf

12. AARC Library.org, Carlos Marcello, http://www.aarclibrary.org/publib/jfk/hsca/reportvols/vol9/pdf/HSCA Vol9 3 Marcello.pdf

13. *Case Closed*, 461, 462

14. *Case Closed,* 462

15. *Vanity Fair*, Legacy of Mystery by Rob Sheffield, http://www.vanityfair.com/politics/features/2008/11/conspiracy200811

16. *The JFK Myths: A Scientific Investigation of The Kennedy Assassination* by Larry Sturdivan, (2005)

17. *Case Closed*, 464

18. Warren Commission Report, 369-370, 802; also see C-Span video with Tony Zoppi, November 20, 1993, http://jfk-archives.blogspot.com/2012/05/ tony-zoppi.html

19. HSCA Final Report, 3

20. *Texas Monthly,* Who Was Jack Ruby? by Gary Cartwright, November 1975, http://www.texasmonthly.com/story/who-was-jack-ruby

21. HSCA, Testimony of Santos Trafficante, JFK Exhibit F-411 http://jfkassassination.net/russ/jfkinfo2/jfk5/traff.htm

22. *True Detective*, The Jack Ruby I knew, Why I Didn't Put Him On The Stand by Melvin Belli, June 1964, 44

23. Seth Kantor, *Who Was Jack Ruby?* Everest House 1978, 210

24. HSCA Report V – Possible Associations Between Jack Ruby and Organized Crime, http://jfkassassination.net/russ/jfkinfo/jfk9/hscv9c.htm

25. *Case Closed*, 361

26. *Case Closed*, 353

27. *Case Closed*, 353

28. *Case Closed,* 354

29. *Case Closed,* 360

30. *True Compass – A Memoir* by Edward M. Kennedy, Little Brown, 2009

31. John McAdams, *JFK Assassination Logic: How To Think About Claims Of Conspiracy*, 2011, 203

32. Assignment: Oswald, 30, On Trial: Lee Harvey Oswald, Testimony of James P. Hosty, London Weekend Television, 1986

33. *History Will Prove Us Right* by Howard P Willens, 152

34. PBS, Frontline, Interview with Robert Oswald, 1993, http://www.pbs.org/wgbh/pages/frontline/shows/ oswald/interviews/oswald.html

35. *New York Times*, The Warren Commission: Why We Still Don't Believe It by David Belin, 20 November 1988, http://www.nytimes.com/1988/11/20/ magazine/the-warren-commission-why-we-still-dont-s-believe- it.html?pagewanted =all&src=pm

36. *Reclaiming History*, 923

37. *The Daily Beast*, May 14, 2013, Roger Stone's New Book 'Solves' JFK Assassination: JohnsonDid It! http://www.thedailybeast.com/ articles/2013/05/14/roger-stone-s-new-book-solves-jfk-assassination-johnson-did-it.html

38. JFK Facts, GOP Consultant : Nixon Hinted That He Thought LBJ Killed JFK, 17 May 2013, http:// jfkfacts.org/assassination/ news/gop-consultant-

39. *New York Times,* Wayne King, Estes Links Johnson to Plot, New York Times, 24 March

1984, http:// www.nytimes.com/1984/03/24/us/estes-links-johnson-to-plot.html

40. *Reclaiming History,* 1280

41. Caro, 353

42. Ibid

43. Caro, 450

CHAPTER 8: THE CIA-DID-IT THEORY

1. *Legacy of Ashes* by Tim Weiner, 228

2. *Robert Kennedy and His Times* by Arthur M. Schlesinger, 614

3. HSCA Report, 181

4. *Reclaiming History*, 1044

5. HSCA Volume 4, 353, 355

6. *The Very Best Men* by Evan Thomas, 1995, 11

7. *Honourable Men* by William Colby, 221

8. *Brothers In Arms*, Russo and Molton, 360

9. JFK Facts, *CIA translator on the missing Oswald Mexico City call*, 6th April 2013, http://jfkfacts.org/ assassination/quote/cia-translator-on-the-missing-oswald-mexico-city-call/

10. In City Times, Oswald and the CIA by John Newman – Book review by Steven R. Maher, 14th July 2009, http://incitytimesworcester.org/2009/07/14/oswald-and-the-cia-by-john-newman/

11. *Reclaiming History*, 1189, 1214 Flawed Patriot: The Rise and Fall of CIA Legend Bill Harvey by Bayard Stockton, 228

12. *Flawed Patriot:The Rise and Fall of CIA Legend Bill Harvey* by Bayard Stockton, 228

13. *Mind Control, Oswald & JFK: Were We Controlled*? by Lincoln Lawrence and Kenn Thomas; *The Perfect Assassin: Lee Harvey Oswald, the CIA and Mind Control* by Jerry Leonard

14. The Kennedy Assassination by John McAdams, Truth or Dare – The Lives and Lies of Richard Case Nagell, http://mcadams.posc.mu.edu/nagell3.htm

15. *Programmed to Kill: Lee Harvey Oswald, the Soviet KGB and the Kennedy Assassination* by Ion Mahai Pacepa

16. *Reclaiming History*, 1259

17. *They Call It Hypnosis* by Robert Allen Baker, 23–27

18. *American Psychologist*, August 1979, Hypnosis and Risks to Human Subjects by W. C. Coe and K. Ryken, 23

19. *They Call It Hypnosis*, 23–27

20. The Skeptic's Dictionary, Hypnosis by Robert Todd Carroll November 27, 2006, http://skepdic.com/ hypnosis.html

21. Dr. Graham Wagstaff, letter to the author with attachment, Hypnosis and Forensic Psychology, March 15, 2003

NOTES & SOURCES

22. *Brainwash – The Secret History of Mind Control* by Dominic Streatfeild, 2007, 177; Black Op internet radio, show 376, May 29, 2008, with James DiEugenio http://www.blackopradio.com/archives2008.html)

23. *Search for the Manchurian Candidate* by John Marks, 110

24. *Search for the Manchurian Candidate*, 154

25. *Search for the Manchurian Candidate*, 200

26. *Search for the Manchurian Candidate*, 196

27. *Search for the Manchurian Candidate*, 198

28. *Search for the Manchurian Candidate*, 223

29. *Secrets and Lies: A History of CIA Mind Control and Germ Warfare* by Gordon Thomas, 264, 321

30. National Geographic Channel, *CIA Secret Experiments*, written, produced, and directed by Tria Thalman

31. *Sabotage Times*, Don't Believe In Derren Brown by Tom Law, 2 November 2012 http://sabotagetimes. com/reportage/dont-believe-in-derren-brown/

32. *Sabotage Times*, Don't Believe In Derren Brown by Tom Law, 2 November 2012 http://sabotagetimes. com/reportage/dont-believe-in-derren-brown/

33. James Randi Educational Forum, Derren Brown – Hypnotism, November 2010, http://forums.randi. org/showthread.php?t=222219

34. Derren Brown: Science Trick or Treat? By Tom Law, http://www.hoofindan.co.uk/blog/ derren-brown-science-trick-or-treat/

35. *The Guardian*, Police expose Derren Brown hoax by Steven Morris, 8 October 2003, http://www.guardian.co.uk/media/2003/oct/08/broadcastin g. channel41

36. *The Daily Telegraph*, 10 June 2003, I'll Bet £1000 That Derren Can't Read My Mind, http://www.telegraph.co.uk/science/science-news/3309267/Ill-bet-1000-that-Derren-cant-read-my-mind.html

37. Warren Commission Report, 321-325

38. *Case Closed*, 180

39. *Assignment Oswald*, 133

40. *A Cruel And Shocking Act*, 465

41. *Oswald Talked*, 250

CHAPTER 9: THE NEW ORLEANS DEBACLE

1. Interview with Carlos Bringuier, November 22, 1963, NBC Radio Network, http://jfk-archives.blogspot.com/2013/05/interview-with-carlos-bringuier-11-22-63.html

2. *The Men Who Killed Kennedy,* Part 4; "The Patsy", 1988

3. *A Look Over My Shoulder* by Richard Helms, 287

4. *False Witness*, 239

5. LIFE, The Mob and Carlos Marcello: King Thug of Louisiana, 95, http://books.google.co.uk/books?id=T1YEAAAAMBAJ&printsec=frontcover&dq=LIFE,+'The+Mob'+and+'Carlos+Marcello:+King+Thug+of+Louisiana'&hl=en&sa=X&ei=p2x-UYv7DOeY1AXuuYH4DQ&ved=0CDAQ6AEwAA#v=onepage&q&f=false

6. Ibid

7. Ibid

8. Ibid

9. *False Witness*, 40

10. *False Witness*, 30

11. The Kennedy Assassination, New Orleans and the Garrison Investigation http://mcadams.posc. mu.edu/garrison.htm

12. NBC Television Special, The JFK Conspiracy: The Case of Jim Garrison, 1967, http://dvp-video-audio-archive.blogspot.com/2012/03/jfk-conspiracy-case-of-jim-garrison.html)

13. The Kennedy Assassination, New Orleans and the Garrison Investigation, http://mcadams.posc. mu.edu/garrison.htm; see also http://jfk-archives.blogspot.com/2010/09/david-ferrie.html)

14. *False Witness*, 62

15. *Case Closed*, 428-429

16. Secret Service report, December 13, 1963, Anthony Gerrets, New Orleans, Warren Commission Document 87; cited in House Select Committee Hearings Vol. IX, pages 105-106

17. *Case Closed*, 139

18. The Kennedy Assassination, Ferrie's Library Card, http://mcadams.posc.mu.edu/garrison.htm

19. *Road To Dallas* by David Kaiser, 183.

20. *Washington Decoded*, Road to Nowhere by John McAdams, http://www.washingtondecoded.com/site/2008/03/road-to-nowhere.html

21. *Case Closed*, 137

22. *Case Closed*, 142

23. *Case Closed*, 140

24. Warren Commission Document 75, page 285, http://www.maryferrell.org/mffweb/archive/viewer/showDoc.do?docId=10477&relPageId=287   A Look Over My Shoulder, 288

25. *A Look Over My Shoulder*, 288

26. The Kennedy Assassination, Was Clay Shaw a CIA Operative? – What do the Documents Say? – He was Not, http://mcadams.posc.mu.edu/shawcia.htm)

27. *American Grotesque: An Account of the Clay Shaw-Jim Garrison Affair in the City of New Orleans* by James Kirkwood, 220

28. *False Witness*, 185-200

29. The JFK Conspiracy: The Case of Jim Garrison, NBC-TV, 1967, http://dvp-video-audio-archive.blogspot.com/2012/03/jfk-conspiracy-case-of-jim-garrison.html

30. *American Grotesque*, 618-633

31. *False Witness*, 173

32. *Reclaiming History*, 1379-1380

33. The Jim Garrison Investigation, Who Speaks For Clay Shaw by Dave Reitzes, http://www.jfk-online. com/garrison.html)

34. *Fair Play Magazine*, Bearing the Unbearable? by Clay Shaw, Clay Shaw Journal, March 1, 1967, http:// www.acorn.net/jfkplace/09/fp.back issues/19th Issue/shaw diary.html

CHAPTER 10: OSWALD'S DEFENDERS

1. *Case Closed*, 308

2. Warren Commission Volume 5, 191

3. Warren Commission Volume 5, 204; see also *Case Closed*, 400

4. The Controversy-The Death-The Warren Report, 12" LP Record, Capitol Records, 1967

5. The Controversy-The Death-The Warren Report, 12" LP Record, Capitol Records, 1967

6. *Oswald's Game,* 17-19; *Reclaiming History*, 1003

7. Warren Commission Hearings, Volume 7, 502, http://history-matters.com/archive/jfk/wc/wcvols/wh7/html/WC_Vol7_0255b.htm

8. *Case Closed*, 228

9. *Reclaiming History*, 1001, 1002-1011

10. E-mail to author, May 19, 2012

11. *JFK: Breaking The News* by Hugh Aynesworth with Stephen G. Michaud, 231

12. *New York Times* Book Review, Mark Lane: Smearing America's Soldiers in Vietnam by Neil Sheehan, December 27, 1970

13. HSCA Final Report, 424, footnote 16

14. *JFK Assassination Logic*, 198

15. The John F Kennedy Assassination, John McAdams, Jean Hill: The Lady In Red; http://mcadams.posc.mu.edu/jhill.htm, David Perry, *Roger Craig: The Rambler Man*, http://mcadams. posc.mu.edu/craig.htm

16. The Nation, *The Rosenberg Variations* by Victor Navasky, November 15, 2010, http://www.thenation.com/article/155633/rosenberg-variations

17. Mary Ferrell Foundation, Warren Commission Executive Session of 30 April http://www.maryferrell.org/mffweb/archive/viewer/showDoc.do?absPageId=172830

18. *Last Word* by Mark Lane 43, 113, 143; *The Forgotten Terrorist: Sirhan Sirhan and the Assassination of Robert F. Kennedy* by Mel Ayton 2007, 80

19. *Last Word*, 103, 111, 126, 127, 129, 134, 135, 137, 139, 195, 230

20. *Last Word*, 113; Michael O'Dell, The Kennedy Assassination, The Acoustic Evidence in the Kennedy Assassination, http://mcadams.posc.mu.edu/odell/

NOTES & SOURCES

21. The Kennedy Assassination, JFK Assassination: A Hobo Hit? The Three Tramps, http://mcadams.posc. mu.edu/3tramps.htm

22. *Plausible Denial* by Mark Lane, 322

23. *Miami Herald*, Hunt-JFK Article 'Trash' But Not Libellous, Jury Finds by Stephen K. Doig, February 7, 1985, http://www.scribd.com/doc/203430875/ Hunt-v-Spotlight-Articles

24. *American Spy: My Secret History in the CIA, Watergate, and Beyond*, E. Howard Hunt with Greg Aunapu, 126–147

25. United States Court of Appeals Seventh Circuit. 355 F.2d 453 United States of America, Plaintiff-Appellee, v. Abraham W. BOLDEN, Defendant-Appellant. No. 14907. Dec. 29, 1965, Rehearing Denied Feb. 25, 1966, En Banc, http://federal-circuits.vlex.com/vid/america-abraham-w-bolden-defendant-36715337

26. The Kennedy Assassination, *Marita Lorenz: Tying Hunt To A Conspiracy by* John McAdams, Ed Dolan, and Jean Davison, http://mcadams.posc.mu.edu/ denial.ht

27. *Case Closed*, 465

28. The JFK and RFK Assassinations and the Bogus 'Manchurian Candidate Theories by Mel Ayton, http://mcadams.posc.mu.edu/Manchurian.htm

29. Black Op Radio, Show 234, August 18, 2005, http:// www.blackopradio.com

30. *The Lie That Linked The CIA to the Kennedy Assassination*,

https://www.cia.gov/library/center-for-the-study-of-intelligence/csi-publications/ csi-studies/studies/fall_winter_2001/article02.html and Washington Decoded, September 9, 2002, *Oliver Stone on Jim Garrison, the KGB, and the CIA*, http://www.washingtondecoded.com/site/jfk_assassination/

31. *Washington Decoded*, 11 February 2002, Was Jim Garrison Duped by the KGB? http://www.washingtondecoded.com/site/jfk_assassination/

32. E-mail to the author from Don Bohning, October 9, 2005

33. The Lie That Linked The CIA to the Kennedy Assassination by Max Holland, https://www.cia.gov/ library/center-for-the-study-of-intelligence/csi-publications/csi-studies/studies/fall_winter_2001/article02.html

34. The Kennedy Assassination, Garrison Ripples – The La Fontaines and Big Jim by Dave Reitzes, http://mcadams.posc.mu.edu/ripples.htm#jackmartin

35. The Kennedy Assassination, Truth or Dare – The Lives and Lies of Richard Case Nagell by Dave Reitzes, http://mcadams.posc.mu.edu/nagell1.htm

36. Don Bohning E-mail to the author, October 3, 2005

37. *Case Closed*, 138

CHAPTER 11: THE CASTRO CONNECTION

NOTES & SOURCES

1. *Live By The Sword* by Gus Russo, 375

2. Author's Note: After three decades of debate there is a consensus amongst historians that JFK and his brother Bobby knew (and sanctioned) CIA attempts to kill the Cuban leader – see *Legacy of Ashes – A History of the CIA* by Tim Weiner, 583

3. *New Orleans Times-Picayune*, Castro Blasts Raids On Cuba, 9 September 1963

4. HSCA Final Report, 127

5. HSCA Final Report, 126

6. *Castro's Secrets* by Brian Latell, 230

7. The New Republic, When Castro Heard the News By Jean Daniel, 7 December 1963, 7–9, http://karws.gso.uri.edu/jfk/history/wc period/ pre-wcr reactions to assassination/prewcr reactions by the left/When Castro Heard TNR. html

8. Email to the author from Rudy Apocada, 12 June 2013

9. Emails to the author from source who wishes to remain anonymous, 6 May 2013, 9 May 2013, 5 June 2013

10. Assignment: Oswald, 220 National Archives, JFK Assassination Records, Assassination Records Review Board, Series 4: Research and Analysis 4.0.2 Subject Files *SOLO SAC New York to Director, FBI*, June 12 1964, NARA 124-10274-10338 released March 30 1995 and 4.0.2 Subject Files Cuba, Castro's Knowledge http://www.archives.gov/research/jfk/review-board/series-04.html)

11. National Archives, JFK Assassination Records, Assassination Records Review Board, Series 4: Research and Analysis 4.0.2 Subject Files SOLO SAC New York to Director, FBI, June 12, 1964, Nara 124-10274-10388 released March 30, 1995 and 4.0.2 Subject Files Cuba, Castro's Knowledge http://www.archives.gov/research//jfk/review-board/series-04.html)

12. *Castro's Secrets*, 221

13. *Rendezvous With Death* by Wilfried Huismann, Film Documentary 2006

14. Ibid

15. CUBAN INFORMATION ARCHIVES, The Sordid History of Cuba's Spy Apparatus by Gus Russo and Stephen Molton, http://cuban-exile.com/doc 451-475/doc0451.html

16. Email to the author from Gus Russo, 25 April 2013, See also: Cuban Information Archives, *The Sordid History of Cuba's Spy Apparatus* by Gus Russo and Stephen Molton, http://cuban-exile. com/doc 451-475/doc0451.html In their words, Oswald "did it with the aid and comfort of Fidel and Raúl Castro", *Brothers in Arms*, 237

17. *The Miami Herald*, Fresh meat forJFKassassination hounds, by Glen Garvin, 17 March 2012, http://www.miamiherald.com/2012/03/17/2700191/ fresh-meat-for-jfk-assassination.html

18. *Castro's Secrets*, 231

19. *The Miami Herald,* The Kennedy assassination: Did Castro know in advance? Glenn Garvin, 17

NOTES & SOURCES

March 2012, http://www.miamiherald.com/201 2/03/1 7/27001 86/the-kennedy-assassination-did.html

20. *Castro's Secrets*, 191

21. *Castro's Secrets,* 103

22. *Castro's Secrets*, 144

23. *The Miami Herald*, Fresh meat forJ FK assassination hounds, by Glen Garvin, 17 March 2012, http://www.miamiherald.com/2012/03/17/2700191/fresh-meat-for-jfk-assassination.html

24. *Miami Herald*, The Kennedy Assassination – Did Castro Know in Advance? by Glenn Garvin, 17 March 2012, http://www.miamiherald.com/2012/03/17/2700191/fresh-meat-for-jfk-assassination.html

25. *Washington Decoded*, Concocting the Dots by Brian Latell, 11 January 2009, http://www.washingtondecoded.com/site/2009/01/concocting-the-dots.html

26. *Miami Herald*, The Kennedy Assassination – Did Castro Know in Advance? by Glenn Garvin, 17 March 2012, http://www.miamiherald.com/2012/03/17/2700191/fresh-meat-for-jfk-assassination.html

27. *The Miami Herald*, What did Castro know? (an opposing view) By Arnaldo M. Fernandez, June 30, 2012,
    http://www.miamiherald.com/2012/06/30/v-fullstory/2876687/what-did-castro-know-an-opposing.html

28. *Castro's Secrets*, 216

29. *The Miami Herald*, What Did Castro Know – An Opposing View by Arnaldo M. Fernandez,

30. *Reclaiming History*, Bugliosi Endnotes, 1288

31. *Reclaiming History*, Bugliosi Endnotes, 1288

32. Anthony Summers, email to the author, January 9, 2006

33. *Brothers in Arms*, 224

34. *Case Closed*, 203

35. *Mrs Paine's Garage*, 41

36. *Marina and Lee*, 376

37. Warren Report, 736

38. *Reclaiming History*, Bugliosi Endnotes, 1288

39. Warren Report, 736

40. *Reclaiming History*, Bugliosi Endnotes, 1288

41. Warren Commission Hearings Volume 5 Testimony of Marina Oswald, http://www.history-matters.com/archive/contents/wc/contents wh5. htm

42. CUBAN INFORMATION ARCHIVES, The Sordid History of Cuba's Spy Apparatus, by Gus Russo and Stephen Molton (http://cuban-exile. com/doc 451-475/doc0451.html

43. *Marina and Lee*, 376

44. *Final Disclosure*, 217

45. *Assignment: Oswald*, 249

46. *Brothers in Arms*, 308

47. *A Cruel and Shocking Act*, page 553

48. Email to the author from Anthony Summers, 9th January 2006

49. *Enemies*, 210

50. *Reclaiming History*, Bugliosi Endnotes, 1291

51. *Mrs Paine's Garage*, 44

CHAPTER 12: THE JFK ASSASSINATION LEGACY

1. Daniel Pipe's Middle East Forum, Lee Harvey Oswald's Malign Legacy by Daniel Pipes, Jerusalem Post, November 22, 2007, http://www.danielpipes. org/5136/lee-harvey-oswalds-malign-legacy

2. Reviews in American History 22, After Thirty Years – Making Sense of the Assassination by Max Holland, (1994), pages 191-209, The Johns Hopkins University Press. Posted on the web with permission of Reviews in American History, http://mcadams.posc.mu.edu/holland.htm

3. National Review, Murder Heaven: The Law Is A Quagmire by William F. Buckley Jr, November 18, 2003, http://old.nationalreview.com/buckley/buckley200311181428.asp

4. *Shadow Play*, xiii

5. *Killing The Dream*, 287-289

6. *Killing The Dream*, 318

7. *Killing The Dream*, 266

8. *Slate Magazine,* Of Conspiracies and Kings by David Greenburg, 10th May1998, http://www.slate.com/ articles/news and politics/backstory/1998/05/ of conspiracies and king.html)

9. *Chief – My Life In The LAPD* by Daryl Gates, 153

10. *Dead Reckoning* by Michael Baden and Marion Roach, 227

11. *The Forgotten Terrorist*, 78

12. *The Assassinations* by James DiEugenio and Lisa Pease, 538

13. The Forgotten Terrorist, 247-263

14. A CBS News Inquiry: The Warren Report, Part 4, CBS Television Network, June 1967, http://dvp-video-audio-archive.blogspot.com/2012/03/ cbs-news-inquiry-warren-report-1967.html

15. US News and World Report, The Inner Worlds of Conspiracy Believers By Bruce Bower, Science News, 26 May 2009, http://www.usnews.com/ science/articles/2009/05/26/the-inner-worlds-of-conspiracy-believers?page=2)

16. Huffington Post, Oliver Stone Talks US In Denial Of JFK Assassination, Hitler's Rise by Michael Casey, January 25, 2010 http://www.huffingtonpost.com/2010/01/25/oliver-stone-us-in-denial_n_435147.html

17. *Reclaiming History*, 925

18. *The Guardian*, Did the CIA Kill Bobby Kennedy? by Shane O'Sullivan, 20 November 2006, 8

19. Washington Decoded, Still Guilty After All These Years: Sirhan B. Sirhan By Mel Ayton May 11, 2008, http://www.washingtondecoded.com/site/2008/05/still-guilty-af.html

20. Washington Decoded, Still Guilty After All These Years: Sirhan B. Sirhan By Mel Ayton , 11 May 2008, http://www.washingtondecoded.com/site/2008/05/still-guilty-af.html and History News Network, November 20, 2007 – *How the Discovery Channel Duped the American Public About the RFK Assassination Acoustics Debate* http://hnn.us/ articles/44466.html

21. History News Network, CNN's Conspiracy Bias in the Robert F. Kennedy Assassination By Mel Ayton , 7th May 2012, http://hnn.us/articles/cnns-conspiracy-bias-robert-f-kennedy-assassination

22. BBC Documentary, Who Killed Martin Luther King?, 1993

23. *Intelligencer: Journal of US Intelligence Studies*, JFK Evidence and the Conspiracy Industry – To Be A Player-Some Invent Facts, Winter/Spring 2009, page 61

24. ARRB, Testimony of David Belin, Los Angeles, California — September 17, 1996, http://mcadams.posc.mu.edu/arrb/index36.htm

BEYOND REASONABLE DOUBT

APPENDIX 1

ADDITIONAL CONTROVERSIAL ISSUES SURROUNDING THE JFK ASSASSINATION
By David Von Pein

WAS CE399 A PLANTED BULLET?:

Conspiracy theorists like to postulate the theory that Warren Commission Exhibit No. 399 was planted or substituted for the actual bullet that was found by Darrell Tomlinson at Parkland Hospital.

One of the primary reasons for the conspiracists believing that CE399 is a phony bullet is due to the *supposed* lack of a complete and firm chain of possession for the bullet as it made its way into the hands of several individuals from Parkland Hospital in Dallas to the FBI laboratory in Washington, D.C., on November 22, 1963.

It has long been accepted as undisputed fact, even among lone-assassin believers, that the two Secret Service men who handled CE399 prior to the bullet being turned over to the FBI on the day of the assassination (Richard E. Johnsen and Chief James J. Rowley) did not mark the bullet with their initials (or any other markings).

But in September 2012, I acquired some intriguing new information about this topic from former Secret Service agent Gerald Blaine, who was a part of the Kennedy Detail of Secret Service agents assigned to protect President Kennedy, although Mr. Blaine was not assigned to provide protection during the Dallas motorcade.

Below are some portions of a conversation I had with Mr. Blaine via e-mail in late September of 2012:

"I'm writing today to ask you a couple of questions. As you no doubt know, many JFK conspiracy theorists think that the stretcher bullet (CE399) found at Parkland Hospital after President Kennedy was killed is a 'fake' or 'planted' bullet. And part of the reason the theorists believe that it's a fake is because neither of the Secret Service representatives who handled the stretcher bullet on 11/22/63 marked it in any way. ... What was the normal policy of the Secret Service in 1963 when it came to Secret Service agents marking pieces of evidence in criminal cases? Did they normally mark evidence themselves, or was evidence only marked by FBI agents and local police authorities? Also: If it was the policy of the Secret Service to mark evidence that went through their hands, then what would your explanation be for why SS agent Richard Johnsen and SS Chief James Rowley failed to mark CE399 when each man handled that bullet on 11/22/63?" -- E-mail from David Von Pein to Gerald Blaine; September 23, 2012

"The bullet found on the stretcher was retrieved and marked by SA Richard Johnsen and submitted as evidence. ... [Former Secret Service agent] Clint Hill

APPENDIX 1

talked to Dick [Johnsen] a month or two before he passed away and Clint told me that Dick had marked the evidence. Sounds like he must have put it in an envelope rather that initiating it [the bullet itself]. ... It is very unusual for WHD [White House Detail] agents to get involved in investigative work, but Dick...studied Criminal Justice, so he should have known the rules of evidence. James Rowley once worked for the FBI and he too should have understood the rules. I have no doubt that it was the bullet that came from the stretcher." -- Two E-mails from Gerald Blaine to David Von Pein; September 27, 2012

"There was, indeed, an envelope involved with the transfer of Bullet CE399 as it went from the possession of the Secret Service to the FBI lab in Washington on 11/22/63. That 'envelope' fact is confirmed in Commission Document No. 7 [page 288]. ... So, if Richard Johnsen marked the envelope, rather than the bullet itself, it would certainly explain why he said he could not 'positively identify' the bullet that was later shown to him by Elmer Todd of the FBI in June of 1964. Because in such a circumstance, Johnsen wouldn't have placed his initials on the bullet itself, but instead would have marked only the container (envelope) that Johnsen put the bullet into." -- E-mail from David Von Pein to Gerald Blaine; September 27, 2012

http://JFK-Archives.blogspot.com/2012/09/the-secret-service-and-ce399.html

So, per Gerald Blaine (and, via Blaine, former Secret Service agent Clint Hill), it would seem that Richard Johnsen, the first person other than civilian witnesses

Darrell Tomlinson and O.P. Wright to touch the stretcher bullet at Parkland Hospital, might very well have marked the envelope which contained Bullet CE399 on 11/22/63. Which, in effect, would be the same as Johnsen (and possibly Rowley too, if Rowley had also marked the envelope) marking the bullet itself.

The envelope in question has been seen (and photographed) by assassination researcher John Hunt, who made a trip to the National Archives on July 30, 2004, to examine various pieces of evidence connected with the Kennedy case. Hunt took a picture of one side of the envelope (the other side was evidently not photographed), and there is no sign of Johnsen's or Rowley's markings on the side of the envelope that was photographed.

The envelope in Hunt's picture [which can be seen at the link provided above] contains the initials of three of the FBI agents who ultimately handled and examined CE399, and it has the signature and written words of FBI agent Elmer Todd at the very bottom, which really is tantamount to having Rowley's initials on the envelope as well, since Todd is telling us on that very envelope that he received that exact envelope from Chief James Rowley on the night of the assassination. The exact words that Agent Todd wrote on the envelope are: "Received from Chief Rowley, USSS, 8:50 p.m. 11-22-63. E.L. Todd."

http://JFKLancer.com/hunt/mystery.html

In addition to the envelope, there is also an often-overlooked document pertaining to the chain of custody

APPENDIX 1

of the Parkland stretcher bullet that appears on page 800 of Warren Commission Volume 18. It's a copy of a typewritten note from Secret Service agent Richard Johnsen. In the note, Johnsen says the following:

"The attached expended bullet was received by me about 5 min. prior to Mrs. Kennedy's departure from the hospital. It was found on one of the stretchers located in the emergency ward of the hospital."

The note is not signed with a handwritten signature, but is "signed" in typewritten form in this manner:

*"Richard E. Johnsen
Special Agent
7:30 p.m.
Nov. 22, 1963"*

The original note, typed on White House stationery, was photographed at the National Archives by John Hunt in 2004 [see the link below].

http://JFK-Archives.blogspot.com/2012/09/the-secret-service-and-ce399.html

Logic and common sense would therefore dictate that the note written by Agent Johnsen concerning the Parkland bullet was physically attached to the envelope which contained stretcher bullet CE399. Hence the words *"the attached expended bullet"* at the beginning of the note. And a staple hole is clearly visible in the original note that was written by Johnsen on White House stationery, which is a staple hole that dovetails nicely with the staples that can also be seen in the envelope that was photographed by John Hunt in 2004

417

at the National Archives, making it obvious that something was, indeed, stapled to that envelope. There are, in fact, *three* different staples (or staple holes) visible in the picture of the envelope, leading to the distinct possibility that perhaps James Rowley also attached a note to the envelope as well.

But even without definitive proof of a similar note written by Rowley concerning his handling of CE399, since that very same envelope is telling us, via the handwritten words of FBI agent Elmer Todd, that Rowley *was* most certainly in possession of that envelope (with or without Rowley's own initials being present on the envelope), it would indicate that there *is* documentation in the official records of this case that shows a complete chain of custody of the stretcher bullet -- from Tomlinson/Wright....to Johnsen....to Rowley....to Todd....to Frazier.

To firm up the bullet's chain of possession even more, there are also two official FBI documents that were made available by the Warren Commission (Commission Exhibit No. 2011 and Commission Document No. 7). And while James Rowley said he could not *positively* identify CE399 as the bullet he handled on 11/22/63, the document known as CE2011 does show that Rowley did definitely receive a bullet from Richard Johnsen on November 22nd:

"On June 24, 1964, James Rowley, Chief, United States Secret Service, Washington, D.C., was shown Exhibit C1 [CE399], a rifle bullet, by Special Agent Elmer Lee Todd. Rowley advised he could not identify this bullet as the one he received from Special Agent Richard E. Johnsen

APPENDIX 1

and gave to Special Agent Todd on November 22, 1963."
-- CE2011 (Pages 2 and 3)

"At 8:50 p.m. [on 11/22/63], Mr. JAMES ROWLEY, Chief, United States Secret Service, gave to SA ELMER LEE TODD an envelope containing a bullet. This envelope and its contents were taken directly to the FBI Laboratory and delivered to SA ROBERT A. FRAZIER. The envelope was opened and initials of both SA TODD and FRAZIER were etched on the nose of the bullet for identification purposes." -- Warren Commission Document No. 7 (Page 288)

Conspiracy theorists will, of course, argue that the "chain" shown above is still extremely weak and that it doesn't constitute a "chain" of custody at all--particularly since the Johnsen typewritten note is not signed with his handwritten signature or initials and is not still physically attached to the envelope that contains Todd's remarks about receiving the bullet from Rowley.

So, yes, maybe this issue about the chain of possession of the bullet will always provide fertile ground for continued debate and argument. It seems quite obvious that it will. No issue in this case seems to ever go unchallenged by conspiracists, even the ones that have been thoroughly debunked by lone-assassin proponents over the years.

But if a person digs into the records deep enough, that person *can* and *will* find documentation to support the idea, which is totally foreign to most conspiracy theorists, that Bullet CE399 *was* the bullet that made its

BEYOND REASONABLE DOUBT

way from Parkland Memorial Hospital in Dallas to the FBI laboratory in Washington on November 22, 1963.

It's also important to consider this fact -- both the Warren Commission *and* the House Select Committee on Assassinations (comprised chiefly of lawyers) had no problem at all accepting CE399 as *the exact bullet* that went through the bodies of both President Kennedy and Governor Connally on November 22, 1963.

No other scenario has ever come close to matching the Warren Commission's "Single-Bullet Theory" in the evidence department. Nor has any alternate theory come close to equalling the SBT in the *reasonable*, *believable*, and *common sense* categories as well.

But, to quote President John F. Kennedy himself, *"Reason does not always appeal to unreasonable men."* [JFK; November 16, 1961]

THE MOTORCADE ROUTE:

In the years since JFK's assassination, a whole bunch of people have latched onto the myth that the President's motorcade route was changed at the eleventh hour just prior to Kennedy's drive through downtown Dallas on November 22, 1963.

But the allegation about the route being changed at the last minute is pure malarkey--and provably so. That is, unless the conspiracists who continually tout such an unsupportable theory actually believe, and can prove, that the Warren Commission somehow faked

APPENDIX 1

Commission Exhibits 1362 and 1363, which consist of photographs of two Dallas newspapers, both from November 19, 1963, which verify the finalized motorcade route, including the turn from Houston Street onto Elm Street, which is a turn that took JFK's car directly in front of the Texas School Book Depository Building, from where Lee Harvey Oswald shot and killed President Kennedy.

CE1362 and CE1363 were utilized as official exhibits by the Warren Commission to demonstrate the fact that the motorcade route was never changed [Warren Report, p.643], and also to demonstrate the fact that JFK's assassin, Lee Oswald, could very easily have had ample foreknowledge as to the precise motorcade route through Dallas that the President would travel on November 22 [WR, p.642].

And those two Warren Commission exhibits aren't the only things that prove that the motorcade route was not changed. There is also a videotaped news broadcast of President Kennedy's arrival at Love Field Airport in Dallas which aired live on all of the local Dallas television stations on the morning of 11/22/63. That video includes this narration by WFAA-TV reporter Bob Walker, which perfectly matches the detailed route that was shown in both Dallas newspapers three days earlier on November 19:

"Thousands will be on hand for that motorcade now, which will be downtown Dallas, down Cedar Springs to Harwood, and on Harwood it will turn on Main, from which point it will go all the way down to the courthouse area which is the end of Main; it'll turn on Houston

421

BEYOND REASONABLE DOUBT

Street to Elm, under the Triple Underpass, out to the [Trade] Mart where the President talks at approximately one o'clock, which will also be carried live right here on most of these channels."

Plus, in addition to Bob Walker's TV narration of the motorcade route, there is also a November 22 radio report by Joe Long of Dallas radio station KLIF. In Long's report from Love Field, these words were spoken:

"For those of you who plan to try and catch a glimpse of the fast-moving President and First Lady, here's the route of travel they're going to be covering from Love Field to the Trade Mart, where the President will make his luncheon speech. The motorcade departs Love Field, then it goes Mockingbird Lane to Lemmon Avenue, south on Lemmon to Turtle Creek, Cedar Springs, then through the downtown area on Harwood to Main. The main route of travel will be west on Main to Houston, then through the Triple Underpass to Stemmons Freeway, and on to the Trade Mart."

http://JFK-Arrives-In-Dallas.blogspot.com

So it's plainly evident that the motorcade route was never changed from its original configuration. To begin with, the route wasn't even finalized until November 18th [WR, p.32], just four days prior to Kennedy's visit to Dallas. The route was then published in both Dallas papers, the *Dallas Morning News* and the *Dallas Times Herald*, on November 19.

On November 20 and November 22, the Dallas papers then mentioned the general routing of the motorcade (but lacing specific street details). But this lack of "Elm

APPENDIX 1

Street" detail in the two later papers on the 20th and the 22nd can't possibly be used by conspiracy buffs to promote a "Route Was Changed" theory, unless those buffs actually want to believe that the route was changed *twice* -- with the last change mirroring the exact Houston-to-Elm route that was already published in the November 19 papers.

Here's a direct passage from page 40 of the Warren Commission Report:

"On November 19, the Times-Herald afternoon paper detailed the precise route: 'From the airport, the President's party will proceed to Mockingbird Lane to Lemmon and then to Turtle Creek, turning south to Cedar Springs. The motorcade will then pass through downtown on Harwood and then west on Main, turning back to Elm at Houston and then out Stemmons Freeway to the Trade Mart'."

The Warren Commission's source note that is attached to the above words points to CE1362, which shows a page from the November 19, 1963, edition of the *Dallas Times Herald*, which positively proves that the turn onto Elm Street was being planned as of the date of that newspaper.

Page 40 of the Warren Report also tells us that the Dallas morning paper on November 19 also mentioned the specific turn onto Elm Street -- *"Main to Houston, Houston to Elm."* [CE1363]

As those Warren Commission exhibits show, Oswald had ample time to read about the motorcade route (including the specific details regarding the turn onto Elm Street)

423

BEYOND REASONABLE DOUBT

prior to his November 21 trip to Ruth Paine's home in Irving to retrieve his rifle.

Plus, it's also quite possible that Oswald would have attempted the assassination even if the President's limousine didn't proceed down Elm Street. If the car had gone straight down Main Street, Oswald could still have attempted the shooting. It would have been a longer and more difficult shot, that's true. But he still could have tried it. Sadly, he had an even better chance to commit his heinous act when the President's car made its slow turn onto Elm Street, right in front of the building where Oswald and his gun were waiting.

EDDY BENAVIDES AND OTHER "MYSTERIOUS DEATHS":

Some people who promote the "Mysterious Deaths" conspiracy theory seem to believe that Eddy Benavides belongs on that ever-growing list of individuals who, per the conspiracists, were bumped off by evil plotters after the assassination of President Kennedy.

Eddy Benavides was the brother of Domingo Benavides. Domingo was one of the witnesses to the murder of Dallas policeman J.D. Tippit, which is a murder that was committed by Lee Harvey Oswald and occurred approximately 45 minutes after President Kennedy had been slain.

According to some conspiracists, the theory goes like this: Eddy Benavides was murdered in order to send a message to his brother, Domingo, very shortly prior to

APPENDIX 1

Domingo testifying in front of the Warren Commission. (Apparently the "death squad" didn't want to kill Domingo himself. I guess that would have looked too obvious. So they murdered his brother instead. An alternative version of this theory, which is actually the version that most conspiracy buffs likely place their faith in, has Eddy being killed as a result of mistaken identity. Evidently, Eddy looked quite a bit like his brother, Domingo.)

But, as it turns out, this chapter in the "Mysterious Deaths" log book should have never appeared there in the first place, because in April 2010 I garnered some additional information supplied on the Internet by JFK researchers Jean Davison and John McAdams.

It turns out that Eddy Benavides was shot and killed in February of **1965**, not February of **1964**. That one-year difference is important, because it means that at the time of Eddy's death, Domingo had already given his testimony to the Warren Commission (which disbanded in September 1964).

[See the death notice for Edward H. Benavidez in the February 18, 1965, edition of the *Dallas Morning News*. Eddy's last name is spelled with a "z" in the death notice, but there is ample additional information contained in the newspaper's death notice to indicate that Edward H. Benavidez was, in fact, Eddy Benavides. See the newspaper clippings at the webpage below.]

http://JFK-Archives.blogspot.com/2010/09/mystery-deaths.html

So, it seems as though the "Mystery Deaths" list now has one less person on it (or it should have anyway), even from the viewpoint of most conspiracy theorists. Because for anybody to still maintain that Eddy's death was sinister and related in some way to a conspiracy surrounding the events of 11/22/63, we'd have to believe that the "Death Squad" would have wanted to rub out witness Domingo Benavides (or his brother) almost one year *after* that witness had already told the Warren Commission everything he knew about the Tippit shooting, and almost a full year after Domingo had gone on record as saying that the man he saw shoot and kill Officer Tippit *"looked like"* Lee Harvey Oswald [6 H 452]. He had essentially fingered Oswald (the so-called "patsy" in the case) as the killer of Tippit, so why on Earth would any conspirators consider Domingo's testimony to be a threat to any conspiracy plot?

In addition to the ridiculous contention that Eddy Benavides was rubbed out by evil forces, many other deceased persons who currently occupy space on various researchers' "Mystery Deaths" lists are equally as ridiculous and ludicrous. Here are just a few examples (taken from a list containing dozens of names compiled by Jim Marrs and Ralph Schuster; the sections in quotation marks are direct quotes copied from the Marrs/Schuster list):

"Charles Mentesana -- Filmed rifle other than Mannlicher-Carcano being taken from Depository."

Ever see this film? Mentesana's film does not prove a second rifle was found in the Texas School Book Depository at all. Plus, why in the world would anyone

APPENDIX 1

bother killing the person who filmed a short clip of a rifle? Merely because he *filmed* footage of a rifle? Does killing the filmmaker eliminate the film?

"Abraham Zapruder -- Took famous film of JFK assassination."

Of course, the death squad waited seven years to take care of Abe. And what was the reason again? Merely because he filmed the assassination?

Or maybe it was because Zapruder knew George DeMohrenschildt's future wife in 1959, years prior to the assassination. Or it could just be because Jim Marrs needed a name beginning with "Z" to fill out an alphabet quota.

"William Whaley -- Cab driver who reportedly drove Oswald to Oak Cliff. (The only Dallas taxi driver to die on duty.)"

Again, why kill William Whaley? For what possible reason? We know Whaley took Lee Harvey Oswald to Beckley Avenue in Oak Cliff on 11/22/63 by taxicab. What does Whaley know that can blow the case wide open?

"Henry Delaune -- Brother-in-law to coroner Chetta."

Yeah, this guy must have been a much better choice to knock off than, say, S.M. Holland or Jean Hill or J.C. Price. How far down the family tree is considered too far for Marrs and Company?

BEYOND REASONABLE DOUBT

"J. Edgar Hoover -- FBI director who pushed 'lone assassin' theory in JFK assassination."

Therefore, by always pushing the lone assassin theory, this meant that J. Edgar was a *threat* to the conspirators? Why not just rub out all of Washington?

"Earl Warren -- Chief Justice who reluctantly chaired Warren Commission."

Can the "Mystery Deaths" get any sillier than this one? Does anyone seriously believe that the man who headed up the Warren Commission, which was a commission that concluded that Lee Harvey Oswald had, indeed, acted alone in assassinating President Kennedy in Dallas, was going to suddenly go on Perry Mason and belt out a confession that the *"Warren Report is nothing but a pack of lies! Hoffa did it!"*?

"Lee Bowers Jr. -- Witnessed men behind picket fence on Grassy Knoll."

Why would any conspirators want to bother knocking off Mr. Bowers? Bowers, a few months prior to his 1966 death, had *already talked* (on camera) to Mark Lane (in Lane's film *"Rush To Judgment"*), with Bowers saying things to Lane (*on film* no less!) that many conspiracy theorists believe lead down a path toward conspiracy.

So what's the point of killing a person who has already spilled his guts? Did murdering Bowers in a car crash suddenly *undo* his filmed remarks in the *"Rush To Judgment"* motion picture?

"Marguerite Oswald -- Mother of accused assassin."

APPENDIX 1

Marguerite Oswald died of cancer in January 1981. (I guess the conspiracists must think it was cancer of the "injected" variety.) And the goon squad waited more than 17 years to bump her off too, after this highly visible person has had ample opportunity to blow the case sky high. That makes a lot of sense, doesn't it? Well, apparently it does to people like Jim Marrs, et al.

In short, these "Mysterious Deaths" lists are nothing but a crock. Such lists are invented by conspiracy buffs who desperately *want* some kind of conspiratorial and sinister activity to exist revolving around the death of President Kennedy.

I'm surprised that Judy Garland doesn't show up on Marrs' list. She and JFK were good friends. So she probably knew something conspiracy-related. Right, Jim?

"Mystery Deaths" Source:

http://www.assassinationresearch.com/v1n2/deaths.html

THE "SECRET SERVICE STAND-DOWN" MYTH:

For many years now, it's been theorized by certain assassination buffs that the United States Secret Service was in some way connected with the murder of JFK. And it's also been further stated by some conspiracists that there was some form of "Secret Service standdown" or "security stripping" at Love Field Airport in Dallas.

BEYOND REASONABLE DOUBT

But, in reality, the whole Secret Service "stripping" topic is total nonsense, mainly because it can be proven that the security for President Kennedy's motorcade in Dallas on 11/22/63 was absolutely no different in *any substantial way* from other pre-November 22nd motorcades that JFK rode in during his 1,037 days as the 35th U.S. Chief Executive.

Some conspiracy theorists like to harp on the fact that the Secret Service agents did not continuously ride on the back bumpers of JFK's limousine in Dallas (and particularly, of course, in Dealey Plaza)

But the Secret Service configuration in Dealey Plaza was no different than many other pre-November 22 parades, as the photos shown on the webpage below amply demonstrate (and JFK is even *standing up* in the Presidential limousine in several of these pictures, making himself an even bigger target in the car, and there are no Secret Service agents riding the back bumpers at all):

http://Kennedy-Photos.blogspot.com/2013/05/kennedy-gallery-321.html

So, do the conspiracy theorists think that the plot was so sophisticated and elaborate so as to have the Secret Service agents avoiding JFK's bumper in many motorcades *prior* to November 22, just to make it seem like the security was no different at all in Dallas? Obviously, nobody can believe such a nonsensical thing.

Therefore, the argument that is frequently heard from conspiracists about the fact that the agents weren't on the bumper of JFK's car in Dealey Plaza is an argument

APPENDIX 1

that goes absolutely nowhere and proves nothing, because the practice of the Secret Service was to only ride on the bumper of the President's car on those occasions when it was determined that an agent needed to be in closer proximity to President Kennedy.

Quoting from Secret Service agent Clint Hill's Warren Commission testimony [2 H 136]:

"It is left to the agent's discretion more or less to move to that particular position [on the bumper of the President's car] when he feels that there is a danger to the President, to place himself as close to the President--or the First Lady as my case was--as possible."

In addition, the *"all windows along the President's motorcade route would (or should) have been closed"* mantra that is also often dredged up by conspiracy buffs is nonsense, too.

Just look at how many times that (supposed) rule was broken during JFK's administration—during virtually every motorcade I've ever seen in pictures, including Dallas on 11/22/63 (as illustrated in the photo at the webpage below).

http://Kennedy-Photos.blogspot.com/2012/06/kennedy-gallery-032.html

That's just one more example of the Dallas parade being no different whatsoever from other Kennedy motorcades.

With respect to the so-called "Secret Service Stand-down" at Love Field, new information surfaced in 2010

431

BEYOND REASONABLE DOUBT

that should be weighed when attempting to reach a conclusion regarding the identity of a particular "shrugging" Secret Service agent who appears briefly in a videotaped clip just as President Kennedy's motorcade was leaving Love Field Airport.

In the 2010 book *"The Kennedy Detail"*, co-written by former Secret Service agents Gerald Blaine and Clint Hill, it is revealed that the Secret Service agent who appears to be bewildered and who is holding his arms out to his side in the television footage is not the person that most people for years believed him to be--Henry Rybka. Instead of Rybka, however, the bewildered agent is most likely an agent by the name of Donald Lawton, whose assignment on 11/22/63 was to **remain at Love Field**. He was never scheduled to be a part of the actual motorcade through the city of Dallas that day [see Warren Commission Exhibit No. 2554].

Gary Mack, the curator at the *Sixth Floor Museum at Dealey Plaza*, told me this in 2010:

"A [Tom] Dillard photo a few seconds before departure shows an agent behind the right front fender of 679-X [the Secret Service follow-up car], another agent, apparently Rybka, at the bumper on the back end of 100-X [JFK's car], and a third agent wearing a darker suit standing even with JFK. All three men have their left hand on the car they are next to but, unfortunately, their faces cannot be seen. Since the source isn't in the book ["The Kennedy Detail"], I asked writer Lisa McCubbin how the Lawton identification was confirmed and here is what she wrote: 'Confirmed by Clint Hill, Paul Landis, and Don Lawton.' The logical explanation is

APPENDIX 1

that Rybka was farther behind 100-X and just barely out of camera range before and shortly after the motorcade departed. Rybka's report stating he 'moved along with' the motorcade makes sense if he had dropped behind 679-X when that car appeared on camera, thus putting himself impossible to see at that moment." -- E-mail from Gary Mack to David Von Pein; November 16, 2010

The information about the "shrugging" Secret Service man very likely being Don Lawton instead of Henry Rybka is important, because such a discovery should forever silence the conspiracy theorists who like to talk about how the security for JFK's motorcade was being "stripped away" at Love Field.

Why should it silence them with respect to the shrugging agent?

Because, as mentioned previously, Agent Donald Lawton was never assigned to be a part of the team of agents in the follow-up car. [See Emory Roberts' assignment sheets, http://mcadams.posc.mu.edu/russ/m_j_russ/Sa-rober.htm]

Lawton's assignment was *"to remain at the airport to effect security for the President's departure"* (a direct quote from Lawton's 11/30/63 report). [CE2554]

The conspiracy theorists have always been able to argue that Emory Roberts had initially penciled in Henry Rybka's name to be one of the agents assigned to sit in the follow-up car during the Dallas parade. But no such argument can be made regarding Don Lawton, because Lawton knew what his assignment that day was going to

433

be--to stay at Love Field and help out with security at the airport.

Therefore, we can know with 100% certainty that if Lawton is the shrugging agent who looks confused and bewildered just as the motorcade is departing Love Field, then his actions cannot possibly have anything to do with any kind of "security stripping" at the airport. The conspiracy believers can, of course, continue to use their previous "security stripping" argument when it comes to Rybka specifically, but not with Lawton.

There is also video footage taken from a position on the left-hand side of the cars as the motorcade began to move out. That particular footage can be found in a 1963 WBAP-TV special called *"President Kennedy In Texas"*.

[See: http://JFK-Archives.blogspot.com/2010/11/secret-service.html#The-Agents-Near-The-Cars]

The WBAP footage clearly shows two different Secret Service agents walking next to the cars (and probably even *three* different agents), rather than just the one "shrugging" agent that can be seen just a few seconds later in the WFAA-TV videotape footage.

Therefore, all but one of those agents *must* have peeled off and stopped walking beside the cars within just seconds of the WBAP film being shot. Now, whether one of the agents who peeled off was Henry Rybka or not, I cannot say for sure. But it's quite clear that more than just one Secret Service agent was walking next to the cars at Love Field when the motorcade began to roll.

APPENDIX 1

HAPPENSTANCE OR CONSPIRACY?:

So many different things, both large and small, could have occurred leading up to the fateful date of November 22, 1963, that would have almost assuredly kept the assassination of President Kennedy from taking place. For example:

1. If Texas School Book Depository boss Roy Truly had not hired Lee Harvey Oswald (or if Truly would have assigned Oswald to the other TSBD warehouse building at 1917 North Houston Street, which was not located along the Presidential motorcade route), then the assassination would very likely have never taken place. It certainly wouldn't have occurred from where it did take place at any rate, and probably not at all.

2. If Linnie Mae Randle hadn't suggested to Ruth Paine and Marina Oswald in mid-October 1963 that a job might be available at the TSBD, then Lee Oswald would never have even gone to the Book Depository for his interview with Roy Truly on October 15th. It's certainly not likely Lee would have found that Depository job without the aid of Randle and Paine, that's for sure.

   http://JFK-Archives.blogspot.com/2013/04/dvp-vs-dieugenio-part-87.html

3. If Buell Wesley Frazier had never been hired at the TSBD shortly before Lee was hired there, then (again) there's very little chance that

Oswald would have been hired there in October either, because if Frazier hadn't worked there prior to Lee, the whole subject of a possible job opportunity at the Book Depository would never have surfaced during the conversation between Linnie Randle, Ruth Paine, and Marina Oswald at Dorothy Roberts' house in October.

4. If Randle and Frazier had only lived just a few blocks from where they did live in Irving, Texas, then it's very likely that the coffee-break get-together at neighbor Dorothy Roberts' house would never have taken place at all, and the possible job opening at the Depository would never have been brought to the attention of Ruth Paine (or Lee Harvey Oswald) in October.

5. If the Texas Employment Commission would have called Lee Oswald and informed him of the job opening at an airline company (Trans-Texas Airways) just a day or two earlier, then Oswald would have quite possibly been hired by the airline company and would not have applied for work at the TSBD in October [Warren Report, p.247]. (This item here has a little bit more doubt attached to it, since we can never know for sure whether Lee would have made a favorable impression when interviewed by the airline company and been hired there, or even if Oswald would have gone there to seek the work. It stands to reason, though, that he probably would have tried to get that job, since he was looking for work and needed a job badly as of early to mid-October 1963.)

6. If Oswald had been caught while trying to kill General Edwin Walker on the night of April 10,

APPENDIX 1

1963, then, quite clearly, Lee would never have had an opportunity seven months later to take that same rifle he used to try and kill Walker and use it on President Kennedy in Dealey Plaza. He'd have been in prison for the Walker attempt instead.

http://JFK-Archives.blogspot.com/2012/12/edwin-walker-and-lee-harvey-oswald.html

7. If Oswald had been successful in his suicide attempt in Russia in October 1959, then he would have been graveyard dead when President Kennedy visited Dallas four years later.

In a nutshell, these are the things that resulted in a President being killed in Dallas:

Fate, coincidence, happenstance, a good deal of luck, a rifle that was handy, Lee Harvey Oswald's rifle training in the Marine Corps, a job in a seven-story building that just happened to command a perfect view of the slow-moving President's car, Oswald having easy and legitimate access to all seven floors of the Book Depository Building, Mother Nature's cooperation with the Dallas weather on 11/22/63 (resulting in clear skies at noontime for JFK's motorcade, meaning that the limousine's bubbletop roof would not be required, which was a roof that, while not bulletproof, might have served to deflect Oswald's bullets or might have altered Oswald's plan to fire any shots at all at an enclosed vehicle which might have been, for all the assassin knew, a bulletproof enclosure), a bleak-looking future for Lee Oswald, an

437

BEYOND REASONABLE DOUBT

unresolved spat with his wife the night before, the President driving by the TSBD at noontime (the normal lunchtime for the employees, meaning that the sixth floor would stand a better chance of being totally free of workers, since most of them ate their lunch on the lower floors), and Lee Harvey Oswald's hatred of authority and his hatred of American society in general.

All of these things played a part in what occurred at 12:30 PM in Dealey Plaza on November 22, 1963. If any one of the above factors had been different, then perhaps the President would have been able to make that speech at the Trade Mart that Friday in Dallas.

Also see -- http://JFK-Archives.blogspot.com/2010/08/if-only.html

THREE SIMPLE QUESTIONS FOR CONSPIRACY THEORISTS:

1. Where does *all* of the physical evidence lead in the JFK and J.D. Tippit murder cases (e.g., the guns, the bullets, the bullet shells, the fingerprints, and the fibers), plus Lee Harvey Oswald's own movements, actions, and statements before and after the murders?

2. Is it even remotely possible (or doable) -- in the real world -- that every piece of evidence in both the JFK and Tippit murder investigations could have been faked or manufactured so that all of it became neatly (and almost immediately) stacked up into a perfect *"Oswald did it"* pile?

3. Who amongst the current population of millions of conspiracy theorists worldwide would have

APPENDIX 1

actually attempted to set up and frame Lee Harvey Oswald as the patsy in President John F. Kennedy's assassination by utilizing a *multi-gun* frame-up plot in Dallas, Texas, on November 22, 1963?

The only conceivable answers to the above inquiries are, of course:

1. To Lee Harvey Oswald.
2. No, it is not.
3. Nobody.

I'd thoroughly enjoy seeing just one conspiracy theorist answer the above three questions in a believable manner, while using common sense and reasoned thinking along the way. However, I fear that being able to do that would be even more problematic than the task that was facing the after-the-shooting "Fake Everything In Sight" conspiracy crew in Dallas, Texas, on 11/22/63.

A simple and basic fact should probably be placed in front of the eyes of many JFK conspiracy theorists, and that fact is this one: If only a *small portion* of the physical evidence in the JFK and J.D. Tippit murder cases has *not* been tampered with or planted or faked in some manner, then it's very likely that Lee Harvey Oswald was guilty of shooting and killing President Kennedy and/or Officer Tippit. The above "real world" fact, however, doesn't seem to enter the heads of a lot of the conspiracy believers around the world. Along this same line of thought, lawyer and author Vincent Bugliosi said this -- *"If you're innocent of a crime, chances are there's not going to be any evidence pointing toward your guilt. Why? Because you're innocent."*

WEBLINKS:

Here is a list of useful Internet websites relating in a variety of ways to President John F. Kennedy and his assassination:

- MelAyton.com
- DavidVonPein.blogspot.com
- JFK-Archives.blogspot.com
- JFK-Assassination-As-It-Happened.blogspot.com
- Oswald-Is-Guilty.blogspot.com
- Single-Bullet-Theory.blogspot.com
- Kennedy-Photos.blogspot.com
- Quoting-Common-Sense.blogspot.com
- JFK-Press-Conferences.blogspot.com

APPENDIX 2

REPLICATION OF THE HSCA WEISS & ASCHKENASY ACOUSTIC ANALYSIS BY MICHAEL O'DELL

Replication of the HSCA Weiss & Aschkenasy Acoustic Analysis

> "Scientific researchers propose hypotheses as explanations of phenomena, and design experimental studies to test these hypotheses via predictions which can be derived from them. These steps must be repeatable, to guard against mistake or confusion in any particular experimenter." – Wikipedia article on "Scientific method".

History

In 1978 the House Select Committee on Assassinations (HSCA) concluded that there was probably a conspiracy involved in the assassination of President Kennedy, a conclusion primarily based on the acoustic evidence contained on the Dallas Police Department radio recordings.

An unknown motorcycle tuned to channel I had a defective microphone button that caused it to continuously transmit over a five minute period during which the assassination took place. If this motorcycle had been part of the motorcade it might have picked up sounds of the gunshots. If true, those sounds could be used to determine how many shots were fired, their timing, and using echo location methods, the source of the shots.

Working for the HSCA, a team (BRSW) from Bolt, Beranek and Newman Inc. (BBN) headed by James E. Barger, studied the recordings. BRSW performed a series of test shots in Dealey Plaza and used recordings of these shots to compare with signals on the DPD recordings. BRSW concluded that channel I contained impulses probably caused by the gunshots, with a 50% probability that one shot came from the grassy knoll in front of the President. Because of the level of uncertainty in this finding the HSCA asked another team try to raise the confidence level of the results. Weiss and Aschkenasy (W&A) used an acoustic modeling method and concluded there was a 95% probability of a shot from the grassy knoll.

Science and Reproducibility

The BBN tests compared impulse patterns from the Dictabelt recording to patterns from live test firings done in Dealey Plaza. Recordings or other records of those test firings are no longer available. Without them there is no practical way to attempt a replication of the BBN procedure. However, it was not the BBN tests that determined there was a shot from the grassy knoll or a fourth shot. The BBN tests were inconclusive on these points. Those conclusions came from the W&A analysis. For this reason, although it may be enlightening to obtain those test fire recordings and they may be necessary to replicate the BBN test, they are not necessary for evaluating the evidence for a grassy knoll shot. It is also why any falsification of the BBN tests does not automatically falsify the HSCA acoustic evidence conclusion.

Despite the historic significance of these tests and despite years of back and forth scientific debate about them since they were done, nobody has replicated the experiments. It does seem to be a strange oversight.

Reproducibility is a fundamental principle of the scientific method. An experiment performed only once has little significance. Science is a human endeavor and subject to human frailties. Replication is one of the ways that science controls for human error.

The Current Effort

Six years ago I was provided a full sized copy of the Drommer & Associates survey map by Anthony Marsh. This is the same map that Weiss & Aschkenasy used to perform their analysis. It gave every appearance of being the same map, to the same scale. It matches the image of the map that was presented in Weiss & Aschkenasy's testimony before the committee. Known distances of features, like the widths of buildings, were confirmed on the map. It has the same scale, 1 inch equal to 10 feet.

Since acquiring the map it has been a goal to one day attempt a replication of the W&A analysis. There has been discussion for years about additional tests that could be done to help clarify our understanding of the acoustic evidence. There have been efforts to acquire the test shot recordings that were made in Dealey Plaza in 1978. There have been suggestions about analyzing the other suspect shots the same way Weiss & Aschkenasy did for the suspect Grassy Knoll shot. These could be worthwhile efforts, but replication of the Weiss & Aschkenasy experiment could have been done at any time.

Not long after receiving the map I made some preliminary calculations of some echo paths presented in the W&A report and got results indicating buildings might be in the wrong place. This was puzzling, and I wanted to double check the accuracy of the map. I asked Dale Myers to confirm some long distance measurements of buildings in Dealey Plaza. Dale made his own extensive surveys of the plaza while building his virtual recreation so this would be independent confirmation. Again measurements on the map were confirmed. The discrepancies with the W&A report remained unexplained, but I did not pursue them further at the time.

I assumed that replication would not be a problem. The strange initial results I had gotten that prompted confirmation with Dale I attributed to some unknown error that would work out once I really got into it. There are some easily observed errors in the W&A report as well, but I thought those could be resolved and not be a barrier to replication. The intention was to build a computer model to calculate echoes in Dealey Plaza, replicate the W&A results, and then use the model to test additional scenarios and locations that W&A were unable to check. However, this subject is just one of many things in which I'm interested and there are always projects to be done. The enthusiasm to start on this just wasn't there and years went by without doing anything.

In late 2012 I began receiving inquiries from media people and authors that were working on projects for the 50th anniversary in 2013. I realized that it was time to get this project done.

Using Excel for the model was always one of the goals. When Jefferson Morley came out to interview me in 2006 for his Playboy article I showed him a crude Excel spreadsheet calculating echo paths. I doubt he thought much of it, it wasn't very impressive.

I started by measuring the positions of objects on the map and entering those into a table on a spreadsheet, then writing formulas to calculate distances, echo paths, conversions to millimeters and milliseconds, and the other necessary functions.

APPENDIX 2

Before long I realized the results of runs could be plotted directly on the map image, and that it would run orders of magnitude faster if all of the calculation were removed from cell functions and run in background VBA code. The model gradually evolved into a very sophisticated tool that could test possibilities Weiss & Aschkenasy could never have attempted.

The W&A report cites a single live fire test shot for calibration purposes and the data for that impulse pattern is provided in the report. The rest of the procedure required the survey map of Dealey Plaza and a recording of the Dictabelt, both of which are now readily available. Measurements W&A made using the map are published in the report.

I have made every effort to reproduce the process as laid out in the report, using the same materials and techniques but with more powerful tools. Numerous errors have been found with the data provided in the report, including basic errors involving the measurement of delay times, waveform peaks, and object positions. Some of the errors are necessary to the finding of an echo correlation to the suspect Dictabelt pattern. The Weiss & Aschkenasy report does not stand up to even limited scrutiny, and the results it contains cannot be reproduced.

Materials

1. Drommer & Associates survey map prepared for the HSCA, provided by Anthony Marsh (image: http://the-puzzle-palace.com/DP1280.jpg). Scale: 1 inch = 10 feet
2. Copy of the Weiss & Aschkenasy report to the HSCA (http://www.history-matters.com/archive/jfk/hsca/reportvols/vol8/pdf/HSCA_Vol8_AS_1_Weiss.pdf)
3. Copies of the Dallas Police Department recordings, provided by Dr. Norman Ramsey and Dr. Paul Horowitz.
4. A copy of the Dictabelt recording used in the Court TV program in 2003, provided by Robert Berkovitz of Sensimetrics.

Methods

The Weiss & Aschkenasy procedure involved measuring distances on the survey map and converting those to time in milliseconds based on the speed of sound, and comparing those values to delay times derived from either the Dictabelt or a test fire recording.

In 1978 this was done manually using a ruler and lengths of string. Locations were measured on a high resolution scan (4923 x 3596) of the survey map. Map locations were identified by two dimensional coordinates, as number of pixels from the upper left corner of the map, using Adobe Photoshop. Coordinates and other variables were entered into a Microsoft Excel 2010 spreadsheet, in which Excel VBA code was written to handle conversions and the computations of echo paths, and other functions.

W&A measured distances on the map in millimeters. For this effort distances were measured as individual pixels from the upper left corner of the image on the scanned map. A ratio has to be established to convert pixels to millimeters. That was done by taking measurements of long distances directly on the paper map and comparing those with pixel measurements on the image. The conversion ratio was also later cross-checked with fixed location data in the W&A report. The ratio was determined to be 3.92 pixels/mm.

Calibration

The W&A analysis was an effort to match a suspect impulse pattern on the Dictabelt recording to a specific location on the survey map of Dealey Plaza, using echo location. The assumption was that it would be very unlikely to be able to pin a specific location to the pattern if it was not in fact a real gunshot sound, recorded in Dealey Plaza.

To do this they first had to establish which objects on the map should be used to calculate echoes. They took a test shot recording made in Dealey Plaza by BBN, and matched up the echo peaks on that impulse pattern with objects on the map. This generated the list of echo producing objects and echo paths that are used in the succeeding steps.

The calibration procedure involved the following steps:

1. Establish the position of the rifle and microphone used for the test shot.
2. Measure echo times of peaks on the test shot recording.
3. Identify echo objects, using pins at the rifle and microphone locations on the map and strings cut to the distance each echo would travel, to draw an ellipse. Each ellipse should intersect the object that produced the echo peak.
4. Generate a numbered list of echo paths using objects identified on the map. Some peaks may be produced by compound echoes, and their paths will involve two objects.

Rifle and Microphone positions

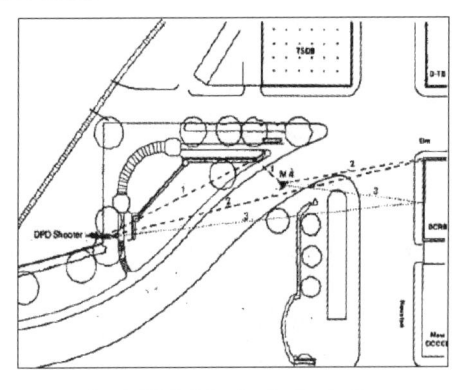

Figure 1: W&A Fig. 5, depicting microphone location.

APPENDIX 2

W&A placed the test rifle north of the corner of the wooden fence on the grassy knoll, where the shooter fired during the reconstruction tests. The microphone was the fourth in the third array, as depicted in their Figure 4 diagram. The report documents these positions in text accompanying their Figure 5.

Page 22 of the report cites the path of echo 2 in this diagram and gives the following measurements:

    Rifle to diffraction point: 499 mm.
    Rifle to microphone: 213 ft. or 185.2 ms.
    Diffraction point to microphone: 92 mm.

These are fixed measurements for three sides of a triangle, with one apex on the diffraction point and another touching the fence line. This is enough information to geometrically determine the positions of the rifle and microphone.

One problem I noticed with the report early on is that the diagram does not match the description. Echo path 2 as depicted in the illustration diffracts off of the northwest corner of the Dallas County Records Building. The distance between the fence and that building is easily checked on the map. The DCRB is about 930 mm from the fence, not 499 mm.

There is however only one object on the list of objects that is 499 mm away from the fence. It is not labeled on the illustration. It is "Wall A, Corner 2" on the object list. That is very near "Wall A, Corner 1", which is the path depicted by path 1 on the illustration.

If we ignore the W&A illustration and use the provided dimensions, the rifle is along the fence line 499 mm from "Wall A, Corner 2". That position is 892 pixels right and 1750 pixels down from the corner of the map. This also corresponds to 15 mm north of the corner of the fence.

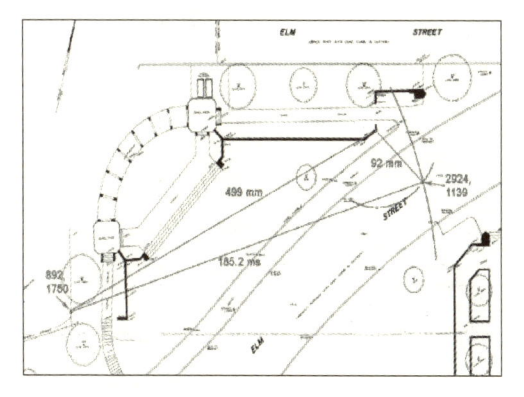

Figure 2: Corrected diagram for microphone location.

445

BEYOND REASONABLE DOUBT

The microphone position for the test would be 92 mm from "Wall A, Corner 2", and 185.2 ms. from the rifle. Given the rifle position, the microphone coordinates are 2924 pixels right and 1139 pixels down.

Echo Times of Test Shot Peaks

The test shot recordings are unavailable. The only evidence of the test shot used by W&A is Figure 6 in their report, a poor quality copy of the waveform without a scale. However W&A provide measurements from the waveform in their Table 3. That data is used here.

Identify Echo Objects and Paths

Table 2 is a list of echo paths. Each path is a line connecting the rifle position, to an object position, and then to the microphone position. Some paths use two object positions making a compound echo. Each path is made using objects listed in Table 1.

Table 1 contains another of the obvious errors. Both object 16 and 20 are described as the same object, "DCRB : Southwest corner." Yet the echo times for these two paths are different. One or both must be labeled incorrectly.

TABLE 1.— *List of structures in Dealey Plaza that would have produced echoes of sufficient strength to have been recorded on the DPD tape*

Object No.:	Identification
1	South shelter : South door, east post.
2	South shelter : East door, south post.
3	South shelter : East door, north post.
4	North shelter : South door, west post.
5	North shelter : South door, east post.
6	North shelter : East door, south post.
7	North shelter : East door, north post.
8	Wall "A." [1]
9	Wall "A" : Corner 1.
10	Wall "A" : Corner 2.
11	Column "A" [2] : Southwest corner.
12	Wall "B" [3] : Corner 1.
13	Wall "B" : Corner 2.
14	Column "B" [4] : West corner.
15	Wall at the north end of the reflecting pool.
16	DCRB : Southwest corner.
17	DCRB : Northwest corner.
18	DCRB : West wall (front of building).
19	DCRB : Roof edge on west wall.
20	DCRB : Southwest corner.
21	New DCCCB : Northwest corner.
22	DCRB—New DCCCB : Alley wall between buildings.

[1] Wall "A" is a concrete wall on the north side of Elm St. that runs in an east-west direction. Corners 1 and 2 are at the east end of the wall. The direction of the wall changes from east to northeast at corner 1, and from northeast to north at corner 2.

[2] Column "A" is a concrete column on the north side of Elm St. near the intersection with Houston St.

[3] Wall "B" is a concrete wall on the south side of Elm St. near the reflecting pool. It runs in a generally north-south direction. Corners 1 and 2 are at the northern end of the wall. The direction of the wall changes from north to northeast at corner 1 and from northeast to east at corner 2.

[4] Column "B" is a concrete column on the south side of Elm St., at the northern end of Wall "B."

446

APPENDIX 2

Table 2 contains a third obvious error. Path 26 is said to bounce off of object 23. There are only 22 objects in the object list.

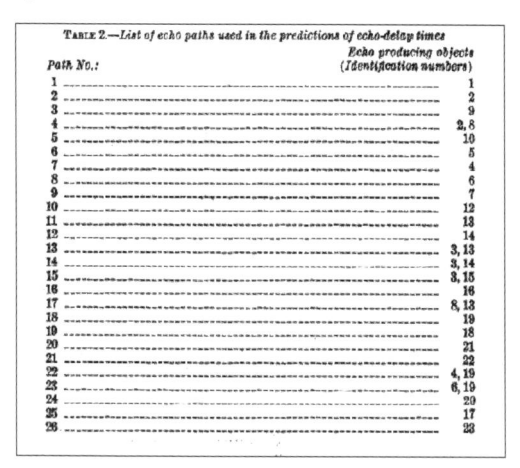

TABLE 2.—*List of echo paths used in the predictions of echo-delay times*

Path No.:	Echo producing objects (Identification numbers)
1	1
2	2
3	9
4	2, 8
5	10
6	5
7	4
8	6
9	7
10	12
11	13
12	14
13	3, 13
14	3, 14
15	3, 15
16	16
17	8, 13
18	19
19	18
20	21
21	22
22	4, 19
23	6, 19
24	20
25	17
26	23

Each of the 26 numbered paths is listed in Table 3, along with the relevant measurements. Since each echo path was supposed to correspond to one of the peaks on the test shot pattern, each path has an associated echo travel time and delay times. Weiss & Aschkenasy used the echo travel times to draw ellipses on the map, using pins and string. If an ellipse intersects a potential echo producing object on the map then it is an indication that the object produced the echo.

We can do the same and use the model to plot the ellipses for each path to check the object selections and record their map coordinates.

Most echo time ellipses do in fact match with an object recorded in the object list, confirming those objects and also the accuracy of the model. But there are problems with some of the identifications used by W&A.

447

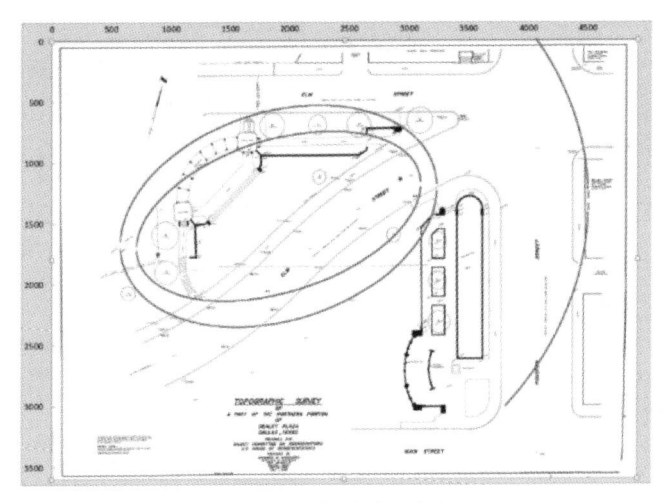

TABLE 3.—MEASURED AND PREDICTED DELAY TIMES OF ECHOES FOR A GUNSHOT FIRED ON AUG. 20, 1978

[In milliseconds]

Echo path	Echo travel time	Echo-delay time [1] Predicted	Echo-delay time [1] Measured	Deviation
1	192.3	7.0	7.3	0.3
2	196.0	10.8	11.2	.5
3	196.6	13.4	13.1	.3
4	201.7	16.5	16.9	.3
5	202.4	17.2	16.9	.3
6	213.0	27.8	28.3	.5
7	213.0	27.8	29.8	2.0
8	215.4	30.1	29.8	.0
9	218.1	32.9	32.9	.0
10	228.4	43.2	42.1	1.1
11	229.4	44.7	45.6	.9
12	232.5	52.3	52.9	.6
13	243.4	58.2	60.0	1.8
14	252.7	67.5	66.3	1.2
15	259.9	74.7	76.9	2.2
16	267.1	81.9	82.5	.6
17	267.4	82.2	83.1	.9
18	451.0	266.7	266.6	.1
19	455.0	269.8	269.2	.6
20	458.1	272.9	272.2	.7
21	469.2	284.0	282.2	1.7
22	482.8	297.6	297.7	.1
23	482.8	297.6	297.7	.1
24	487.2	302.0	303.2	1.2
25	497.8	312.6	313.0	.4
26	541.3	356.1	354.0	2.1

[1] For the calculated locations of the gun and the microphone, the muzzle blast travel time is computed to be 185.2 ms.

Figure 3: Echo time ellipses for three echo times.

APPENDIX 2

Object 1, used in path 1, is labeled as, "South shelter : South door, east post.". In fact, the ellipse for path 1 crosses the west post.

Object 2, used in path 2, is labeled as, "South shelter : East door, south post". In fact, the ellipse identifies the north post.

Object 4, used in path 7, is labeled as, "North shelter : South door, west post.". In fact, the ellipse for path 7 misses all the posts in both shelters. The only potential object with which it intersects is the end of a wall just north of Wall "A" that does not appear on the object list at all.

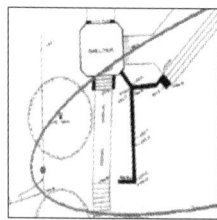

Figure 4: For object 1, path 1

Object 6, used in path 8, is labeled as, "North shelter : East door, south post.". However, it uses the same echo time as object #4 and therefore draws the same ellipse, which intersects no posts.

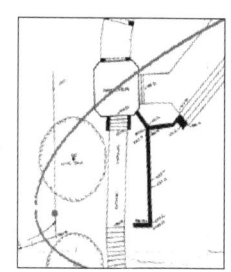

Figure 5: For object 2, path 2

An interesting pattern emerges when checking objects numbered higher than 10. When a path cites an object higher than 10, the ellipse for that path will intersect the object that is numbered one less. That is, when a path cites object 13, it really intersects at object 12. A path cites object 18 but really intersects object 17.

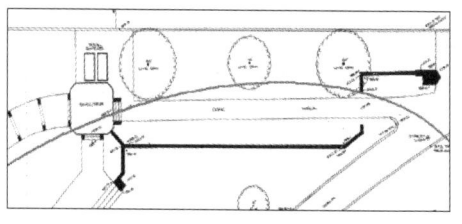

Figure 4: For objects 4 and 6, paths 7 and 8.

This observation helps explain the obvious mistake in the path list regarding object 23. Path 26 cites object 23 when there is no object 23. No path cites object 11, when the only reason an object appears on the list is because it is used in a path.

The objects in the path list are numbered incorrectly. They can be corrected by subtracting one from every object number higher than 10, wherever the object number appears. For example, instead of path 19 using object 18, it should use object 17.

The duplicate labeling of objects 16 and 20 can now be corrected. Object 16 is now cited by path 25. The echo time ellipse for path 25 intersects only one potential object, the southwest corner of the Dal-Tex building.

449

BEYOND REASONABLE DOUBT

There are two additional ambiguities on the object list. First, object 19 is, "DCRB : Roof edge on west wall.". The west wall of the DCRB is already used as object 18, with a different echo time. The "roof edge" would be at the top of this tall building. This introduces the third dimension into W&A's work for the only time, and there are no notations on the map regarding the height or position of the "roof edge". It is possible they used another source for that information. Ignoring the doubts raised by choosing to introduce the third dimension for this one and only echo, we can resolve the ambiguity by giving them the benefit of the doubt. A position for the unknown roof edge was used that would give the result cited by W&A.

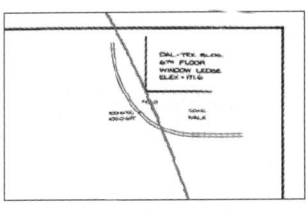

Figure 5: For object 16, path 25.

Another ambiguity involves object 22. The table calls this, "DCRB—New DCCCB : Alley wall between buildings". No such alley wall is depicted on the survey map. We might assume they used other sources for that information as well, but there is a problem with that. The ellipse drawn for this object would place it significantly off the right edge of the map. Even if there is a wall that far back in the alley the walls of the alley would prevent any echoes coming from it from reaching most of the plaza, including the part of the street we are interested in. That cannot be the real object. However the ellipse for path 26, object 22 does identify one potential object, the southwest corner of the New DCCCB.

After corrections to objects 1, 2, 16, 22, and fixing the incorrect numbering in the path list, only objects 4 and 6 are unresolved. Those are both based on the same reported echo time of 215 ms. which does not map to either of the objects reported in the list but does at the end of an unidentified wall.

One resolution would be to assign this wall as the echo producing object instead of the two shelter posts they were supposed to be.

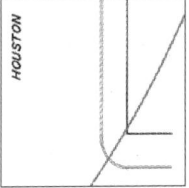

Figure 6: For object 22, path 26.

The conservative option would be to use a resolution that favors W&A if one is available. Their Table 3 also lists other echo times for the paths. The "Predicted" column is the number they calculated from the map after assigning an object position. The "predicted" echo time for path 7 is two milliseconds less than the value reported for the waveform measurement. That in itself is strange since two milliseconds would qualify it to be a different echo. However, since we don't have good data for the test shot recording, it's possible the error is in recording the "measured" value. The conservative option is therefore to plot the ellipse with the "predicted" value. When that's done it does intersect with the object described in the list for object 4, "North shelter : South door, west post".

This does not help resolve object 6. The difference between the "Predicted" and "Measured" column values is only 0.4 milliseconds, and it does not move the ellipse enough to make a difference. The only

450

APPENDIX 2

object that intersects this line is the south end of the unidentified wall. The choice is to use that object, or to strike the path from the list for possible matching.

The procedure being used here is the same one prescribed by W&A for selecting all of the objects, and it does in fact point to an object. What reason would we have for not using it, other than the fact that W&A didn't?

One reason might be that W&A believed this object would be occluded by structures between it and the rifle. That's very possible, Wall "A" runs just south of this object. However, object 10 appears to be equally occluded by the wall and it made the list. Such objections might be raised about the several post objects in the two shelters. To get to the position reported for object 7 sound from the rifle would have to pass through the south shelter (through what appears to be solid wall) and barely pass through the south doorway of the north shelter. This analysis is not intended to dispute the physical plausibility of these echo paths however, so such potential occlusion is not grounds for dismissing an echo path. According to the procedure defined by W&A we should use the object indicated by the ellipse.

After replicating the W&A procedure for selecting echo producing objects and echo paths, 5 objects have been found to be incorrect, and 17 of the path definitions have to be altered. In addition the diagram depicting the microphone placement is found to be in error.

Some of these mistakes may just be errors in compiling the report. Renumbering the object numbers in the paths, or changing a label on an object would have no material effect if W&A used the correct values when they performed the experiment.

However, if W&A selected the wrong objects and used those positions going forward, then they weren't comparing the right values to the echo peaks on the Dictabelt. Testing of the echoes for object 1 does indicate that they used the incorrect post.

Figure 10 depicts results from the model when the parameters were set up for the Dictabelt test. The two colored areas are plots of the possible microphone locations where Dictabelt peak 1 would match the predicted value (+/- 1 ms.) for echo path 1. The only difference between them is which post

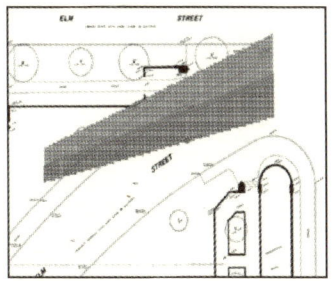

Figure 10: Possible microphone positions with alternative selections for object 1.

is selected for the echo path. The green area uses the correct post shown by plotting the echo time ellipse. The lower purple area uses the incorrect post cited by Weiss & Aschkenasy.

Using the incorrect post is required to get the reported Dictabelt correlation.

BEYOND REASONABLE DOUBT

Dictabelt Pattern

The ultimate purpose of this entire calibration procedure was to create sets of predicted echoes for comparison to the Dictabelt recording. Using the echo paths that were defined, the microphone and rifle locations could be altered and a new pattern of echo peaks generated. These could then be compared to the Dictabelt pattern. It is just as important to measure the Dictabelt pattern accurately as it is to generate a proper set of comparison peaks.

W&A Figure 7 depicts the Dictabelt pattern with labels for each of the 26 echoes that were assigned to paths. The echo time measurements for these peaks were recorded in W&A Table 4. The "Impulse delay time" column of Table 4 would be the time elapsed from the muzzle blast to each labeled peak.

TABLE 4.—MEASURED DELAY TIMES OF IMPULSES AND PREDICTED DELAY TIMES OF GUNSHOT ECHOES FOR NOV. 22, 1963
[In milliseconds]

Echo path	Echo travel time	Echo delay time	Impulse delay time	Deviation
1	202.4	6.5	6.3	0.2
2	206.9	10.9	10.5	.4
3	211.0	15.1	14.7	.4
4	214.7	18.8	19.3	.5
5	217.0	21.1	20.1	1.0
6	224.3	28.4	27.4	1.0
7	225.2	29.3	30.3	1.0
8	227.1	31.2	31.6	.4
9	230.6	34.7	34.1	.6
10	244.1	48.2	48.7	.5
11	241.5	45.6	45.4	.2
12	250.3	54.4	54.2	.2
13	255.2	59.3	59.7	.4
14	266.0	70.1	69.4	.7
15	273.4	77.5	77.4	.1
16	281.0	85.9	85.3	.6
17	276.7	80.8	80.2	.6
18	473.9	278.0	278.6	.6
19	479.8	283.9	283.7	.2
20	479.8	283.9	283.7	.2
21	489.1	293.2	292.1	1.1
22	506.8	310.9	310.5	.4
23	507.9	312.0	312.4	.4
24	509.6	313.7	313.1	.6
25	524.0	328.1	327.5	.6
26	565.0	369.1	369.2	.1

¹ For the calculated locations of the gun and the microphone, the muzzle blast travel time is computed to be 195.9 ms.

Figure 7 has no scale of any kind so the measurements can't be completely confirmed by referring to that illustration. One check that can be made with Figure 7 is to see if the measurements are accurately made regardless of scale. To do that we can assume peak 26 represents the 369.2 ms. mark as the table says, and compare all the other peaks relative to that. When I did, many of the peaks were found to produce measurements that were significantly different than those presented in the table.

Other peaks were tried as the anchor with similar results. Even a sliding scale was used to find the best possible match, which minimized the sum of all the differences. However no such adjustments could reconcile all of the peak measurements. Even when using a scale with minimum differences many of the peaks differed by more than the 1 ms. tolerance that W&A claimed to be allowing.

APPENDIX 2

Considering the possibility that the printed Dictabelt pattern may have been distorted in the production process, I needed to check the measurements against the actual recording. Figure 8 is the suspect pattern taken from a digital copy of the Dictabelt recording.

Visually the two patterns confirm each other. Once they are scaled to the same size the two images could be placed on transparent backgrounds and laid over each other and the peaks will line up. There is no significant distortion in the printed pattern.

The digital recording has the advantage of being directly measureable. Each peak in Figure 8 can be measured very precisely in the audio software. When measurements of all 26 peaks were made very large differences from the Table 4 values were observed. This is best seen by looking at the longest echo delay, the one for peak 26.

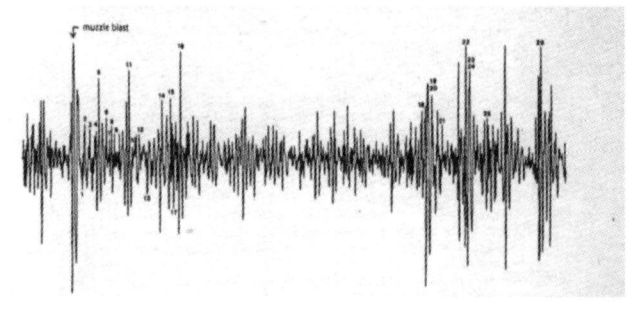

Figure 7: W&A Dictabelt pattern of suspected grassy knoll shot.

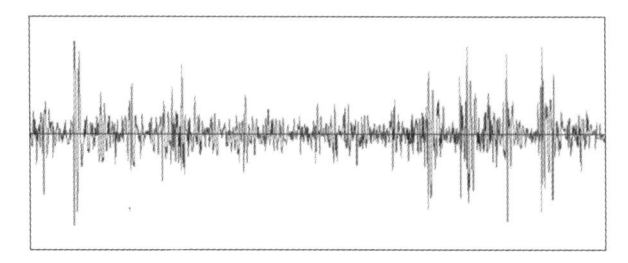

Figure 8: Pattern seen in digital recording of Dictabelt.

Table 4 records the value of the echo delay for peak 26 as 369.2 ms. The same peak measured directly in the recording is 337.1 ms after the muzzle blast. That's a difference of almost 10%.

453

BEYOND REASONABLE DOUBT

On average W&A Table 4 gives delay times that are 13.4% greater than those measured off the recording. That's only the average. Some peaks have a much greater difference, as much as 34% for peak 1. If it were only a matter of using different scales, or playback speeds, the percentage of difference would be the same for every peak.

Playback speed is an issue in the reports, but cannot explain the discrepancies I observed. W&A explained that they adjusted Dictabelt times by a factor of 1.043 because that gave the best match. This was said to be justified because BBN found that the recorder was running at, "0.95 of correct speed."

However the recording I used to measure the peaks had already been established as very close to real time. The very same digital recording was used in the 2003 Court TV analysis performed by Robert Berkovitz. Berkovitz created pattern detection software to evaluate possible matches between W&A's echo pattern and the Dictabelt recording. He reported that there was no match of any significance. For his analysis he made the 5% correction to the playback speed called for by BBN. Don Thomas and I both found that this was an error because the recording he used had already been speed corrected, and his software produced a better correlation with a 0% speed correction.

I performed another check on the playback speed by comparing signals between recordings. Both channel 2 and channel 1 contain a simulcast announcement that is almost 10 seconds long. The speed of channel 2 can be calculated with some certainty because of the prominent power hum that was unmistakably deposited at record time (see: http://mcadams.posc.mu.edu/odell). This test showed that perhaps a correction to Dictabelt times as much as 1.5% may be justified, but in the opposite direction. That adjustment would only increase the differences with Table 4.

There is also a conflict between W&A and BBN regarding the total span of the Dictabelt impulses. In the relevant test BBN says W&A found, "14 impulses in a 320 msec time span", and that value forms a part of the probability calculation upon which the 95% chance of "gunfire from the knoll" is based. Table 4 contains peaks out to 369.2 ms.

Because the range of differences runs from 8% to 34%, the values in Table 4 cannot be completely reconciled by any adjustment for speed.

The bottom line is that the values presented in Table 4 for the Dictabelt pattern do not appear to be valid measurements of the peaks on the recording. A test that supposedly identifies a gunshot on the Dictabelt recording must, at a minimum, correctly measure the sound being tested on the Dictabelt. If it does not then it is not a real test.

Peak	DB.wav	Table 4	%
0	0	0	
1	4.717	6.3	134%
2	8.164	10.5	129%
3	11.157	14.7	132%
4	15.511	19.3	124%
5	18.594	20.1	108%
6	24.309	27.4	113%
7	26.667	30.3	114%
8	28.3	31.6	112%
9	30.386	34.1	112%
10	43.538	48.7	112%
11	41.089	45.4	110%
12	48.254	54.2	112%
13	54.15	59.7	110%
14	64.127	69.4	108%
15	70.204	77.4	110%
16	77.461	85.3	110%
17	72.563	80.2	111%
18	251.52	278.6	111%
19	258.232	283.7	110%
20	258.232	283.7	110%
21	265.851	292.1	110%
22	283.084	310.5	110%
23	285.533	312.4	109%
24	285.533	313.1	110%
25	298.413	327.5	110%
26	337.143	369.2	110%

Figure 9: Comparison of W&A Table 4 peaks to Dictabelt recording.

APPENDIX 2

Conclusions About the Attempt to Reproduce Weiss & Aschkenasy

The Weiss & Aschkenasy report to the HSCA formed the basis for the scientific finding a gunshot from the grassy knoll. The analysis depended upon measuring distances on a survey map, identifying echo producing structures on that map, predicting echoes that would be made at various locations on the map, and measuring the Dictabelt pattern to compare those projected echoes.

This attempt to reproduce that experiment has demonstrated significant errors in Weiss & Aschkenasy's results at every step. An attempt to completely reproduce the process without any dependence on data from the report may require additional sources, like the calibration shot recording, that are not currently available.

Someone with a religious devotion to belief in the acoustic evidence might say that falsifying the report does not prove there was no shot from the grassy knoll on the Dictabelt recording. Maybe Weiss & Aschkenasy did the test correctly and everything got all messed up when the report was written. True, maybe that happened. Maybe it didn't. We also can't prove there was no shot from the Dal-Tex building, or the overpass, or the storm drain. We are not often required to prove negatives such as that. The basis for believing the Weiss & Aschkenasy result is the report. A hypothetical experiment conducted in private and not written down does not count.

Falsifying the Weiss & Aschkenasy report basically puts us back where things were before the HSCA hired them to do the analysis. We have a report from BBN that is unable to say whether there was a shot from the grassy knoll, or even a fourth shot. That report also has never been reproduced and relied on data we can no longer examine.

There is another point that needs to be emphasized here. Explaining that a scientific experiment needs to be reproduced to be credible is not an insinuation of fraud. The reproducibility of experiments is a fundamental tenet of the scientific method, for good reason. It is just as important as the idea that a theory must be falsifiable in principle. In my own personal experience of dealing with the acoustic evidence I have been accused of calling the HSCA scientists frauds for simply observing these tests have not been duplicated. I would like to preempt more of that now.

I have corresponded with Dr. Barger over the years and have read all of his HSCA testimony and reports. My personal opinion is that he is honest and that he tried to restrict his statements to those that could be supported by the evidence. Weiss & Aschkenasy were not as careful and clearly they made mistakes. That does not mean they acted fraudulently.

BEYOND REASONABLE DOUBT

BIBLIOGRAPHY

Report of the President's Commission on the Assassination of President John F. Kennedy, 26 accompanying volumes of Hearings and Exhibits published by the US Government Printing Office in 1964. Also 'The Warren Report', without supporting volumes, published by Doubleday with forward by Louis Nizer and afterword by Bruce Catton (1964)

The Investigation of the Assassination of President John F. Kennedy, conducted by the Senate Select Committee to Study Governmental Operations, Published by the US Government Printing Office in 1976.US Senate Select Committee on Intelligence, http://www.history-matters.com/archive/contents/hsca/contents_hsca_report.htm

Report to the President by the Commission on CIA Activities Within the United States, Vice President Nelson A. Rockefeller, Chairman. Washington, D.C.: U.S. Government Printing Office, June, 1975, p. 262, http://www.history- matters.com/archive/church/rockcomm/html/Rockefeller_0137b.htm

Investigation of the Assassination of President John F. Kennedy, conducted by the Select Committee on Assassinations of the US House of Representatives, published by the US Government Printing Office in 1979. http://www.history-matters.com/archive/contents/hsca/contents_hsca_report.htm

Final Report of the Assassination Records Review Board September 1998 http://www.fas.org/sgp/advisory/arrb98/

National Archives, JFK Assassination Records, Assassination Records Review Board, Series 4: Research and Analysis 4.0.2 Subject Files SOLO SAC New York to Director, FBI, June 12 1964, NARA 124-10274-10338 released March 30 1995 and 4.0.2 Subject Files Cuba, Castro's Knowledge http://www.archives.gov/research/jfk/review-board/series-04.html

BOOKS

Andrew, Christopher. *For The President's Eyes Only – Secret Intelligence and the American Presidency from Washington to Bush* (HarperCollins) 1995

Anson, Robert Sam. *They've Killed The President* (Bantam Books) 1975

Aynesworth, Hugh (with Stephen G. Michaud). *JFK: Breaking The News*, 2003

Ayton, Mel. *The Forgotten Terrorist* (Potomac Books) 2007

Baden, Michael and Roach, Marion. *Dead Reckoning – The New Science of Catching Killers* (London Arrow) 2002

Robert Allen Baker, *They Call It Hypnosis*, Buffalo New York (Prometheus Books) 1990

BIBLIOGRAPHY

Baughman, U.E. (with Leonard Wallace Robinson) *Secret Service Chief* (Harper and Brothers) New York 1962

Belin, David W. *Final Disclosure* (Charles Scribner's Sons) 1998

Bishop, James A. *The Day Kennedy Was Shot* (HarperPerennial) 1992.

Blumenthal, Sid, and Yazijian, Harvey, eds. *Government by Gunplay: Assassination Conspiracies from Dallas to Today,* (New American Library) New York 1976.

Bradlee, Ben. *A Good Life – Newspapering and Other Adventures* (Simon and Schuster) 1995

Brennan, Howard. *Eyewitness To History* (Texian Press) 1987

Brown, Walt. *Treachery In Dallas* (Carroll and Graf) 1996

Bugliosi, Vincent. *Helter Skelter* (Dell Publishing) 1994

------------- *Reclaiming History* (WW Norton) 2007

Canal, John. *Silencing The Lone Assassin* (Paragon House) 2000

Colby, William, with Peter Forbath. *Honourable Men – My Life in the CIA* (Hutchinson) London 1978

Cornwell, Gar. *Real Answers* (Paleface Press) 1998

Davis, John H. *Mafia Kingfish – Carlos Marcello and the Assassination of John F. Kennedy* (McGraw-Hill Publishing Company) 1989

Davison, Jean, *Oswald's Game* (WW Norton) 1983.

DeFrank, Thomas M. *Write It When I'm Gone – Remarkable Off-the-Record Conversations With Gerald R. Ford* (Putnam Publishing Group - U.S.) 2007

Demaris, Ovid, and Willis, Gary B. *Jack Ruby*, (DaCapo Press N.Y.) 1994

DiEugenio, James and Pease, Lisa. *The Assassinations* (Feral House) 2012 .

Duffy, James R., *The Web – Kennedy Assassination Cover-Up* (Alan Sutton Publishing) 1988.

Eddowes, Michael. *November 22: How They Killed Kennedy* (Spearman) London 1976

Epstein, Edward J. *Legend: The Secret World of Lee Harvey Oswald* (Hutchinson) 1976

-------------- *Inquest: The Warren Commission and the Establishment of Truth* (Viking) New York 1966.

Fetzer, James H. (Editor) *Murder In Dealey Plaza* (Catfeet Press) 2000

-------------- *Assassination* (Catfeet Press) 1998

Fonzi, Gaeton. *The Last Investigation* (Thunder's Mouth Press) 1994

Gates, Daryl, *Chief – My Life In The LAPD* (Bantam Books) New York 1993

Garrison, Jim. *On The Trail Of The Assassins* (Penguin Books) 1992.

Gentry, Curt. J. *Edgar Hoover – The Man and the Secrets* (WW Norton and Co.) 1991

Giancana, Sam and Chuck. *Double Cross – The Story of the Man Who Controlled America* (MacDonald) 1992

Giancana, Antoinette. *Mafia Princess* with Thomas C. Renner (George Allen and Unwin) 1984.

Gordon, Thomas. *Secrets and Lies: A History of CIA Mind Control and Germ Warfare* (JR Books Ltd) 2008

Groden, Robert J. *The Search For Lee Harvey Oswald* (Bloomsbury) 1995

--------------- *The Killing of A President* (Bloomsbury) 1993

Grose, Peter. *Gentleman Spy – The Life of Allen Dulles* (Andre Deutsch) 1995.

Helms, Richard. *A Look Over My Shoulder* (Random House) 2003

Hinckle, Warren (with William Turner). *Deadly Secrets – The CIA-Mafia War Against Castro and the Assassination of JFK* (Thunder's Mouth Press) New York 1992

Hosty James P.,Jr. *Assignment Oswald* (Arcade Publishing) 1996

Hunt E. Howard with Greg Aunapu. *American Spy: My Secret History in the CIA, Watergate, and Beyond* (John Wiley and Sons) 2007

Hurt, Henry. *Reasonable Doubt – An Investigation Into The Assassination of John F. Kennedy* (Sidgewick and Jackson) 1986

Jeffreys-Jones, Rhodri. *The CIA and American Democracy* (Yale University Press) 1989.

Joesten, Joachim. *Oswald: Assassin or Fall Guy?* (Merlin Books) 1964.

Kaiser, David. *Road To Dallas* (Belknap Press) 2009

Kantor, Seth. *Who was Jack Ruby?* (New York-Everett House) 1978

Kennedy, Edward M. *A Memoir – True Compass* (Little Brown) 2009

Kirkwood, James. *American Grotesque: An Account of the Clay Shaw-Jim Garrison Affair in the City of New Orleans* (HarperPerennial) 1992

Klaber, William and Melanson, Philip H. *Shadow Play – The Murder of Robert F. Kennedy, The Trial Of Sirhan Sirhan and the Failure of American Justice* (St Martin's Press) New York 1997

Kunhardt, Philip B. *Life in Camelot – The Kennedy Years* (Little Brown and Co.) 1988

Kurtz , Michael L. *Crime of the Century – The Kennedy Assassination from an Historian's Perspective* (The University of Tennessee Press) 1993.

LaFontaine, Ray and Mary. *Oswald Talked – The New Evidence in the JFK Assassination* (Pelican Publishing Co. Gretna) 1996.

Latell, Brian. *Castro's Secrets* (Palgrave Macmillan) 2012

Lambert, Patricia, *False Witness* (M. Evans and Co.) 1998

Lane, Mark. *Rush To Judgment* (Holt Rinehart) 1966

-------------- *Plausible Denial – Was the CIA Involved in the Assassination of JFK?* (Plexus) London 1992.

-------------- *Last Word* (Skyhorse Publishing) 2011

Lawrence, Lincoln Thomas, Kenn. *Mind Control, Oswald & JFK: Were We Controlled?* (Adventures Unlimited Press; 2nd Revised edition) 1997

Leamer, Laurence. *The Kennedy Women – The Saga of An American Family* (Villard Books) New York 1994

Leonard, Jerry. *The Perfect Assassin: Lee Harvey Oswald, the CIA and Mind Control* (AuthorHouse) 2002

Lewis, Richard Warren. *The Scavengers and Critics of the Warren Report* (Delacorte) New York 1967.

Lifton, David. *Best Evidence: Disguise and Deception in the Assassination of John F. Kennedy* (Carroll and Graf Publishers) 1982.

Livingstone, Harrison Edward. *High Treason 2* (Carroll and Graf Publishers Inc) 1992

Lorenz, Marita. *Marita – From Castro To Kennedy: Love and Espionage in the CIA* (Warner) 1994

McAdams, John. *JFK Assassination Logic: How To Think About Claims Of Conspiracy* (Potomac Books) 2011

Mailer, Norman. *Oswald's Tale* (Random House) 1995

Mallon, Thomas. *Mrs Paine's Garage* (Harvest Books) 2003

Manchester, William R. *The Death of a President: November 20-November 25, 1963* (Michael Joseph) 1967

Mangold, Tom, *Cold Warrior – James Jesus Angleton* (Simon and Schuster) 1991

Marchetti, Victor, and Marks, John D. *The CIA and the Cult of Intelligence* (Jonathan Cape), 1974.

Marks, John. *Search for the Manchurian Candidate* (Norton) 1979

Marrs, Jim. *Crossfire – The Plot That Killed Kennedy,* (Carroll and Graf Publishers) 1992

McDonald, Hugh. *LBJ and the JFK Conspiracy* (with Robin Moore) (Condor) 1979

McMillan, Priscilla Johnson. *Marina and Lee* (Collins) 1978.

Mellen, Joan. *A Farewell To Justice* (Potomac Books) 2005

Menninger, Bonar. *Mortal Error – The Shot That Killed JFK* (Sidgewick and Jackson) 1992

Miller, Merle. *Lyndon – An Oral Biography* (Ballantine Books, N.Y.)1987

Moldea, Dan. *The Hoffa Wars – The Rise and Fall of Jimmy Hoffa* (SPI Books) 1994

Morrow, Robert D. *First-hand Knowledge How I Participated in the CIA-Mafia Murder of President Kennedy* (SPI Books) 1994.

Myers, Dale. *With Malice* (Oak Cliff Press) 1998

Nechiporenko, Oleg M. *Passport To Assassination: The Never-Before-Told Story of Lee Harvey Oswald by the KGB Colonel Who Knew Him* (Todd P. Bludeau Translator) (Birch Lane) 1993.

Newman, John. *Oswald and the CIA* (Carroll and Graf) 1995

North, Mark. *Act of Treason – The Role of J. Edgar Hoover in the Assassination of President Kennedy* (Carroll and Graf Publishers inc.) 1992

Oglesby, Carl. *The JFK Assassination – The Facts and the Theories* (Signet) 1992

Oswald, Robert L. with Myrick Land, Barbara Land. *Lee: A Portrait of Lee Harvey Oswald* (Coward-McCann) 1967

Pacepa, Ion Mahai. *Programmed to Kill: Lee Harvey Oswald, the Soviet KGB and the Kennedy Assassination* (Ivan R Dee, Inc.) 2007

Pepper, William. *An Act Of State* (Verso Books) 2003

Posner, Gerald. *Case Closed – Lee Harvey Oswald and the Assassination of JFK* (Warner Books) 1993.

-------------*Killing The Dream* (Little Brown and Company) 1998

Prouty, L. Fletcher. *JFK – The CIA, Vietnam and the Plot to Assassinate John F. Kennedy* (Carol Publishing Group) 1992.

Quirk, Robert E. *Fidel Castro* (WW Norton and Co.) 1993.

Ranelagh, John. *The Agency – The Rise and Decline of the CIA* (Sceptre) 1988

Reeves, Richard. *President Kennedy-Profile In Power* (Simon and Schuster) 1993

Russo, Gus. *Live By The Sword* (Bancroft Press) 1998

-------------*Brothers In Arms* (With Molton, Stephen) Bloomsbury Publishing PLC) 2008

Sabato, Larry J. *The Kennedy Half Century – The Presidency, Assassination, And Lasting Legacy Of John F Kennedy* (Bloomsbury) 2013

Savage, Gary. *JFK: First Day Evidence* (The Shoppe Press) 1993

Scheim, David E. *Contract on America – The Mafia Murder of President John F. Kennedy* (Shapolsky Publishers Inc.) 1988.

Schlesinger, Arthur M. *A Thousand Days – John F. Kennedy In The White House* (Andre Deutsch) 1965

Scott, Peter Dale. *Deep Politics and the Death of JFK* (University of California Press) 1993

Shenon, Philip. *A Cruel And Shocking Act – The Secret History Of The Kennedy Assassination* (Little, Brown) 2013

Short, Martin, *Crime Inc.* (Thames Methuen) 1984

Sloan, Bill. *JFK – Breaking the Silence* (Taylor Publishing Co.) 1993.

Smith, Matthew. *JFK – The Second Plot* (Mainstream Publishing) 1992

--------------*Vendetta – The Kennedys* (Mainstream Publishing) 1993

Sorensen, Theodore. *Kennedy* (Harper and Row) 1965

Stafford, Jean. *A Mother in History* (Chatto and Windus) 1966

Stockton, Bayard. *Flawed Patriot: The Rise and Fall of CIA Legend Bill Harvey* (Potomac Books) 2006

Streatfeild, Dominic. *Brainwash – The Secret History of Mind Control* (Thomas Dunne Books) 2007

Sturdivan, Larry. *The JFK Myths: A Scientific Investigation of The Kennedy Assassination* (Paragon House Publishers) 2005

Summers, Anthony. *The Kennedy Conspiracy* (Sphere Books), 1998

Thomas, Evan. *The Very Best Men* (Simon and Schuster) 1995.

Thomas, Gordon. *Secrets and Lies – A History of CIA Mind Control and Germ Warfare* (Konecky, William S. Associates, Inc.) 2007

Twyman, Noel. *Bloody Treason* (Laurel Publishing) 1997

Wecht, Cyril. *Cause of Death* (With Mark Curriden and Benjamin Wecht) (Dutton) 1993

Weiner, Tim. *Legacy of Ashes – The History of the CIA* (Allen Lane) 2007

------------*Enemies – A History of the FBI* (Randon House New York) 2012

Weisberg, Harold. *Case Open – The Omissions, Distortions and Falsifications of Case Closed* (Carroll and Graf) 1994

-----------*Never Again* (Carroll and Graf Publishers) 1995.

White, Theodore H. *In Search of History* (Jonathan Cape) 1978

Willens, Howard P. *History Will Prove Us Right Inside The Warren Commission Report On The Assassination Of John F. Kennedy* (The Overlook Press) NY 2013

Wills, Gary, Demaris, Ovid. *Jack Ruby: The Man Who Killed the Man Who Killed Kennedy* (Ishi Press) 2011

DOCUMENTARY VIDEOS AND RECORDED NEWS PROGRAMS

ABC-TV and BBC Timewatch, The Kennedy Assassination – Beyond Conspiracy, http://jfk.timewatch.org.uk/BBC/bbc-beyond-conspiracy.html

On Trial: Lee Harvey Oswald, http://www.amazon.co.uk/ Trial-Harvey-Oswald-Region-NTSC/dp/B001CDLASU/ref=sr_1_1?s=dvd&ie=UTF8&qid=1363431009&sr=1-1

PBS, Frontline, Who Was Lee Harvey Oswald? http://www.pbs.org/wgbh/pages/frontline/shows/oswald/etc/credits.html

JFK: First Day Evidence, by Gary Savage, The Shoppe Press, http://karws.gso.uri.edu/marsh/jfk-conspiracy/1stDayEvidence.txt

UK, The Mysterious Career of Lee Harvey Oswald, Written and Produced by William Cran and Ben Loeterman, Invasion Productions for the BBC, 1993

Discovery Channel, Unsolved History JFK: Beyond The Magic Bullet Discovery Communications, Inc. 2004

Oswald's Ghost Directed by Robert Stone PBS (2007)

The KGB Secret JFK Assassination Files, 1998, directed by David McKenzie

Secrets of a Homicide – JFK Assassination website, Dale Myers – http://www.jfkfiles.com/

Peter Jennings Reporting—The Kennedy Assassination: Beyond Conspiracy, ABC-TV, 2003

PBS, Frontline, Interview With Robert Oswald, 1993, http://www.pbs.org/wgbh/pages/frontline/biographies/oswald/interview-robert-oswald/

National Geographic Channel, CIA Secret Experiments, written, produced, and directed by Tria Thalman 2008

Rendezvous With Death, Wilfried Huismann 2006 First aired on January 6, 2006 on German television station Westdeutscher Rundfunk

CNN 1992 "Larry King Live" Larry King Interviews Dr.Lundberg, Editor Of 'The Journal Of The American Medical Association.'(JAMA).

CNN November 1993 "Larry King Live" Kal Korff and Gaeton Fonzi

interviewed by Larry King.

CNN November 1993 "30 Years later: Reflections of the FBI" James Hosty, Vincent Drain and Cartha (Deke) DeLoach interviewed by Larry Woods.

PBS, 'NOVA' Documentary 1988. "Who Shot President Kennedy?" Hosted By Walter Cronkite.

Reasonable Doubt – The Single-Bullet Theory and the Assassination of John F. Kennedy Produced and Directed by Chip Selby CS Films Inc/Castle Communications 1988

BIBLIOGRAPHY

The Day The Dream Died, Exposed Films Ltd. 1988

The JFK Assassination: The Jim Garrison Tapes, Blue Ridge/Film Trust/Brave World Videos 1992

Best Evidence:The Research Video, Fabulous Films Ltd. 1990

The Men Who Killed Kennedy-The Incredible True Facts" Produced and Directed By Nigel Turner, Central Independent Television Ltd

BBC "The Nazis" television series (Broadcast September 1997)

Capitol Records EMI Records, The Controversy:The Voices of President John F. Kennedy

Warren Report. Produced By Lawrence Schiller 1967.

NBC Television Special, The JFK Conspiracy: The Case of Jim Garrison, 1967, http://dvp-video-audio-archive.blogspot.com/2012/03/jfk-conspiracy-case-of-jim-garrison.html